15 X
10/02
6/04
18x 4/10 - 3/11
19 x 2/12 - 1/14
21 X 4/15
_____
10-18

WITHDRAWN

SAN DIEGO PUBLIC LIBRARY
NORTH PARK

DEC   1996

D1505925

THE LIFE AND TIMES
EINSTEIN

THE LIFE AND TIMES
EINSTEIN
AN ILLUSTRATED BIOGRAPHY

BY RONALD W. CLARK

WINGS BOOKS

NEW YORK • AVENEL, NEW JERSEY

8 1336 04122 5716

DIEGO PUBLIC

Project Manager: Lois Brown

Design: Samuel N. Antupit and
Melissa Feldman

Frontispiece: Einstein at the California
Institute of Technology, Pasadena.
(California Institute of Technology)

The author and publisher gratefully
acknowledge permission to quote
from the following works:

The Questioners by Barbara Lovett
Cline, copyright © 1965 by Barbara
Lovett Cline, reprinted by permission
of the publishers, Thomas Y. Crowell
Company (c/o Harper & Row,
Publishers, New York).

Einstein: His Life and Times, by
Philipp Frank, translated by George
Rosen, copyright © 1947, 1953 by
Alfred A. Knopf, Inc. Reprinted by
permission of the publisher.

*The Relativity Theory Simplified and
the Formative Period of Its Inventor,*
by Max Talmey, published 1932,
used with permission of
McGraw–Hill Book Company.

The text of this edition is abridged
from *Einstein: The Life and Times*
published by Hodder and Stoughton
Limited, copyright © 1973 by
Ronald W. Clark.

Text copyright © 1984 by
Ronald W. Clark.

Illustrations copyright © 1984 by
Harry N. Abrams, Inc.

All rights reserved. No part of
the contents of this book may be
reproduced without the written
permission of the publisher.

This 1995 edition is published
by Wings Books, distributed by
Random House Value Publishing, Inc.,
40 Engelhard Avenue, Avenel, New Jersey 07001,
by arrangement with Harry N. Abrams, Inc.

Random House
New York • Toronto • London • Sydney • Auckland

Drawings in Chapter Four
and Five commissioned by
Harry N. Abrams, Inc.

Printed and bound in the United States of America

**Library of Congress
Cataloging-in-Publication Data**

Clark, Ronald William.
    Einstein: the life and times / by Ronald W.
    Clark.
        p. cm.
    Originally published: New York:
    H.N.Abrams, 1984.
    Includes bibliographical references and
    index.
    ISBN 0-517-14718-1
    1. Einstein, Albert, 1879-1955.
    2. Physicists--Biography. I. Title.
QC16.E5C5   1995
530'.092—dc20   95-22819
    [B]   CIP

8 7 6 5 4 3 2 1

CONTENTS

FOREWORD

The story of Albert Einstein, scientist, philosopher and contemporary conscience, with all its impact and influence, would fit better within the walls of a library than between the covers of a single book. For Einstein was far more than the scientist who confidently claimed that space and time were not what everybody thought, including the most sophisticated heirs of Newton, and who shrugged it off when he was found to be right. In his technical language, the universe was four-dimensional, while fallible human beings thought they had a right to no more than three. He passionately indulged in pacifism, and as passionately indulged out when Hitler began to show that he really meant what he said about the Jews and the master-race. Throughout it all he stuck to the job in hand, determined to squeeze the next secret from Nature.

The different facets of Einstein's life and work will long continue to be explored. Deeper and deeper theses on ever smaller aspects of his science will continue to be written. The impact of his support for pacifism between the two world wars will one day get the detailed and possibly disillusioning analysis it warrants; so will the result of that honest enthusiasm for Zionism which for long led him to believe that the promised land could be reached without force of arms. In theology he is likely to remain something of an enigma, even among those who do not take his cosmic religion too seriously. As a peg on which to hang an argument on science and government, he is less useful than might be expected; even so, the real relevance of his famous letter to Roosevelt in 1939, and of his lesser-known actions in the winter of 1944, provide the substance of more than one might-have-been which could be explored in detail. Einstein the philosopher is certain to get even more critical study as the deeper implications of his work continue to be investigated. And few can read his correspondence—whose publication is long over-due—without feeling that Einstein's wit is worth a slim volume on its own. All this will come one day.

But something more than these specialist portraits, each with Einstein at the center of a technical argument, emerges from digging hard into the documents, and from a critical appraisal of the myth and reminiscence which have grown around his memory in the last two or three decades. It is the picture of a man who can, without exaggeration, be called one of the great tragic figures of our time. It is the picture of a man who while still young abandoned, with all the passion of the convinced monastic, much of what life had to offer—and who was shot back into the struggle by the unobliging stumble of history. Thus the youth who relinquished his nationality at the age of 15 returned to the fold later; opted out of German nationality a second time in middle life; and even in old age, when reconciliation had become respectable, refused to return to "the land of the mass murderers." The dedicated pacifist, who after his change of stance was reviled for his apostasy, believed himself to be among those who pressed the buttons which destroyed Hiroshima and Nagasaki. The Zionist who put peace with the Arabs as a first essential was forced finally to agree that it was necessary to fight. In science the greatest physicist in three centuries, or possibly of all time, found himself after middle age pushed by the advance of quantum theory into a backwater, "a genuine old museum-piece" as he described himself.

These ironies not only gave Einstein's life a great personal poignancy; they also combined to keep him in the glare of the public limelight, first switched on with such spectacular results in 1919 when, in Whitehead's words, "a great adventure in thought had at length come safe to shore." In this glare, the human figure has tended to be enlarged into the Delphic oracle. The aureole of white hair helped. So did the great luminous eyes. So did the brave stand which Einstein made for civic and academic freedoms. After his death, all this encouraged a biographical molly-coddling which was less than his genius deserved. It also tended to encourage the belief that, as he once put it, all men dance to the tune of an invisible piper. This is not so. "Wherever a system is really complicated, as in the brain or in an organized community," Sir George Thomson has said, "indeterminacy comes in, not necessarily because of h [Planck's constant] but because to make a prediction so *many* things must be known that the stray consequences of studying them will disturb the *status quo,* which can never therefore be discovered. History is not and cannot be determinate. The supposed causes only *may* produce the consequences we expect."*

This has rarely been more true than of Albert Einstein, whose thought and action in science and life became interrelated in a way no dramatist would dare to conceive. His extraordinary story has itself some quality of the indeterminacy which in physics he was so reluctant to accept. He would not have liked it. But he would have appreciated the situation. He might even have laughed about it.

RONALD W. CLARK
New York

*From a letter to the author from Sir George Thomson, February 16, 1970.

1. THE MAKING OF A MISSION

1. GERMAN BOY

The earliest known photograph of Einstein, believed to have been taken in Munich in the 1880s. *(Bilderdienst Süddeutscher Verlag)*

The life of Albert Einstein has a dramatic quality that does not rest exclusively on his theory of relativity. For the extravagant timing of history has linked him with three shattering developments of the twentieth century: the rise of modern Germany, the birth of nuclear weapons, and the growth of Zionism. Their impact on his simple genius combined to drive him into a contact with the affairs of the world for which he had little taste. The result would have made him a unique historical figure even had he not radically altered man's ideas of the physical world. Yet Einstein was also something more, something very different from the Delphic, hair-haloed oracle of his later years. To the end he retained a touch of clowning humor as well as a resigned and understanding amusement at the follies of the human race. Behind the great man there lurked a perpetual glint in the eye, a fundamental irreverence for authority, and an unexpected sense of the ridiculous that could unlatch a deep belly laugh that shook the windows; together with decent moral purpose it combined to make him a character rich in his own nonscientific right.

German by nationality, Jewish by origin, dissenting in spirit, Einstein reacted ambivalently against these three birthday gifts. He threw his German nationality overboard at the age of fifteen but twenty years later, after becoming Swiss, settled in Berlin, where he remained throughout the First World War; after Germany's defeat in 1918 he took up German civic rights again, one of the follies of his life as he later called it, only to renounce his country a second time when Hitler came to power. His position as a Jew was buttressed by his support of Zionism, yet he offended more than once by his insistence that Jews were, more importantly, members of the human species. Moreover, his Zionism conflicted at times with his pacifism; and to his old friend, Lord Samuel, he commented that he was, despite anti-Semitic attacks, "pas très Juif." The free-thinking ideals of his youth continued into old age; these included a belief in the ordered and orderly nature of the universe that was by no means in conflict with the idea of a God— even though what Einstein meant by the word was peculiar to himself and to a small number of others. In these and other ways, in his private and his professional life, Einstein became the great contradiction: the German who detested the Germans; the pacifist who encouraged men to arms and played a significant part in the birth of nuclear weapons; the Zionist who wished to placate the Arabs; the physicist who with his "heuristic viewpoint" of 1905 suggested that light could be both wave and particle and who was ultimately to agree that all matter presented the same enigma. Yet Einstein himself supplied part of the answer to his own riddle. In ordinary life, as well as in the splendid mysteries of physics, absolutes were to be distrusted; events were often relative to circumstance.

8

He was born in Ulm, an old city on the Danube with narrow winding streets and the great cathedral on which workmen were then building the tallest spire in Europe. In 1842 the old fortifications were restored by German engineers, and with the creation of the new German Empire in the Hall of Mirrors in 1870, Prussian discipline began to reach down from the north German plains toward the free-and-easy Swabians of which the Einsteins were commonplace examples.

The Einsteins came from Buchau, a small town between Lake Constance and Ulm, comfortable and complacent on the Federnsee, a minor marsh of prehistoric interest whose story is admirably told in the fine new Federnsee Museum and whose shores are today thronged with weekend tourists. Since 1577 the Jews had formed a distinguished and respectable community in the area. They prospered down the centuries; they hung on, despite the burning of the synagogue in 1938 and all that followed it, until 1968. Only then could the local papers report: "Death of the Last Jew in Buchau." His name was Siegbert Einstein, a relative, many times removed, of the most famous Jew in modern history.

Industrious and mildly prosperous, the Einsteins had lived in Buchau at least since the 1750s. By the middle of the nineteenth century they were numerous, and eleven of that name are shown on the roll of those who subscribed to the new synagogue in 1839. Albert Einstein's great-grandfather had been born in the town in 1759, and the Jewish registers record his marriage to Rebekka Obernauer; the birth of their son Abraham in 1808; and Abraham's marriage to Helene Moos. Their son Hermann, father of Albert, was born in Buchau on August 30, 1847. Nineteen years later Abraham and his family moved to Ulm, thirty miles to the north, and in 1876 Hermann married Pauline Koch, born in Cannstadt, only a few miles away, and eleven years his junior.

Like the Einsteins, the Kochs had been part of the Württemberg Jewish community for more than a century, a family with roots rather more to the north—in Goppingen, Jebenhausen, and Cannstadt. Like her husband, Pauline Koch spoke the soft Swabian dialect, hallmark of an ancient duchy that had once spread from Franconia to Switzerland, from Burgundy to Bavaria, and whose inhabitants lacked both the discipline of Prussia and the coarseness of Bavaria.

The differences between Einstein's parents, a devoted, cheerful couple who faced the results of the husband's happy-go-lucky character with resignation, were largely those of emphasis. The picture of the father that comes through, secondhand, from a grandson he never knew, is of a jovial hopeful man—fond of beer and good food, of Schiller and Heine. This fits the description that Einstein himself presented to his friend Philipp Frank, who wrote of Hermann: "His mode of life and his *Weltanschauung*

9

Einstein's father, Hermann Einstein.
(Hebrew University of Jerusalem)

Einstein's mother, Pauline Koch.
Undated photograph, probably
taken at the turn of the century.
(E.T.H., Zurich)

differed in no respect from those of the average citizen in that locality. When his work was done, he liked to go on outings with his family into the beautiful country round Munich, to the romantic lakes and mountains, and he was fond of stopping at the pleasant, comfortable Bavarian taverns, with their good beer, radishes and sausages." More than half a century later Albert Einstein remembered those Sunday excursions with enjoyment, the discussions between his father and his mother as to which way they should go, and the husband's careful selection of a route that would end up where his wife wanted. "Exceedingly friendly, mild and wise," was how he spoke of his father as he approached the age of seventy. Easygoing and unruffleable, a large optimistic man with a thick moustache who looks out from his portraits through rimmed pince-nez with all the quiet certitude of the nineteenth century, Hermann Einstein would have thought it slightly presumptuous to have fathered a genius.

To the union, Pauline Koch, with even features and a mass of dark hair piled high above a broad forehead, brought more than the comparative affluence of a woman whose father was a Stuttgart grain merchant and Court Purveyor. She brought also a breath of genuine culture, a love of music that was to be inextricably entwined with her son's work and, in the pursuit of her ambition for him, a touch of the ruthlessness with which he followed his star. She appears to have had a wider grasp than her husband of German literature and, while for him Schiller and Heine were an end in themselves, for her they were only a beginning.

For a year the young Einsteins lived in Buchau. Then in 1877 they moved back to Ulm where Hermann set up, in a building on the south side of the Cathedral Square,

Munich, the capital of Bavaria, at the turn of the century. Lying on the banks of the Isar, a tributary of the Danube, the city is one of the handsomest in Europe, and famous for its churches and art collections. *(The Mansell Collection)*

which later became the "Englander" wine tavern, a small electrical and engineering workshop financed by his more prosperous in-laws. He and his wife lived a few hundred yards away in an apartment at No. 135, city-division B, an undistinguished four-story building renumbered 20 Bahnhofstrasse in 1880 and destroyed in an Allied air raid sixty-four years later. Below it, one of the tributaries of the river Blau flowed in a cutting beside the street, past the over-jutting windows of houses that had not changed much since the fifteenth century, turning before it reached the cathedral and entered the Danube. Here, in the town whose inhabitants proudly claimed that *"Ulmense sunt mathematici"* (the people of Ulm are mathematicians), Albert Einstein was born on March 14, 1879.

Within a year of the birth Hermann's small business had collapsed, a victim of his own perpetual good nature and high hopes. He now moved to Munich and with his brother Jakob opened a small electrochemical works. Thus for Einstein Ulm was merely a vestigial memory, a town from whose winding medieval streets the open country could still be seen, a town where the Jews retained their own identity yet lived at ease with the rest of the community; a smallish place through whose squares the cows with their great clanging bells were driven, and into which there drifted, on summer evenings, the scent of the forests and the surrounding hills.

The move to Munich brought the Einstein family from an almost rural environment into the capital of Bavaria, already more than a quarter of a million strong, still fresh from the architectural adornments added to it by the mad King Ludwig at a cost of seven million thalers. Overwhelmingly Catholic, its air was heavy with the sound of bells from numerous churches: the cathedral of the archbishopric of Munich-Freising, with its

The site of Einstein's birth in Ulm (right). It was rebuilt during the early years of the present century, then destroyed by bombing during the Second World War. (*Stadtarchiv Ulm*)

unfinished towers; the Jesuit St. Michael's; the Louis, with Cornelius' fresco of the Last Judgment; and St. Mariahilf with its gorgeous glass and fine woodwork. The city was rich in art galleries, proud of its seven bridges across the Isar, and of the Konigsbau built in the style of the Pitti Palace in Florence; a city still epitomizing the baroquerie of southern Germany before it bowed to the Prussians from the north.

In the University of Munich there had begun to work in 1880 a man whose influence on Einstein was to be continuous, critical, and, in the final assessment, enigmatic. This was Max Karl Ernst Ludwig Planck, then aged twenty-two. Born in Kiel while the port was still part of Danish Schleswig-Holstein, aged eight at the time of Prussia's conquest of the province, Max Planck was born into a professional German family that had moved south to Munich the following year. Later he studied at the University before going north to Berlin. Then, dedicated to the task of discovering how nature worked, Planck returned to Munich where he served as a *privatdozent* for five years; as he walked daily to the University, the young private tutor may have brushed shoulders with a boy whose life was to be intimately linked with his own. Two decades later Einstein was to provide a revolutionary development to Planck's own quantum theory. Another decade on, and Planck was to attract Einstein from the Switzerland he loved to the Germany he detested. Planck was to encourage him into becoming a German citizen for the second time, and, more than once during the 1920s, to dissuade him from leaving the Fatherland. In these and in other ways, the two men's lives were to be ironically linked in a way that reads like nature aping art.

The first Einstein home in Munich was a small rented house. After five years the family business had prospered sufficiently for a move to be made to a larger home in the suburb of Sendling, surrounded by big trees and a rambling garden, usually unkempt, that separated it from the main road. Only a short distance away were buildings that were soon converted into a small factory for the manufacture of electrical equipment. Here, Hermann attended to the business, while brother Jakob, with more technical knowledge, ran the works.

A year after the family's arrival in Munich, Albert's sister Maja was born. Only two years younger, she was to become his constant companion and unfailing confidant. Himself unconcerned with death, he faced the loss of two wives with equanimity; but the death of his sister, at the age of seventy, dented the hard defensive shell he had built around his personal feelings.

In one way the Einsteins failed to fit any of the convenient slots of their history and environment. In a predominantly Catholic community—eighty-four percent in Munich—they were not merely Jews, but Jews who had fallen away. Many deep-grained Jewish characteristics remained, it is true. The tradition of the close-knit intermarrying community is well brought out in the family tree, and Einstein himself was to add to it when, after his divorce, he married a double cousin. The deep respect for learning that the Jew shares with the Celt ran in the very marrow of the family. And Einstein was to

Einstein at five years of age with his three-year-old sister, Maja. *(Lotte Jacobi Collection)*

become but one more witness to the prominent part that Jews have played in the revolutionary developments of science—from Jacques Loeb in physiology to Levi-Civita and Minkowski in mathematics; Paul Ehrenfest in the quantum theory; Haber in chemistry; and Lise Meitner, Leo Szilard, and many others in nuclear physics.

Despite this, the essential Jewish root of the matter was lacking: the family did not attend the local synagogue. It did not deny itself bacon or ham, nor certain seafoods. It did not demand that animals must be slaughtered according to ritual, and it did not forbid the eating of meat and dairy products together. All this was to Hermann Einstein but "an ancient superstition," and equally so were the other customs and traditions of the Jewish faith. There was also in the family one particularly hard-bitten agnostic uncle, and Einstein used him as peg for the old Jewish joke. Einstein would always describe with relish how he had surprised his uncle one day in full formal dress preparing to go to the synagogue. The uncle had responded to the nephew's astonishment with the warning: "Ah, but you never know."

Thus Einstein was nourished on a family tradition that had broken with authority; that disagreed, sought independence, had deliberately trodden out of line. Sent first to a Catholic elementary school apparently on the grounds that it was convenient, he was there a Jew among Christians; among Jews he was, like the members of his family, an outsider. The pattern was to repeat itself through much of his life.

Nothing in Einstein's early history suggests dormant genius. Quite the contrary. The one feature of his childhood about which there appears no doubt is the lateness with which he learned to speak. Even at the age of nine he was not fluent, while reminiscences of his youth stress hesitancies and the fact that he would reply to questions only after consideration and reflection. This is in line with the family legend that when Hermann Einstein asked his son's headmaster what profession his son should adopt, the answer was simply: "It doesn't matter; he'll never make a success of anything."

His boyhood was straightforward enough. From the age of five until the age of ten, he attended a Catholic school near his home, and at ten he was transferred to the Luitpold Gymnasium, where the children of the middle classes had drummed into them the rudiments of Latin and Greek, of history and geography, as well as of simple mathematics. The choice of a Catholic school was not as curious as it seems. Elementary education in Bavaria was run on a denominational basis. The nearest Jewish school was some distance from the Einstein home, and its fees were high. To a family of little religious feeling the dangers of Catholic orientation were outweighed by the sound general instruction that the school gave.

According to some sources he was here confronted for the first time with his Jewishness. As an object lesson a teacher one day produced a large nail with the words: "The nails with which Christ was nailed to the cross looked like this." Almost sixty years later Einstein gave his seal to the tale: "A true story." But Frank, to whom he appears to have told it, comments that the teacher "did not add, as sometimes happens, that the

13

Crucifixion was the work of the Jews. Nor did the idea enter the minds of the students that because of this they must change their relations with their classmate Albert."

Before Einstein left his Catholic elementary school for the sterner Luitpold Gymnasium, he received what appears to have been the first genuine shock to his intellectual system. The "appears" is necessary. For this was the famous incident of the pocket compass, and while he confirmed that it actually happened, he was also to put a gloss on its significance.

The story is simply that when the boy was five, ill in bed, his father showed him a pocket compass. What impressed the child was that since the iron needle always pointed in the same direction, whichever way the case was turned, it must be acted upon by something that existed in space—the space that had always been considered empty. The incident, so redolent of "famous childhoods," is reported persistently in the accounts of Einstein's youth that began to be printed after he achieved popular fame at the end of the First World War. Whether it always had its later significance is another matter. Einstein himself, answering questions in 1953 at the time of his seventy-fourth birthday, seemed uncertain.

Soon afterward, another influence entered Einstein's life. From the age of six he began to learn the violin. The enthusiasm this evoked did not come quickly. He was taught by rote rather than inspiration, and seven years passed before he was aroused by Mozart into an awareness of the mathematical structure of music. His delight in the instrument grew steadily and became a psychological safety valve; it was never quite matched by performance. In later years the violin became the hallmark of the world's most famous scientist; but it was Einstein's supreme and obvious enjoyment in performance that was the thing. Amateur, gifted or not, remained amateur.

Hermann Einstein with his compass and Pauline Einstein with her insistence on music lessons brought two influences to bear on their son. A third was provided by his Uncle Jakob, the sound engineer without whom Hermann would have foundered even faster in the sea of good intentions. Jakob Einstein is a relatively shadowy figure, and his memorial is a single anecdote, remembered over more than thirty years and recalled by Einstein to his early biographers. "Algebra is a merry science," Uncle Jakob would say. "We go hunting for a little animal whose name we don't know, so we call it x. When we bag our game we pounce on it and give it its right name." Uncle Jakob may or may not have played a significant part in making mathematics appear attractive, but his influence seems to have been long lasting. In many of Einstein's later attempts to present the theory of relativity to nonmathematicians, there is recourse to something not so very different: to analogies with lifts, trains, and ships, that suggest a memory of the stone house at Sendling and Uncle Jakob's "little animal whose name we don't know."

The Einstein family also included an in-law more important than father, mother, or Uncle Jakob. This was Cäsar Koch, Pauline Koch's brother, who lived in Stuttgart and whose visits to the Einstein family were long remembered. In January,

1885, Cäsar Koch returned to Germany from Russia, where part of his family was living. With him he brought as a present for Albert a model steam engine, handed over during a visit to Munich that year, and drawn from memory by his nephew thirty years later. Soon afterward Cäsar married and moved to Antwerp—where the young Albert was subsequently taken on a conducted tour of the Bourse. A well-to-do grain merchant, Cäsar Koch appears to have had few intellectual pretensions. But some confidence was sparked up between uncle and nephew, and it was to Cäsar that Einstein was to send, as a boy of sixteen, an outline of the imaginative ideas that foreshadowed the Special Theory of Relativity.

Nothing so precocious appeared likely, however, when Einstein in 1889 made his first appearance at the Luitpold Gymnasium. Within the climate of the time, the school seems to have been no better or no worse than most establishments of its kind. It is true that it put as great a premium on a thick skin as any British public school, but there is no reason to suppose that it was particularly ogreish. Behind what might be regarded as no more than normal discipline, it held, in reserve, the ultimate weapon of appeal to the unquestionable Prussian god of authority. But boys, and even sensitive boys, have survived as much; some have even survived Eton.

The Gymnasium was to have a critical effect on Einstein in separate ways. The first was that its discipline created in him a deep suspicion of authority in general and of educational authority in particular. This feeling lasted all his life, without qualification. The Gymnasium also taught him the virtues of skepticism. It encouraged him to question and to doubt, always valuable qualities in a scientist and particularly so at this period in the history of physics. Here, the advance of technology was bringing to light curious new phenomena that, however hard men might try, could not be fitted into the existing order of things. Yet innate conservatism presented a formidable barrier to the discussion, let alone acceptance, of new ideas. If Einstein had not been pushed by the Luitpold Gymnasium into the stance of opposition he was to retain all his life, he might not have questioned so quickly so many assumptions that most men took for granted, nor have arrived at such an early age at the Special Theory of Relativity.

A third effect was of a very different kind. There is no doubt that he despised educational discipline and that this, in turn, nourished the radical inquiring attitude that is essential to the scientist. It was only years later, as he looked back from middle life to childhood, that he expressed his dislike of the Gymnasium so vehemently. Until then, according to one percipient biographer who came to know him well, "he could not even say that he hated it. According to family legend, this taciturn child, who was not given to complaining, did not even seem very miserable. Only long afterwards did he identify the tone and atmosphere of his schooldays with that of barracks, the negation, in his opinion, of the human being."

By the end of the First World War this school environment had become a symbol in an equation whose validity Einstein never doubted. The Luitpold Gymnasium as he looked back on it equaled ruthless discipline, and the Luitpold Gymnasium was German. The boyhood hardships thus became transformed into the symbol of all that was worst in the German character—a transformation that was to produce dire and ironic consequences. With the stench of Auschwitz and Belsen still in the nostrils, it is easy enough to understand the near-paranoia that affected Einstein when in later life he regarded his own countrymen. It is easy enough to understand his reply when, at the age of sixty-nine, he was asked: "Is there any German person towards whom you feel an estimation and who was your very personal friend among the German born?" "Respect for Planck," Einstein had replied. "No friendship for any real German. Max von Laue was the closest to me." All this is understandable. Yet Germans were among the first to die in the concentration camps, and it is remarkable to find in Einstein, normally the most compassionate of men, what must reluctantly be identified as a trace of Vansittartism. The Luitpold Gymnasium, transmogrified by memory, thus has a lot to answer for as it convinced Einstein that the Prussians had been handed a double dose of original sin. Later experiences tended to confirm the belief.

At the Gymnasium there appears to have been, as there frequently is in such schools, one master who stood apart, the odd man out going his nonconformist way. His name was Reuss. He tried to make his pupils think for themselves, while most of his colleagues did little more—in Einstein's later opinion—than encourage an academic *Kadavergehorsamkeit* (the obedience of the corpse), that was required among troops of the Imperial Prussian Army.

There was to be an unexpected footnote to Einstein's memory. After his first work had begun to pass a disturbing electric shock through the framework of science, he himself visited Munich and called on his old teacher, then living in retirement. But the worn suit and baggy trousers that had already become the Einstein hallmark among his colleagues, merely suggested poverty. Reuss had no recollection of Einstein's name, and it became clear that he thought his caller was on a begging errand. Einstein left hurriedly.

The influence that initially led Einstein on to his chosen path did not come from the Luitpold Gymnasium but from Max Talmey, a young Jewish medical student who in 1889 matriculated at Munich University. In later life Talmey was seized with the idea for a universal language, an Esperanto that he felt would be particularly valuable for science. He tried to enlist Einstein's support, became interested in relativity, and then, like so many others, attempted to explain the theory. More important, he included in his book his own impressions of Einstein at the age of twelve:

He was a pretty, dark-haired boy…a good illustration…against the theory of Houston Stewart Chamberlain and others who try to prove that only the blond races produce geniuses [Talmey wrote]. He showed a particular inclination toward physics and took pleasure in conversing on physical phenomena. I gave him therefore as reading matter A. Bernstein's *Popular Books on Physical Science* and L. Buchner's *Force and Matter*, two works that were then quite popular in Germany. The boy was profoundly impressed by them. Bernstein's work especially, which describes physical phenomena lucidly and engagingly, had a great influence on Albert, and enhanced considerably his interest in physical science.

Einstein (front row, third from right) with his Munich schoolfellows. Undated photograph, believed to have been taken in the early 1890s. *(Stadtarchiv Ulm)*

Soon afterward, he began to show keenness for mathematics, and Talmey gave him a copy of Spieker's *Lehrbuch der ebenen Geometrie*, a popular textbook. Thereafter, whenever the young medical student arrived for the midday meal on Thursdays, he would be shown the problems solved by Einstein during the previous week. His protégé also read Darwin. There is no evidence that he was particularly moved. One reason was that the battle for evolution had by this time been fought and won. Yet even in his youth, Einstein may have believed, as he was to write years later, that living matter and clarity were opposites. The same feeling that "biological procedures cannot be expressed in mathematical formulae," gave him a lifelong skepticism of medicine, according to his later friend Gustav Bucky, and it certainly tended to concentrate Einstein's interests on nonbiological subjects. This attitude, a sense almost of annoyance with the Creator at having produced things that could not be easily quantified, explains at least something of the invisible barrier that so often rises to separate Einstein, the intuitively understanding and kind human being, from Einstein ordering his daily life. The bugle calls of science were always sounding, and he could rarely devote much time to individual men and women.

By the time he was twelve, Einstein had attained, in his own words, a deep religiosity. His approval of this translation of the original German in his autobiographical notes is significant; for religiosity, the "affected or excessive religiousness" of the dictionary, appears to describe accurately the results of his education so far. Always sensitive to beauty, abnormally sensitive to music, Einstein had no doubt been deeply impressed by the splendid trappings that decked out the Bavarian Catholicism of those days. But if his emotions were won over, his mind remained free—with considerable results, for through the reading of popular scientific books he soon reached the conviction that most of the stories in the Bible could not be true.

If there were no order or logic in the man-made conceptions of the world based

Einstein and his sister Maja, about
1893. *[Hebrew University of Jerusalem]*

on revealed religion, surely order and logic could be discovered in the external world. The young Einstein, like the Victorian ecclesiastic who wished "to penetrate into the *arcana* of nature, so as to discern 'the law within the law,'" picked up science where religion appeared to leave off. Later he was to see both as different sides of the same coin, as complementary as the wave and corpuscle conceptions of light, and both just as necessary if one were to see reality in the round. All this, however, developed in the decades after conversion.

Conversion did not come in a day. Common sense, together with what little evidence exists, suggests that Einstein's determination to probe the secrets of the physical world did not appear like a Pauline vision on the Damascus road but crystallized over a period of time. Nevertheless, it was a conversion that began in early youth, quickly hardened, and set fast for the rest of his life.

Brooding on the "lies" he had been told in the Luitpold Gymnasium, Einstein decided on the work to which he would be willing to devote everything and sacrifice anything with a steely determination that separated him from other men. On two occasions he put down in simple words what that work was. The first occasion came during an hour's meeting with the Jewish philosopher Martin Buber, who pressed him hard "with a concealed question about his faith." Finally, in Buber's words, Einstein "burst forth," revealingly. "'What we (and by this 'we' he meant we physicists) strive for,' he cried, 'is just to draw His lines after Him.' To draw after—as one retraces a geometrical figure." The second occasion came years later when, walking with a young woman physicist to his Berlin University office, Einstein spelled out the same task in more detail. He had no interest in learning a new language, nor in food, nor in new clothes. "I'm not much with people," he continued, "and I'm not a family man. I want my peace. I want to know how God created this world. I am not interested in this or that phenomenon, in the spectrum of this or that element. I want to know His thoughts, the rest are details."

This aim was matched by a belief: "God is subtle but he is not malicious." With these words he was to crystallize his view that complex though the laws of nature might be, difficult though they were to understand, they were yet understandable by human reason. If a man worried away at the law behind the law—if, in Rutherford's words, he knew what questions to ask nature—then the answers could be discovered. God might pose difficult problems but He never broke the rules by posing unanswerable ones. What is more, He never left the answers to blind chance—"God does not play dice with the world."

Einstein's God, however, was not the God of most other men. When he wrote of religion, as he often did in middle and later life, he tended to adopt the belief of Alice's Red Queen that "words mean what you want them to mean," and to clothe with different names what to more ordinary mortals—and to most Jews—looked like a variant of simple agnosticism. Years later, asked by Ben-Gurion whether he believed in God, "even he, with his great formula about energy and mass, agreed that there must be something behind the energy." No doubt. But much of Einstein's writing gives the impression of belief in a God even more intangible and impersonal than a celestial machine-minder, running the universe with undisputable authority and expert touch. Instead, Einstein's God appears as the physical world itself, with its infinitely marvelous structure operating at atomic level with the beauty of a craftsman's wristwatch, and at stellar level with the majesty of a massive cyclotron. This was belief enough. It grew early and rooted deep. Only later was it dignified by the title of cosmic religion, a phrase that gave plausible respectability to the views of a man who did not believe in a life after death and who felt that if virtue paid off in the earthly one, then this was the result of cause and effect rather than celestial reward. Einstein's God thus stood for an orderly system obeying rules that could be discovered by those who had the courage, the imagination, and the persistence to go on searching for them. And it was to this task that he began to turn his mind soon after the age of twelve. For the rest of his life everything else was to seem almost trivial by comparison.

Einstein had three more years at the Gymnasium, uninterested in the classics, increasingly able at mathematics, precocious in philosophical matters, which one can assume he discussed only rarely with his masters and not at all with his fellow pupils. This time in Munich would have been longer still had not the family business failed again. For now the Einsteins decided to cross the Alps to Milan. A wealthy branch of the family lived in Genoa, and it may well have been their stipulation that the new business enterprise should start where they could keep a watchful eye on the happy-go-lucky optimism of Hermann Einstein.

The family moved from Munich in 1894, taking their daughter Maja with them and leaving Albert in a boardinghouse under the care of a distant relative. It was anticipated that he would in due time finish his course, acquire the diploma that would ensure entry to a university, and would then enter the profession of electrical engineering that his father had vaguely chosen for him. The son had other views and within six months had followed his family across the Alps.

Little is known about the period that the young Einstein spent in Italy, but he looked back on it as extremely happy. "I was so surprised, when I crossed the Alps to Italy, to see how the ordinary Italian, the ordinary man and woman, uses words and expressions of a high level of thought and cultural content, so different from the ordinary Germans," he remembered nearly forty years later. "This is due to their long cultural history. The people of northern Italy are the most civilized people I have ever met."

There is little doubt that he enjoyed the people and the air of freedom, both very different from what he had known in the Munich Gymnasium. When his father's business failed yet again, almost as expected, and was restarted in Pavia, his own travels began to take him farther afield to Padua, Pisa, Siena, and Perugia.

This freedom, however, could not last since the continuing precariousness of the family finances made it necessary for him to prepare for a career. The only record of how he was prodded into this comes secondhand from his son: "At the age of sixteen," he has said, "his father urged him to forget his 'philosophical nonsense,' and apply himself to the 'sensible trade' of electrical engineering." The lack of a necessary Gymnasium certificate at once made itself felt since entry to a university was barred without it.

There was one possible way out. Conveniently over the Alps from Milan, there existed in Zurich the Eidgenossische Technische Hochschule (E.T.H.) [the Swiss Federal Institute of Technology], outside Germany the best technical school in central Europe. The Institute demanded no Gymnasium diploma, and all a candidate had to do was pass the necessary examination. There was one difficulty, however. In the spring of 1895 Einstein was only sixteen, at least two years younger than most scholars when they joined the E.T.H. It was decided, however, that the risk should be taken, and in the autumn he was dispatched over the Alps.

Before he went—probably a few weeks or months earlier, although the date is uncertain—he sent to his Uncle Cäsar in Stuttgart a "paper," an augury of things to come, in which he proposed tackling one of the most hotly disputed scientific subjects, the relationship between electricity, magnetism, and the ether, that hypothetical non-material entity that was presumed to fill all space and to transmit electromagnetic waves.

Neither letter nor paper is dated, but in 1950 Einstein recalled that they were written in 1894 or 1895, while the internal reference to the E.T.H. in Zurich suggests that the latter was the more likely year.

The accompanying essay, written in sloping and spidery Gothic script on five pages of lined paper, was headed: "Uber die Untersuchung des Aetherzustandes im magnetischen Felde" ("Concerning the Investigation State of Ether in Magnetic Fields") and began by outlining the nature of electromagnetic phenomena and stressing the little that was known concerning their relationship with the ether, a situation that, it was suggested, could be remedied by experiment.

It was a remarkable paper for a boy of sixteen, and if it is straining too far to see in it the seeds of the Special Theory, it gives a firm enough pointer to the subject that was to remain constantly at the back of his mind for a decade. As he wrote in old age, at the age of sixteen he had discovered a paradox by considering what would happen if one could follow a beam of light at the speed of light. He did not put it quite like that to Uncle Cäsar; but it was no doubt still in his mind as he arrived in Zurich, carrying the high hopes of the family and, judging from the odd hint, a firm determination that he would not become an electrical engineer.

2.

STATELESS PERSON

Einstein at the age of seventeen.
[E.T.H., Zurich]

Einstein arrived in Zurich, the bustling mercantile capital of Switzerland, in the autumn of 1895. Set on its long finger of lake among the foothills of the Alps, the city was half cultural remnant from the Middle Ages, half commercial metropolis, a center whose nonconformist devotees were within the next few years to include Lenin, Rosa Luxembourg, and James Joyce. Einstein, for whom the attractions of Zurich never palled, was to be another.

During this first visit as a youth of sixteen and a half he stayed with the family of Gustav Meier, an old friend of his father and a former inhabitant of Ulm. Einstein took the normal entrance examination for the E.T.H. shortly afterward. He did not pass. Subsequently, he admitted that failure in Zurich "was entirely his own fault because he had made no attempt whatever to prepare himself"; and, asked in later life whether he might have been forced into choosing a "profitable profession" rather than becoming a scientist, he bluntly replied, "I was supposed to choose a practical profession, but this was simply unbearable to me." Although the horse had been brought to the water in Zurich, nothing could make it drink. But the principal of the E.T.H., Albin Herzog, had been impressed by Einstein's mathematical ability. Reading between the lines, he had also been impressed by Einstein's character. With the support of Meier, it was arranged that the boy should attend the cantonal school at Aarau, twenty miles to the west, where a year's study might enable him to pass the E.T.H. entrance exam.

A small picturesque town on the Aare, from whose banks the vineyards climb the slopes of the Jura, Aarau could justifiably boast of its cantonal school run by Professor Winteler. But wherever Einstein had been sent in Switzerland, he would have been impressed by the contrast with the Munich Gymnasium. For in spite of the Swiss tradition under which every man appears eager to spring to arms, and has his rifle on the wall, the spirit of militarism is singularly absent. Contrariwise, the practice of democracy, about which Einstein early showed what was to be a lifelong enthusiasm, had for centuries been an ingrained feature of the country. Even so, he was lucky with Aarau and with Winteler, with whose family he lived during his stay at the school.

A slightly casual teacher, as ready to discuss work or politics with his pupils as with his fellow teachers, Winteler was friendly and liberal-minded, an ornithologist never happier than when taking his students and his own children for walks in the nearby mountains. Teaching resembled university lectures rather than high school instruction. There was a room for each subject rather than for each class, and in one of them Einstein was introduced to the outer mysteries of physics by a first-class teacher, August Tuchschmid. More than half a century later he remembered the school as a pleasant place. Instruction was good, authority was exercised with a light hand, and it is clear that in this friendly climate Einstein began to open up, even though the details that have survived are scanty and tantalizing. On a three-day school outing during which pupils climbed the 8,000-foot Santis above Feldkirch, he slipped on a steep slope and was saved from destruction only by the prompt move of a colleague who stretched out his alpenstock for the boy to grasp, a quick action that helped change the course of history. When, on another school outing, a master asked: "Now, Einstein, how do the strata run here? From below upwards or vice versa?" the reply was unexpected: "It is pretty much the same to me whichever way they run, Professor."

The story may well have been embroidered by recollection. But it reflects an attitude that juts out during Einstein's youth from beneath the layers of adulation that increased with the years. The description of "impudent Swabian," given by his fellow pupil Hans Byland, belongs to this period. "Sure of himself, his grey felt hat pushed back on his thick, black hair, he strode energetically up and down in a rapid, I might almost say crazy, tempo of a restless spirit which carries a whole world in itself," Byland has said. These rougher corners eventually became smoothed off so that he would bite back the comment he might consider natural and others might consider bitter; but the essential attitude remained, an intellectual disinclination to give a damn for anybody. Like a rock never very far below the surface, it was as likely to capsize Einstein as anyone else.

This prickly arrogance appears increasingly throughout his student years. The gentle philosopher, benignly asking questions of the universe, was always to be one part of the complete Einstein. But there was another part during youth. He knew not only the clanging existence of metropolitan Munich but the delights of northern Italy. He was, judged by the experience of his contemporaries, a young man of the world, well filled with his own opinions, careless of expressing them without reserve, regarding the passing scene with a sometimes slightly contemptuous smile. Had it not been for his deep underlying sense of the mystery of things, a humility that at this age he was apt to conceal, he would have been the model iconoclast.

Life in Aarau was to have one specific and far-reaching result: the antagonism to all things German that had been burning away in Einstein for years now came to the surface in what was, for a boy, a remarkable explosion. He refused to continue being German. The usual story is that on arriving in Milan from Munich the youthful Einstein told his father that he no longer wished to be German and at the same time announced that he was severing all formal connection with the Jewish faith. In general, it is the second half of the story, which would have caused his religiously happy-go-lucky family little worry, that is given most credence; the first has been considered a later magnification of youthful disenchantment and wishful thinking. In fact, the reverse is true.

Right: Einstein (front row, far right) in the classroom at Aarau, with Dr. Jost Winteler, toward the end of the nineteenth century. [AIP Niels Bohr Library]

Left: The University of Zurich (center), Zurich Cathedral (left), and the Zurichberg hill (background) seen from the lake. [Swiss National Tourist Office, London]

As far as the Jewish faith is concerned, the boy had as little to renounce as the grown man. Although Einstein the Zionist speaker of adult life had an intense feeling for Jewish culture, a dedication to the preservation of the people, and a deep respect for the Jewish intellectual tradition, his feelings for the faith itself rarely went beyond kindly tolerance and the belief that it did no more harm than other revealed religions.

The question of German nationality was different. At first, the idea of a sixteen-year-old renouncing his country appears slightly bizarre, while in the modern world the mechanics of the operation would be complicated. So much so that the story has been taken rather lightly and André Mercier, head of the Department of Theoretical Physics in the University of Berne, and secretary general of the International Committee on General Relativity, has gone on record as saying that when Einstein arrived in Switzerland, "he was by nationality a German and remained so until he became of age." It has also been pointed out that if the young Einstein did "give up his passport at the age of fifteen," as has been claimed by Dr. Walter Jens of the University of Tubingen, then this act would have been of no legal consequence.

In fact, no passport was involved. On birth, Einstein had become a citizen of the state of Württemburg and, as a result, a German national. According to a letter in the Princeton archives he had pleaded with his father, even before the latter had crossed the Alps to Milan, to renounce this nationality on his behalf. Nothing appears to have been done. But the boy returned home from Switzerland to Milan to spend the Christmas of 1895 with his parents. And soon after his return to Aarau early in 1896, Hermann Einstein, presumably yielding at last to his son's renewed badgerings, wrote to the Württemburg authorities. They acknowledged the application, and on January 28, 1896, formally ended Einstein's German nationality. Two memoranda sent by them to Ulm on January 30 and February 5 confirmed this with various departments in the city. Thus he completed his education in Switzerland and obtained his degree in Zurich as a stateless person, merely "the son of German parents," as he put it on official forms. Once free of Germany, he succeeded in switching academic horses in midstream: despite the family decision that he should become an electrical engineer, it was now agreed that he should study for a teacher's degree.

He sat for his examination at the E.T.H. in the summer of 1896; passed; returned to his parents in Italy; and in October left them for Switzerland, now dedicated to a four-year course that would, if he were successful, qualify him for a post on the lowest rung of the professional teacher's ladder.

On October 29, 1896, he settled down in Zurich, first in the lodgings of Frau Kagi at 4 Unionstrasse. There he was to remain for two years before moving to Frau Mark-

The small manufacturing town of Aarau on the banks of the River Aare where Einstein went to school before entering the Zurich Polytechnic. [Swiss National Tourist Office, London]

walder in 87 Klosbach and then, after twelve months, returning to Frau Kagi at a new address. At the end of each term he visited his family in Milan or, later, Pavia, while in Zurich he was under the watchful but discreet eye of the Karr family, moderately well-to-do people distantly related to Einstein's mother, whose relatives now provided the one hundred francs a month on which he lived.

His fellow students came mainly from the families of minor professional people or small businessmen. There was also a group of young girls from Hungary, one of whom joined the class of '96 with Einstein. This was Mileva Maric, born 1875 and like the rest of the class a few years older than Einstein, daughter of a Serbian peasant from Titel in southern Hungary, who had labored her way to Zurich by dogged determination, handicapped by a limp, anxious to succeed.

Einstein was casual of dress, unconventional of habit, with the happy-go-lucky absentmindedness of a man concentrating on other things, which he was to retain all his life. "When I was a very young man," he once confided to an old friend, "I visited overnight at the home of friends. In the morning I left, forgetting my valise. My host said to my parents: 'That young man will never amount to anything because he can't remember anything.'" And he would often forget his key and have to call up to his landlady late at night: "It's Einstein—I've forgotten my key again."

He followed the normal student pursuits, picking up on the Zurichsee a passion for sailing that never deserted him, taking occasional walks among the mountains. On the water he would invariably have a small notebook. Fraülein Markwalder, who sometimes accompanied him, remembered years later how when the breeze died and the sails dropped, out would come the notebook, and he would be scribbling away. "But as soon as there was a breath of wind he was immediately ready to start sailing again."

The picture is almost prosaic. But a hint of something to come is suggested by the barely concealed arrogant impatience that showed itself even during the musical evenings to which he was often invited by the parents of his Swiss friends. If attention to his performance was not adequate, he would stop, sometimes with a remark that verged on boorishness. To a group of elderly ladies who continued knitting while he played, and who then asked why he was closing his score and putting his violin back in its case, he explained: "We would not dream of disturbing your work." And when, politely asked on one occasion: "Do you count the beat?" he quickly replied, "Heavens, no. It's in my blood." Perhaps there was always something a little risky in questioning Einstein. The "not much with people," as he later put it, was true despite his personality, not because of it. Even as a youth, moodily aloof at times from his companions, he had a quality that attracted as certainly as it could rebuff. As a man, he was the kind who made heads turn

25

Einstein at the school at Aarau. [E.T.H., Zurich]

when he entered the room, and not merely because the founder of relativity had come in. If the word "charisma" has a modern meaning outside the public relations trade, Einstein had it.

It is noticeable that he appears to have been particularly happy in the company of women. The feelings were often mutual. The well set-up young man with his shock of jet-black wavy hair, his huge luminous eyes, and his casual air, was distinctly attractive. More than one young Zurich girl, more than one Swiss matron, were delighted that the young Herr Einstein was such an excellent performer on the violin and was agreeable to accompany them at evening parties. And he was a frequent visitor to the house of Frau Bachtold, where several of the women students lodged, sitting in the living room and attentively listening as Mileva Maric played the piano.

26

Einstein's pleasure in the company of women lasted all his life. But there was little more to it than that. Like most famous men he attracted the hangers-on, the adorers, and the semicharlatans. On at least two occasions women claimed him as the father of their children. In one instance, the claimant was insane; the case of the other appears to have been equally groundless. His doctor-friend, Janos Plesch, suggested in a letter after Einstein's death that Einstein may have formed a liaison during the First World War when he had been left by one wife and had not yet acquired another. Other comparably vague suggestions have been handed down from the early Berlin days. Although they cannot be ignored, it would be wrong to give them more weight than unsubstantiated observations deserve—suggestions that tended to be kept afloat by Einstein's own personal attitude. According to Vera Weizmann, wife of the Jewish leader Chaim Weizmann, Einstein's second wife did not mind him flirting with her since "intellectual women did not attract him; out of pity he was attracted to women who did physical work." The same comment has been made in strikingly similar terms by more than one of his friends, who have drawn attention to the fact that he preferred to have women rather than men around him. All this is true. But the implications remain unsubstantiated. As a young man he tended to keep his women friends at arm's length since he wished to devote the maximum energy and resource to the one great game; later on, as youth merged first into middle and later into old age, he still tended to like having women around, but in an almost old-maidish way. He had, after all, resigned himself to the necessary priorities: first research, second Einstein.

This lifelong dedication set him apart in a number of ways. As Bertrand Russell once wrote, "Personal matters never occupied more than odd nooks and crannies in his thoughts." Other men allowed themselves to become implicated in the human predicament, on one level willingly dealing with the trivia of life and on another being swept off course by the normal passions. Einstein avoided such energy-wasting complications at all levels. To this extent his self-imposed task, the determination to keep first things first, forced him into abdicating his human position. He felt an intuitive sympathy with human beings in the mass, and many of his letters—notably those to his friends Max and Hedi Born—reveal a deeply compassionate nature. Throughout much of his life he could find little time to express this, while his own isolation from the normal run of human feelings did not make its expression any easier or any more frequent. Yet many of the things that moved most men failed to move Albert Einstein. "He was devoid of the human feelings that can cause trouble and misery," wrote the son of Dr. Bucky, whom Einstein knew for almost a quarter of a century. "In the twenty-three years of our friendship I never saw him show jealousy, vanity, bitterness, anger, resentment, or personal ambition. He seemed to be immune to these emotions." This fact of nature certainly lightened his personal burden; it also created a gulf that he had to leap before he could fully understand the emotions of others.

Einstein's obsession with exploring and understanding the physical world

Einstein (seated at left) with his graduating class at Aarau, 1896. [E.T.H., Zurich]

caught him early. He followed it, as André Mercier has noted, as the result of a double experience, "the experience of the exterior world, revealing material facts, numberless and numerical; and the revelation of an interior or spiritual world which showed him the path he should follow." But there was another dichotomy about the early years. A good deal of his genius lay in the imagination, which gave him courage to challenge accepted beliefs. This quality has been rightly stressed, and his old friend Morris Cohen went so far as to claim that "like so many of the very young men who have revolutionised physics in our day [Einstein] has not been embarrassed by too much learning about the past or by what the Germans call the literature of the subject." Yet the "too much" is relative. Einstein's ability to soar up from the nineteenth century basis of physics, and his own dislike of the routine involved in understanding that basis, has tended to undervalue the four-year slog of routine that he went through at the E.T.H. But this routine was demanding enough.

It was physics to which he turned, working most of the time in the physical laboratory. This was in strange contrast with the period when he would answer a question about his laboratory by pointing to his head and a question about his tools by pointing to his fountain pen. Despite this he never ceased to emphasize that the bulk of his work sprang directly and naturally from observed facts; the coordinating theory explaining them might arise from an inspired gleam of intuition, but the need for it arose only after observation.

In June, 1899, Einstein seriously injured his hand in the Zurich laboratories— typically enough after tearing up a chit of paper telling him how to do an experiment one way and then attempting to do it another way. From the first, however, it was theoretical physics that attracted him, and here he was unlucky. Subsequently, he was to write of the excellent teachers of these Zurich days. It is significant that he omitted reference to Heinrich Weber, who held the physics course. According to Einstein's fellow student Louis Kollross, this course was designed primarily for engineers. Certainly, it taught nothing of Maxwell, whose theory of electromagnetism was already changing not only men's ideas of the physical world but the practical applications of physics to that world. Of the two sets of notes made by Einstein at Weber's own lectures, one dealt with heat and dynamics, the other with technical problems and with electricity from Coulomb's law to induction; Maxwell's work was not touched upon. This was not as startling as it sounds, for Maxwell's theory was symptomatic of the radically new ideas that were about to transform the face of physics.

Only a few years earlier, as the nineteenth century moved toward its close, the empire of the physical sciences had appeared to be on the edge of the millennium. Just as

Left: Michael Faraday (1791–1867), discoverer of electromagnetism, whose "Experimental Researches on Electricity" greatly affected Einstein's early thinking. [AIP Niels Bohr Library]

Right: James Clerk Maxwell (1831–1879), the Scottish mathematician and physicist who gave mathematical form to Faraday's speculations on magnetic lines of force. His equations expressed and bound together magnetic and electric phenomena and showed that neither magnetism nor electricity could exist in isolation. [AIP Niels Bohr Library]

there seemed no possible limit to the industrial development of the United States, to the political advances in Europe, over much of which the liberal spirit still reigned, or to the technological progress that could be achieved in the world's workshops, so did physical science seem to be moving toward a solution of its final problems. Almost a century earlier Laplace had made his fine boast: "An intelligence knowing, at a given instance of time, all forces acting in nature, as well as the momentary position of all things of which the universe consists, would be able to comprehend the motions of the largest bodies of the world and those of the lightest atoms in one single formula, provided his intellect were sufficiently powerful to subject all data to analysis; to him nothing would be uncertain, both past and future would be present in his eyes."

This prophecy from the Newton of France had been in some ways an extrapolation from the spectacular success of Newton's own celestial mechanics, with whose help the motions of moon, comets, asteroids, and satellites could be computed with splendid accuracy. The confidence appeared to be justified, not only by the advances made throughout the nineteenth century but by the ease with which these could be seen as intelligible parts of one vast but finite *corpus* of knowledge whose final understanding must be only a few years away. Mechanics, acoustics, and optics were all set on firm foundations during this heroic age of classical physics. Faraday's work on electromagnetism from 1831 onward produced the dynamo and the first shoots of what was to become the great electrical industry. The first scientific knowledge of electricity led to the electric telegraph. And to crown the fine structure there came Maxwell in the 1860s with the synthesis of his electromagnetic equations, giving the answer to so many natural phenomena and forecasting the radio waves to be discovered by Heinrich Hertz twenty-five years later.

Throughout the last decades of the nineteenth century the problem of the luminiferous ether, through which Maxwell's electromagnetic waves appeared to be transmitted like shakings in an invisible jelly, began to sap the foundations of classical science and to reveal the electromagnetic theory as the revolutionary theory it was. But this was not the only worm in the apple. The imposing structure that had been built on Newtonian mechanics, the solid edifice of knowledge utilized by so many of the sciences to which it had seemed that man was now putting the finishing touches, had in fact been undermined by a score of experimental physicists tunneling along their own separate routes from a dozen different directions. Their work was continuing, and the repercussions from it were beginning to be felt.

In the world of Newtonian physics an obstinate planet had failed to conform to the calculations, for it had been confirmed that the motion of the perihelion of Mercury's

Left: Henri Poincaré (1854–1912), French mathematician and philosopher of science, whose paper at the first International Congress of Mathematicians in Zurich in 1897 concluded: "Absolute space, absolute time, even Euclidean geometry, are not conditions to be imposed on mechanics; one can express the facts connecting them in terms of non-Euclidean space." [AIP Niels Bohr Library]

Right: Ernst Mach (1838–1916), the Austrian physicist whose "Science of Mechanics" shook Einstein's dogmatic faith in mechanics. "[It] exercised a profound influence upon me in this regard when I was a student," he once said. "I see Mach's greatness in his incorruptible skepticism and independence." [AIP Niels Bohr Library]

orbit was advancing by a small but regular amount for which the Newtonian hypothesis could provide no explanation. From Vienna there came the heresy of Ernst Mach who was skeptical of the very foundations of Newton's universe, absolute space, and absolute time. In the United States Albert Michelson and Edward Morley had performed an experiment that confronted scientists with an appalling choice. Designed to show the existence of the ether, at that time considered essential, it had yielded a null result, leaving science with the alternatives of tossing aside the key that had helped to explain the phenomena of electricity, magnetism, and light, or of deciding that the earth was not in fact moving at all. Wien, in Berlin, was investigating discrepancies in the phenomena of heat and radiation, which stubbornly refused to be explained by the concepts of classical physics. In Leiden the great Dutch physicist, Hendrik Lorentz, had formed a new theory of matter in which atoms—still regarded as John Dalton's solid billiard balls of matter when their existence was credited at all—contained electrically charged particles. In the Cavendish Laboratory, Cambridge, J. J. Thomson—about to be joined by a young New Zealand graduate, Ernest Rutherford—was showing that these extraordinary bits of electricity, or electrons, not only had an existence of their own but a mass and an electric charge that could be measured. If this were not enough to strike at the very vitals of accepted ideas, Becquerel in Paris had found that at least one element, the metal uranium, was giving off streams of radiation and matter, an awkward fact that appeared to make nonsense of contemporary ideas. These were only the more important of a disturbing new group of discoveries made possible as much by technological advance as by exceptionally nimble minds, which were about to destroy the comfortable complacency into which physics had worked itself. It is hardly surprising that in this climate, "Maxwell's theory of the electro-magnetic field was…not a part of the ordinary syllabus of a provincial German university," as Max Born has pointed out. The reluctance of the more conservative men of science to acknowledge this revolutionary concept—marking a change from Newton's idea of forces operating at a distance to that of fields of force as fundamental variables—was no more surprising than any other human weakness for things as they are. The embrace of Newtonian mechanics had continued for so long, and was still so firm, that those who either saw or suspected the fundamental incompatability of Maxwell's theory with these long-accepted ideas tended to look the other way and, above all, to avoid discussion of such a potentially disturbing subject. This was physics as presented to Einstein and his fellow students and accepted by all except the few contemporaries fortunate enough to fall under the influence of a few questioning minds in Berlin, in Leiden, in Paris, or in Cambridge.

Einstein thus comes on to the scene as a student at a moment when physics was about to be revolutionized but when few students were encouraged to be revolutionaries. Without his own basically dissenting spirit he would have got nowhere. With it, the almost inevitable consequence was that he rubbed along with his formal work just as much as he had to and found his real education elsewhere, in his own time. At home he studied the works of Kirchhoff, Helmholtz, and Hertz. Maxwell was another of the scientific revolutionaries whose works he read in his lodgings, or on the banks of the Zurichsee while his friend Marcel Grossmann attended lectures on his behalf, took notes, and later passed these on so that when examination questions had to be faced Einstein was adequately briefed.

There was also Henri Poincaré, "the last man to take practically all mathematics, both pure and applied, as his province." Poincaré's influence on Einstein has sometimes been exaggerated. It has rarely been noted, however, that the first International Congress of Mathematicians was held in Zurich at the end of Einstein's first year as a student there; that Poincaré was due to attend; and that while he was prevented from doing so, there was read at the conference his famous paper containing the prophecy: "Absolute space, absolute time, even Euclidean geometry, are not conditions to be imposed on mechanics; one can express the fact connecting them in terms of non-Euclidean space." There is no evidence that Einstein attended the conference; but it seems unlikely that news of such an expression, so in tune with the freedom of his own way of thinking, should entirely have passed him by.

Whatever the exact weight of Poincaré's influence on Einstein, at Zurich or after, there is no doubt about the significance of Ernst Mach, that disappointed man who ran a close second to Maxwell himself in Einstein's estimation. Now mainly remembered for the eponymous Mach Number of supersonic flight, he believed that all knowledge is a matter of sensations and that what men delude themselves into calling "laws of nature" are merely summaries of experiences provided by their own—fallible—senses. "Colours, space, tones, etc. These are the only realities. Others do not exist," he had written in his daybook.

Einstein's views on the importance of such purely observational factors in discovering the way in which the world is built changed considerably throughout the years. His formulation of the Special Theory of Relativity, he was never tired of emphasizing, "was not speculative in origin; it owes its invention entirely to the desire to make physical theory fit observed facts as well as possible." As the years passed, the value of pure thought, objective and dissociated from exterior circumstance, appeared to increase.

The renunciation of almost all that Mach stood for began only in Einstein's midlife, the final stage in a long philosophical pilgrimage. During the first or second year of his studies in Zurich, there was nothing but awed enthusiasm when his attention was drawn to Mach's *The Science of Mechanics* by Michelangelo Besso, an Italian engineering student six years older than Einstein, who had come to the E.T.H. from Rome. One expression of Mach's independence lay in his analysis of Newtonian mechanics and his conclusion that it contained no principle that was self-evident to the human mind. The nub of this criticism was that Newton had used expressions that were impossible to define in terms of observable quantities or processes—expressions such as "absolute space" and "absolute time," which to Mach were thus quite meaningless. One result was that in Mach's view the Newtonian laws would have to be rewritten in more comprehensible terms, substituting in the law of inertia, for instance, "relative to the fixed stars" for "relative to absolute space." This critical attitude to the whole Newtonian framework as it had been utilized for more than two centuries helped to prepare Einstein's mind for things to come; for if Mach could claim, with at least a measure of plausibility, that men had been misled about the definition of the material world, then a similarly audacious venture was not beyond Einstein. Realization that accepted views could be so readily challenged came as a revelation to the student who intuitively felt that the world of degree courses was at the best incomplete and at the worst wrong. If he were really to discover how God had made the world, he could take nothing for granted—not even Newton.

This skepticism was a useful scientific qualification, but one side effect was inevitable: Einstein became, as far as the professorial staff of the E.T.H. was concerned, one of the awkward scholars who might or might not graduate but who in either case was a great deal of trouble. In such a situation it was natural that he should be asked by Professor Pernet, responsible for practical physics, why he did not study medicine, law, or philology rather than physics. It was natural that Pernet, faced with the young man's assertion that he felt he had a natural talent for physics, should reply: "You can do what you like: I only wish to warn you in your own interest." And it was natural that Weber, who disliked the young man addressing him as "Herr Weber" instead of "Herr Professor," should add, after admitting Einstein's cleverness: "But you have one fault: one can't tell you anything."

The situation throughout his four academic years at the E.T.H. from 1896 until 1900 was not improved by his own attitude toward examinations. After passing his finals, he was put off scientific work for a whole year. But graduate he did, in August, 1900, receiving an overall mark of 4.91 out of 6.00; celebrating with his particular friends, of whom all except Mileva Maric had been successful; and expecting that he would now be offered, as was the custom of the time, a place on the lowest rung of the academic ladder, an appointment in the physics department of the E.T.H. The laws of human nature, however, worked as rigorously for Albert Einstein as for others. Weber the physicist took on two mechanical engineers but overlooked the physicist Einstein. Other colleagues were given posts. For the difficult fellow, no opening could be found.

One of the first results of Einstein's failure to gain a post in the E.T.H. was the summary ending of his allowance from the Koch relations in Genoa. Having come of age, he would have to stand on his own feet. He crossed the Alps once more to join his parents in Milan, and from here, in September, 1900, wrote the first of numerous letters asking for work. It went to Adolf Hurwitz, the Zurich professor under whom he had read differential and integral calculus, and asked whether there was any chance of becoming his assistant. Shortly afterward, a further letter followed; but the post went elsewhere.

Later that autumn, Einstein was back in Zurich, working with Professor Alfred Wolfer under whom he had studied astrophysics and astronomy and who was now a director of the Swiss Federal Observatory. The work, though temporary, served its purpose, as shown in Einstein's first letter to Hurwitz. In this he revealed that he was applying for Zurich citizenship, but for this he had to have a job.

Citizenship—in effect, Swiss nationality—had been one of Einstein's objectives since the first weeks of 1896. Almost half a century later he remembered how he had been "happy in Switzerland because there men are left to themselves and privacy is respected," and throughout his student days he regularly set aside twenty francs a month toward the cost of obtaining Swiss naturalization. Now at last he had the necessary cash, the necessary residential qualifications, and the necessary job. He had made his formal application to the Zurich authorities the previous autumn, on October 19, 1899, enclosing a testimonial of good character and proof of unbroken residence in the city since October 29, 1896. But the wheels of the Zurich authorities ground as slowly as God's, and it was the following summer before the necessary declaration was demanded of his father. It was given on July 4, Hermann Einstein formally stating that he was "perfectly in agreement with the request of his son, Albert Einstein, regarding immigration to Switzerland and [the granting of] civic rights of the city of Zurich."

Einstein made only passing references to the formalities in later years. But the "duly accurate" biography by his stepson-in-law, Anton Reiser, contained details that can only have come from himself. Even though they came thirty years later, they have an interest in showing Einstein as seen by Einstein:

> The process had not been simple [Reiser wrote]. The Zurich city fathers definitely mistrusted the unworldly dreamy young scholar of German descent who was so bound [sic] to become a citizen of Switzerland. They could not be too sure that he was not engaged in dangerous practices. They decided to examine the young man in person and to question him rigorously. Was he inclined to drink, had his grandfather been syphilitic, did he himself lead a proper life? Young Einstein had to give information on all these questions. He had hardly expected that the acquisition of Swiss naturalisation papers was so morally involved a matter. Finally, the authorities observed how

Einstein in his early twenties. Undated photograph, believed to have been taken in Zurich or Berne shortly before Einstein joined the Swiss Patent Office in Berne. [E.T.H., Zurich]

harmless and how innocent of the world the young man was. They laughed at him, teased him about his ignorance of the world, and finally honoured him by recognising his right to Swiss citizenship.

On February 21, 1901, Einstein was granted the threefold citizen rights of the Swiss—of the city, of the canton, and of the Swiss confederation. As such he became due for his three-month military service like all other young Swiss men. Thirty years later, he was to be among those who signed a protest against this system, but in 1901 he felt differently, dutifully presenting himself to the authorities, who rejected him for military service because of flat feet and varicose veins. According to contemporaries he was shocked and distressed. He certainly kept his *Dienstbüchlein*, or Service book, for many years, at least until the 1930s.

The formality over, Einstein was now a fully fledged Swiss, a status he was to retain all his life and of which he was always proud. There is little doubt that his chances of permanent employment were now greater than they had been as a German Jew. Yet his move had been far from merely utilitarian. He felt a basic attachment to Switzerland and to the Swiss that continued throughout the years and grew with self-imposed exile in the United States into reminiscent affection. The reasons for it are revealing.

The people were humane, and there was also their pacific political record. As Morris Cohen has stressed, "Like other opponents of military imperialism, Einstein [was] inclined to look upon the smaller European nations as on the right path" while tending to ignore the fact that "their present attitude is in part at least due to the fact that the path of military aggrandisement is no longer open to them." Quite apart from this record, which on the political level gave Switzerland an honorable place among nations, the country had physical and psychological characteristics that helped to make it a national example of all that Einstein felt the world might be if only men behaved sanely. Within its frontiers were French- and Italian-speaking peoples as well as German-speaking, and within these boundaries the rough corners of national attitudes tended to be smoothed off by mutual contact. The Swiss, therefore, tended to be tolerant of national idiosyncracies and of personal ones as well. In the early years of the century, moreover, before the country had become the home of international agencies, before the reputation of Swiss bank accounts and of Swiss bankers gave it an aura of power, Switzerland existed in a European backwater that was particularly satisfying to Einstein, a man anxious only to be left to his work. Here, he could carry on with minimum interruption. This was the prospect, although it was not to be enjoyed immediately. His expectations of quickly getting a permanent job were still not justified, and in March he was back with his parents in Milan.

However, his hopes were rising. In 1901, as much as today, publication pro-

34

duced the rungs of the ladder up which scientists climbed to fame, and in December of the previous year Einstein set up the first rung. This was "Folgerungen aus den Capillaritätserscheinungen" ("Deductions from the Phenomena of Capillarity"), which appeared on December 13, 1900, in the *Annalen der Physik*. Shortly after the issue appeared, he sent a copy to Wilhelm Ostwald, the German physical chemist who was carrying out his pioneer work on the principles of catalysis. The paper had been inspired by Ostwald's own work, and Einstein inquired whether there was a job in Ostwald's laboratory. He appears to have received no reply, either to this first letter, or to a second that was, unknown to Einstein himself, supported by an appeal from his father. Certainly he got no job.

Before sending the second letter he also wrote to Kamerlingh Onnes, the Dutch physicist, who in Leiden was already probing down toward the depths of ultimate cold. He had heard through a student friend, Einstein wrote on a simple reply-paid card, that there was a vacancy for a university assistant. He outlined his qualifications and added that he was putting in the same post a copy of his treatise published in the *Annalen der Physik*. This card, now in the Leiden Museum for the History of Science, was the first link between Einstein and the Dutch university city, dreaming away among its canals and its great past, most of its honest burghers unaware that Kamerlingh Onnes was founding under their patronage the science of cryogenics and that Lorentz was dramatically introducing atomic ideas into Maxwell's electromagnetic theory. Two decades later Einstein was to become an honored visiting professor to the University. In its great hall he was to give some of his first lectures on the General Theory of Relativity. But his first contact with Leiden was of a different kind. Kamerlingh Onnes did not even answer, and the reply-paid second half of the card, self-addressed to "A. Einstein, Via Bigli 21, Milano," remains blank in the Museum's archives.

But rescue was at hand, and on May 3 he wrote from Milan to Professor Alfred Stern of Zurich, who had taught him history in the E.T.H., telling him that from mid-May to mid-July he would be teaching mathematics in a technical school at Winterthur, while the regular professor did national service.

A few days later he was off, crossing the Alps and walking down through the valleys of the Grisons to Coire and eastern Switzerland.

Einstein's stand-in for Professor Gasser at the Winterthur Technical School was uneventful. But no cause was found for keeping his services after Gasser's return, and once again he found himself back in Zurich, looking for work.

He was now saved by a combination of persistence and personal wire-pulling. In a Zurich newspaper he read that a teacher was required in a boarding school run by a Dr. Jakob Nuesch of Schaffhausen, the little town on the Swiss frontier famous alike for its Rhine falls and its position astride the narrow neck of land joining the main body of Switzerland to its "island" on the right bank of the Rhine. In Schaffhausen there lived Conrad Habicht, a former fellow student from the E.T.H. and a young man able to drop the right word in the right place. With Habicht's help, Einstein was given the post that turned out to be, for the most part, coaching a young English boy, Louis Cohen. He held it for only a few months and by the end of the year was back once more in his old Zurich "digs," out of work again.

By this time, however, there were two gleams of light on the horizon. Before he left Schaffhausen he had completed a thesis on the kinetic theory of gases for his Ph.D. and sent it to the University of Zurich. He had also made formal application for the post in the Swiss Patent Office, which was to be his first regular job.

The Office had been founded only in 1888 and still went its official if individual way under the control of its original director, Herr Friedrich Haller. A large, friendly, rough diamond, Haller was an engineer who had won his professional spurs during the seventies and eighties when the Swiss were establishing their reputation for driving railways through mountains, across mountains, and, if really necessary, up the near-vertical sides of mountains. Success was the yardstick, and if success were attained by a leavening of by-guess-and-by-God to formal scientific work, Haller saw little harm in that. He ran the Patent Office on his own unconventional lines, "with a whip in one hand and a bun in the other," according to a much later Patent Office official, and it was largely his own idiosyncratic rule, which appears eventually to have brought Einstein to the Swiss capital as a minor civil servant.

Among Haller's personal friends was Herr Grossmann, father of Einstein's former colleague Marcel Grossmann of the E.T.H. The Grossmanns' intervention on Einstein's behalf is certain, although the details are not clear; yet it seems likely that a casual talk between the two older men brought a generous promise that when a vacancy arose Marcel's friend would be favorably considered. Einstein learned of such an opening in December, 1901, and a few months after applying was among those selected for interview.

Shortly afterward, he traveled to Berne for the all-important personal meeting with Haller. The only evidence of that meeting that remains consists of a brief paragraph in Reiser. "Albert was examined for two full hours," this says. "The Director placed before him literature on new patents about which he was required to form an immediate opinion. The examination unfortunately disclosed his obvious lack of technical training." This minor detail was no embarrassment to a man such as Haller, intent on helping an old friend. On June 16 Einstein was formally appointed, together with a J. Heinrich Schenk, as Technical Expert, at a salary of three thousand five hundred francs a year. But Haller's goodwill could stretch only so far. The post for which Einstein had applied was Technical Expert (Second Class). He was made Technical Expert (Third Class).

Two legends have grown up around the appointment. One is that Einstein was employed because a knowledge of Maxwell's equations was considered essential and he was the only applicant who had it. The second is that the authorities in Zurich had already noted Einstein as a genius and passed on the good news to Haller, who had then seized the chance of bringing on to his staff a young man whose fame and fortune would all come in good time.

The first of these legends is easily disposed of. The vacancy officially advertised in the Swiss *Gazette* listed the qualifications for the Patent Office post merely as follows: *"Gründliche Hochschulbildung in mechanischtechnischer oder speciell physikalischer Richtung, Beherrschung der deutschen und Kenntnis der französischen Sprache oder Beherrschung der französischen und Kenntnis der deutschen Sprache, eventuell auch Kenntnis der italienischen Sprache."* ("Thorough academic education in technical mechanics, or special leaning towards physics, a mastery of German and knowledge of French, or mastery of French and knowledge of German and possibly knowledge of Italian.") The *"speciell physikalischer Richtung"* is the nearest that the requirement comes to a knowledge of Maxwell's laws, and it is unlikely that Haller would—as is sometimes suggested—have pulled them into his interviews of candidates to eliminate everyone but Einstein.

It is easy to see the way in which the second legend, of long standing in the Patent Office, quietly grew throughout the years. In retrospect, it must have been maddening for the authorities to reflect that they had taken an ordinary, if not an ugly, duckling under their wing without realizing that he would develop into the most amazing swan of the scientific world. What more natural than that a legend of prescience, of inner awareness of the young man's potential genius, should steadily grow? The picture of Haller, nodding sagely in his retirement whenever the name of Einstein arose, is a picture that one hardly likes to shatter. Yet there appears not the slightest evidence for it.

A week after being formally appointed, he took up his post in the Patent Office.

3.

SWISS CIVIL SERVANT

Einstein in the Swiss Patent Office, Berne, in the early 1900s. *[E.T.H., Zurich]*

The city to which Einstein moved in the summer of 1902 was very different in character from Zurich. Standing on its high sandstone ridge, three parts encircled by the swift waters of the Aare, looking toward the fine prospect of the Oberland, Berne was less tied to technology and industry, more tuned to the arts, than the city to the east. Embassies and legations occupied many of the fine houses to the south of the river across the Kirchenfeld Bridge. Summer tourists came to gaze at the famous clocktower with its midday procession of model bears that was the pride not only of the city but of all Switzerland. The British had already begun to make the huge main hotel, standing cheek by jowl with the Swiss Parliament house, a base from which they moved into the mountains for the fashionable sport of skiing, which they had introduced. In Berne the wrappings of the Swiss cocoon, which tended to shelter the country from the brute buffets of a Europe already being polarized toward Paris or Berlin, were slightly less protective. Here, Einstein was to spend the first creative years of his life, transforming the face of physics from the small back room of an apartment behind the arcades of Kramgasse into which there vibrated the chimes of the city clocktower.

His work as a technical officer in the Swiss Patent Office began on June 23, 1902. The details of his seven-year career there are simple enough. The initial appointment was provisional, and it was agreed that when this was confirmed his salary should be "regularised to suit that of his work at the time." Confirmation did not come until September 5, 1904, when Haller wrote to the Federal Council, noting that Einstein had "proved himself very useful" and proposing that his salary should be raised from three thousand five hundred to three thousand nine hundred francs. He should, however, remain Class III rather than be promoted to Class II since "he is not yet fully accustomed to matters of mechanical engineering (he is actually a physicist)."

Upgrading to a higher class followed in 1906, when his salary was increased by another six hundred francs. Since the autumn of 1904, Haller then wrote, Einstein had "continued to familiarise himself with the work, so that he now handles very difficult patent applications with the greatest success and is one of the most valued experts in the Office." The director went on to note that his young technical officer had "acquired the title of Dr. Phil. from the University of Zurich this winter, and the loss of this man, who is still young, would be much regretted by the administration of the Office."

Three points are of interest. The first is that Einstein had won his academic spurs in 1905. They had come after his presentation to the University of Zurich of a twenty-one-page paper on "Eine neue Bestimmung der Moleküldimensionen" ("A New Definition of Molecular Dimensions"), dedicated to his friend Marcel Grossmann. Judging by the records, it was touch and go whether he would get his doctorate. Professor

Alfred Kleiner, director of the Zurich Physics Institute, recommended acceptance of the dissertation. But "as the principal achievement of Einstein's work consists of the treatment of differential equations, it is thus of a mathematical nature and belongs to analytical mechanics," and Kleiner recommended two more opinions. That of Professor Burckhardt appears to have been decisive; despite "crudeness in style and slips of the pen in the formulae which can, and must, be overlooked," he noted that Einstein's paper showed "thorough mastery of mathematical methods."

Director Haller's remark about his young technical officer not only notes his academic advance but also implies that Einstein was by this time already searching around for another post and had not concealed the fact from his employers. Circumstantial evidence—casual references to teaching posts in Einstein's correspondence of this period—confirms that this was so. Third, it is significant that the director of the Patent Office, writing about his employee's progress in the spring of 1906, did not even comment on the three papers that the young man had by this time contributed to a single issue of the *Annalen der Physik*—one important enough to take him into the history books, one that helped to bring him the Nobel Prize sixteen years later, and a third containing the outline of the Special Theory of Relativity.

Einstein's first home in Berne was one small room in Gerechtigkeitsgasse, and from this he walked every morning the few hundred yards to the building in whose third-floor office he learned his routine duties.

The work of the Patent Office at the turn of the century was strikingly different from what it later became. The difference is illustrated by one fact: until 1907 patents were granted only for inventions that could be represented by a model. The model, it is difficult not to feel, may have been as important as the specification that described, in words that ideally should allow of no dispute, the duties the device was intended to perform. These inventions, ideas, and proposals that were directed to the Office consisted largely of suggestions for practical, utilitarian, basically simple and often homely applications of technology to the mundane affairs of everyday life. At first glance, all this appears to be singularly unrelated to Einstein's special genius. Despite the apparently esoteric quality of the theories on which his fame was founded, these theories sprang, as he was never tired of stressing, from observation of facts and from deductions that would account for these facts. This demanded an intuitive discernment of essentials, and it was just this that was sharpened during his days at the Patent Office. For the work frequently involved rewriting inventors' vague applications to give them legal protection; this, in turn, required an ability to see, among sometimes tortuous descriptions, the basic idea or ideas on which an application rested. The demand was not so much for the routine

Left: Berne's sixteenth-century *Zeitglockenthurm* (clock tower), whose puppets—a crowing cock and bears—revolve daily. Einstein lived to the left. *[The Mansell Collection]*

Right: The Swiss capital of Berne seen from the northwest. Behind the city and the surrounding countryside rise the Bernese Alps. *[Swiss National Tourist Office, London]*

application of a routine mind to routine documents, as for perceptive intuition. "It is no exaggeration," says a member of the Patent Office staff, "to say that Einstein's activity was, at least in the first few months, literally an apprenticeship in the critical reading of technical specifications and in understanding the drawings that went with them."

Observation and analysis were, therefore, brought to a sharper edge, as from the summer of 1902 onward Einstein sat in the long narrow room of the government office with his fellow technical officers sorting, reading, and putting into intelligible German the specifications for typewriters and cameras, engineering devices, and the hundred and one curious appliances for which inventors wished to claim legal protection. He himself was in no doubt of what he learned at the Patent Office. "More severe than my father," was how he described the director to his colleague Joseph Sauter. "He taught me to express myself correctly."

But there was more to it than that. It was the opportunity to think about physics that mattered. For while the Patent Office work helped to tickle into first-class condition Einstein's ability to discern the essentials of a scientific statement, it acted also as an undemanding occupation that released his mind for creative work at a different level. The process is not uncommon, and there had been an example in the very city in which he worked—that of Albrecht von Haller, the scientist who as secretary of the Berne City Council had in the 1700s kept the council minutes. Reprimanded one day by the Council chairman for writing a scientific treatise as a meeting proceeded, Haller was able to read out the detailed minutes that he had, simultaneously, been correctly keeping. Many men of genius need an occupation that keeps the wolf from the door while their intellectual work continues undisturbed: Trollope working in the Post Office while concentrating on the Barchester novels; Maurice Baring helping Trenchard plan the bombing offensive of 1918 while continuing his work as man of letters; Churchill politicking away through the inter-war years while producing *Marlborough*—these are examples of great men immersing part of themselves in a routine that helped to release their creative genius. In Berne, Einstein was another, unobtrusively trotting from Gerechtigkeitsgasse to the Patent Office each morning, usually lunching at his desk, returning to his lodgings each evening with the orthodoxy of the city clerk, then setting himself down in a quiet corner to discover the laws of nature.

His first original papers had no connection with the theory of relativity that was to make him world famous. They concerned, instead, the nature of the forces that hold together the molecules of a liquid. A number of eminent scientists—notably Mach and Ostwald—did not believe in the physical existence of atoms as such; for them it was almost as if Dalton had lived in vain. It was typical that Einstein, still in his early twenties, should set about educating them.

The first five papers in which he started to do this were published between 1901 and 1904. They were followed by a sixth, which came in his *annus mirabilis* of 1905 and which applied several of his earlier results in a dramatically conclusive way. The first two

Plaque on Einstein's house, Berne: "In this house lived Albert Einstein in the years 1903–1905, when he made his greatest contribution, the Theory of Relativity." [AIP Niels Bohr Library]

papers dealt with capillarity and potential differences. Neither was particularly successful, but the attraction of their subject for Einstein, dealing as it did with the links between intermolecular and other forces, was made clear in a letter he wrote to Marcel Grossmann in April, 1901. Even at this early stage, when dealing with a subject far removed from his shattering new concept of space and time to be embodied in relativity, Einstein revealed two aspects of his approach to science that became the keys to his work: the search for a unity behind disparate phenomena, and the acceptance of a reality distinct from what could be seen.

The subject matter of this early work was the immense numbers of particles that made up the liquids or the gases being considered. It is not possible to deal with the movements of individual particles and therefore statistical methods, which could handle the averaged-out movements of vast numbers, had to be used. If man had time enough, and equipment sensitive enough, it would be possible to calculate the movement of each molecule and each atom since these movements were the result of cause and effect. But statistics, as in life insurance, provided a handy short cut. As yet they provided no more.

His methods in the first two papers were those of thermodynamics. When he had completed them, he turned to the statistical foundations of the subject, attempting in three more papers to derive the laws describing equilibrium and irreversibility from the general equations of mechanics and the theory of probability. He believed his methods to be new, although they had, unknown to him, already been used by the American, Josiah Willard Gibbs; however, it can be claimed that this work was in some ways more profound than that of Gibbs.

Between the first of these early papers, written in Zurich, and the last of them, written in Berne, Einstein's circumstances changed. He became the center of a small coterie of young students who were to remain his friends for life; and, soon after this was formed, he married the friend of his Zurich days, Mileva Maric.

The group came into being shortly after Einstein moved to Berne. He had arrived a few weeks before taking up his Patent Office appointment, and he was doubtful whether his funds would last until the first payday. What he really loved and really understood was physics. Berne was a university city, and it was thus the most natural thing in the world that he should set up shop as a private tutor, offering to teach physics at so much an hour.

His first pupil was Maurice Solovine, a young Rumanian studying at Berne University a ragbag of subjects that included literature, philosophy, Greek, mathematics, and geology. "Walking in the streets of Berne one day during the Easter holidays of 1902, and having bought a newspaper, I noticed an advertisement saying that Albert Einstein,

The Olympia Academy: Conrad
Habicht, Maurice Solovine, and
Albert Einstein.

former pupil of the École Polytechnique of Zurich, gave lessons in physics at three francs an hour," he has written. Solovine sought out the house, climbed the stairs to the first story, and rang the bell.

The second visit was followed by a third, and on Solovine's suggestion it was agreed that they should read some of the standard works and discuss the problems they presented. The two men were soon joined by Conrad Habicht, Einstein's former friend from Zurich, who had now arrived in Berne to continue his mathematical studies. The faint line between teacher and taught, between the twenty-three-year-old Einstein and his companions of twenty, soon disappeared, and the lessons dissolved into discussions that were continued week by week and month by month.

At times they would top off their argument with a long walk. Sometimes a Sunday would be enlivened by an eighteen-mile tramp to the Lake of Thun, by whose side they would camp for the day before returning to Berne on the evening train.

Einstein himself was the natural leader, and not only by virtue of the elder-statesman advantage that a year or two's seniority gave him. Even in his early twenties, the force of character, which was so to impress observers later on, made itself felt. Something of this shows through even in the factual description given by Lucien Chavan, a young electrical engineer in the Federal Post and Telegraph Administration, who was an occasional member of what became the self-styled "Olympia Academy." "Einstein is 1.76 metres tall," he wrote beneath a picture of Einstein, which was given to the Swiss postal library after Chavan's death, "broadshouldered, with a slight stoop. His short skull seems remarkably broad. His complexion is swarthy. He has a narrow moustache above a large sensitive mouth, an acquiline nose. His brown eyes have a deep benign lustre. He has a fine voice, like the vibrant tones of a cello. Einstein speaks a good French with a slight foreign accent."

42

Discussion was the magnet that held the group together, and when it was in full swing little else mattered. Solovine has recorded how shortly before Einstein's birthday he saw caviar displayed in a shop window in the city. Knowing it from his earlier days in Rumania, he decided with Habicht to buy some as an expensive birthday treat. When it was put on the table, Einstein was talking about the problems of Galilean inertia. He went on talking, eating the caviar without comment.

This carefree, almost undergraduate existence, was drastically changed when in January, 1903, Einstein married Mileva Maric. The daughter of a Slav peasant, four years his senior, Mileva was to remain his wife until, early in 1919, a divorce was agreed on when the prospects of a Nobel Prize, whose thirty thousand kroner he promised to pass on to her if he won it, seemed likely to secure her own future and that of their two sons. She had left him in the summer of 1914; but she was wife and companion during the decade that brought him from the anonymity of the Patent Office to a secure position in international science and to the threshold of worldwide fame. Thus, the part that Mileva played in helping him up the ladder of success, or in holding him back, is important in Einstein's own story; it has remained untold partly because of his reluctance to reveal details of his personal affairs; partly because Mileva lived on, despite crippling illness, until 1948; and partly because legal problems have prevented publication of a long series of letters between the couple. The story, also told in many dozens of letters that Einstein wrote to his colleague and confidant Michelangelo Besso, is one of incompatability rather than conflict; of a couple who respected one another as long as they did not have to live together. And it is a story that makes all the more remarkable the intellectual accomplishment of a man who, as he wrote on one occasion, would have become mentally and physically exhausted if he had not been able to keep his wife at a distance.

According to some accounts the couple had become engaged while still students, an event frowned upon by Hermann Einstein, who had apparently never met Mileva when he died in Italy in 1902. Certainly Einstein crossed the Alps to be present at his father's deathbed, and certainly he married Mileva a few months after his return to Berne. The photographs that survive show her as a not unattractive woman of pleasant features, broadish nose above a good sensual mouth, and with an aura of thick dark hair. She had a limp, but this was not serious; and judging by the generally unkind descriptions of her, her deficiencies, such as they were, lay elsewhere. "A modest, unassuming creature" was the best that Fräulein Markwalder, daughter of Einstein's landlady, could muster. Carl Seelig, who, like Mileva, lived in Zurich for the greater part of his life, comments that "her dreamy, ponderous nature often curdled her life and her studies. Her contemporaries found Mileva a gloomy, laconic, and distrustful character. Whoever got to know her better began to appreciate her Slav openmindedness and the simple modesty with which she often followed the liveliest debates from the background." He notes, in addition, that she was "hardly the typical Swiss-German house-sprite, the height of whose ambition is a constant war against dust, moths and dirt." There is more than a touch of race bias in some of this, and it is fair to assume that, to many Teutons, Mileva had the unpardonable Slav tendency of letting things slip. There was one compensation. Einstein, hearing a friend comment, "I should never have the courage to marry a woman unless she were absolutely sound," replied, "But she has such a lovely voice."

Einstein himself has given various accounts of why he did, in fact, marry her. One old friend to whom he confided his own account, says, "How it came about he doesn't seem to know himself," and to another he said that he married despite his parents' determined opposition but out of a feeling of duty. In old age he also tried to rationalize his action, claiming that what he called this tragedy in his life probably explained his immersion in serious work. However, whether the emotional crises of an unhappy marriage are likely to affect the work of the theoretical physicist in the same beneficent way that they can affect the artist is a moot point; certainly Einstein, writing not years later but as the rift with Mileva developed, gives little sign of it.

In many ways Einstein would have been happier in 1903 with a dedicated housekeeper; instead, he tumbled into marriage, almost by accident, possibly while thinking of more important things. But even in those days, before pacifism, before Zionism, before the anti-bomb movement, he was a decent man beneath the determination of his scientific exterior. Just as, even then, he felt a responsibility toward the human race, so did he feel a responsibility toward those with whom circumstance had joined him. He hardly had time or inclination to be a family man, but he did his best.

Relations worsened as the years passed, particularly after 1905 when the Special Theory of Relativity began to make him famous. His acquaintances, the men and women against whom he was brushed by the chances of everyday life, were only too ready to admit that relativity was beyond them; his second wife was to say so with an air of relief. With Mileva the situation was different, for was she not a physicist like her husband? Had she not, in fact, got just enough "little learning" to enter the new world he had created, if only he would spare time to explain things? The answer was "No," but she would never believe it.

Another factor was quite as important. When Einstein married, he expected to win more time for work; he expected to shuffle off the domestic detail that hangs around bachelor necks. The physicist who in later life was to discard socks as unnecessary complications and who insisted that washing and shaving with the same soap made life that much simpler, had one basic desire, even in the early 1900s: to transfer to other shoulders the tiresome tasks that diverted time from more important things. Many men have married for worse reasons; and many have found that, failing the grand passion, such mundane considerations have enabled a couple to rub along happily enough.

It is true Einstein could always isolate himself from surrounding trivia with an enviable ease. In a mob, at a concert, listening to speeches, he could follow the exterior pattern of events while an essential part of his mind worked away at the problem of the

Einstein and his first wife, Mileva Maric, taken in 1911 when both were in their early thirties. *[E.T.H., Zurich]*

moment. But it would, even so, be useful if marriage removed the clutter of workaday duties and diversions. That it failed to do so, that it merely exchanged the preoccupations of bachelordom for those of a family man, is clear from the pictures of his early family life that have survived.

"He was sitting in his study in front of a heap of papers covered with mathematical formulae," says one student who visited him a few years after his marriage. "Writing with his right hand and holding his younger son in his left, he kept replying to questions from his elder son Albert, who was playing with his bricks. With the words, 'Wait a minute, I've nearly finished,' he gave me the children to look after for a few moments and went on working." A similar picture is painted by David Reichinstein, one of the Zurich professors. "The door of the flat was open to allow the floor which had just been scrubbed, as well as the washing hung up in the hall, to dry," he says. "I entered Einstein's room. He was calmly philosophic, with one hand rocking the bassinet in which there was a child. In his mouth Einstein had a bad, a very bad cigar, and in the other hand an open book. The stove was smoking horribly. How in the world could he bear it?"

The home life of a poorly paid academic in Switzerland in the first decade of the century must be kept in perspective. All the same, a colleague felt it necessary to ask: "How could he bear it?" The answer is that he had to.

Einstein married Mileva Maric in Berne on Tuesday, January 6, 1903. The two witnesses at the quiet wedding were the original members of the Olympia Academy, Maurice Solovine and Conrad Habicht. There was no honeymoon, and after a celebratory meal in a local restaurant the couple returned to their new home, a small flat in 49 Kramgasse, only a hundred yards from Berne's famous clocktower. Here there was a minor incident. Many stories were to arise, or to be invented, of the absentminded professor; but here, on his wedding day, Einstein did find on arriving back home that he had forgotten the key to his flat.

In March, 1905, Einstein was twenty-six. Only his papers on intermolecular forces distinguished him from hundreds of other young men serving their time in Government offices, and they did not distinguish him all that much. When, early in 1905, he rounded off the series in an inaugural dissertation for Zurich University, he had a total of six papers to show for the five years that had passed since his graduation.

Up to now, Einstein had no academic status. He had the run of the Patent Office Library, strong on engineering but weak on physics, and he read the leading physics journals published in German. But he had access to little else. Neither did he work, nor could he talk and debate even on social occasions, inside a university environment with its incessant point counterpoint of argument, its constant cross-fertilization of ideas and its stimulating climate of inquiry. The Olympia Academy, lively as it was, was no substitute for this. He corresponded with his former student friends in Zurich, and he occasionally visited them. But that was all. Thus from 1902 until 1905 Einstein worked on his own, an outsider of outsiders, scientifically provincial and having few links with the main body of contemporary physics. This isolation accounts for his broad view of specific scientific problems—he ignored the detailed arguments of others because he was unaware of them. It also shows a courage beyond the call of scientific duty, submission to the inner compulsion that was to drive him on throughout life and for which he was willing to sacrifice everything.

Any one of the main papers that he published in 1905 would alone have assured him a place in the textbooks. Three were published in the single famous Volume 17 of *Annalen der Physik*—today a bibliographical rarity that changes hands at many hundreds of dollars—and the fourth was published in Volume 18. All were comparatively short, and all contained the foundations for new theories even though they did not elaborate on them—"blazing rockets which in the dark of the night suddenly cast a brief but powerful illumination over an immense unknown region," as they have been described by Louis de Broglie. Yet in science there had been one burst of genius strikingly similar to Einstein's. Almost two and a half centuries earlier Newton had been driven by the plague at Cambridge to the quiet of Woolsthorpe and had there produced the calculus, an explanation of the spectral nature of white light, and the law of gravitation.

In the spring of 1905 Einstein gave a resume of things to come in a letter to his friend Conrad Habicht. He would soon, he said, be able to let him see four different papers, the first of which was very revolutionary and dealt with radiation and the energy of light. The next discussed different ways of discovering the real dimensions of atoms. The third dealt with the Brownian movement, discovered earlier in the century by a Scottish biologist, while the fourth was based on concepts of the electrodynamics of moving bodies and modified current ideas of time and space.

The promised papers were a peculiar mixture—as though a competently executed watercolor from the local art society had been thrown in with three Rembrandts. The "second work" was merely Einstein's inaugural dissertation for Zurich University, which he was having printed in Berne, interesting enough in its own way, but a minnow among the whales of the other three papers. Of these, that dealing with Brownian motion sprang most obviously from earlier work. For his doctoral dissertation had discussed various methods of statistical thermodynamics, and it was these tools that he used to predict not only that in certain circumstances the results of molecular movement could actually be seen under the microscope, but also the mass and the numbers of molecules in any particular volume.

This motion had been reported some seventy years earlier by Robert Brown, the Scottish naturalist, who had discovered that when pollen dust was suspended in water and studied under the microscope, the individual particles exhibited a continuous, zigzag, and apparently random motion. "These motions," he wrote, "were such as to satisfy me, after frequently repeated observation, that they arose neither from current in the fluid nor from its gradual evaporation, but belonged to the particle itself." Many men discovered more about the Brownian motion in the years that followed. M. Gouy saw that as the viscosity of the liquid increased, so did the sluggishness of the movements; Franz Exner noted that speed of movement increased with a rise in temperature but decreased if bigger particles were used.

When Einstein later observed this motion through the microscope for himself, he was fascinated since it seemed to him contrary to all experience. It was the explanation of this "contrary" experience that Einstein now gave in his paper "Über die von der molekularkinetischen Theorie der Wärme geforderte Bewegung von in ruhenden Flüssigkeiten suspendierten Teilchen" ("On the Motion of Small Particles Suspended in a Stationary Liquid According to the Molecular Kinetic Theory of Heat"). The random motion of the individual particles was due to the kinetic energy of the invisible molecules with which they were constantly colliding. From this point he went on to use his new statistical machinery to predict the mass and numbers of molecules involved. It was the essence of his theory that the mean kinetic energy of agitation of the particles would be exactly the same as the roughly known energy of agitation in a gas molecule, and this was, in fact, shown experimentally only a few years later—by Jean Perrin in Paris in 1908 and by Fletcher and Millikan four years later in Chicago.

"To appreciate the importance of this step," Max Born has written of Einstein's successful attempt to quantify the Brownian motion, "one has to remember that at that time [about 1900] atoms and molecules were still far from being as real as they are today—there were still physicists who did not believe in them." The latter included both Mach and "the old fighter against atomistics, Wilhelm Ostwald" who, Arnold Sommerfeld has stated, "told me once that he had been converted to atomistics by the complete explanation of the Brownian motion." Thus Einstein's figures for the invisible molecules had something in common with the Hertzian sparks that showed the existence of the radio waves postulated by Maxwell two decades earlier.

But Einstein's paper was also to have an important consequence for scientific methodology in general:

> The accuracy of measurement depends [as Max Born has pointed out] on the sensitivity of the instruments, and this again on the size and weight of the mobile parts, and the restoring forces acting on them. Before Einstein's work it was tacitly assumed that progress in this direction was limited only by experimental technique. Now it became obvious that this was not so. If an indicator, like the needle of a galvanometer, became too small or the suspending fibre too thin, it would never be at rest but perform a kind of

Brownian movement. This has in fact been observed. Similar phenomena play a large part in modern electronic technique, where the limit of observation is given by irregular observations which can be heard as "noise" in a loud-speaker. There is a limit of observability given by the laws of nature themselves.

Einstein's virtual proof of the existence of molecules, invisible to the human eye, postulated by theory rather than produced by experimental evidence, was symptomatic of the line that he was to take throughout the career on which he was now embarking. He believed that theories into which facts were later seen to fit were more likely to stand the test of time than theories constructed entirely from experimental evidence. This was certainly the case with the first paper, which he had described in his letter to Habicht, a paper that "fell like a bolt from the blue, so much so that the crisis which it ushered in some fifty years ago is not yet passed today," as Louis de Broglie described it in 1955. It was to help bring Einstein the Nobel Prize for Physics sixteen years later. It was to play a key part in the development of modern technology since the photoelectric effect whose law it propounded was to become a cornerstone of television. It contained Einstein's first implied admission of the duality of nature, which was to haunt his life, and an early hint of the indeterminacy problem that drove him, as De Broglie has put it "to end his scientific life in sad isolation and—paradoxically enough— apparently far behind the ideas of his time." Moreover, with the sense of theater that chance was to utilize so often in Einstein's life, it linked his scientific work at the age of twenty-six with two men whose nonscientific beliefs and attitudes were to influence him, and on some occasions to dominate him, for more than forty years—Max Planck, that devoted upholder of the German State, who was also the founder of the quantum theory, and Philipp Lenard, composed in almost equal parts of Nobel Prize winner and Jew-baiter.

This famous paper, "Über einen die Erzeugung und Verwandlung des Lichtes betreffenden heuristischen Gesichtspunkt" ("On a Heuristic Viewpoint Concerning the Production and Transformation of Light"), explained one particular phenomenon, the photoelectric effect, which had been puzzling scientists for years, and it suggested answers to a number of other less important scientific riddles. But it did a great deal more, and while it is usually known as Einstein's "photoelectric paper" it did not spring from consideration of this specific problem but from something far more fundamental. For Einstein, mulling over his previous work on thermodynamics and statistical mechanics, noted a discrepancy in current scientific beliefs and wondered how it could be removed: the photoelectric riddle was merely a particularly convenient one that could apparently be resolved by applying a revolutionary explanation of the discrepancy. To understand its importance it is necessary to consider briefly how the nature of light was regarded at the start of the twentieth century.

To the Greeks the idea that light consisted of minute grains in rapid movement appeared to be borne out by the fact that it traveled in straight lines and bounced off

Max Karl Ernst Ludwig Planck (1858–1947), the German physicist whose revolutionary quantum theory was based on the assumption that energy is emitted not in a continuous flow but as discrete bursts. These he named *quanta*, which means "how much" in Latin. While walking in the woods around Berlin in the winter of 1900, he turned to his son and said, "Today I have made a discovery as important as that of Newton." [AIP Niels Bohr Library, W.F. Meggers Collection]

mirrors in the same way that balls bounce off walls. Only in the early 1600s was there made the first of a series of discoveries that culminated, in the last third of the century, in the theory put forward by Huygens: that light was composed of waves propagated through a medium that he called the ether and that permeated all space. Newton, in his *Opticks*, apparently favored the corpuscular theory, although he also outlined a scheme in which corpuscles of light were associated with waves that influenced them—an idea revived some two and a half centuries later in the form of wave mechanics to explain the nature of matter. Not until the nineteenth century did the work first of Fresnel and then of Maxwell provide a wave explanation of light that appeared—at least for a few years—to deal satisfactorily with all the experimental evidence.

It was Hertz who raised one of the first questions that were to bring this comfortable state of affairs to an end. What he found was that when a sheet of glass was put between his wave-transmitter and his receiver, the sparks produced in the transmitter failed to produce as large a group of sparks in the receiver. He decided, naturally enough, that the receiving loop must be affected by the sparks' ultraviolet light, which does not penetrate glass, and that in some inexplicable way this light was thus increasing the electrical discharge from his metal receiver. Other scientists discovered that this photoelectric effect, as it came to be known, could be produced by visible as well as by ultraviolet light; that it was produced with some metals more easily than with others; and that the receiving metal acquired a small positive electrical charge.

Now elucidation of the nature of light by Maxwell's electromagnetic equations had been paralleled by another, and apparently contradictory, development. For while it had been found that light was radiated as electromagnetic waves, other physicists—Hendrik Lorentz in Leiden and J. J. Thomson in Cambridge among them—had been discovering that what could only be considered particles, the negatively charged electrons, played an important part in the constitution of electrified matter. It is at this stage that Lenard comes on the scene. A scientist of great skill, Lenard was a German whose desperation at his country's defeat in 1918 was to lead him into the welcoming arms of the

Nazi party; in addition his paranoic hatred of the Jews brought him, after 1919, into the movement that attempted to discredit both Einstein's honesty and his work. At the turn of the century Lenard put forward a simple explanation of the photoelectric effect; it was that photoelectrons, or negative charges, were knocked out of the metal by the light that hit it. Soon, however, he reported another less easily explicable phenomenon. Since electrons were ejected from the sensitive metal solely as a result of light falling upon it, then it might surely be assumed that an increase in light would produce an increase in the speed at which the electrons were thrown from the metal. This was not the case, however. If the intensity of the light was increased, then a greater number of electrons would be ejected from the metal, but they would continue to be ejected at the same speed. But—and this appeared even more inexplicable—if there was a change in the color of the light, or in other words in its frequency, then there would be a change in the speeds at which the electrons were thrown out; and the higher the frequency, the higher the speed of ejection.

While Lenard was thus occupied in the familiar scientific operation of answering one riddle and creating another in the process, Max Planck, by this time professor of theoretical physics in the University of Berlin, was grappling with a problem that at first glance seemed to be only indirectly concerned with the photoelectric effect. Planck had taken the chair after the death of Kirchhoff in 1887, and it was from a continuation of Kirchhoff's work that he produced the theory that was to alter man's idea of energy as drastically as Einstein's theory of relativity was to alter ideas of time and space.

Kirchhoff had been interested, like many of his contemporaries, in discovering more about the mechanism by which radiant energy was emitted by electromagnetic waves, already known to include not only the spectrum of visible light but the infrared and ultraviolet rays either side of them, as well as the newly discovered radio waves. It was known that as a body was heated its maximum energy was produced at shorter and shorter wavelengths, and its color passed from red to yellow and then to bluish-white. But all experiments appeared to be affected by the nature of the emitting body, only overcome by Kirchhoff's ingenious method of using "black body radiation," which utilized a closed container with blackened inner walls and one tiny pinhole. When the container was heated to incandescence, genuinely pure light of all the visible wavelengths could, in theory at least, be observed coming from the pinhole. This primitive equipment was supplemented in 1881 by the bolometer, invented by Samuel Langley, whose aerodynamic work led on to the Wright brothers and Kitty Hawk. With Langley's bolometer, which depended on the electrical measurement of minute quantities of heat set up in a blackened platinum wire, it was possible to record temperature changes as little as one millionth of a degree under the impact of specific wavelengths; thus there was now, it appeared, a route to an adequate description of the way that energy was radiated.

During the 1890s Planck found that this was far from being the case. Despite the efforts of physicists throughout Europe, it became clear that while one set of distribution formulas, produced by Wilhelm Wien, served well enough to explain radiation at low wavelengths, those at high wavelengths demanded the different mathematical explanation produced by Lord Rayleigh—as though nature had changed the rules of the game at half time. No one could explain it. "The discrepancy," Sir Basil Schonland has stated, "suggested that something fundamental had been missed by both. The affair, which was extremely closely examined by the best minds of the time, presented something like a scientific scandal."

It was to this discrepancy that Planck turned during the latter half of the 1890s. In the autumn of 1900 he thought he had solved the problem and on October 14 read a paper to the Berlin Physical Society that proposed a single neat expression to explain how radiation worked. This satisfied the Wien distribution formula at low wavelengths and Rayleigh's distribution formula at high ones; in fact, it fitted experimental observations between infrared measurements toward one end of the spectrum and ultraviolet measurements toward the other so well that some men working on ultraviolet found it necessary to repeat their experiments and amend their figures.

For Planck, this was not enough. Intuitively, he felt that something more or something different was required. "After some weeks of the most intense work of my life, clearness began to dawn upon me, and an unexpected view revealed itself in the distance," he later said.

Some weeks after his October address, Planck found the explanation. Walking in the Grunewald woods in Berlin, he turned to his son. "Today," he said, "I have made a discovery as important as that of Newton."

On December 14, 1900, Planck appeared again before the Physical Society. This time he announced that his earlier expression could best be derived from an entirely new hypothesis. It was not only new but startling. Planck now stated that his whole theory was based on one assumption: that energy was emitted not in the continuous flow that everyday common sense suggested but as discrete bursts, for which he used the Latin "how much," or quanta. The size of quanta was, moreover, directly related to the frequency of the electromagnetic wave with which they are associated; violet light, which has twice the frequency of red light, had associated quanta twice as large as those associated with red light. Linking the frequency of the radiation and the size of the quantum, there was, in the units current in Planck's time, which are still widely but not exclusively used, the magic quantity of $h = 6.6 \times 10^{-27}$, erg. sec., quickly known as Planck's constant and soon recognized as one of the fundamental constants of nature.

At first sight this revolutionary idea appeared to stick a dagger between the ribs of the accepted view that light consisted of waves rather than particles. But not even Planck could go as far as that. His theory, he stressed, was concerned with the relationship between radiation and matter, not with the nature of radiation on its journey between emission and reception; he allowed the discontinuous bursts of energy to join up in some inexplicable way and produce waves that dissolved into particulate entities as they were absorbed. Thus the "scientific scandal," as Schonland was later to describe it, had been removed only by creating a fresh one.

In 1903 J. J. Thomson, giving the Silliman Lectures at Yale University, appears to have been on the verge of dissipating it when he suggested that some form of localized radiant energy might account for a number of unexplained experimental facts, including the manner in which ultraviolet light ejected electrons from a metal surface. But the idea was taken no further. This preserved the wave-nature of light; it also left the way open for Einstein. For just as Niels Bohr was later to use the quantum theory to explain the structure of the atom, so did Einstein now use it to justify the idea that light could have characteristics of both wave and particle.

Until 1905 his published papers had dealt almost exclusively with thermodynamics and statistical mechanics; they were essentially studies in which the laws of nature were considered by reference to the random movements of vast numbers of individual particles that obeyed Newton's laws as obediently as the planets. But there were also Einstein's unpublished thoughts; and these were obsessed with the reality of light and its associated electromagnetic waves, a reality conceived not in terms of Newtonian particles but of the field that had been proposed by Faraday and developed by Maxwell. No one had up until now thought of asking the awkward questions that the contradiction begged; or if they had thought of it they had not dared. Einstein both thought and dared.

The formal difference between the theoretical ideas that physicists had formed about gases and other ponderable bodies, and Maxwell's theory of electromagnetic processes in so-called empty space, could be resolved, he suggested, if for some purposes light could be considered as a collection of independent particles that behaved like the particles of a gas—the "heuristic viewpoint" of his title. When Einstein began to consider this new concept in the light of his earlier work, he found that it provided some startlingly useful results. The photoelectric explanation was one of them.

For the size of Planck's quanta depended on the frequency of the light concerned, and the small quanta of a low-frequency light would, if they were considered as discrete packages of particulate energy, therefore eject the electrons they hit with a comparatively low speed; the bigger "packets of energy," as the quanta making up the higher-frequency colors could be considered, would of course eject at higher speeds the electrons they hit. This explanation would also account for what happened when the intensity of the light of any specific color was decreased. Each individual quantum that went to make it up would have the same power to eject an electron that it hit. But there would be fewer quanta, fewer "hits," and fewer electrons ejected. As Sir James Jeans said in describing the photochemical law that Einstein produced, his explanation of the photoelectric effect "not only prohibits the killing of two birds by one stone, but also the killing of one bird with two stones."

In his paper Einstein did more than put forward a theory that was, as he said, "in perfect agreement with observation"—and that was later to be confirmed experimentally. In addition, he calculated the maximum kinetic energy of the electron that was emitted, giving this by the use of the formula $hv\text{-}e$ where h is Planck's constant, v is the frequency of the light, and e is the energy lost by the electron in its escape from the metal surface, called the work function. Thus Einstein's conception of light as being formed of light quanta—or photons as they were later christened—in itself involved a paradoxical contradiction from which a man of lesser mental stature might have edged away. For while light, consisting of discrete packets of energy as indivisible as the atom was still thought to be, conformed—if it conformed to anything—to the corpuscular theory of Newton's day, the idea also utilized frequency, a vital feature of the wave theory. As Bohr was later to write, physics was thus "confronted with a novel kind of complementary relationship between the applications of different fundamental concepts of classical physics." Physicists began to study more closely these contradictory ideas that alone seemed to explain verifiable facts, and eventually, in the 1920s, they began to see the limitations of deterministic description. At the level of simple atomic processes, nature could be described in terms of statistical chance—the case of "God playing dice with the world" that Einstein would never accept. Yet he had pushed the stone that started the avalanche.

This was not clear in 1905. Even so, Einstein had to face the embarrassing contradiction that Planck had tried to avoid: for some purposes light must be regarded as a stream of particles, as Newton had regarded it; for others, it must be considered in terms of wave motion. But he believed that eventually, if men were only persistent enough, a satisfactory explanation for the contradiction would emerge. This was, in fact, to be the case some two decades later when De Broglie and Schrödinger, Born and Heisenberg, were to produce a conception of the physical world that could be regarded in terms either of waves or of particles—or, as one humorist called it, of "wavicles."

Planck himself was reluctant to accept Einstein's development of his theory, and as late as 1912 was rejecting, in Berlin lectures, the idea that light traveled through space as bunches of localized energy.

Einstein's record was thus an unusual one. He had applied Planck's revolutionary theory with apparent success to a physical phenomenon that classical physics could not explain. He had been more revolutionary than his elders, and they would not credit him with what he had done. It needed courage; but this was to be expected from the man who could, in the same volume of the *Annalen der Physik*, explode the bomb that was his new theory of relativity.

4. EINSTEIN'S RELATIVITY

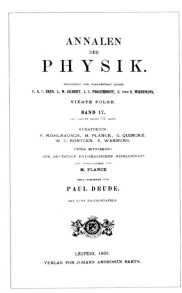

The title page of Volume 17 of *Annalen der Physik*, in which three of Einstein's four famous papers of 1905 were published: "Über einen die Erzeugung und Verwandlung des Lichtes betreffenden heuristischen Gesichtspunkt"; "Über die von der molekularkinetischen Theorie der Wärme geforderte Bewegung von in ruhenden Flüssigkeiten suspendierten Teilchen"; and "Zur Elektrodynamik bewegter Körper."

The Special Theory of Relativity that was to give Einstein his unique position in history was outlined in the third paper that he wrote for the *Annalen der Physik* in the summer of 1905. Entitled simply "Zur Elektrodynamik bewegter Körper" ("On the Electrodynamics of Moving Bodies"), it was in many ways one of the most remarkable scientific papers that had ever been written. Even in form and style it was unusual, lacking the notes and references that give weight to most serious expositions and merely noting, in its closing paragraph, that the author was indebted for a number of valuable suggestions to his friend and colleague, M. Besso. This dissertation of some nine thousand words overturned man's accepted ideas of time and space in a way that was, as *The Times* of London once put it, "an affront to common sense" and drastically altered the classical concepts of physics still held by the overwhelming majority of scientists. In addition, it provided such an accurate blueprint for the way in which the physical world was built that within a generation men could no more ignore relativity in the teaching of physics than they could ignore grammar in the teaching of language.

During the seventy-odd years that have passed since Einstein tossed this rock into the pool, an immense literature and exegesis have spread out around the paper, the theory, and its history. This literature does more than describe, explain, and criticize what Einstein wrote, and attempts with varying degrees of success to outline his theory to the layman. It also gives differing assessments of Einstein's debt to his predecessors and shows scientific historians to be as practiced as their less specialized colleagues in the gentle art of blacking an opponent's eye. This is natural enough. Most revolutionary theories—scientific as well as political—have roots deep in the past, and relativity is no exception to the rule. Today, nearly eighty years after Einstein posted the manuscript of his paper to *Annalen der Physik*, the dust is still stirred by discussion of what inspired him. The controversy about how much he owed to his predecessors complicates still further the problem of explaining a complicated subject to a lay public. However, it is not insuperable and is best tackled by outlining briefly the background against which his paper was written; by describing first the daring propositions he put forward and then their implications; and by surveying the sometimes contradictory evidence of the paper's genesis.

Over the background of the scientific world as it existed in the first years of the twentieth century, there still towered, as the central ornament, the bold figure of Sir Isaac Newton. Driven in 1666 from Cambridge to his Lincolnshire home by the plague when only twenty-four, he had been almost of an age with Einstein; and, like Einstein, he had in a single summer delivered three hammer blows at the foundations of contemporary science. The formulation of the law of gravity was the greatest of the three, showing that the fall of the apple and the passage of the moon in its orbit were governed by the same natural laws. For, starting with an explanation of the forces that kept the planets on their tracks, Newton constructed the first modern synthesis of the physical world, a logical explanation of the universe. Judged by contemporary standards, his universe was a simple and comforting place through which planets and stars, men and animals, the smallest particles of matter, and even the particles of which light was deemed to consist, moved in accordance with the same mathematical laws:

> From the time of Newton up to the end of the last century [Robert Oppenheimer has noted] physicists built, on the basis of these laws, a magnificently precise and beautiful science involving the celestial mechanics of the solar system, involving incredible problems in the Cambridge Tripos, involving the theory of gases, involving the behaviour of fluids, of elastic vibrations, of sound—indeed, a comprehensive system so robust and varied and apparently all-powerful that what was in store for it could hardly be imagined.

In the first pages of his *Philosophiae Naturalis Principia Mathematica*, which enshrined these laws, Newton used two words whose definitions formed the basis not only of his whole system but of everything that had been constructed as a by-product of it—two words that between them formed the bottom layer of the house that science had been building for two and a half centuries. One was "time," the other was "space." "Absolute, true and mathematical time," as Newton put it, "of itself and from its own nature, flows equably, without relation to anything external, and by another name is called duration." Space could be "absolute space, in its own nature, without relation to anything external," which "remains always similar and immovable"; or relative space, which was "some movable dimensions or measure of the absolute spaces."

From these definitions Newton went on to illustrate the principle of the addition of velocities, a principle so obvious that at first there seems little point in repeating it. Yet it was to be radically amended by Einstein's Special Theory, and it is salutary to consider how Newton expressed it:

> Absolute motion [he wrote], is the translation of a body from one relative place into another. Thus in a ship under sail the relative place of a body is that part of the ship which the body possesses; or that part of the cavity which the body fills, and which therefore moves together with the ship; and relative rest is the continuance of the body in the same part of that immovable space, in which the ship itself, its cavity, and all that it contains, is moved. Wherefore, if the earth is really at rest, the body which relatively rests in the ship, will really and absolutely move with the same velocity which the ship

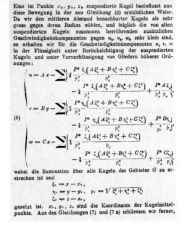

Extract of Einstein article published in *Annalen der Physik,* 1905.

has on the earth. But if the earth also moves, the true and absolute motion of the body will arise, partly from the true motion of the earth, in immovable space, partly from the relative motion of the ship on the earth; and if the body moves also relatively in the ship, its true motion will arise, partly from the true motion of the earth, in immovable space, and partly from the relative motions as well of the ship on the earth, as of the body in the ship; and from these relative motions will arise the relative motion of the body on the earth. As if that part of the earth where the ship is, was truly moved towards the east, with a velocity of 10,010 parts; while the ship itself, with a fresh gale, and full sails, is carried towards the west, with a velocity expressed by 10 of those parts; but a sailor walks in the ship towards the east, with 1 part of the said velocity; then the sailor will be moved truly in immovable space towards the east, with a velocity of 10,001 parts, and relatively on the earth towards the west, with a velocity of 9 of those parts.

Newton's sailor—pacing three miles an hour east on the deck of his ship while the ship sails past the coast at twelve miles an hour in the same direction and therefore moving past the land at fifteen miles an hour—has his modern counterpart: the train passenger traveling at forty miles an hour whose carriage is passed by a second train traveling at fifty miles an hour, to whom a passenger in the faster train is moving at only ten miles an hour. In both cases it is possible to describe the movement of a person—or a particle—in one frame of reference (the sailor relative to the ship) and then to describe it in a second frame of reference (the sailor relative to the land) by the simple addition of velocities.

Newton's sailor and the train movements of the twentieth century have one other important thing in common. Newton himself gives a clue to it when he writes: "The motions of bodies included in a given space are the same among themselves, whether that space is at rest or moves uniformly forward in a straight line." In other words, the mechanical laws that are applicable in a ship—or a train—when at rest are also applicable when it is moving uniformly. Nature does not give special preference to one situation or the other, and any measurements or experiments made on a vehicle in uniform motion will produce the same results as when it is at rest.

During the second half of the nineteenth century, attacks began to be made on this mechanical view of the universe. From one side came those prepared to strike at its epistemological roots and those who sought to deny that the apparently sound mechanical structure was anything more than a convenient illusion.

But if men were able to cast doubt on Newton's absolute space and time, an equally dangerous attack was to come from a different quarter, as confusing and sometimes conflicting evidence on the nature and behavior of light accumulated during the nineteenth century. To Newton, light was a stream of particles moving according to mechanical laws, although his contemporary, Christiaan Huygens, thought it might be instead a vibration in an unspecified medium, much as sound was a vibration in the air. The problem looked as if it had been solved in mid-century when the French physicists Dominique Arago, followed by Jean Foucault, produced evidence supporting the wave

Isaac Newton (1642–1727), who transformed man's ideas of the universe with his law of universal gravitation, his three laws of motion, and his development of the calculus independently of Leibnitz. [AIP Niels Bohr Library]

theory. If any doubt remained, it appeared to be dispelled during the next few decades. Maxwell's theoretical calculations showed that the vibrations associated with light were due to very rapid oscillations of electric and magnetic fields; twenty years later Hertz, with his demonstration of electromagnetic radio waves, seemed to put this beyond question.

But there was one particular way in which Maxwell's electromagnetism operated in a manner totally different from Newtonian mechanics. Newton had built his law of gravitation on the idea of action-at-a-distance, believing that the pull of gravity between the apple and the ground, the moon and the earth, the earth and the sun, in fact between all the components of the universe, operated as a mysterious and instantaneous force across empty space. Maxwell utilized instead the idea of "the field" that had been conceived by Faraday: a region of space in which certain physical conditions were created and through which forces were transmitted; somewhat like ripples through an invisible jelly, the electromagnetic waves of light being propagated through the field in straight lines at a finite speed, and the pull of the magnet for iron filings being a property of the field that the magnet had itself created.

Largely due to the concept of the field, it was believed during the last decades of the nineteenth century that electromagnetic waves required a medium through which they could travel, just as sound needs the molecules of air before it can be heard and seismic waves require the medium of the earth before they can be recorded. Scientists decided that this medium was the ether, vaguely postulated since the time of the Greeks. But the presence of the ether had never been confirmed, and there was a doubt about its existence, like the pea under the princess's mattress—minute, yet sufficient to prevent peace of mind. It was to resolve this doubt that the famous—indeed, almost legendary—

Michelson-Morley experiment was designed in 1887. How much Einstein knew of this before 1905 is questionable, and even more so is the importance to his thinking of what he did know. The awkward results of the experiment permeated the scientific climate of the 1890s, and its implications must even have been noted by Einstein in the Berne Patent Office. Later, moreover, it could be seen as a linchpin of the whole theory of relativity. As Einstein said years later, talking to Sir Herbert Samuel in the grounds of Government House, Jerusalem, "If Michelson-Morley is wrong, then relativity is wrong."

By the time that Einstein came on the scene, other experiments had been carried out in an effort to show the existence of the ether by recording the effects of the earth's passage through it. Trouton and Noble had tried to discover experimentally the torque that should, in theory, have been shown by the charging of a condenser hung from a fine filament with its plates inclined to the ether drift. Both Lord Rayleigh and Brace had looked for double refraction in a transparent body produced by the passage of the ether through it. All these experiments had failed to produce any evidence for the existence of the ether. It was, however, the Michelson-Morley experiment that lodged in the scientific gullet, partly because it seemed impossible to escape from its implications, partly on account of its basic simplicity.

What Michelson and Morley set out to discover was the effect of the earth's passage through the postulated ether on the speed of light. Long known to be roughly 186,000 miles per second, it was so great as to present technical problems that would have ruled out the experiment before the last decades of the nineteenth century. On the other hand, the experiment's basic mathematics are quite simple.

To understand them one has merely to consider the case of two oarsmen rowing respectively across a river four hundred yards wide and four hundred yards up and down the same stream of water, an analogy that is one of many littering the pages explaining Einstein's work. Both oarsmen have the same speed—which can be arbitrarily given as five hundred yards a minute, with the stream running at an equally arbitrary rate of three hundred yards a minute. The first oarsman starts from one bank, aiming to arrive at a point on the far bank directly opposite—in other words, four hundred yards away. If there were no current, he would reach it in four-fifths of a minute. But since there is a current, he must point his boat upstream. Now an observer starting at the same point as the oarsman but allowing himself merely to float downstream will see the "aiming-point" on the far bank moving "back" at a rate of three hundred yards a minute (the rate of the stream's movement), while the oarsman is moving away from him at a rate of five hundred yards a minute (the speed at which he is rowing). The construction of a simple right-angled triangle, using this information plus an equally simple use of Pythagoras, will show that the oarsman will have traveled five hundred yards before he reaches the far bank and that the time he takes will be one minute for the single journey or two minutes there and back.

Now what of the oarsman given the comparable task of rowing four hundred yards upstream and returning to the same point? During the first minute he will have covered five hundred minus three hundred yards, which is two hundred yards. So he will take two minutes for the journey against the stream. On his return his speed of five hundred yards a minute will be aided by the three-hundred-yard-a-minute stream so that the four hundred yards will take him only half a minute. That is, the time for the double journey measured up and down the stream is more than the double journey measured across the stream, and it always will be more except in a currentless river. And by measuring the times both oarsmen take, it is possible to calculate both the speed at which they row and also the speed of the river. Similarly, Michelson and Morley proposed, it should be possible to confirm the existence of the ether.

In their experiment the ether, presumably streaming past the earth at twenty miles a second as the earth moved in its orbit around the sun, would represent the current. A ray of light, split into two, would represent the two oarsmen. These two rays would be directed along two paths identical in length but at right angles to one another, then they would be reflected back to the "test-bed" of the experiment—after having made journeys that would be respectively "across," and "up" and then "down," the presumed flow of the ether. If the "ether flow" had an effect on light comparable to the normal mechanical effects, the two returning rays would be out of phase. The result would be interference-fringes, or bands of alternately light and dark color, and from these it would be possible to calculate the speed of the ether wind relative to the movement of the earth. Nearly forty years later, Edward Appleton used a comparable technique with radio waves to pinpoint the height of the ionosphere from which such waves are reflected back to the earth.

The huge difference between the speed of light and the mere twenty miles per second of the earth's orbit around the sun presented considerable problems, and an earlier experiment carried out in 1881 by Michelson alone had failed. Now these inherent problems had been solved, and "pure" science was able to move forward once again on the vehicle provided by technology. This has happened frequently. From the days of William Herschel, whose discovery of infrared rays in 1800 was aided by sensitive thermometers, through the work of Oersted, Von Fraunhofer, Wheatstone, and Joule, knowledge of the physical world has marched steadily forward on the achievements of the craftsmen. Maxwell, on arriving at Aberdeen, had stated significantly: "I am happy in the knowledge of a good instrument maker, in addition to a smith, an optician and a carpenter." In another field, accurate gravimetric analysis was made possible by improvements in the chemical balance. Hermann Bondi has emphasized that "the enormous stream of discoveries at the end of the nineteenth century that gave us such insight as the discovery of X-rays, working with radioactivity, and all that, is entirely due to the fact that the technologists developed decent vacuum pumps."

The process of pure science moving forward with the packhorses of technology was now illustrated by Michelson and Morley, who set up their apparatus in the Case

Institute of Technology in Cleveland, Ohio. The massive stone test-bed, nearly five feet square, was floated in a bowl of mercury to obviate vibrations. The light rays used were ingeniously lengthened by a system of mirrors. The experiments were carried out at various times of day to lessen the chances of experimental error. The results, however they were considered, told one incontrovertible story: light that traveled back and forth across the ether stream did the journey in exactly the same time as light traveling the same distance up and down the ether stream.

The problem that now faced science was considerable. For there seemed to be only three alternatives. The first was that the earth was standing still, a scuttling of the whole Copernican theory, which was unthinkable. The second was that the ether was carried along by the earth in its passage through space, a possibility that had already been ruled out to the satisfaction of the scientific community by a number of experiments, notably those of the English astronomer, James Bradley. The third solution was that the ether just did not exist, which to many nineteenth century scientists was equivalent to scrapping current views of light, electricity, and magnetism and starting again.

The only other explanation must surely lie in some perverse feature of the physical world that scientists had not yet suspected, and during the next few years this was sought by three men in particular—George Fitzgerald, professor of natural and experimental philosophy at Trinity College, Dublin; Hendrik Lorentz of Leiden, the kindly humanitarian physicist whose lifetime spanned the closing days of Newtonian cosmology and the splitting of the atom—the man who, wrote Einstein within a few weeks of his own death, "for me personally…meant more than all the others I have met on my life's journey"; and the French mathematician, Henri Poincaré.

The Fitzgerald explanation came first. To many it must have seemed that he had strained at a gnat and swallowed an elephant. For while Fitzgerald was unwilling to believe that the velocity of light could remain unaffected by the velocity of its source, he suggested instead that all moving objects were shortened along the axis of their movement. A foot-rule moving end forward would be slightly shorter than a stationary foot-rule, and the faster it moved the shorter it would be. The speed of the earth's movement was all that was involved, so the contraction would be extremely small, and it would only rise to appreciable amounts as the speed involved rose to a sizable proportion of the speed of light itself. But it was not this alone that made the proposal apparently incapable of proof or disproof. Any test instruments would adjust themselves in the same way, shortening themselves as they were turned into the direction of the earth's movement through the ether. For some years this explanation appeared to be little more than a plausible trick—"I have been rather laughed at for my view over here," Fitzgerald wrote to Lorentz from Dublin in 1894—and it was only transformed into something more when Lorentz turned his mind to the question.

Lorentz had been among the first to postulate the electron, the negatively

Hendrik Antoon Lorentz (1853–1928).
[AIP Niels Bohr Library]

charged particle whose existence had finally been proved by J. J. Thomson at Cambridge. It now seemed to him that such a contraction could well be a direct result of electromagnetic forces produced when a body with its electrical charges was moved through the ether. These would disturb the equilibrium of the body, and its particles would assume new relative distances from one another. The result would be a change in the shape of the body, which would become flattened in the direction of its movement. The contraction would thus be explained, as Philipp Frank has put it, as "a logical consequence of several simultaneous hypotheses, namely the validity of the electro-magnetic field equations and laws of force and the hypothesis that all bodies are built up of electric charges."

Lorentz' invocation of electromagnetism thus brought a whiff of sanity into the game. Here, at least, was a credible explanation of how a foot-rule in motion could be of a different length from the foot-rule at rest. However, if this solved one problem it created others; and it played havoc with the simple transformation that had hitherto been used to describe events taking place in one frame of reference in terms of a different one. This had served well enough throughout the centuries for sailors on ships, for men on horseback, and for the early railways. It serves well enough for flight and even for contemporary space travel. Yet if Lorentz' hypothesis was correct, the simple addition of velocities could no longer hold water. For if distances contract with relative speed, then the yards paced out on the deck by Newton's sailor will be slightly shorter than the relatively stationary yards on the shore that his ship has sailed past. The smallness of the difference, so minute that it can be disregarded for practical purposes, can be gauged by even a nonmathematician's comparison of the simple equations, or "transformations," of the Newtonian world with those that Fitzgerald had provided and that were given a fresh significance by Lorentz. In the old Galilean transformation, the new place of the sailor on his deck is given by his old position plus or minus the speed of his walking multiplied by the time he has been on the move—in other words his old position x, plus or minus vt. But using the new set of equations that Lorentz now developed—and that soon became known as the Lorentz transformations—the sailor's new position is represented by this $x \pm vt$ divided by $\sqrt{1 - (v^2/c^2)}$.

In the case of the sailor walking at three miles an hour, v^2 will be nine, and in most examples from everyday life it will be a similarly humble figure; but c is the speed of light in miles per second, and c^2 is measured in millions of miles per hour. Once this is realized, two things become immediately clear: that the sailor need not be worried by the Lorentz transformations, and that these will, as Fitzgerald had forecast, begin to have significant applications only when the speeds concerned are a significant percentage of the speed of light.

While Fitzgerald and Lorentz were struggling to produce these explanations for physical experiments, Henri Poincaré was making a different approach. He was concerned not so much with the awkward specific problem of the speed of light as with the conglomeration of problems being presented to physicists at the turn of the century. He was, moreover, tackling them from an angle more philosophical than that of Fitzgerald and Lorentz. "Suppose," he argued, "that in one night all the dimensions of the universe became a thousand times larger. The world will remain *similar* to itself if we give the word *similitude* the meaning it has in the third book of Euclid....Have we any right, therefore, to say that we know the distance between two points?" Poincaré's answer was "No"—the concept of space being relative to the frame of reference within which its distances were measured.

Poincaré reached the climax of his reputation in the 1900s, and in 1904 he was among those invited to a Congress of Arts and Sciences at the Universal Exposition, St. Louis, held to commemorate the Louisiana Purchase a century earlier. Here, in a speech that was part of a symposium surveying human thought in the nineteenth century, he dealt with the contemporary crisis in physics. "Perhaps," he said, "we should construct a whole new mechanics, of which we only succeed in catching a glimpse, where, inertia increasing with the velocity, the velocity of light would become an impassable limit." The Lorentz transformation would no doubt be included in the new structure, and it might well form part of a new principle of relativity that would replace, or supplement, the restricted principle that was epitomized by the Galilean transformation. Poincaré was, as he stressed, doing his best to fit such new ideas as were required into the existing classical principles—"and as yet," he concluded at St. Louis "nothing proves that the principles will not come forth from the combat victorious and intact."

His speech was an indication of the scientific unrest and philosophical distrust created not only by the Michelson-Morley experiment but by others made during the preceding two decades in Cambridge and Berlin, in Leiden and Paris. But there was no hint of the Special Theory, created by Einstein for different reasons, after an approach across different territory.

While Fitzgerald, Lorentz, and Poincaré were trying to rescue physics from the cul-de-sac into which it appeared to have been led by the Michelson-Morley experiment, Einstein was wondering about the world, gaining a basic grounding in physics at the E.T.H. and giving special attention to what he realized, early on, were the revolutionary implications of Maxwell's electromagnetic theory, based on continuous fields. This was a new idea of the way in which the world had been made, and it continued to exercise Einstein for a decade, working away like a fermenting yeast in contrast to the boring material with which the Zurich masters tried to fill the stockpot of his mind.

As early as the age of sixteen, he had considered what he would see were he able to follow a beam of light at its own velocity through space. Here is a problem-picture as graphic as any of the number with which he was to explain his ideas. What, in fact, would be seen by anyone who could travel as fast as the oscillating electromagnetic waves that by the turn of the century were known to cause the phenomenon of light? The answer, believed Einstein, was a spatially oscillatory electromagnetic field at rest. But this was a contradiction in terms of which Maxwell's equations gave no hint. Quite as important, if such a conception were feasible, it would mean that the laws of electromagnetism would be different for observers at rest and for those on the move—at least for those moving at the speed of light. But it seemed soundly established that the mechanical laws of the Newtonian universe were the same for all observers, and Einstein saw no reason for thinking that the laws of electromagnetism would be any different. Thus it looked as certain as the QED at the end of a theorem that the laws of nature would prevent anyone or anything moving at the speed of light. But this idea, in turn, raised its own problems. For in the mechanical Newtonian world it was always possible to add a little more force and thus make the billiard ball, or the cannonball, go a little faster. What was there to prevent addition plus addition pushing up speeds above that of light?

Einstein himself has given more than a hint of how he worked away at the problem. "I must confess," he told Alexander Moszkowski in Berlin in 1915, "that at the very beginning, when the Special Theory of Relativity began to germinate in me, I was visited by all sorts of nervous conflicts. When young, I used to go away for weeks in a state of confusion, as one who at that time had yet to overcome the stage of stupefaction in his first encounter with such questions." To R. S. Shankland, professor at the Case Institute of Technology, Cleveland, Ohio, he said in old age that he had "worked for ten years; first as a student when, of course, he could only spend part-time on it, but the problem was always with him. He abandoned many fruitless attempts, 'until at last it came to me that time was suspect.'"

He worked alone, or almost alone. His earlier papers had brought him into the physicists' world—or, more accurately, into contact with it by correspondence. But he had none of the stimulus of university life, he played no part in any scientific group or society. For all practical purposes he was a scientific loner, trying out his ideas not on sharp minds of professional equals but on the blunt edges of the Swiss civil service. His only two confidants were two colleagues, Josef Sauter and the Michelangelo Besso whom he had eased into the Patent Office the previous year.

Sauter, eight years older than Einstein, was given the young man's notes to criticize after the two had walked home from the office one evening. "I pestered him for a whole month with every possible objection without managing to make him in the least impatient, until I was finally convinced that my objections were no more than the usual judgments of contemporary physics," Sauter has written. "I cannot forget the patience and good temper with which he listened, agreeing or disagreeing with my objections. He went over it again and again until he saw that I had understood his ideas. 'You are the second to whom I have told my discovery,' he said."

Besso's version of events was: "Einstein the eagle took Besso the sparrow under his wing. Then the sparrow fluttered a little higher." Certainly Besso was the only person given a niche in history in the famous paper outlining the Special Theory.

Einstein began by doing exactly what he had done when dealing with the photoelectric effect: he noted a contradiction in contemporary scientific beliefs apparent for years but conveniently ignored. In the first case it was the contradiction between the Newtonian world of corpuscles and the Maxwellian world of fields. Here, it was something perhaps even more fundamental: the contradiction implicit in Faraday's law of induction. This had for years been one of the accepted facts of life, and to raise awkward questions about it was to spit in a sacred place. Yet, Einstein pointed out, the current induced between a magnet and a conductor depends according to observation only on the relative motion of the conducting wire and the magnet "whereas the customary view," in other words, the accepted theory of currents, drew a distinction according to which of the two bodies was in motion. Faraday had discovered the induction law in 1834 but, as Born has put it, "everybody had known all along that the effect depended only on relative motion, but nobody had taken offense at the theory not accounting for this circumstance." Even had they done so, few would have had the temerity to pass on, in Einstein's grand style, to what he saw as the inevitable consequences: the destruction of the idea of absolute rest and the proposal that the same laws of electrodynamics and optics would be valid for all frames of reference for which the equations of mechanics held good.

This linking of electrodynamics and mechanics was the crux of the matter. In the world of electromagnetism, governed by the field-laws of Faraday and Maxwell, light was propagated at a constant speed that could not be surpassed; but there seemed to be little connection here with Newtonian mechanics, which made it possible to increase the speed of an object indefinitely by adding more energy to it. What Einstein now proposed was that the velocity of light was a constant and a maximum in the electromagnetic and the mechanical worlds and that light would thus travel with a constant velocity that was independent of the bodies emitting or receiving it. This would explain the failure to discover the movement of the earth through the ether, and it would also answer Einstein's boyhood riddle of how a beam of light would look if you traveled at its own speed. The answer to the riddle was that this would be impossible since only light could reach the speed of light.

The inclusion of Newton's mechanical world within that of Maxwell's electromagnetism is difficult to conceive. For what it says is this: that while a cricket ball thrown forward at x miles an hour from a train traveling at y miles an hour will apparently be traveling at x plus y miles an hour, something very different happens with light. Whatever the speed of the train from which it is being emitted, light will travel at the same constant speed of some 186,000 miles a second. Furthermore, it will be received at this same constant speed, whatever the speed of the vehicle that receives it—as though the cricket ball thrown from the speeding train would arrive at the fielder on the ground with the same speed whether he was standing still, running in the direction of the train, or running toward it.

This, of course, appeared to be ridiculous. As Bertrand Russell has said, "Every-

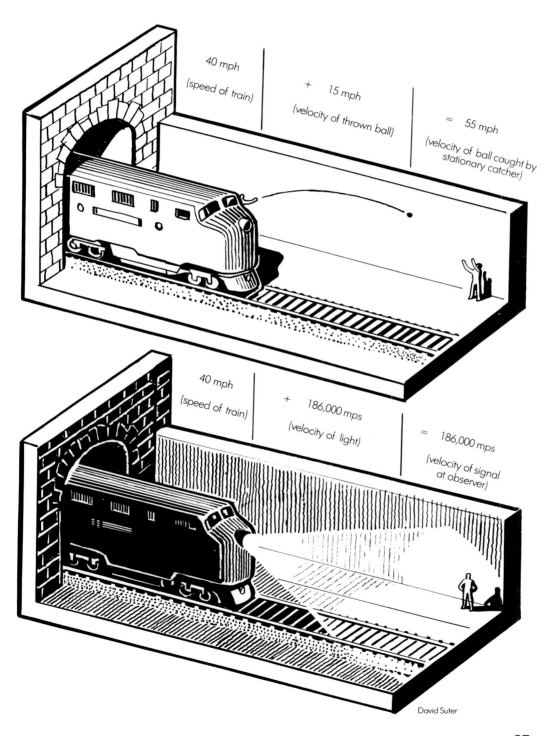

40 mph

(speed of train)

+ 15 mph

(velocity of thrown ball)

= 55 mph

(velocity of ball caught by stationary catcher)

40 mph

(speed of train)

+ 186,000 mps

(velocity of light)

= 186,000 mps

(velocity of signal at observer)

David Suter

Constancy of the Speed of Light

Einstein's Special Theory of Relativity stated that the velocity of light was a constant that was independent of the uniform motion of the bodies emitting it or receiving it. Thus, while a ball thrown forward at x miles per hour from a train traveling at y miles per hour would be traveling at x plus y miles per hour, something very different happens with light. Whatever the speed of the train, a flash of light emitted from it would travel at a constant speed of some 186,000 miles per second. Furthermore, it would be received at this same constant speed. If this rule applied to the ball thrown from the moving train, it would arrive at a receiver on the ground with the same speed whether he was standing still, running toward the train, or running away from the train.

body knows that if you are on an escalator you reach the top sooner if you walk up than if you stand still. But if the escalator moved with the velocity of light you would reach the top at exactly the same moment whether you walked up or stood still." But Einstein went on to link this assumption with his initial idea—that all the laws of nature are identical to all observers moving uniformly relative to one another. It required more than vision and audacity—qualities demanded of Blondin crossing the Falls, of Whymper nonchalantly tackling the unclimbed Matterhorn, of Whittle, confident that the jet would work. It required also the quality of intuition, a feel for nature as indefinable as a poet's sense of words or the artist's knowledge of what his last dab of materialistic paint can unlock in the human mind.

Einstein once wrote with his collaborator, Leopold Infeld, of "the eternal struggle of the inventive human mind for a fuller understanding of the law governing physical phenomena." Sir Basil Schonland, writing of Maxwell—whose relaxation was writing verse—has no hesitation in describing him as "fey," a word not commonly used to describe scientific genius. Einstein himself was always ready to agree that inventiveness, imagination, the intuitive approach—the very stuff of which artists rather than scientists are usually thought to be made—played a serious part in his work. And when his friend Janos Plesch commented years later that there seemed to be some connection between mathematics and fiction, a field in which the writer made a world out of invented characters and situations and then compared it with the existing world, Einstein replied that there might be something in this idea.

The problems created by linking Einstein's two assumptions—the similarity of all natural laws for all observers and the constancy of the speed of light in both the electromagnetic and the mechanical worlds—become evident when one reconsiders Newton's handy sailor. Consider him standing on deck as his ship sails parallel to a long jetty. At each end of the jetty there stands a signal lamp, and midway between the two lamps there stands an observer. As the sailor passes the observer, flashes of light are sent out by the two lamps. They are sent out, so far as the stationary observer on the jetty is concerned, at exactly the same time. The light rays coming from each end of the jetty have to travel the same distance to reach him, and they will reach him simultaneously. So far, so good. But what about the sailor on the ship—who will have been at an equal distance from both lamps as each sent out its light signal? He knows that both flashes travel with the same speed. Although this speed is very great, it is finite, and since he is moving away from one lamp and toward the other he will receive the light signals at different times. As far as he is concerned, they will not have been switched on simultaneously.

Here is the first extraordinary result of linking Einstein's two assumptions. If they are correct—and there is now no doubt about this—the old idea of simultaneity is dethroned; for events that are simultaneous to the observer on the jetty are not simultaneous to the sailor on deck. If the nub of Einstein's Special Relativity can be considered

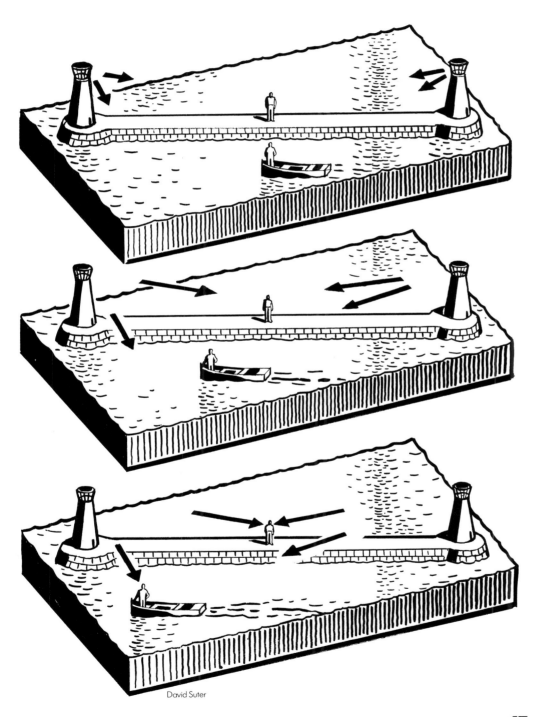

The Relativity of Simultaneity

If an observer standing on a long jetty, midway between two signal lamps, sees flashes of light sent out from both lamps at the same time, they will reach him simultaneously. However, a sailor standing on a ship sailing parallel to the jetty will be a different distance from each lamp when the flashes reach him, since he has been, and is, moving away from one lamp and toward the other. Since the speed of light is constant, he will receive the signals at different times. "So we see," as Einstein put it, "that we cannot attach any *absolute* significance to the concept of simultaneity, but that two events which, viewed from a system of coordinates, are simultaneous, can no longer be looked upon as simultaneous events when envisaged from a system which is in motion relatively to that system."

David Suter

as resting within any one sentence, it rests in this realization that one man's "now" is another man's "then"; that "now" itself is a subjective conception, valid only for an observer within one specific frame of reference.

Despite the apparent chaos that this appears to cause, there is one stable factor that it is possible to grasp as thankfully as a rock climber grasps a jug-handle hold in a dangerous place. That factor is the constancy of the speed of light, and with its aid all natural phenomena can be described in terms that are correct for all frames of reference in constant relative motion with each other. All that was needed, Einstein went on to demonstrate, were the Lorentz transformation equations. Using these instead of the earlier and simpler Newtonian transformations, it was still possible to connect events in any two frames of reference, whether the difference in their relative speeds was that between a sailor and the deck, between a ship and the coast, or between a physicist in the laboratory and the electrons of atomic experiments that were already known to move at a sizable proportion of the speed of light.

But a price had to be paid for resolving this difference between two conceptions of simultaneity; or, put more accurately, it had to be admitted that if the constancy of the speed of light was allowed to restore order from chaos, then not one but two factors in the equations were different from the simple stable things that man had always imagined. For velocity is provided by distance divided by time, and if velocity was invariant in the Lorentz transformations, not only distance but time itself could be variable. If the Newtonian world of mechanics as well as the Maxwellian world of electromagnetism were subject to the invariant velocity of light, both distance—or space—and time were no longer absolute.

It is at this point that the difference between the ideas of Fitzgerald, Lorentz, and even Poincaré, and the ideas of Einstein, begin to appear. For Einstein's predecessors, the Lorentz transformation was merely a useful tool for linking objects in relative motion. For him it was not a mathematical tool so much as a revelation about nature itself.

The difference between the earlier view and that of Einstein was exemplified by what Max Born, one of the first expositors of relativity, called "the notorious controversy as to whether the contraction is 'real' or only 'apparent.'" Lorentz had one view. "Asked if I consider this contraction as a real one, I should answer 'Yes,'" he said. "It is as real as anything we can observe." Sir Arthur Eddington, the later great exponent of Einstein, held a rather different view. "When a rod is started from rest into uniform motion, nothing whatever happens to the rod," he has written. "We say that it contracts; but length is not a property of the rod; it is a relation between the rod and the observer. *Until the observer is specified the length of the rod is quite indeterminate.*"

But it was not only distance but also time that was now seen to be relative. The idea was not entirely new. Voigt had suggested in 1887 that it might be mathematically convenient to use a local time in moving reference systems. But just as Einstein transformed earlier ideas of the curious "contraction" by showing that it was space itself that was altered by relative speed, so was his concept of relative time far more than a mathematical convenience. It was, in fact, more than a concept in the proper meaning of the word. For with his Special Theory Einstein was not so much propounding an idea as revealing a truth of nature that had previously been overlooked. And as far as time was concerned the truth was that a clock attached to any moving system in relative movement ran more slowly than a clock that was stationary. This was not in any sense a mechanical phenomenon; it was not in any way connected with the physical properties of the clock and—as was to be shown less than half a century later—it was as true of clocks operated by atomic vibrations as of those operated by other methods; it was a property of the way in which God had made the world.

Once it is accepted, as it was during the years that followed 1905, that space and time are relatively different in moving and in stationary systems, and that both can be linked by the Lorentz transformations, the position of the velocity of light as the limiting velocity of the universe becomes clear. For the stationary measuring rod that shrinks at an ever-faster rate as its speed increases, and reaches half its original length at nine-tenths the speed of light, would shrink to nothing as it reached ten-tenths. Similarly, the recordings on a clock would slow to a standstill as it reached the same speed.

Three questions arise. One is the question of which is the "real" dimension and which the "real" time. Another is the riddle of why the extraordinary characteristic of the universe revealed by the Special Theory had escaped man's notice for so long. The third is the question of what difference the Special Theory could make to the world. The answer to the first is simple. The "real" dimension and the "real" time is that of the observer, and the stationary and the moving observers are each concerned with their own reality. Just as beauty lies in the eye of the beholder, so does each man carry with him his own space and his own time. But there is one rider to this, a restriction put even on relativity. For while the time at which something happens is indeed a relative matter, there is a limitation: if two events happen at different places in such a way that a light signal starting at the first event could reach the second before it took place, then no use of the Lorentz transformations will make the first event take place after the second one. In other words, relativity does not claim that if a man is hit by a bullet, then it is possible for an observer somewhere else in the universe to have seen the gun being fired after the bullet landed. This, however, does not invalidate the famous "thought-experiment"—an experiment possible in theory but ruled out by experimental difficulties—concerning the alleged twin-paradox. Here, two twins, one of whom "stays at home" while the other travels through the universe at great speed, age differently—an outcome still disputed by a few who refuse to accept the restrictions on "common sense" that Einstein showed to be necessary.

The answer to the second question is that the human physiological apparatus is too insensitive to record the extremely minute changes in space and time that are produced by anything less than exceptionally high speeds. In other and better known ways, the five senses have their limitations. The unreliability of touch is exemplified by the "burn" that cold metal can give. Taste is not only notoriously subjective—"one man's meat, another man's poison"—but is also governed, to an extent not yet fully known, by genetic inheritance. So, too, smell is an indicator whose gross incapacity in humans is thrown into relief by insects who can identify members of their species at ranges of up to a mile. Sound is hardly better. The pattern of "reality" heard by the human is different from that heard by the dog—witness the "soundless" dog whistles of trainers; while the "real" world of the near-sightless bat is one in which "real" objects are "seen"—and avoided—by ultrasonic waves that play no part in the construction of the external human world.

And sight, a stimulation of the human retina by certain electromagnetic waves, is perhaps the most illusory of all senses. "Seeing is believing," and so it is difficult to appreciate that the light of common day—all that unaided human physiology allows in the visual search for the world around—comes through only a narrow slit in a broad curtain. At one end of this curtain there exist the cosmic rays, a trillionth of a centimeter in wavelength; at the other end, the infrared, heat radiations, and the even longer wavelengths used for radar, radio, and television. In between lies the narrow band of the visible spectrum, for long the only source of man's incomplete visual picture, supplemented but slowly as he used instruments to increase his own limited powers. The landscape seen with human eyes is dramatically different, yet no more "real," than the scene captured on the infrared plate and showing a mass of detail beyond human vision; the "real" world of the partially colorblind is the same "real" world seen more colorfully by most humans, and both worlds are composed of the same objects that make up the "real" but again different world of totally colorblind animals.

Thus the human species is unconsciously and inevitably selective in describing the nature of the physical world in which it lives and moves. Once this is appreciated, the implications of Einstein's Special Theory begin to take on a more respectable air. His achievement showed beyond all reasonable doubt that there existed a further limitation, so far unnoticed, produced by man's lack of experience of speeds comparable to that of light. Until such speeds were reached, the variability of space and time that was a product of relative motion was so small as to be unobservable. Thus it was, as Professor Lindemann was later to point out, "precisely because the old conceptions are so nearly right, because we have no personal experience of their being inaccurate in everyday life, that our so-called common sense revolts when we are asked to give them up, and that we tend to attribute to them a significance infinitely beyond their deserts." In fact, the human concepts of absolute space and time, which Einstein appeared to have violated so brusquely, had been produced simply by the rough-and-ready observation of countless generations of men using a physiological apparatus too coarse-grained to supply any better approximation of reality. As Bertrand Russell once wrote in describing the speeds at which relativity is significant, "since everyday life does not confront us with such swiftly moving bodies, Nature, always economical, had educated common sense only up to the level of everyday life."

Thus Special Relativity did not so much "overthrow Newton" as show that Newtonian ideas were valid only in circumstances that were restricted even though they did appear to permeate everyday life.

Einstein's revelation was one that only a very few could ever hope to prove by experiment in the laboratory and that would remain forever outside the experience of most people. To the nonscientist—as well as to some physicists—Einstein had really offended against common sense, the limited yardstick with which men measure the exterior world. In addition, the mental effort required before the theory could be fully grasped turned it for the general public, when they were eventually forced to notice it, into a fantasy that further separated the world of science from the world of ordinary men and women. Only Einstein could have transformed amused skepticism of the theory into a veneration for its author, which no one deplored more than Einstein himself.

Yet even when it is accepted that the theory of special relativity is not a metaphysical concept but, as Einstein was never tired of pointing out, an explanation of certain observable features of the universe, even when it is appreciated how this explanation had hitherto slipped through the net of human understanding, the third question remains. For at first glance the Special Theory appears to deal with matters that are outside the range of human experience. Nevertheless, there are two answers, one general and the other specific, to the question of what difference the Special Theory was to make to the world.

The general answer has been concisely given by Eddington, the British astronomer who was to play an important role in Einstein's later life:

Distance and duration are the most fundamental terms in physics; velocity, acceleration, force, energy, and so on, all depend on them; and we can scarcely make any statement in physics without direct or indirect reference to them. Surely then we can best indicate the revolutionary consequences of [relativity] by the statement that distance and duration, and all the physical quantities derived from them, do not as hitherto supposed refer to anything absolute in the external world, but are relative quantities which alter when we pass from one observer to another with different motion. The consequence in physics of the discovery that a yard is not an absolute chunk of space, and that what is a yard for one observer may be eighteen inches for another observer, may be compared with the consequences in economics of the discovery that a pound sterling is not an absolute quantity of wealth, and in certain circumstances may "really" be seven and sixpence.

However, the differences in these varying values of time and space were so small as to become significant only when the speeds involved were far beyond the range of human experience. How, then, could they really affect the world? It is here that one comes to the more specialized answer, and to what, in the light of history, can be considered as either an extraordinary coincidence or as part of the natural evolution of science.

For Einstein's Special Theory was evolved just as the investigations of physicists were reaching into the subatomic world of the nucleus, and as astronomers were for the first time peering out beyond the confines of the galaxy in which the earth is a minute speck toward the immensities of outer space. In the atomic world there were already known to be particles such as the electron that moved at speeds that were a sizable percentage of the speed of light; and in outer space, beyond our own galaxy, it was soon to be discovered that there were others that were moving at similar speeds. Thus in both of the fresh fields that were opening up during the first decades of the twentieth century, the microscopically small and the macroscopically large, the revelations of relativity were to have a significant place.

But there was another, and in some ways more important, result that flowed directly from the acceptance of Einstein's theory that during the next decade was seen as inevitable. For the absolute quality of space and time had not only been generally accepted up to now but had been confirmed by the overwhelming bulk of observational evidence. Now it was realized that the conventional belief, so soundly induced from observation, was gravely lacking, a circumstance with important philosophical implications. It underlined, more strongly than had previously been the case, that science might really be a search not for absolute truth but for a succession of theories that would progressively approach the truth. It suggested, furthermore, that the best path to be

Galileo Galilei (1564–1642), the Italian mathematician, astronomer, and physicist who demonstrated that falling bodies of different weights descend at the same rate. His development of the refracting telescope, leading to the discovery of Jupiter's satellites and of the craters on the moon, marked the beginning of telescope astronomy. "The four men who laid the foundations of physics on which I have been able to construct my theory," Einstein once said, "are Galileo, Newton, Maxwell, and Lorentz." [AIP Niels Bohr Library]

followed might not be that of observation followed by the induction of general laws, but the totally different process of postulating a theory and then discovering whether or not the facts fitted it. A theory should thus start with more scientific and philosophical assumptions than the facts alone warranted. A decade later the method was to provide the startling results of the General Theory.

How much, it is now necessary to ask, did these revelations owe to Einstein's predecessors? It should be clear by this time that the problem he tackled was different from that faced by Fitzgerald and Lorentz, who were mainly concerned with explaining the awkward result of an important experiment, and different in many ways from that faced by Poincaré, whose problem was largely a philosophical one. Einstein, not overly concerned with specific experiments, or with philosophy, had a grander aim: to penetrate the fog and discern more clearly the principles on which the material world had been built. "The theory of relativity," he once said, "was nothing more than a further consequential development of the field theory." Asked by Hans Reichenbach, later a Berlin colleague and later still a professor of philosophy at the University of California, how the theory of relativity had been arrived at, he "replied that he had discovered it because he was so firmly convinced of the harmony of the universe."

Yet in science as elsewhere, "no man is an island entire of itself." Einstein himself spoke repeatedly in later life of his debt to Lorentz—"the four men who laid the foundations of physics on which I have been able to construct my theory are Galileo, Newton, Maxwell and Lorentz" he said during his visit to the United States in 1921. In more general terms he emphasized that "in science...the work of the individual is so bound up with that of his scientific predecessors and contemporaries that it appears almost as an impersonal product of his generation."

Einstein himself made a number of statements on the subject. At first, when he spoke of relativity in Berlin, in the United States and in London, he was apt to stress, as in London in 1921, merely "that this theory is not speculative in origin; it owes its invention entirely to the desire to make physical theory fit observed fact as well as possible." At Columbia University, the same year, he noted that "to start with, it disturbed me that electrodynamics should pick out *one* state of motion in preference to others, without any experimental justification for this preferential treatment. Thus arose the Special Theory of Relativity." Both statements tended by implication to sustain the idea that the Michelson-Morley experiment had played a part in his thinking.

Later evidence provided by Einstein is contradictory and is probably influenced by the fact that, as Maitland put it, "events now long in the past were once in the future." "When I asked him how he had learned of the Michelson-Morley experiment," says R. S.

Shankland, who visited Einstein on February 4, 1950, from the Case Institute of Technology, while preparing a historical account of the work, "he told me he had become aware of it through the writings of H. A. Lorentz, but *only after 1905* had it come to his attention. 'Otherwise,' he said, 'I would have mentioned it in my paper.' He continued to say that the experimental results which had influenced him most were the observations of stellar aberration and Fizeau's measurements of the speed of light in moving water. 'They were enough,' he said." Yet when Shankland again visited Princeton on October 24, 1952, Einstein was not so certain. "This is not so easy," Shankland quotes him as saying;

> "I am not sure when I first heard of the Michelson experiment. I was not conscious that it had influenced me directly during the seven years that relativity had been my life. I guess I just took it for granted that it was true." However, Einstein said that in the years 1905 to 1909, he thought a great deal about Michelson's result, in his discussions with Lorentz and others in his thinking about general relativity. He then realized (so he told me) that he had also been conscious of Michelson's result before 1905 partly through his reading of the papers of Lorentz and more because he had assumed this result of Michelson to be true.

In 1954, for Michael Polanyi's *The Art of Knowing*, Einstein personally approved the statement that "the Michelson-Morley experiment had a negligible effect on the discovery of relativity." Furthermore, a supplementary note from Dr. N. Balazs, who was working with Einstein in Princeton in the summer of 1953, and who questioned him on the subject for Polanyi, runs as follows: "The Michelson-Morley experiment had no role in the foundation of the theory. He got acquainted with it while reading Lorentz' paper about the theory of this experiment (he of course does not remember exactly when, though prior to his paper), but it had no further influence on Einstein's consideration and the theory of relativity was not founded to explain its outcome at all."

To David Ben-Gurion, who asked whether the theory of relativity was the result of thought only, Einstein confirmed that this was so but added: "I naturally had before me the experimental works of those preceding me. These served as material for my thoughts and studies." And finally there is a letter from Einstein to Carl Seelig, published in the *Technische Rundschau* N°. 20, 47, Jahrgang, Berne on May 6, 1955, two months after Einstein's death, in which he stresses that the Special Theory of Relativity was ripe for discovery in 1905.

From this not entirely satisfactory evidence two general conclusions have been drawn. One is the view of the popular eulogy, in which Einstein is seen as the inspired genius, working in an intellectual vacuum and drawing the Special Theory from his brain like the conjuror producing the rabbit from the hat. The other is typified by Sir

Edmund Whittaker, the notable British physicist who in Einstein's biographical memoir for the Royal Society wrote that he had "adopted Poincaré's Principle of Relativity (using Poincaré's name for it) as a new basis of physics," a view which tends to produce enraged speechlessness in some scientists.

The truth appears to be different from both tidy black-and-white versions. It is rather that Einstein, traveling from his own starting point to his own lonely destination, noted Lorentz' work as bearing on his own, different, problems. When light dawned, during that creative fortnight in 1905, what Einstein had already heard of the Michelson-Morley experiment fell into place. But it was no more than an interesting piece of evidence that gave comforting confirmation of the theory that he had already decided could provide a more accurate picture of the material world than that provided by Newtonian mechanics alone. What he had produced was, as he wrote in *The Times* in 1919, "simply a systematic extension of the electrodynamics of Clerk-Maxwell and Lorentz." Certainly Lorentz himself had no doubt about whose theory it was. "To discuss Einstein's Principle of Relativity here in Göttingen..." he said when he spoke there in 1910, "appears to be a particularly welcome task."

If there are any missing acknowledgements in Einstein's work, they belong not to Michelson-Morley, to Lorentz, Fitzgerald, or Poincaré but to August Föppl, a German administrator and teacher whose *Introduction to Maxwell's Theory of Electricity* was almost certainly studied by Einstein. The famous relativity paper has similarities in style and argument with Föppl's treatment of "relative and absolute motion in space"; and Föppl himself writes of "a deep-going revision of that conception of space which has been impressed upon human thinking in its previous period of development" as presenting "perhaps the most important problem of science of our time."

Thus Föppl, like the Lorentz equations, can justifiably be considered as another of the useful instruments lying to hand that Einstein was able to utilize. As *The Times* was later to say of Einstein's General Theory, there is no need to defend his originality. "The genius of Einstein consists in taking up the uninterpreted experiments and scattered suggestions of his predecessors, and welding them into a comprehensive scheme that wins universal admiration by its simplicity and beauty."

The "comprehensive scheme" of 1905 had shown that space and time, previously thought to be absolute, in fact depended on relative motion. Yet these are but two of the three yardsticks used to measure the nature of the physical world. The third is mass. Was this, also, linked in some hitherto unexpected way with the speed of light? Einstein considered the question.

The result was a brief paper, "Ist die Trägheit eines Körpers von seinem

Ernest (later Lord) Rutherford (1871–1937), whose work in the first decades of the twentieth century transformed man's knowledge of the atomic nucleus. [AIP Niels Bohr Library]

Energieinhalt abhängig?" ("Does the Inertia of a Body Depend upon Its Energy-content?"), which appeared in the *Annalen der Physik* later in 1905, almost as a footnote to his earlier relativity paper. It asked whether the inertia of a body depended on its energy content, and concluded with the comment that the theory might be put to the test by the use of such materials as radium salts, whose energy content was very variable, and that radiation appeared to convey inertia between emitting and absorbing bodies. Yet the immediately important conclusion was that mass increased with relative speed. There had already been laboratory examples of this awkward process. Both J. J. Thomson in Cambridge and subsequently W. Kaufmann in Göttingen, had investigated the ways in which fast cathode rays, the streams of electrons whose existence had been postulated by Lorentz and confirmed by Thomson, could be electromagnetically deflected; both had found that mass of the particle appeared to depend on velocity. Some years later F. Hasenöhrl had shown that light radiation enclosed in a vessel increased that vessel's resistance to acceleration—and that its mass was altered in the process. Finally, in 1900, Poincaré had suggested that this inertia or resistance to acceleration was a property of all energy and not merely of electromagnetic energy.

Now Einstein leapfrogged one jump ahead, ignoring the separate experimental results that had been puzzling individual workers and coming up with a simple overall explanation that, almost staring them in the face, had appeared too simple to be true. All mass was merely congealed energy; all energy merely liberated matter. Thus the photons or light quanta of the photoelectric effect were just particles that had shed their mass and were traveling with the speed of light in the form of energy; while energy below the speed of light had been transformed by its slowing down, a transformation that had had the effect of congealing it into matter. There had been a whiff of this very idea from Newton, who in his *Opticks* had asked: "Are not gross Bodies and Light convertible into one another, and may not Bodies receive much of their Activity from the Particles of Light which enter their Composition?" The apparent rightness of this was underlined by his comment, a few lines lower, that "the changing of Bodies into Light, and Light into Bodies, is very conformable to the Course of Nature, which seems delighted with Transmutations."

The nub of this revelation—which involved two separate things, the difference between the mass of a body at rest and its mass in motion, and the transformation of a material body into energy—linked the previously separate concepts of conservation of energy and conservation of matter, and was embodied in two equations. One showed that the mass of a body moving at any particular velocity was its mass at rest divided by $\sqrt{1 - v^2/c^2}$. This quickly provides a clue to man's long ignorance of the difference between the mass of a body at rest and in movement; for the difference will be very small indeed until the velocity concerned leaves the speeds of ordinary life and begins to approach the velocity of light.

As with space and time, the changes are too small to be noted by man's inadequate senses. The second equation follows on from the fact that the motion whose increase raises the mass of a body is a form of energy. This is the famous $E = mc^2$ that states, in the shorthand of science, that the energy contained in matter is equal in ergs to its mass in grams multiplied by the square of the velocity of light in centimeters per second. Here again, one needed no mathematical expertise to see the essence of the argument: the velocity of light being what it is, a very small amount of mass is equivalent to a vast amount of energy.

Einstein's "follow-through" from his Special Theory of Relativity thus explained how electrons weighed more when moving than when at rest since this was the natural result of their speed. It helped to explain how materials such as radium, whose radioactivity still puzzled the men experimenting with them, were able to eject particles at great speeds and to go on doing so for long periods since creation of the comparatively large amounts of energy involved could be attained by the loss of a minute amount of mass. It helped to explain, furthermore, the ability of the sun—and of the stars—to continue radiating a large amount of light and heat by losing only a small amount of mass.

Forty years on, the facts of nature as revealed by Einstein's equation were to be demonstrated in another way. By then it had been discovered that if the nucleus of a heavy atom could be split into two parts, the mass of its two fragments would be less than that of the original nucleus. The difference in mass would have been transformed into energy; its amount would be minute, but the energy released would be this minute mass multiplied by the square of the speed of light—the energy that, released from vast numbers of nuclei by the fission process, destroyed Hiroshima and Nagasaki.

The chances of splitting the atom appeared minute in 1905. But the equation was there. And for writers and cranks, for visionaries and men who lived on the borderland of the mind, a new pipedream became possible. A few scientists thought along similar lines, and in 1921 Hans Thirring commented: "…it takes one's breath away to think of what might happen in a town, if the dormant energy of a single brick were to be set free, say in the form of an explosion. It would suffice to raze a city with a million inhabitants to the ground." Most of his professional colleagues did not speculate thus far. Rutherford maintained almost to the end of his life, in 1937, that the use of the energy locked within the atom was "moonshine." And when a young man approached Einstein

Ernest Rutherford with his assistant Johannes Geiger (left) in Rutherford's laboratory in Manchester in 1907, when Rutherford was investigating the structure of the atom. *[Bildarchiv Preussischer Kulturbesitz]*

in Prague in 1921, wanting to produce a weapon from nuclear energy based on $E = mc^2$, he was told to calm himself. "You haven't lost anything if I don't discuss your work with you in detail," Einstein said. "Its foolishness is evident at first glance. You cannot learn anything more from a longer discussion."

The demonstration of Einstein's mass-energy equation in the destruction of Hiroshima and Nagasaki has naturally given this by-product of his Special Theory a popular predominance over all others. But it should be emphasized that nuclear fission, whose utilization made nuclear weapons possible, was "discovered" by other men moving along very different paths. Fission illustrated—dramatically in the case of the atomic bombs—Einstein's mass-energy equation rather than being based on it.

But the atomic bomb came forty years after Einstein had cut at the foundation of classical physics, and the effects of relativity during these four decades were to be all-pervasive. So much so that while the immense effects of evolution and communism, those two other revolutionary ideas of the last hundred years, are as toughly debated as they are freely admitted, a different attitude exists about relativity. So much has it been assimilated into human knowledge that it is sometimes overlooked altogether.

There are three ways in which man's relationship with his physical world has been changed by relativity. The first, and possibly the least important, is that it has helped him to understand some phenomena that would otherwise have been incomprehensible. The behavior of nuclear particles discovered during the last half-century is only the most obvious example. "We use it," Oppenheimer has said of Special Relativity, "literally in almost every branch of nuclear physics and many branches of atomic physics, and in all branches of physics dealing with the fundamental particles. It has been checked and cross-checked and counter-checked in the most numerous ways and it is a very rich part of our heritage."

In addition to supplying this very practical tool, relativity has enabled man to give more accurate, more descriptive accounts of the world of which he is a part. As

Philipp Frank has pointed out, the plain statement that a table is three feet long is not only incomplete but meaningless when compared with the statement that it is three feet long relative to the room in which it stands. "Relativism," he says, "means the introduction of a richer language which allows us to meet adequately the requirements of the enriched experience. We are now able to cover these new facts by plain and direct words and to come one step nearer to what one may call the 'plain truth about the universe.'"

It is this "plain truth about the universe" that suggests the third and most important change that relativity has produced. Its epistemological implications are still hotly debated. Nevertheless, it is indisputable that while the theory has enabled man to describe his position in the universe with greater accuracy it has also thrown into higher relief the limitations of his own personal experiences.

> Physical science [Sir James Jeans has emphasized] does not of course suggest that we must abandon the intuitive concepts of space and time which we derive from individual experience. These may mean nothing to nature, but they still mean a good deal to us. Whatever conclusions the mathematicians may reach, it is certain that our newspapers, our historians and story-tellers will still place their truths and fictions in a framework of space and time; they will continue to say—this event happened at such an instant in the course of the ever-flowing stream of time, this other event at another instant lower down the stream, and so on.
>
> Such a scheme is perfectly satisfactory for any single individual, or for any group of individuals whose experiences keep them fairly close together in space and time—and, compared with the vast ranges of nature, all the inhabitants of the earth form such a group. The theory of relativity merely suggests that such a scheme is private to single individuals or to small colonies of individuals; it is a parochial method of measuring, and so is not suited for nature as a whole. It can represent all the facts and phenomena of nature, but only by attaching a subjective taint to them all; it does not represent nature so much as what the inhabitants of one rocket, or of one planet, or better still an individual pair of human eyes, see of nature. Nothing in our experiences or experiments justifies us in extending either this or any other parochial scheme to the whole of nature, on the supposition that it represents any sort of objective reality.

Relativity has thus helped human beings to appreciate their place in the physical world just as T. H. Huxley's *Man's Place in Nature* gave them context in the biological world. It is significant that one of the most hard-headed remarks on relativity made after Einstein's death should come from a religious journal. His theory has shown, remarked *The Tablet*, that "space and time for the physicists are defined by the operations used to measure them, and that any theory in which they appear must implicitly take these operations into account. Thus modern science looks at nature from the viewpoint of a man, not from that of an angel."

5.

FRUITS OF SUCCESS

Einstein's papers of 1905 revealed to the small handful of leading European physicists that they had a potential leader in their midst; only the next decade would show whether that potential was to be realized. Other men, in the arts as well as in science, in politics, and in war, had sent up sparks of genius during their early years yet failed to set the world ablaze. And even if Einstein did have the qualities needed to carry through and exploit his early promise, there were still a dozen ways in which chance might circumscribe or cut short his future—the Great War, taking Hasenöhrl on the German side and Moseley on Britain's, was only one pitfall lying ahead.

However, Einstein's statistical work, which led to his paper on the Brownian motion, his conception of photons, and his adventurous theory of relativity, were all soon seen as more than isolated efforts. Instead, it became clear that they were logically consequential operations, each of which could be further developed to throw fresh light on the current problems of physics. In this development he was to be helped by the climate of the times. From 1905 until 1914 he was able to think and read and move in a truly international scientific society that was shattered with the outbreak of the Great War and was not fully restored for almost half a century. Traveling from Berne or Zurich to Leiden or Salzburg, to Brussels or Vienna, he crossed frontiers that were political but not cultural. Talking with Lorentz in Holland, with Mach in Austria, and in Belgium with Rutherford from England, Madame Curie and Langevin from France, Planck and Nernst from Berlin, he was embraced as a full member of that small group whose work was concentrated on the single task of discovering the nature of the physical world.

The story of his life for the decade is therefore first of scientific consolidation and then of scientific exploration, of increasing contact with the men and women who produced the twentieth century's scientific revolution. In it there appear rarely, and as if by accident, the figures of his family and the everyday emotions that move most ordinary men. He was kind, but in a slightly casual way; amiable as long as people allowed him to get on with his work; and totally uninterested in what he regarded as the superficialities of life. Thus when his wife returned from Serbia, where she had been on holiday, with his two sons, and announced that she had become a Catholic, the news left him unmoved, as he made clear in a comment to Professor Hurwitz. He did not care.

In the summer of 1905 he visited Belgrade with Mileva. They stayed with her relatives and friends, spending a week in the lakeside holiday resort of Kijevo, and then traveling on to Novi Sad, where he met his wife's parents for the first time. It was one of numerous holiday journeys to what is now Yugoslavia but was then part of the Austro-Hungarian Empire, holidays that were long remembered by his elder son Hans as pleasant rambling interludes during which the odd character of a father amiably visits his in-laws from another world, accompanied first by his small son and, later, by a baby second son as well. Einstein never forgot his Serbian hosts and kept up an intermittent correspondence with them for nearly half a century—mentioning only casually, they recounted after his death, that he had been awarded a Nobel Prize.

Other holidays were spent in the nearby Oberland, sometimes in Murren, not yet overfashionable—quiet holidays of a minor civil servant who superficially seemed likely to spend the rest of his life on much the same local round. He would occasionally visit Cäsar Koch in Antwerp. He kept in touch with his former colleagues of Aarau or Zurich, and to friends and relations he jotted off the postcards with their spidery writing that were later to become collectors' items. It was all rather low key. Yet it was this that still seemed to be the genuine Einstein. Surely, the real person was the slightly shabby, poor man's Bohemian of the rather broken down apartment in Märktgasse. Surely, the potential genius of which whispers began to come from Planck and the great names in Berlin was merely a dream-figure that had stepped down from one of Paul Klee's early landscapes.

The only hint that the potential genius might be the real Einstein came from his ferocious concentration on the task to be done and his determination that nothing should be allowed to divert him from it. A few years earlier it might have been only a hangover from graduate enthusiasm; now it began to look as though it was part and parcel of the mature man. Here, there is a similarity—first pointed out by C. P. Snow—between Einstein and Churchill. The comparison is not surprising once the picture-book image of both scientist and statesman is scraped away to reveal the machinery beneath. Of Churchill it has been written that almost obsessional concentration "was one of the keys to his character. It was not always obvious, but he never really thought of anything but the job in hand. He was not a fast worker, especially when dealing with papers, but he was essentially a non-stop worker." Einstein, with the black notebook in his pocket, handy for the moment when the sails began to hang limp, reading while he rocked the cradle in his Berne apartment, was much the same.

He had his music. But this, as he would explain on occasions, was in some ways an extension of his thinking processes, a method of allowing the subconscious to solve particularly tricky problems. "Whenever he felt that he had come to the end of the road or into a difficult situation in his work," his elder son has said, "he would take refuge in music, and that would usually resolve all his difficulties."

There was also his sailing, and here a remark by his second wife is pertinent: "He is so much on the water that people cannot easily reach him." On the Zurichsee, on the Lake of Thun, or on any of Switzerland's myriad of small lakes, where the hand

Einstein, his wife Mileva, and their son Hans Albert, in 1904. *[Hebrew University of Jerusalem]*

responded instinctively to the demands of the breeze and an able man could let a boat sail itself, the mind could get on with the job without fear of interruption. What is more, the surroundings helped. "He needed this kind of relaxation from his intense work," says his elder son. And with relaxation there would often come the solution. For his work needed neither laboratory nor equipment.

During the years that immediately followed 1905, Einstein is thus outwardly the minor Jewish civil servant of slightly radical ideas, the professional odd man out, with a Slav wife and illusions of grandeur that had actually gained him a doctorate of philosophy. But slowly, and as surely as the tide comes in, the other image began to harden, the picture of the man who for some inexplicable reason really was being sought out by those who had made their way in the world. This metamorphosis was nothing to do with the popular acclaim that brought Einstein international renown after the First World War. As far as the outside world was concerned, he remained totally unknown until 1912, when some aspects of relativity became headline news in Austria, and almost totally unknown until 1919. But in the academic world the significance of the relativity papers soon began to be appreciated.

First off the mark seems to have been Wilhelm Wien, who as editor of the *Annalen der Physik* had accepted the papers. Another man who soon realized the significance of Einstein's work was the Pole, Professor Witkowski, who after reading the famous Volume 17 of *Annalen der Physik* exclaimed to his friend, Professor Loria in Cracow, "A new Copernicus is born! Read Einstein's paper." But there was a sequel— apparently in 1907—according to Einstein's future collaborator, Leopold Infeld. "Later, when Professor Loria met Professor Max Born at a physics meeting, he told him about

Einstein and asked Born if he had read the paper," writes Infeld. "It turned out that neither Born nor anyone else there had heard about Einstein." They went to the library, took from the bookshelves the seventeenth volume of *Annalen der Physik* and started to read the articles. "Although I was quite familiar with the relativistic idea and the Lorentz transformations," Born has said of the incident, "Einstein's reasoning was a revelation to me." Elsewhere he has said that the paper "had a stronger influence on my thinking than any other scientific experience."

It is clear that during the years immediately following 1905 the concept of relativity percolated slowly through accepted ideas like rain through limestone rather than breaking them down like the weight of water cracking a dam. But as water slowly penetrates the myriad channels, so did the Special Theory begin to affect the whole body of physics. There were some setbacks, and one early reaction to the theory was of unqualified rejection. It came as a paper by W. Kaufmann on the constitution of the electron, and it included the following blunt statement: "I anticipate right away the general result of the measurements to be described in the following: *the results are not compatible with the Lorentz-Einsteinian fundamental assumptions.*" The results had been obtained experimentally in Kaufmann's laboratory and were in line with other theories that had given plausible accounts of the electron's characteristics without invoking relativity. But neither Einstein nor anyone else fully realized that the technology of the times was incapable of delivering results accurate enough to support or refute the theory of relativity.

The scientific world awaited Einstein's reply with some interest—much as central Europe held its breath after Tetzel had committed Luther's theses to the flames. It came the following year in the first of two articles in the *Jahrbuch der Radioaktivität und Elektronik.* Taking the theory of relativity a number of important steps further forward, the articles were to be of great importance for other reasons. Here, it is only necessary to note the way, suggesting assurance or arrogance according to point of view, with which Einstein handled Kaufmann. For while he agreed that Kaufmann's results could not apparently be faulted, he refused to take this too seriously. The great scientific theories that mattered, he inferred, explained a blueprint of nature as revealed in general terms; only then was a search made to see whether minor details supported it. Einstein's attitude was not that of *tant pis pour les faits*; but to some skeptics it must have looked dangerously like it.

The theory of relativity remained the central scientific problem with which he concerned himself. He saw it, rightly most scientists feel today, as one of the vital factors in man's understanding of the natural world, a factor whose omission had distorted ideas across the whole spectrum of physical knowledge. But there was another of equal importance; this was the conception of quanta that Planck had seen as accounting for certain characteristics of radiation and that Einstein with his light quanta, or photons, had adventurously developed. The subject, which seemed to present numerous and almost insuperable problems, continued to exercise him. For while the theory of the photon helped to clarify heat, radiation, and the photoelectric effect, it totally failed to explain interference, the diffraction of light, or other phenomena. There was something, if not wrong, then at least incomplete about the explanations that had so far been put forward, and during these years in Berne Einstein worked hard to lessen this.

Meanwhile, his thoughts were increasingly preoccupied with the looming problem of causality, taken for granted in one shape or form for centuries by the majority of scientists who believed that the explanation of every event could be found in its antecedent conditions. The billiard balls on the green baize tables moved along paths that could be predicted once the vectors imposed on them were known; and if the equations involved had for strict accuracy to be those of the Special Theory rather than of Newtonian mechanics, effect yet followed cause in exactly the same way. Surely, the motions of the atoms, and of their components, infinitely small though they were, could be comparably predicted once it became possible to quantify the forces imposed upon them?

This was not to be so. Doubts had been raised with the discovery of radioactivity and of the way in which the atoms comprising an element disintegrated—apparently without reason and in a pattern that enabled the statistician to forecast the future of a collection of atoms but not of an individual atom. At first, it had appeared that this statistical forecast might be similar to the prediction of how a tossed coin would fall— used only because sufficient factors were not known with enough accuracy to allow the use of anything better. Once enough was known, it would surely be possible not merely to predict statistically the outcome of a series of coin tossings, but to predict in terms of cause and effect the result of each particular toss. Surely, it was argued, the grand designs of nature operated along similar causal lines, with all that was required being merely sufficient information on the causes.

On this question, which grew steadily in importance as the century advanced, Einstein became increasingly separated from the bulk of his colleagues. While they moved on, he remained faithful to the attitude he had adopted as early as 1907 and which he revealed in a letter of that year to Philipp Frank, a young Austrian who had just taken his doctorate at the University of Vienna. In a paper entitled "Kausalgesetz und Erfahrung" ("Causality and Knowledge") Frank had set out to show that the law of causality "can be neither confirmed nor disproved by experience; not, however, because it is a truth known *a priori* but because it is a purely conventional definition." Einstein, who developed a rich correspondence with any scientist who had similar interests, wrote to Frank.

> He approved the logic of my argument [Frank has said] but he objected that it demonstrates only that there is a conventional element in the law of causality and not that there is merely a convention or definition. He agreed with me that, whatever may happen in nature, one can never prove that a violation of the law of causality has taken

place. One can always introduce by convention a terminology by which this law is saved. But it could happen that in this way our language and terminology might become highly complicated and cumbersome.

What Einstein was saying was this: if all the details of a coin's velocity, mass, moment of inertia, and other relevant factors were known as soon as it was in the air, and if it was still impossible to tell only by statistics which way it would fall, this was due not to a failure of causality. There was simply another causative factor that had not been considered. So with the laws of nature. Current ability to understand events in the atomic world only in statistical terms sprang from the limitations imposed by ignorance. In due course, scientists might learn all the necessary facts, and the mysteries would then be removed. In 1907 it was difficult to dispute that this would eventually be so. The arguments were not developed until more than a decade later when the progress of physics slowly revealed that at the atomic level the laws of cause and effect give way to the laws of chance. Einstein remained unmoved, acknowledging that the work of his earlier years had led to the new situation, confident that "God did not play dice with the world."

All this lay two decades away as Einstein the scientist built up his connections with Europe's leading physicists and Einstein the Patent Office employee played the role of minor civil servant. The situation was growing more incongruous. The first steps to remedy this were taken in 1907—mainly at the instigation of Professor Kleiner who in 1905 had helped to push through Einstein's Ph.D. in Zurich. Kleiner wanted Einstein on his staff. But during the early years of the century it was impossible for a man to be appointed professor in Switzerland—or in most other Continental countries—before serving a spell as *privatdozent*. The holders of such posts, which have no equivalent in Britain or the United States, lecture as much or as little as they like and normally receive only nominal sums from the students whom they serve.

In 1907 Kleiner proposed that Einstein should apply for a post as *privatdozent* in the University of Berne, a post in which the looseness of obligations would enable him to combine it easily with his Patent Office job. Einstein applied for entry to the faculty of theoretical physics, submitting as proof of his ability the printed version of the paper that had won him his Zurich doctorate. With his usual mixture of impatience and optimism he did not wait for the outcome before writing to the dean and suggesting what he might do. However, he was to receive a shock. His application was rejected; partly because it was too short, an example of academic red tape, as he later noted; partly because Professor Aimé Forster did not want a *privatdozent* on his staff. There were probably other reasons. The aura of the great man that has surrounded Einstein's name since 1919, when his work on the General Theory suddenly became well known, has overshadowed his position and his nature during the years before the First World War. The Einstein of the early 1900s was not only a scientist of minor academic qualifications who had launched an obscure theory on the world. He was also the man who failed to fit in or to conform, the nonrespecter of professors, the dropper of conversational bricks, the awkward Jewish customer, the man who although approaching the age of thirty still seemed to prefer the company of students. However, help was at hand. Shortly afterward, the decision was revised and Einstein appointed.

Thus he started on his academic career at the age of twenty-nine. His first lectures, on "The Theory of Radiation," were delivered in the winter term of 1908-9. He had only four students, and during the following term the numbers shrank to a single man. Formality was abandoned, and the session continued in Einstein's own rooms. The contradictions of his life still obstinately continued. The genius who had at first been rejected by the E.T.H. had been succeeded by the minor Patent Office official who in a single issue of the *Annalen der Physik* had delivered three major blows at the accepted body of physics. Now this picture was succeeded by that of the apparently unsuccessful university part-timer. But once again the situation was on the point of being transformed.

The events that combined to give Einstein a new status were his formulation of the Principle of Equivalence, the cornerstone of the Theory of General Relativity, and the arrival of two papers from Hermann Minkowski, who had left Zurich in 1902 for Göttingen, which gave mathematical formality to Special Relativity.

The Principle of Equivalence, which first saw the light of day in "Über das Relativitätsprinzip und die aus demselben gezogenen Folgerungen" ("The Principle of Relativity and the Inferences to be Drawn from It"), published in two issues of the *Jahrbuch der Radioaktivität und Elektronik* in 1907 and 1908, emerged from a problem that had been worrying Einstein since his formulation of the Special Theory in 1905. This theory had been complete in itself. But it was a characteristic of Einstein's whole scientific life that most of his main achievements sprang directly from their predecessors. Each advance was first consolidated and then used as a base for a fresh move into unexplored territory.

In the Special Theory he had shown that there was no place for the word "absolute" when motion was considered. Movement was relative, whether it was the movement of the stars in their courses or of the electrons in the physicist's laboratory. Yet the motion concerned was of a very limited variety—hence the "special" in the description of the theory. For he had dealt only with motion in a straight line at a constant velocity. In the world of everyday life, to which he clung with such determination, this was exemplified by the train moving at constant speed, from which it was impossible to discover the existence of motion except by looking out of the window and relating the train to another frame of reference. But this situation altered radically if there was a change in the speed of the train. Then acceleration thrust a passenger back into a forward-facing seat, or deceleration slumped him forward, while the movement of inanimate objects in the train—a glass of water, for instance—would clearly show that a change of movement was taking place. Similarly, if constant motion were maintained in a circular motion—as in a car on a merry-go-round—then the outward pull on the body (or on the glass of water) would once again provide a yardstick for the movement involved. "Because of this," said Einstein in describing how his argument had progressed from Special to General Relativity, "we feel compelled at the present juncture to grant a kind of absolute physical reality to non-uniform motion."

This discrepancy between the relativity of uniform motion and the apparent nonrelativity of nonuniform motion, between the fact that the first has no meaning unless it is compared to something else, while the second is self-evident within its own frame of reference, greatly worried him. As it has been put by Dr. Sciama, "This was displeasing to Einstein, who felt that the harmony of his theory of relativity required that all motion should be equally relative." He had come to it by considering the empirical equivalence of all inertial systems in regard to light. But he now raised the purely epistemological question: "Why should relativity concern only uniform motion?" Einstein refused to let the discrepancy remain unexplained. What was it, he wondered, that lay at the heart of inertia, that tendency of a body to resist acceleration?

At first, he thought back to Ernst Mach, now in his mid-sixties, still deeply skeptical of the atomic theory, already becoming out-of-touch, bypassed, and half-forgotten. Mach, who attributed the movement of earthly bodies to the influence of the stars—it "savours of astrology and is scientifically incredible" was Bertrand Russell's opinion—had revived Bishop Berkeley's notion that centrifugal forces were governed by the same thing. Einstein arrived at a somewhat similar conclusion by a very different route. But first, he had begun to reflect on one force that had always been taken for granted—the force of gravity.

He began by returning to Newton's conception of inertia, which triggers the senses into knowing when the train has jerked forward or a body is being pulled out of a straight line in a swing or on a merry-go-round. First, "every body continues in its state of rest, or of uniform motion in a straight line, unless it is compelled to change that state by forces impressed thereon"; and, second, the greater the mass of the body, the greater the force needed to accelerate it or to change its course. These formal statements were the quintessence of everyday experience, the scientists' explanation of the fact that it is easier to throw a tennis ball than a cannonball and less difficult to get a small wheelbarrow on the move than a large one. But there was one exception to this otherwise unfailing rule that different forces were necessary to move objects of different masses. That exception was gravity, the mysterious force that appeared to pervade space and tended to draw all objects to the ground. More than three centuries earlier Simon Stevenus, quartermaster of the Dutch army, had shown that different weights—reputedly cannonballs of different sizes—fell to the ground at the same speed. Some years later, Galileo repeated and refined the experiment to produce his revolutionary conclusion: that the force of gravity had the same effect on all objects, regardless of their size or mass. Air resistance prevented cannonballs and feathers from falling at similar speeds, but if this resistance were eliminated, by the use of a perfect vacuum for instance, then cannonballs and feathers would reach the ground at the same time if dropped from equal heights—a proposition subsequently found to be correct.

The explanation proposed by Newton for this curious exception to his laws of inertia was ingenious; to Einstein it was too ingenious. The explanation was that gravity, reaching up into the heavens to attract material objects down to earth, exercised its power precisely in proportion to the mass concerned. On objects of small mass, the "pull" was relatively small; on those of greater mass, the "pull" was increased—to just the extent needed to bring them all down toward the ground at the accelerating speed of thirty-two feet per second per second. Thus the force of gravity operated so that it always counterbalanced inertia—a proposition Einstein found hard to take for granted.

But there was another aspect of Newton's explanation which he found difficult to accept. The effect of gravity was in Newtonian terms transmitted through space instantaneously, a proposition conflicting harshly with Einstein's assumption in the Special Theory that the speed of light is a limiting speed in the universe. The more he contemplated this instantaneous and apparently fortuitous balancing of the effect of gravity and the effect of inertia, the less he liked it. It was an accident of nature that he considered too odd to be truly accidental, a lucky chance that he felt must be the result of something more than luck.

Einstein's reaction was typical. He visualized the situation in concrete terms, in the "man in a box" problem that appears in different guises in most discussions of General Relativity. Einstein's illustration was basically simple—although it appears more so now, when men have been shot out of the earth's gravitational field, than it did more than a half-century ago, when space travel was only a theoretical fancy.

In the first place Einstein envisaged a box falling freely down a suitably long shaft. Inside it, an occupant who took his money and keys from his pocket would find that they did not fall to the floor. Man, box, and objects were all falling freely in a gravitational field; but, and this was the important point, their temporary physical situation was identical to what it would have been in space, far beyond any gravitational field. With this in mind, Einstein then mentally transported both box and occupant to such a point in space beyond the pull of gravity. Here, all would have been as before. But he then envisaged the box being accelerated. The means were immaterial since it was the result that mattered. Money and keys now fell to the bottom of the box. But the same thing would have happened had the box been at rest in a gravitational field. So the effect of gravity on the box at rest was identical with the effect of acceleration beyond the pull of gravity. What is more, it was clearly apparent that if a centrifugal force replaced acceleration, the results would be the same. As it was later described by Professor Lindemann, a friend of Einstein for more than forty years, it would be as impossible for the man in the box "to tell us whether he was in a gravitational field or subject to uniform acceleration, as it is for an aeroplane pilot in a cloud to tell whether he is flying straight or executing a properly banked turn."

Thus logical reasoning showed that the effects of gravitation were equivalent to those of inertia, and that there was no way of distinguishing acceleration or centrifugal force from gravity. At least, this appeared to be so with money and keys and other material objects. But what would happen if one thought, instead, in terms of light? Here it was necessary to change the "thought-experiment." Once again there was the closed box. But this time, instead of dropped keys and money, it was necessary to envisage a ray of light crossing the box from one side to the other while the box was being accelerated. The far side of the box would have moved upward before the ray of light reached it; the wall would be hit by the light ray nearer the floor than the point at which it set out. In other words, to the man in the box there would have apparently been a bend in a horizontal ray of light.

But it was the very substance of Einstein's conception that the two situations—one produced by nonuniform motion and the other produced by gravity—were indistinguishable whether one used merely mechanical tricks or those of electrodynamics. Thus the ray of light, seen as bent by the man in the box when the box was subject to acceleration, would surely be seen in the same way if gravity were involved when the box was at rest. From one point of view this was not as outrageous as it sounded. In 1905 Einstein had given fresh support to the idea that light consisted not of waves but of a stream of minute machine-gun bullets, the light quanta that were later christened photons. Why, after all, should not these light quanta be affected by gravity in the same way as everything else?

But even as the idea was contemplated, its implications began to grow like the genie from the lamp. For a straight line is the path of a ray of light, while the basis of time measurement is the interval taken by light to pass from one point to another. Thus if light were affected by gravity, time and space would have two different configurations—one when viewed from within the gravitational field and one when viewed from without. In the absence of gravitation the shortest distance between A and B—the path along which a light ray would travel from A to B—is a straight line. But when gravitation is present the line traveled by light is not the straight line of ordinary geometry. Nevertheless, there is no way of getting from A to B faster than light gets along this path. The "light-line" then *is* the straight line. This might not matter very much in the mundane affairs of the terrestrial world, where the earth's gravity was for all practical purposes a constant that was a part of life. But for those looking out from the earth to the solar system and the worlds beyond, the Principle of Equivalence suggested that they might have been looking out through distorting spectacles. Einstein's new idea appeared to have slipped a disc in the backbone of the universe.

He still did not know what gravity was. He still did not know the characteristics of the gravitational field in the way that one could know the characteristics of the electromagnetic field by referring to Maxwell's equations. Only two things seemed clear. One was that gravity did not operate as Newton had said it operated. The second was that

The Principle of Equivalence

Einstein's Principle of Equivalence stated that the motion produced by inertial forces such as acceleration or recoil was indistinguishable from that produced by gravitational force. Einstein envisaged a man in a box that was falling freely down a long shaft. If the man dropped his briefcase, it would not fall to the ground since man and briefcase were falling freely in a uniform gravitational field. This would also be the case if the box was in space beyond the pull of gravity. But if the box in space was now accelerated upwards, the briefcase would fall to the bottom of the box—as would happen if the box were at rest in a gravitational field. The effect of gravity on the box at rest is identical to the effect of acceleration beyond the pull of gravity.

David Suter

a reasonable theory of gravitation might be obtained by generalizing the principle of relativity. Just as "Special" Relativity could produce an accurate account of events in a frame of reference that was moving uniformly in relation to the observer, so could a more general version of the theory do the same thing when the frame of reference was moving at accelerating speeds—and then the theory should automatically be able to describe motion in a gravitational field as well.

Einstein now began to look out toward the problems beyond the earth just as he had earlier looked in toward the problems of molecules and atoms. The work took time, and another eight years passed before he produced the General Theory, described in 1919 by J. J. Thomson, the president of the Royal Society, as "one of the most momentous pronouncements of human thought" that the world had known. The delay was due not to Einstein's commitment to other research but to the complexity of the problems involved. Their solution came with the aid of other men, among them Hermann Minkowski who in 1909 transformed Einstein's earlier Special Theory into a convenient mathematical tool.

While Einstein had been at work in his Berne apartment, as unaware of his coming influence as Marx in the Reading Room of the British Museum, important events had been taking place in Göttingen. Standing on the outliers of the Harz mountains, its ancient ramparts planted with lindens, proud of its university and its splendid botanic garden laid out by Albrecht von Haller, the little town still retained a whiff of the Middle Ages. The later memories of Gauss and Riemann were still fresh as there began the "great and brilliant period which mathematics experienced during the first decade of the century...unforgettable to those who lived through it." Among its heroes was Hermann Minkowski, the man who at the E.T.H. had taught Einstein, the "lazy dog" who "never bothered about mathematics at all," as Minkowski described him to Max Born.

Minkowski, Russian by birth, had been in his early thirties when lecturing in Zurich. He had been only a middling teacher but earlier, as a boy of eighteen, had won the Paris Prize for Mathematics and by 1909 was a professor at Göttingen University. His contribution to the development of Special Relativity was in effect a single paper, "Grundlegende Gleichungen für die elektromagnetischen Erscheinungen in sich bewegenden Körpern" ("Basic Equations for the Electromagnetic Phenomena in Moving Bodies"), published in the *Göttinger Nachrichten* in 1907; and, more far-reaching in its effects, "Raum und Zeit" ("Space and Time"), a popular lecture that he read to the Gesellschaft Deutscher Naturforscher und Ärzte in Cologne in September, 1908. The combined effect of the two was to be immense. For Minkowski not only gave a new mathematical formalism to the special theory but also, in some opinions, enabled Einstein to solve the problems of gravitation by means of the General Theory—"whether he would ever have done it without the genius of Minkowski we cannot tell," says E. Cunningham. Yet, contrariwise, Minkowski introduced fresh specialized meanings to old familiar words that brought a new and confusingly esoteric element to an already difficult subject.

Einstein himself described Minkowski's contribution as the provision of equations in which "the natural laws satisfying the demands of the [special] theory of relativity assume mathematical forms, in which the time co-ordinate plays exactly the same role as the three space co-ordinates." To understand the importance of this it is necessary to reconsider exactly what it was that Einstein had already achieved. He had shown that an accurate description of mechanical and optical phenomena is linked with the movement of the observer relative to the phenomena observed. And he had, with his use of the Lorentz equations, been able to demonstrate the mathematical relationship between such observations made by observers moving at different relative speeds. What Minkowski now demonstrated was that a limitless number of different descriptions of the same phenomenon could be provided by a single equation through the introduction, in a certain way, of time as a fourth variable. In this the three space coordinates were used as in the Lorentz transformation; the time variable, however, was no longer represented by t but by $\sqrt{-1}\, ct$. The result was an equation that dealt with the "real" world, of which the differing descriptions as seen from differently moving bodies were but partial and incomplete expressions; moreover, the curve produced from plotting a series of such equations representing phenomena contiguous in time would represent nothing less than a continuum of the real world—much as to the wolf and the dog of George Lewes, "the external world seems a continuum of scents."

Minkowski thus gave a mathematical formalism to what had been the purely physical conception of Special Relativity. But more important in some ways was the language in which he clothed his work—essential in the mathematical context where it was used, but misleading outside it unless sufficient explanation were given. Thus an event that takes place in three-dimensional space at a specific time is described as a "world-point," while a series of consecutive events—the movement of a rocket, of a man, or of an electron—is described as a "world-line." More significantly, and confusingly, time is described as "the fourth dimension."

Einstein was well aware of the bewilderment that such language created. "The non-mathematician," he wrote, "is seized by a mysterious shuddering when he hears of 'four-dimensional' things, by a feeling not unlike that awakened by thoughts of the occult. And yet there is no more commonplace statement than that the world in which we live is a four-dimensional space-time continuum." Here, even Einstein, whose scientific explanations have at times a breathtaking simplicity, does not go quite far enough. For he does not explain that while for the layman the world "dimension" signifies one of the three measurements of a body represented by length, breadth, or thickness, for the mathematician it means a fourth variable that must, naturally enough, be inserted into any equation concerning events, since these occur not only in space but at a certain instant in time.

The change produced by Minkowski was clear enough—"from a 'happening' in three-dimensional space, physics becomes, as it were, an 'existence' in the four-dimensional 'world,'" as Einstein said. Or, as Jeans had written of Einstein's original

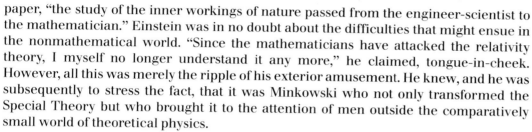

Left: A view of Göttingen. Johann Karl Friedrich Gauss (1777–1855) and Georg Friedrich Bernhard Riemann (1826–1866) were among the mathematicians who made the University of Göttingen, lying in the foothills of the Harz Mountains, a world-famous center of mathematical research before the days of Einstein. Later, it was Hermann Minkowski of Göttingen who, with one paper and one popular lecture, greatly increased knowledge of the Special Theory of Relativity in the first decade of the twentieth century. [Bildarchiv Preussischer Kulturbesitz]

Right: Hermann Minkowski (1864–1909), one of Einstein's professors at the Zurich Polytechnic at the turn of the century. At the University of Göttingen, to which he had moved in 1902, Minkowski wrote "Basic Equations for the Electromagnetic Phenomena in Moving Bodies" in 1907, and the following year gave his influential popular lecture "Space and Time" to the Gesellschaft Deutscher Naturforscher und Ärtzte in Cologne. [Bildarchiv Preussischer Kulturbesitz]

paper, "the study of the inner workings of nature passed from the engineer-scientist to the mathematician." Einstein was in no doubt about the difficulties that might ensue in the nonmathematical world. "Since the mathematicians have attacked the relativity theory, I myself no longer understand it any more," he claimed, tongue-in-cheek. However, all this was merely the ripple of his exterior amusement. He knew, and he was subsequently to stress the fact, that it was Minkowski who not only transformed the Special Theory but who brought it to the attention of men outside the comparatively small world of theoretical physics.

The paper in the *Göttinger Nachrichten* had been important but was of limited influence. Something more significant was involved when in September, 1908, the Versammlung Deutscher Naturforscher und Ärzte, a body rather like the British Association, used by scientists to help spread the knowledge of their individual disciplines among a wider audience, met in Cologne. Here, Minkowski delivered his lecture on "Space and Time," and after half a century his opening words still have a fine ring: "Gentlemen! The ideas on space and time which I wish to develop before you grew from the soil of experimental physics. Therein lies their strength. Their tendency is radical. From now on, space by itself and time by itself must sink into the shadows, while only a union of the two preserves independence."

For Minkowski, relativity had become a central fact of life. After he and David Hilbert had visited an art exhibition at Kassel, Hilbert's wife asked what they thought of the pictures. "I do not know," was the reply. "We were so busy discussing relativity that we never really saw the art." He was among the most austere and dedicated of mathematicians. He was the last man to popularize, to play to the gallery. Yet he had sounded the trumpet for relativity in no uncertain fashion. He was still only forty-four, and in the early winter of 1908 it would not have been too outrageous to speculate on the prospects of future long-term collaboration between Minkowski in Göttingen and Einstein in Berne. Then, toward the end of the year, he fell ill. He was taken to the hospital and died of peritonitis on January 12, 1909—regretting on his deathbed, according to a legend that has more than a touch of plausibility: "What a pity that I have to die in the age of relativity's development."

The increased fame which Minkowski brought Einstein among a larger circle of German scientists looks less surprising today than it did in 1908. In retrospect it is possible to see Einstein's papers of 1905, the almost equally dramatic paper of 1907, and Minkowski's denouement of 1908, as parts of a steady increase of reputation which in the end would inevitably be too great to be contained by the four walls of the Patent Office.

The break came the following year. So did Einstein's first honorary doctorate, his first professional appointment, and his first major invited paper, read to the annual meeting of the same Gesellschaft Deutscher Naturforscher und Ärzte whose members had twelve months earlier listened to Minkowski. The first important event in this year that marked a watershed in Einstein's life was an invitation to Geneva, where the University was celebrating the 350th anniversary of its foundation by Calvin. Einstein, it had been decided, should be awarded an honorary doctorate. He traveled to Geneva early in July and was duly honored together with Marie Curie, steely and determined, the woman who "felt herself at every moment to be a servant of society"; Ernest Solvay, the Belgian whose chemical profits endowed his eponymous congresses; and Wilhelm Ostwald, who a few months later won the Nobel Prize in chemistry for his work on catalysis.

Two months after the Geneva visit came something more important. The previous summer Einstein had been visited in Berne by Rudolf Ladenburg, a physicist from Berlin who was also an official of the Deutscher Naturforscher und Ärzte. The result was an invitation to lecture at the organization's 1909 conference, and in September Einstein left Berne for Salzburg where this was to be held. The next few days were significant; before he was thirty, he told a colleague of this occasion, he had never met a real physicist.

At Salzburg Einstein gave his first major paper, before an informed and critical audience. He thus came under the close-range scrutiny of the pillars of the scientific establishment. But he, in turn, was able to scrutinize them. Judging by what was to follow, it was Planck whom Einstein might have singled out for special mention; for it was he for whom Einstein was to have a near-reverence, which Planck noted and turned to Germany's benefit when he could. The two men had been in correspondence, at first desultory, since 1900, but Planck was increasingly impressed by the young man who had boldly taken his quantum theory into fresh fields. But only at Salzburg did the two men come face to face. Einstein's lasting attitude was illustrated twenty years later. Asked to contribute a preface to Planck's *Where Is Science Going?*, he said that it would be presumptuous on his part to introduce Max Planck to the public, for the discoverer of the quantum theory did not need the reflected light of any lesser luminary to show him off. That was Einstein's attitude toward Planck, expressed with genuine and naïve emphasis.

At Salzburg, relativity as such was dealt with by Max Born, three years younger than Einstein and still with his name to make. "This seems to be rather amusing," Born wrote subsequently. "Einstein had already proceeded beyond Special Relativity which he left to minor prophets, while he himself pondered about the new riddles arising from the quantum structure of light, and of course about gravitation and general relativity which at that time was not ripe for general discussion."

Einstein was still only thirty. He had already shaken the scientific world with an esoteric theory about which some of his elders still retained doubts. It would not have been surprising if he had chosen a comparatively "safe" subject on which to discourse before such a high-powered audience. But that was not the Einstein way. His paper was entitled "Über die Entwicklung unserer Anschauungen über das Wesen und die Konstitution der Strahlung" ("The Development of our Views on the Nature and Constitution of Radiation"). It was subsequently described by Wolfgang Pauli as "one of the landmarks in the development of theoretical physics," and its challenge came quickly.

Einstein began by pointing out that some facts about radiation were more easily explained in terms of Newton's corpuscular theory of light than in terms of the current wave theory. What was therefore necessary, he went on, was a profound change in contemporary views of the nature of light—one that would tend to fuse the two ideas.

So the young man—still a mere "doctor" with not a professorship to his name—was to make the members of his audience profoundly change their views about light and to suggest that it was both particle and wave as well! Planck, rising first when the discussion was opened, probably spoke for the majority: "That seems to me," he said, "to be a step that, in my opinion, is not yet called for."

Einstein's paper lived up to its promise. For he invoked the $E = mc^2$ of his second relativity paper of 1905, showing that the emission of energy in the form of light caused a change of mass and therefore supported the corpuscular theory. And he went on to argue that the elementary process of emission took place not as a spherical wave that classical theory demanded but as directed, or needle, radiation. This was grasping Planck's nettle with a vengeance. With the benefit of hindsight, it is clear that only Einstein would have dared to do it.

In the audience was Lise Meitner, a young woman of thirty-one, studying under Planck in Berlin:

> At that time I certainly did not yet realize the full implications of his theory of relativity [she wrote more than half a century later], and the way in which it would contribute to a revolutionary transformation of our concepts of time and space. In the course of this lecture he did, however, take the theory of relativity and from it derive the equation: energy = mass times the square of the velocity of light, and showed that to every radiation must be attributed an inert mass. These two facts were so overwhelmingly new and surprising that, to this day, I remember the lecture very well.

Almost exactly three decades later, walking at Christmas with her nephew Otto Frisch in the Stockholm woods, Lise Meitner hit upon the explanation of what Otto Hahn, one of Planck's successors, had just discovered in Berlin: nuclear fission, which was the key to nuclear weapons.

Einstein left Salzburg after the conference of 1909 for a short holiday in the surrounding country and then returned to Berne. But this time it was a return with a difference. In 1908 it had been decided to establish a chair of theoretical physics in the University of Zurich, and Professor Kleiner, who had helped Einstein into the post of *privatdozent* in Berne, chose him for the post. There were delays, largely political, but in the early summer Einstein's appointment was formally announced.

MOVES UP THE LADDER

Einstein's appointment in Zurich was that of associate professor, not full professor, and his salary was only the four thousand five hundred francs a year he had been receiving at the Patent Office. It was augmented by lecture fees and was raised by one thousand francs in 1910, but these additions did not compensate for the increased outgoings of a university professor and the higher cost of living in Zurich. By contrast with his position little more than a decade later, when he could have commanded whatever salary he wished, Einstein still lived and worked among the poorly paid, overworked lower professional classes and, to make ends meet, Mileva took in student lodgers. "In my relativity theory," he once said to Frank, "I set up a clock at every point in space, but in reality I find it difficult to provide even one clock in my room."

Even so, Einstein had at last officially broken through into the academic world, and the future seemed plain sailing. The prospect was of a placid life at one or possibly two Swiss universities, of responsibility increasing steadily through the years, of life in an ivory tower safe within the citadel. In the autumn of 1909, with his wife and his son Hans Albert, he moved into an apartment in Moussonstrasse at the bottom of the Zurichberg, and here his second son, Eduard, was born in July 1910.

The Adlers also lived in the same building. Friedrich Adler, the son of Viktor Adler, who had founded the Austrian Social Democratic Party, and a former fellow student with Einstein at the E.T.H., wrote to his parents on October 28:

> We are on extremely good terms with the Einsteins, who live above us, and as things turned out I have become closer to him than to any of the other academics. The Einsteins live the same Bohemian life as ourselves. They have a son the same age as Annika who spends a lot of time with us....The more I speak with Einstein, and this happens often, the more convinced do I become that I was right in my opinion of him. Among contemporary physicists he is not only the clearest but the one who has the most independent of brains, and it is true that the majority of physicists don't even understand his approach. Apart from that, he is a pure physicist, which means that he is interested in theoretical problems which unfortunately is not the case with me.

Einstein was popular as a lecturer. This was due partly to his lack of convention, partly to his humor, partly to memories of the Munich Gymnasium, which made it impossible for him to fit into the usual professorial mold. "He went to a great deal of trouble over his first lecture, in order to help students," recalled his old friend from Aarau, Dr. Adolf Fisch. "He kept stopping and asking whether he was understood. In the pauses he was surrounded by students who wanted to ask questions which he answered in a most patient and friendly way. This contact between lecturer and student was not at all usual at the time."

He lectured in Zurich regularly throughout term-time: on an "Introduction to Mechanics," on thermodynamics, on the kinetic theory of heat, on electricity and magnetism, and on selected topics from theoretical physics. The number of students was usually in single figures—more the result of the tepid interest in physics than of any lack of ability in the master. Adler neatly sums up the situation after Einstein had taken up his appointment: "My mathematics lecture had an audience of only four, which is as good as can be expected in a small university such as this. But people must go and listen to Einstein, as they have to take their examinations with him, and after seven hours they have had more than enough."

He was precise and clear, he rarely used notes, yet he never floundered as even the best extempore lecturer can. His humor was of the quiet, throwaway kind that illustrated points in his thesis, a sometimes quixotic, frequently irreverent humor that delighted his students. He was, moreover, one of the few lecturers who openly invited his listeners to interrupt him if they failed to understand a point, and it was obvious that the memory of the Luitpold Gymnasium was still in his mind. He also cultivated a casual friendship with his students. Taking them to the Terrasse Cafe after the weekly physics colloquium, bringing them home to discuss the riddle of the universe over coffee in the manner of the Olympia Academy little more than a decade before, Einstein appeared a happy man, outwardly satisfied with his financial status and content with the fame he had already achieved.

Friedrich Adler, a fellow student at the Zurich Polytechnic, who later was instrumental in Einstein's appointment to a professorship at the University of Zurich.

The niche in which circumstance had placed him seemed a satisfactory one. He was sixteen and a half when he had arrived in Switzerland. Now he was thirty-one, a whole impressionable lifetime away, a Swiss citizen bound to the country by the strong bonds of all converts, blind to its defects, and soberly convinced that in their system of government the Swiss had found the democratic key to the political millennium. He occasionally traveled outside the frontiers and brushed shoulders with other members of the international physicists' community—Planck from Berlin, Rutherford from England, Poincaré from Paris—the scientific revolutionaries who were already overturning man's idea of the place he lived in. Yet their more rumbustious world—the world of the Berlin laboratories, of the Collège de France, and of the Cavendish, all places against which Zurich had a faintly provincial air—had little attraction for Einstein. He needed no more than pencil, paper, and pipe; peace for relaxation with his violin; a nearby lake to sail on; the opportunity for an occasional not-too-strenuous stroll in pleasant scenery. Switzerland, that happy, happy land, offered it all.

This was outwardly the situation at the end of 1910, when he had been teaching in Zurich for little more than a year. Yet during the first months of 1911 his colleagues

Einstein's first wife, Mileva, and their two sons, Eduard (left) and Hans Albert, in 1914. [Hebrew University of Jerusalem]

heard astounding news: Einstein was about to leave Switzerland for Prague. This was, as his Swiss biographer has noted, "a grievous blow for Swiss science." It would have seemed even more grievous had it been known that Einstein had been considering the move within a few months of coming to the city in October, 1909.

As in Zurich two years previously, two main names had been put forward for the professorship in the German University in Prague. But whereas in Zurich the initial solution had been simple, hacked out by the chopper of political loyalties, the complications in Prague were numerous enough to add an air of farce. On the one hand, there was Einstein. On the other, there was Gustav Jaumann, professor at the Technical Institute in Brno. The choice between them rested on the recommendation of Anton Lampa, head of the physics faculty, and was exercised formally by the Emperor through the Ministry of Education. Lampa favored Einstein, influenced as he was by the belief that the latter was still an unequivocal Machist—and no doubt by Planck's words of advice: "If Einstein's theory should prove correct, as I suspect it will, he will be considered the Copernicus of the twentieth century." The Ministry preferred Jaumann not only because he was a Machist; in addition, he had the virtue of Austrian birth.

The situation was further complicated by university regulations, which laid down that the importance of candidates' publications should govern their positions on the entry list. Einstein's papers from 1902 onward brought him to the top. This was too much for Jaumann, a self-styled unrecognized genius who now withdrew from the race protesting: "If Einstein has been proposed as first choice because of the belief that he has greater achievements to his credit, then I will have nothing to do with a university that chases after modernity and does not appreciate merit." The move appeared to leave the field open for Einstein.

But now another impediment arose. While the Emperor Franz-Joseph had no direct role in the appointment, he could exercise an overriding veto; and it was known that the Emperor would confirm university appointments only of confessing members of a recognized church, a state of grace from which Einstein was self-excluded. Eventually Einstein's appointment to the chair was confirmed. Only, however, after he had reluctantly agreed to take Austro-Hungarian nationality, a necessity since the appointment would make him a civil servant. As a consolation he was allowed to remain a Swiss so that now, for the first but not the last time, he was able to claim the privileges of dual nationality.

The clue to the real attraction of this capital, where the swords of German-Czech animosity were already being sharpened, is to be found in a letter from Einstein to Lucien Chavan written a few months after his arrival. He was having a good time in

Prague, although not so pleasant a time as in Switzerland. He liked Zurich and the Swiss, but what was that against "a fine Institute and a magnificent library."

The move to Prague took place in March, 1911, and Einstein quickly settled down in his new post, considerably helped by Ludwig Hopf, his young assistant in Zurich who had moved east with him. He was to stay in the city less than eighteen months, but the experience was to be important. Here, he was forced to note, however much he tried to push out of his mind all except his work, the ambiguous position of the Jews in a community already divided against itself. He was forced to notice the emotions aroused in many Jewish friends by the very mention of the Zionist cause, as well as the Pan-German feelings that were already moving the Central Powers toward the precipice of the First World War. In Prague he had as pupil Otto Stern, the Silesian physicist who was to follow him to Zurich in 1912, hold a succession of posts in Germany, cross the Atlantic in the great refugee wave of the 1930s, and dramatically reenter Einstein's life during the final months of the Second World War. And in Prague Einstein was introduced to the mathematical machinery that helped him solve the problems of general relativity.

This extension of his powers came through Georg Pick, once an assistant of Ernst Mach and twenty years older than Einstein. Pick and Einstein had a mutual interest in music. They struck up a strong friendship, and when Einstein spoke of the difficulties he was having, Pick proposed that he consider using the absolute differential calculus of Ricci and Levi-Civita. The two men remained in touch long after Einstein had left Prague, and in June, 1939, with the Germans already in occupation of the city, Pick, then aged eighty, sent a long letter to Einstein in Princeton reminiscently discussing the past. He died, a few years later, in Theresienstadt concentration camp.

Comparatively little is known of Einstein's life in the Bohemian capital. But one thing is quite clear both from Frank's account and from the stray reminiscences that Einstein himself passed on to his friends over the years: he responded to "the political air

Top: Prague: the Karlsbrucke (1357) across the River Vltava, a tributary of the Elbe. In the background can be seen fortified Hradcany Palace (sixteenth and seventeenth centuries), formerly the residence of the ancient kings of Bohemia. *[The Mansell Collection]*

Bottom: Emperor Franz-Joseph of Austria (1830–1916), who reigned over the Austro-Hungarian Empire from 1848, when his uncle, Ferdinand I, was forced to abdicate. *[The Mansell Collection]*

99

The old Jewish *rathaus* and synagogue in Prague. When Einstein came to live here in the early twentieth century, the old capital of Bohemia was the third—largest city in Austria-Hungary. *[The Mansell Collection]*

in which the town was steeped" and to the situation in which the Jews of Prague found themselves. For here, Czech and Germans lived in their own closed worlds. The professors of the two universities rarely met, and the Germans isolated themselves from the Czech majority within their own cultural ring of concerts and lectures and theaters. Yet half the Germans were Jews, a fact that tended to drive them toward a mutually supporting alliance.

All this presented a particularly piquant state of affairs for Einstein—a reneged

100

German, Swiss by choice, who by accepting a post at the German University had been forced to take Austro-Hungarian nationality against his own wishes. It was the first of many nonscientific problems that the pursuit of physics was to pose. He resolved it by openly becoming a member of the Jewish community, although tending to ignore his German origin.

The Prague community included Franz Kafka, Hugo Bergmann, and the writer Max Brod. Much of its activity centered on the home of Bertha Fanta, an ardent Zionist and, while its sphere of influence was intellectual and artistic rather than political, the ultimate triumph of Zionism was accepted almost as a fact of nature. Einstein could not be troubled with such an idea. It was one thing to be concerned with the affairs of fellow Jews in a foreign capital; it was quite another to consider Jewry and its problems on a world basis. For, in the words of Philipp Frank, "The problems of nationality and of the relations of the Jews with the rest of the world appeared to him only as a matter of petty significance."

His aloofness from what many fellow Jews regarded as the great cause no doubt affected the interpretation of Einstein that Brod introduced into his novel *The Redemption of Tycho Brahe.*

Here, the portrait of the young Kepler has many of the characteristics of Einstein. Frank claims that Walther Nernst, professor of physical chemistry in Berlin with whom Einstein was to be closely associated, told Einstein on reading the book: "You are this man Kepler." This is significant as suggesting how not only Brod in Prague, but Nernst at a later period, considered the Einstein whom they saw at close quarters and whom both felt they must understand. For the figure of Kepler-Einstein is that of the scientist at the height of his intellectual powers; fully stretched in this case on the generalization of relativity; not concerned with the rest of the human race; only distantly aware of the surrounding turmoil; and regarding the responsibility of science as a responsibility confined to the scientific scene.

Some phrases in Brod's book epitomize Albert Einstein at this central period of his life; others give a clue to his failure as from the 1920s onward he became the supporter of every good cause that could gain his ear. Thus the young Kepler-Einstein begins to inspire the old Tycho Brahe with a feeling of awe:

> The tranquillity with which he applied himself to his labours and entirely ignored the warblings of flatterers was to Tycho almost superhuman. There was something incomprehensible in its absence of emotion, like a breath from a distant region of ice....He had no heart and therefore had nothing to fear from the world. He was not capable of emotion or love. And for that reason he was naturally also secure against the aberrations of feelings.

It would have been easy to consider such a man as an intriguer whose continuing success was due to cunning, but it was clear to Brahe "that Kepler was the very opposite of an intriguer; he never pursued a definite aim and in fact transacted all affairs lying outside the bounds of his science in a sort of dream." The picture of a Kepler working with the instinct of genius within his own scientific shell, but all at sea when he left it, is a not too inaccurate picture of Einstein in his later years, of the man with two Achilles' heels: a too-trusting belief in the goodness of people and a desperately held and innocent belief that the grand investigations of science not only should but could be insulated from the worlds of politics and power. Strangely, the belief survived even Haber and the First World War. It did not survive his desire to beat the Germans twenty-five years later.

But all this was to come. In Prague there was merely the faintest glimmer of awakening in his Jewish consciousness, an awareness that he himself did not recognize until he arrived in Berlin in 1914. This is clear not only from Frank but from the testimony of Dmitri Marianoff, one of Einstein's two stepsons-in-law. Einstein himself protested strongly against Marianoff's biography, but there is little reason to dispute the nonscientific details of the book that have obviously come from Einstein in reminiscent family mood, barriers down.

Marianoff makes a point of the way in which Einstein was thrown up against his inner Jewishness by the daily circumstances of Prague life:

> Once in his strolls through the city he stumbled on a short alley that led to an old high-walled Jewish cemetery, preserved there since the fifth century [he wrote]. The story of his race for a thousand years was told before him on the tombstones. On them were inscriptions in Hebrew with symbolic records of a tribe or a name. A fish for Fisher, a stag for Hirsch, two hands for the tribe of Aaron. Here he found the battered, chipped and crumbling slab of the tomb of Rabbi Loeue, the friend of Tycho Brahe, the sixteenth-century astronomer whose statue with the globe and compass in his hands Einstein had just passed in front of the Svato-Tynsky-Chram.

What Einstein also tended to remember from Prague, according to Marianoff, was "the solemn sounds of the organ in Catholic cathedrals, the chorales in Protestant churches, the mournful Jewish melodies, the resonant Hussite hymns, folk music and the works of Czech, Russian and German composers." This was the world in which he sought relaxation, moving in "a sort of dream" while his mind concentrated on the work that mattered.

Most important within this work was the continuing riddle of gravity. Throughout the whole of his stay in Prague, he worked steadily toward a solution of the problems it presented, returning to the Principle of Equivalence and the "thought-experiment" with light that he had devised to test its validity. The result was another paper for the *Annalen der Physik*, "Über den Einfluss der Schwerkraft auf die Ausbreitung des Lichtes" ("On the Influence of Gravitation on the Propagation of Light"), in which he brought forward his ideas of how gravity affected the matter of the physical world. Matter, as he had already shown, was really congealed energy, while light quanta, or photons, consisted of particles that had changed their mass in the process of reaching the speed of light. Viewed thus it seemed plausible, even without Einstein's logical structure of argument, that light itself should be affected by the tug of gravity as certainly as the cannonball. In fact, Newton had asked in his *Opticks*: "Do not bodies act upon Light at a distance and by their action bend its Rays; and is not this action (*coeteris paribus*) strongest at the least distance?" And the German astronomer Soldner had used Newton's corpuscular theory of light for predicting a similar deviation, although his figure was only half that demanded by Einstein's eventual theory of 1916.

But there was another consequence that Einstein now brought forward for the first time. If light is produced in a star or in the sun, an area of strong gravity, and then streams down on the earth, an area of weak gravity, then its energy will not be dissipated by a reduction of speed, since this is impossible, light always having the same constant speed.

What would happen, Einstein postulated, was something very different: the wavelength of the light would be changed. This "Einstein shift," the assumption that "the spectral lines of sunlight, as compared with the corresponding spectral lines of terrestrial sources of light, must be somewhat displaced toward the red" was spelled out in some detail. However, he was careful to add the qualification that in view of other influences it might be difficult to isolate the effect he was now describing. In fact, the Doppler shift, produced by the motion of the stars relative to the solar system, was to provide an additional and even more important complication. What he concentrated on instead was the deflection of light by the sun, and his paper ended with the proposal that astronomers should try to record this deflection.

The paper had one major limitation. For what it considered was one, and only one, special case of the effects of gravity: that in which gravity had the same force and direction throughout the entire space that was being considered. This was a simplification that helped Einstein to move the theory forward, but it worried him, partly because of its artificiality and partly because he realized that its removal—and the consequent creation of a theory more in accord with reality—would demand a mathematical expertise that was still beyond him.

Despite this limitation, which was eventually to lead him deeper into the mathematicians' world, and which was in some ways to blunt the intuitive feel for physics that was his real genius, the paper of 1911 was important for one special reason. In it, Einstein threw down the gauntlet to the experimentalists. Was light bent by gravity as it passed near the sun? Surely, this was a question to which it should be possible to provide a clear-cut yes-or-no answer. It was not to be quite as simple as that; but from 1911 onward he pointed out with increasing persistence that here was one way of proving or disproving experimentally a theory that had been built up logically but that had as its foundation little more than an intuitive hunch.

Meanwhile he worked on in Prague. And meanwhile the new status he was acquiring began to bring lecture invitations in increasing numbers. In January, 1911, he

was invited to Leiden by Lorentz, and he and Mileva stayed with the Lorentz family the following month. Shortly afterward, he was formally invited to a major scientific conference, the first Solvay Congress, held in Brussels between October 30 and November 3, 1911. Einstein, the ex-German Swiss, attended it as an Austro-Hungarian.

It was the standing of those who came to Brussels that made the Congress more important for Einstein than any other he had attended. Planck, Nernst, and Rubens were among those from Germany; Poincaré, Madame Curie, and Langevin among those from France. James Jeans and Rutherford came from England, while from Austria-Hungary came Einstein and Franz Hasenöhrl, later to be spuriously credited with Einstein's mass-energy equation. Lorentz himself presided over the Congress, which was also attended by Kamerlingh Onnes from Leiden. Louis de Broglie from Paris, Goldschmidt from Brussels, and Frederick Lindemann, then studying under Nernst in Berlin, acted as secretaries. It was very different from the Salzburg meeting. In Brussels Einstein was brought in to an "experts only" conference, whose quality can be gauged from the studied photograph that survived in the Metropole Hotel through two German occupations. It shows a striking group of men—and one woman—the real revolutionaries of the twentieth century.

Einstein now met Planck, Nernst, and Lorentz on equal terms for the first time. He also met Madame Curie, then at the height of her fame, and Ernest Rutherford, the epitome of the huge New Zealand farmer looking around for new land to bring into cultivation—but this time in the unexplored territory of physics.

In Brussels there also met for the first time the two men who occupied such ironically contrasted positions during the Second World War: Einstein popularly credited with the most important influence on the creation of nuclear weapons, and Lindemann, later Lord Cherwell, more correctly credited, as Churchill's *eminence grise*, with a comparable influence on Britain's wartime science. Lindemann, only twenty-five

at the time of the Solvay Congress, facing a distinguished and disgruntled future, as different from Einstein as man-of-the-world from provincial recluse, was to become a firm friend and devoted admirer.

Lindemann's biographer notes that:

> Observing this shy genius at close quarters, [he] formed an opinion of Einstein's character which he never revised. He saw there the towering intellect which made him for Lindemann the greatest genius of the century, but he saw also a pathetic naïveté in the ordinary affairs of life. Einstein appeared to him to be living in a universe of his own creation, and almost to need protection when he touched the mundane sphere. In all matters of politics he was a guileless child, and would lend his great name to worthless causes which he did not understand, signing any ridiculous political or other manifestos put before him by designing people.

The two men were united by one thing: the view that human beings counted for little when weighed against the splendid problems of physics. Lindemann, according to one colleague, "had time for a few dukes and a few physicists, but regarded most of the rest of mankind as furry little animals." Substituting "pacifists" for "dukes," much the same was true of Einstein.

Soon after the Congress ended, Einstein accepted an invitation to return to the E.T.H. in Zurich. But before he left Prague, he had one visitor whose impact was to be considerable. This was Paul Ehrenfest, a man ill-starred for a tragic life, whose work in physics was perpetually to hover round the borders of genius. Ehrenfest had been born in Vienna and had studied and graduated there before obtaining a special professorship at the St. Petersburg Polytechnic. But his position as an Austrian barred the way ahead; so did the fact that he was a Jew, even though he declared himself as without religion. In addition, Ehrenfest's unconventionality, which so mirrored Einstein's, hardly helped him in the clamber up the academic ladder. He was, it has been written, bored by lectures

The first Solvay Congress, held at the Hotel Metropole in Brussels during October and November, 1911. More than twenty of Einstein's contemporaries attended. Seated (left to right): Walther H. Nernst, Léon M. Brillouin, Ernest Solvay, Hendrik A. Lorentz, Emil Warburg, Jean Baptiste Perrin, Wilhelm Wien (behind), Madame Curie, and Henri Poincaré; standing (left to right): Goldschmidt, Max Planck, Heinrich Rubens, Arnold Sommerfeld, Frederick A. Lindemann, Maurice de Broglie, M.H.C. Knudsen, Franz Hasenöhrl, Hostelet, E. Herzen, James Jeans, Ernest Rutherford, Heike Kamerlingh Onnes, Einstein, and Paul Langevin. [AIP Niels Bohr Library]

Left: Paul Ehrenfest (1880–1933), the Austrian physicist who succeeded Hendrik Lorentz at the University of Leiden. He was, it has been written, bored by lectures at which the audience was not expected to interrupt—especially if he was the lecturer. [AIP Niels Bohr Library]

Right: Pieter Zeeman (1865–1943; left), the Dutch physicist awarded the Nobel Prize in 1902 with Hendrik Lorentz for work on the influence of magnetism on radiation; Einstein; and Paul Ehrenfest in Zeeman's Amsterdam laboratory. [AIP Niels Bohr Library]

at which the audience was not expected to interrupt, and especially so if he was the lecturer.

In the autumn of 1912 Ehrenfest decided to tour German-speaking Europe in search of a better post, and almost automatically found his way to Einstein in Prague. The two men had been in professional touch a few years earlier, and by 1912 each admired the other's work.

Ehrenfest arrived on February 23 and stayed with Einstein for a week. They talked only a little about the search for a new appointment. As Einstein wrote later, it was the state of science that took up almost all their time.

Ehrenfest stuck to his nonreligious guns and was not offered the Prague chair. But before the end of the year he had been appointed to Leiden as successor to Lorentz. Soon afterward, Einstein made the first of many journeys to stay with the Ehrenfests, as happy with their children as when he accompanied their parents in playing Bach. What he had found was another man to whom physics was the whole of life and who put everything else firmly in its right place.

Einstein and his family had left Prague for Switzerland in August 1912. His appointment at the E.T.H. was for ten years, and as he moved into his fifth home in Zurich, he may well have looked forward to settling down at last.

In the autumn of 1912 he began holding weekly afternoon colloquia at which new work was discussed. By now his reception was very different from what it had been in the university only three years earlier, and it was not only members of the E.T.H. who attended. Students at the university, and their professors, found ways and means of joining in, and the meetings were usually crowded, Einstein affably discussing the latest developments with anyone who could contrive to be present. He remained unchanged. The meetings over, he would do as he had done years previously, carrying on the discussion outside the building with those who accompanied him to his favorite cafe. He found it difficult to relinquish his grasp on the problem in hand. Years afterward, his students recalled him standing in a snowstorm under a lamp at the foot of the Zurichberg, handing his umbrella to a companion and jotting down formulas for ten minutes as the snowflakes fell on his notebook.

Max von Laue who as Planck's assistant in Berlin had been among the first to take relativity seriously, came to speak on interference of X-rays, an occasion that was followed by Einstein opening the discussion and extemporizing "on the most intricate problems of physics with as much ease as if he were talking about the weather." Many scientists came to Zurich specifically to see him, and Max von Laue recalls one particular visit. "I can still see Einstein and Ehrenfest striding along in front of a great swarm of

Max Theodor Felix von Laue (1879–1960), the German physicist whose path repeatedly crossed that of Einstein for nearly half a century. Awarded the Nobel Prize for Physics in 1914 for work on the diffraction of X-rays in crystals, Von Laue was one of the first supporters of Einstein's Special Theory of Relativity. [Bildarchiv Preussischer Kulturbesitz]

physicists as they climbed the Zurichberg, and Ehrenfest bursting out in a jubilant cry: 'I have understood it.'" Von Laue's words echo the same air of nuclear innocence that then permeated the Cavendish Laboratory where Andrade could offer a toast to: "the useless electron, and long may it remain so."

Another visitor was Madame Curie with whom Einstein and his wife stayed in Paris late in March, 1913, when he addressed the Société Française de Physique. It is clear from Madame Curie's correspondence, and from Einstein and Mileva's "thank you" letters, that she had shepherded an unsophisticated pair through the rigors of a hurried and demanding visit. In return, Einstein hoped that she would allow him to help her about a trip to the Alps later in the year. Typically, he ended the invitation with a brief postscript that dealt only with physics.

The Curies—mother and two daughters—arrived in Zurich in July for a fortnight in the Bregaglia Alps and the Engadine, with Einstein, his wife, and his elder son. The holiday was a great success. Years later Hans Einstein remembered how they had crossed the Maloja Pass on foot; how his father and Madame Curie had inspected the glacier mills, Einstein cogitating on the forces that had carved these deep vertical wells; and how Madame Curie, recalling the fact that Einstein was technically a Swiss, demanded that he name every peak on the horizon.

There was ample reason for her to seek out Einstein and to mull over with him, during the informal talks of a walking holiday, the implications of the new ferment in physics surrounding her own specialized field of radioactivity. Fresh radioactive substances were being discovered, and the key to their characteristics and behavior obviously had to be sought within Rutherford's new concept of the atom, now known to consist of a positively charged central nucleus surrounded, at a comparatively great distance, by one, by a few, or by a cloud of orbiting electrons. Einstein, with his instinctive feel for the nature of things, would obviously have worthwhile views—while it was already clear that subnuclear particles moved at speeds fast enough to make relativistic effects important.

However, it was so far only physicists who were brought into intimate day-to-day contact with the implications of relativity. Many other technical men found it difficult to see that "the new physics" formed part of their world, as was evident when Einstein spoke on the subject during a visit to Göttingen:

I remember watching the engineering professors who were present and who were, of course, horrified by his approach, because to them reality was the wheels in machinery—really solid entities [says Professor Hyman Levy, then a research student at the university.] And here was this man talking in abstract terms about space-time and the geometry of space-time, not the geometry of a surface which you can think of as a physical surface, but the geometry of space-time, and the curvature of space-time; and showing how you could explain gravitation by the way in which a body moves in space-time along a geodesic—namely the shortest curve in space-time. This was all so abstract that it became unreal to them. I remember seeing one of the professors getting up and walking out in a rage, and as he went out I heard him say, *"Das ist absolut Bloedsinn"* ("That is absolute nonsense").

In 1912 Einstein was still trying to generalize his theory of relativity so that it would apply not only to the special case where gravity operated as a force of constant intensity and direction but in all the multiplicity of special cases that existed throughout the universe. In this he was aided by his old friend Marcel Grossmann, the former colleague of a dozen years before, whose notes during student days had enabled him to skip mathematics and concentrate on physics. This particular chicken was coming home to roost, and it was on Grossmann that Einstein now leaned heavily for the mathematical support that he needed. Even so, it was hard going.

There was an ironic outcome of the work. In 1913 Einstein and Grossmann published jointly a paper that came much nearer to the theory of gravity for which Einstein was still groping. This was *"Entwurf einer verallgemeinerten Relativitätstheorie und eine Theorie der Gravitation,"* to which Einstein contributed the physical sections and Grossmann the mathematical. Einstein was dissatisfied with the paper, for its equations appeared to show that instead of a single solution to any particular set of gravitational circumstances, there was an infinitude of solutions. He believed "that they were not compatible with experience." This, together with the conclusion that the results would not agree with the principle of causality, led him to believe that the theory was untenable. Yet the 1913 paper contained the clue to its own apparent discrepancy: what appeared to be an infinitely large number of solutions to one problem was really a single solution applicable to each of an infinitely large number of different frames of reference. Thus the cards of the General Theory of Relativity had been laid face upward on the table in 1913. They were picked up again by Einstein himself in 1915. But they had lain there unnoticed for two years.

By 1913 Einstein had thus reached a temporary impasse. But his views on the need for generalizing the Special Theory aroused great interest, and in September he put them before the eighty-fifth meeting of the Deutscher Naturforscher und Ärtze, held in Vienna. The auditorium was packed with scientists anxious to hear about a theory even more outlandish than Special Relativity. In some ways they were disappointed. Instead of the esoteric explanations they had expected, there came one of Einstein's minor masterpieces of simple statement, an account in which he compared the development of the various theories of gravitation with the development of successive concepts of electricity. As one of his Zionist friends was later to comment, when he wished he could "speak of basic metaphysical concepts such as time or space as matter-of-factly as others speak of sandwiches or potatoes."

The lecture was remarkable, however, not only for the clear exposition that foreshadowed some of Einstein's later scientific writings, so much more understandable than many of his interpreters, but for an incident that well illustrates his character. In his recent work he had used a generally covariant form of the electromagnetic equation first given the previous year by a young Viennese physicist, Friedrich Kottler. In their paper Einstein and Grossmann had acknowledged their indebtedness, but Einstein had never met Kottler personally. On the spur of the moment he asked whether Kottler was in the audience. A young man rose. Einstein asked him to remain standing—so that all could see the man whose help had been so useful.

Although Special Relativity had by this time become incorporated into the new framework of physics with little more than a disapproving grunt from its more conservative critics, the situation was very different with Einstein's still tentative generalized theory. "It was clear in the discussion that followed that many German-speaking men of science were not yet converted to his ideas," says Robert Lawson, a young English physicist then working in the city's Radium Institute, and the man who later translated into English Einstein's first book on relativity. "Doubts were expressed on the validity of his velocity of propagation of gravitational processes, on the possibility of ever being able to detect the deflection of light rays in a gravitational field or the predicted red shift of spectral lines in such a field." At one point the debate grew quite heated, with Felix Ehrenhaft, for long a colleague and later an opponent of Einstein, arguing at length with two of the critics. To relieve the tension, someone pressed the button that automatically shifted the blackboard from one part of the platform to another—calling out as he did so: "Look. The blackboard moves against the lecture hall and not the lecture hall against the blackboard." Einstein remained unperturbed, smiling and noting only that he was prepared to stand or fall by experimental results.

During this visit to Vienna Einstein heard dramatic news of the theory put forward by the Danish physicist Niels Bohr, which united Rutherford's concept of the

A meeting of The German Association of Scientists and Doctors in the Physics Institute, Vienna University, 1913, at which Einstein gave an early outline of what was to become the General Theory of Relativity. *[Bildarchiv Preussischer Kulturbesitz]*

109

Niels Bohr (1885–1962), who united Rutherford's concept of the nuclear atom with the Planck-Einstein quantum theory. [AIP Niels Bohr Library]

nuclear atom with the Planck-Einstein quantum theory. Bohr was still only twenty-eight but already as deeply concerned as Einstein not only with the upheaval in physics through which they were living, but with its underlying philosophical implications. The two were to be friends for nearly forty years, but the matters on which they agreed were more than balanced by those in which each unsuccessfully struggled to convert the other. Both at first failed to appreciate the practical results that would flow from their work; both, when nuclear weapons arrived, appreciated more quickly than many of their fellow scientists the political and moral implications; both, in many ways epitomizing the stock character of absentminded scientist, were anxious to direct nations into decent ways. These motives united them as much as the argument for and against determinacy divided them, an argument that was to lead Einstein into scientific isolation for the later years of his life.

Bohr had been educated as a physicist in Copenhagen and had come under the special influence of Max Planck. But he had also studied and worked in England, first under J. J. Thomson at the Cavendish and then under Rutherford at Manchester. Long afterward, reminiscing on his past, he reflected on his good luck that Denmark had been politically free until the German invasion of 1940, thus allowing him to maintain contacts with both the German and the British schools of thought. One result of these contrasted contacts was the theory, whose confirmation Einstein now heard in 1913, that successfully accounted for some puzzling features of Rutherford's nuclear atom by invoking the idea of Planck's quanta.

According to classical physics the electrons orbiting the nucleus of Rutherford's atom would lose energy by radiation and inevitably spiral into the nucleus itself, giving out as they did so a continuous spectrum of radiation. But this did not happen; instead, free atoms radiated certain specific and discrete frequencies that were characteristic of the atom concerned. Bohr explained this behavior with two suppositions. The first was that atoms exist only at well-defined stationary states or levels, and that at each of these states the electrons circle the nucleus in specific "allowed" orbits. While this continues the atom emits no radiation. Bohr's second supposition was that when an electron jumped—for whatever reason—from one of its "allowed" orbits to another "allowed" orbit nearer the nucleus, then radiation was emitted; by contrast, when an atom absorbed radiation, one or more of its orbiting electrons jumped from its "allowed" orbit to another farther from the nucleus. Both emission of radiation and its absorption took place in discrete units—the light quanta of the Planck-Einstein quantum theory of 1905.

Thus Bohr had shown that electromagnetic radiation was produced not by the oscillation or acceleration of subatomic particles but by changes in their "energy levels"—and had done so by making use both of Planck's conception of radiation by discontinuous surges of energy and Rutherford's idea of the atom as a miniature solar system with electrons orbiting a central nucleus.

He had, moreover, gone further than disembodied theory. He had applied this to

Niels Bohr on his visit to Göttingen in June 1922. Standing (left to right): (unknown), Niels Bohr, James Franck (1882–1964), and Oskar Klein; seated: Max Born (1882–1970). [Bildarchiv Preussischer Kulturbesitz]

the hydrogen atom and, "leaning directly on Einstein's treatment of the photo-electric effect" as he himself wrote, had proposed to Rutherford that the theory was now susceptible to spectroscopic proof. Such proof was provided in Cambridge in the autumn of 1913, and Rutherford passed it on to George de Hevesy, the Hungarian-Danish chemist from the Cavendish who was attending the conference in Vienna. Hevesy, in turn, told Einstein, and on October 14 wrote to Rutherford describing the occasion: "Speaking with Einstein on different topics we came to speak on Bohr's theorie [sic]," he wrote from Budapest. "He told me that he had once similar ideas but he did not dare to publish them. 'Should Bohr's theories be right, so it is from the greatest importance.' When I told him about the Fowler Spectrum the big eyes of Einstein looked still bigger and he told: 'Then it is one of the greatest discoveries.' I felt very happy hearing Einstein saying so."

The result of Bohr's work was, as Planck put it in 1920 when he received the Nobel Prize, that "a stream of knowledge poured in a sudden flood, not only over this entire field but into the adjacent territories of physics and chemistry."

The news of Bohr's breakthrough came as Einstein learned that the following year it should be possible to discover whether light was, in fact, bent by the gravitational pull of the sun. For in the late summer of 1914 an expedition would be traveling from Berlin to southern Russia, where the necessary observations could be made during an eclipse.

The leader of the expedition was to be Erwin Finlay-Freundlich, an astronomer of mixed German and Scottish descent and at this time the youngest assistant at the Berlin University Observatory. Einstein's friendship with Freundlich is interesting and revealing. It had begun in the summer of 1911 when Professor L. W. Pollak, then a student at Prague University, had visited the Berlin Observatory.

Shortly afterward, Freundlich wrote to Einstein in Prague, offering to search for any deflection of light near Jupiter, an ambitious idea that must have been doomed from the start. Einstein welcomed the help but nothing came of these first efforts, nor of Freundlich's subsequent inspections of old photographic plates, which he described in the *Astronomische Nachrichten*. When that failed, he went on to the study of double stars. Einstein still had doubts, saying that if the speed of light was affected by the speed of the light source, then his theory of relativity and of gravity would be false.

When the eclipse of 1914 offered a definite chance of providing experimental proof or disproof, the next step was obvious. The Berlin Observatory was unenthusiastic, but willing to let Freundlich visit the Crimea—at his own expense and in his own time. This was the situation in the summer of 1913. Freundlich, who had not yet met Einstein, was preparing to marry and to spend his honeymoon in the Alps. On August 26 he was delighted to receive a letter from Switzerland. "This morning," he wrote to his fiancée, "I had a nice letter from Einstein in Zurich in which he asked me to meet him in Switzerland between September 9 and 15. This is wonderful because it fits in with our plans."

A fortnight later, as the train pulled into Zurich, Freundlich and his bride saw waiting for them the short figure of Fritz Haber, director of the Kaiser Wilhelm Institute for Chemistry, which had been opened in Berlin two years earlier. Beside him stood an untidy figure in almost sporting clothes, wearing what Frau Freundlich remembers after half a century as a very conspicuous straw hat: Einstein, the maker of new worlds.

Einstein was delighted to meet his friends and insisted that they accompany him to Frauenfeld, a few miles from Zurich, where he was to speak to the Swiss Society of Natural Sciences. Then he invited them to lunch with himself and Otto Stern, now working in Zurich as his assistant. Only at the end of the meal did he discover that he had no money. The situation was saved by Stern who passed him a one hundred franc note under the table.

At Frauenfeld, where both he and Grossmann spoke on the new theory, Einstein announced, to the embarrassment of Freundlich, that the company had among them "the man who will be testing the theory next year." From Frauenfeld they all traveled for the Society's outing to Ermatingen on the shores of Lake Constance, Einstein later insisting that he and the Freundlichs return alone to Zurich. Throughout the entire journey the two men discussed the problems of gravitation while the young bride studied the scenery of a Switzerland she had never before seen.

The Zurich meeting settled details of what Freundlich would do in the Crimea the following summer. Soon afterward, Einstein invoked the aid of Professor George Ellery Hale of the Mount Wilson Observatory, Pasadena, California, a man whose similarity of outlook with Einstein's is shown by an early passage in his autobiography—"Naturally I do not share the common fallacy of an antagonism between science, literature and art, which appeals to me in much the same way. Creative imagination is the vital factor in all of them, and I was fortunate to learn this at an early age." Hale passed on Einstein's letter to Professor Campbell of the Lick Observatory.

> He writes to me [Hale replied to Einstein on November 8] that he has undertaken to secure eclipse photographs of stars near the sun for Doctor Freundlich of the Berlin Observatory, who will measure them in the hope of detecting differential deflections. Doubtless he will send you further particulars, as I requested him to communicate directly with you.

> I fear there is no possibility of detecting the effect in full sunlight.... The eclipse method, on the contrary, appears to be very promising, as it eliminates all... difficulties, and the use of photography would allow a large number of stars to be measured. I therefore strongly recommend that plan.

Einstein also recommended it. So did Freundlich. But the problem of money still remained, as Freundlich pointed out in December. Einstein himself was willing to contribute up to two thousand marks, but in the end he did not have to dig into his own pocket. During the first months of 1914 help came from unexpected sources. The money was provided by Krupp von Bohlen und Halbach and by the chemist Emil Fischer.

Thus Einstein, firmly settled in Zurich, would await the results of a German expedition that in the late summer of 1914 would provide proof or disproof of a theory on whose development he was still hard at work. He had at last achieved full professional status in the establishment that had grudgingly accepted him as a student of sixteen, in a country whose atmosphere and environment he enjoyed. His sister Maja had now settled in Lucerne with her husband, Paul Winteler. To the same city, only thirty miles away from Zurich across the intervening hills, his mother also came. For Mileva, Switzerland seemed the only country in which it was possible to live, and thus family feelings appeared to chime in with professional success. It must have seemed that now, at last, he might finally settle down.

Yet by the autumn of 1913 he was preparing to move to Berlin, capital of a German Empire whose policies he detested and whose inner spirit he deeply distrusted.

7.

A JEW IN BERLIN

Einstein's attendance at the Solvay Congress of 1911 had repercussions that decisively affected the rest of his life. For among those in Brussels most deeply impressed by his ability were Max Planck and Walther Nernst, twin pillars of the Prussian scientific establishment. Following their return to Berlin both men became engaged in a difficult and delicate task that exercised their scientific enthusiasm and their patriotic instincts.

The task was the recruitment of staff for the new and ambitious series of research institutes that the Emperor had graciously allowed to be called the Kaiser Wilhelm Gesellschaft. These institutes were not only to investigate pure science; they would also, it was intended, help increase Germany's lead in the application of scientific discoveries made during the previous half-century. In this field the country was now technologically supreme in Europe, providing much of the continent with dyestuffs, with the tungsten needed for steel making, with magnetos for the gas engines that were revolutionizing land transport and were soon to bring a new dimension to warfare, and providing also the best scientific instruments. Significantly, when war broke out in 1914, the British found much of their artillery using gun sights exclusively made by Goerz of Berlin.

The Germans were well aware that applied technology demands a constant diet of pure research. They were aware that in the United States the General Electric Company had invited Charles Steinmetz, the electrophysicist, to head their laboratories and to do what work he pleased. They knew that in Britain Lord Haldane, secretary of state for war until 1912, had seen the country to be "at a profound disadvantage with the Germans, who were building up their Air Service on a foundation of science" and had, as a result, laid the foundations at Farnborough of what was to become the Royal Aircraft Establishment. All this constituted a warning that was heeded by Friedrich Althoff, the permanent secretary in the Prussian Ministry of Education. His crowning achievement was the Kaiser Wilhelm Gesellschaft, the ambitious plans for which were approved by the emperor himself. The institutes were to be financed by bankers and industrialists who were to be rewarded not merely by a flush of patriotism but by the title of "Senator," the right to wear handsome gowns, and the honor of an occasional breakfast with the emperor.

The scheme was announced in the autumn of 1911, and during the following summer work began at Dahlem, on the outskirts of Berlin, on buildings for the Institute for Physical Chemistry and Electrochemistry that was to be run by Haber. The Physics Institute was to follow, and as little difficulty was expected in staffing it as there had been in attracting men to work under Haber. Indeed, as far as physics was concerned, the

114

scientific atmosphere of the German capital was almost magnet enough. Only the Cavendish Laboratory at Cambridge, forging ahead into the nuclear world under the command of J. J. Thomson, could compare with the physics faculty of the University of Berlin.

Therefore, it was felt in the Prussian capital, there would be little difficulty in attracting Einstein. One possible impediment lay concealed in the word "Swiss," for Einstein had reneged on his German nationality more than a decade and a half previously. And even if the authorities could be induced to accept him, for the sake of German progress if not for the sake of science alone, there was always the chance that Einstein might not accept Berlin. There is little evidence that up to this date he had openly voiced the criticism of the Prussian regime and of the German mentality that later so obsessed him; but such views as he had were almost certainly known, implicitly if not explicitly, to Planck and Nernst. Both were determined men, however, and in the summer of 1913 they decided to visit Einstein in Zurich.

Some of the preliminaries appear to have been dealt with by this time. In the spring of 1912, while still in Prague, Einstein had gone to Berlin for appointments with Nernst, Planck, Rubens, Warburg, and Haber. Later, when his German nationality became an issue on his winning the Nobel Prize, he officially wrote that this question of nationality had been discussed with Haber when his appointment was being considered. It seems likely, therefore, that Planck and Nernst, the subject having already been raised, were visiting Zurich to make sure that if a formal offer were made, it would be accepted.

The high drama of these two major figures in German science traveling south from Berlin to tempt the young Einstein back into the Prussian orbit was equaled by the incongruity of the men themselves—Planck aloof and superbly professional, always master of the situation, the tall, trim man from whom his country could never demand too much; Nernst the businesslike genius, a jolly, plump little man against whom Planck appeared as the epitome of discipline. Both were excellent as fishers for Einstein, who had a respect for Planck only just this side idolatry. For Nernst there was even some warmth.

Planck and Nernst met Einstein in his rooms at the E.T.H. and pleaded their case with him at some length. He was unwilling to give a decision then and there, and the two professors decided to ascend the Rigi, the most famous of nineteenth-century Swiss viewpoints, while Einstein was making up his mind. After their excursion by train and funicular railway they would return to Zurich for his answer. Einstein, exhibiting the quirkish humor with which he often tweaked authority's tail, announced that they would know the verdict as soon as they saw him. If he was carrying a white rose the answer

Einstein and Charles Proteus Steinmetz (1865–1923), an electrical engineer who emigrated to America from Germany and became an American citizen at the end of the last century. Steinmetz' work led to the final victory of alternating current over direct current and made him one of the most important men in electrical engineering during the first decade of the twentieth century. *[United Press International]*

Left: The train from Vitznau to the summit of the Rigi, the mountain Planck and Nernst ascended while Einstein made up his mind whether to leave Switzerland for Berlin. *[Swiss National Tourist Office, London]*

Right: Wilhelm II (1850–1941), Emperor of Germany from 1888 until his abdication in 1918. In 1913 he approved Einstein's appointment to a key post in Berlin. *[The Mansell Collection]*

would be "No"; if the rose was red, then he would accept the offer from Berlin if it were formally made.

When the two men later stepped down from their carriage, they were relieved to see Einstein trotting up the platform carrying a red rose.

The proposal had been that Einstein should become director of the Kaiser Wilhelm Institute for Physics when it was set up, and would meanwhile give advice on research in the subject carried out in other parts of the organization. Had this been the sum total of the offer, however, it seems probable that he would have been carrying a white rose rather than red. But the Kaiser Wilhelm appointment was only one part of an attractive package deal.

Almost exactly three years earlier, Jacobus Hendrikus van't Hoff, the originator of the theory of the spatial structure of molecules, had died at the age of fifty-nine. He had been a member of the Prussian Academy of Sciences, the oldest scientific institution in Germany, planned by Liebnitz and established by Frederick the First as the "Society of Sciences," and his chair remained empty. Planck and Nernst were confident that with the help of their colleagues they could persuade the Prussian Ministry of Education to approve Einstein's appointment to the chair—a necessary move since the Academy existed under the umbrella of the Prussian civil service. Most members occupied only honorary and unpaid positions. A few, however, were endowed from one of various funds, and it was part of the plan that, with such help, Einstein should be offered a salary much in excess of what he was receiving in Zurich. If this were not attraction enough, there was a third item in the offer, which Einstein agreed to accept if it were officially made. This was a nominal professorship in the University of Berlin, nominal since under the proposed special arrangements Einstein would be able to lecture as much or as little as he wished and would have none of the normal duties concerned with university administration.

On their return to Berlin, Planck and Nernst, supported by Heinrich Rubens and Emil Warburg, the founder of modern photochemistry, prepared their draft notice for presentation to the Ministry of Education. The original proposed Einstein "for full membership of the Academy with special personal salary of 6,000 marks," but the figure was subsequently doubled to "12,000," an indication that the Germans were anxious that this particular catch should not slip through their fingers. The draft—in which the German birth and education of this apparently Swiss professor was inserted almost as an afterthought—described Einstein's early years, and the publication of his first relativity paper.

"This new interpretation of the time concept has had sweeping repercussions

Friedrich Wilhelm University, Unter den Linden, Berlin, in 1910. [Bildarchiv Preussischer Kulturbesitz]

on the whole of physics, especially mechanics and even epistemology," it went on. "The mathematician Minkowski subsequently formulated it in terms which unify the whole system of physics inasmuch as time enters the stage as a dimension on completely equal terms with the three conventional dimensions." It then, somewhat surprisingly in the light of later events, turned to what were considered more relevant matters:

> Although this idea of Einstein's has proved itself so fundamental for the development of physical principles, its application still lies for the moment on the frontier of the measurable. Far more important for practical physics is his penetration of other questions on which, for the moment, interest is focused. Thus he was the first man to show the importance of the quantum theory for the energy of atomic and molecular movements, and from this he produced a formula for the specific heat of solids which, although not yet entirely proved in detail, has become a basis for further development of the newer atomic kinetics. He has also linked the quantum hypothesis with photo-electric and photo-chemical effects by the discovery of interesting new relationships capable of being checked by measurement, and he was one of the first to point out the close relationship between the constant of elasticity and those in the optical vibrations of crystals.

> All in all, one can say that among the great problems, so abundant in modern physics, there is hardly one to which Einstein has not brought some outstanding contribution. That he may sometimes have missed the target in his speculations, as, for example in his theory of light quanta, cannot really be held against him. For in the most exact of natural sciences every innovation entails risk. At the moment he is working intensively on a new theory of gravitation, with what success only the future will tell. Apart from his own productivity, Einstein has a special talent for probing peculiar original views and premises, and estimating their inter-relationship with uncanny certainty from his own experience.

> In his treatment and investigation of classical theory, even in the earliest of his publications, as well as in his demonstration and criticism of new hypotheses, Einstein must rank as a master.

The interest in this account, which was to open the gates to Berlin, lies in the way in which it glosses over Einstein's work on relativity and quickly dismisses the "heuristic viewpoint" of the photoelectric paper for which he was to be awarded the Nobel Prize for Physics nine years later. Nernst and Planck, who presumably drew up the document, took into account not only the conservative views of their colleagues but also the character of the minister. And Planck, reluctant to admit that his quanta did not somehow take on wave characteristics during the journey from here to there, still felt it necessary to insist that when it came to photons Einstein had "missed the target."

The Brandenburg Gate in Berlin, built between 1789 and 1793 by K. G. Langhams (1733–1808), is an early example of neoclassical architecture. [The Mansell Collection]

Having been approved by the Academy, the proposal was submitted to the Government on July 28, 1913. It was nearly four months later before the reply came. On November 20 the minister stated that the Kaiser had approved the appointment, that the minister of finance had agreed to grant Dr. Einstein traveling expenses, and that he now wished to be informed if "Professor Einstein actually accepts his new post." Long before this, Nernst took the matter as settled. "At Easter, Einstein will move to Berlin," he wrote to Lindemann on August 18, 1913: "Planck and I were in Zurich to see him the other day and the Academy has already elected him. We have great expectations of him."

Einstein formally accepted on December 7, having by this time asked for his release from the post he had taken up only eighteen months earlier. His acceptance was significant in a number of ways. The most obvious was later stressed by Sommerfeld who wrote that "We owe the completion of his general theory of relativity to his leisure while in Berlin." But there is more to it than that. Had Einstein remained in Zurich until the outbreak of war in August, 1914, it is almost inconceivable that he would have returned to Germany. The anti-Semites in that country would have been deprived both in the postwar chaos of the early 1920s and in the preparations for the Nazi takeover of a ready-made target on which to concentrate their fire. It is almost equally unlikely that Einstein would have moved to the United States in 1933—and thus been available on Long Island in the summer of 1939 to prod America into research that gave them nuclear weapons before the end of the war in the Pacific.

For these reasons, if no other, it is worth considering the pros and cons of what for Einstein must have been a difficult decision. On the credit side there was the enormous attraction of the intellectual climate into which he would be moving. There was also the attraction of the salary. Einstein was never a man to care about money, but he was the father of two growing sons, and he felt responsible for them if not extravagantly affectionate.

"In addition," says one of his generally more reliable biographers, Philipp Frank, "there were also personal factors that entered into the decision. Einstein had an uncle in Berlin, a fairly successful businessman, whose daughter, Elsa, was now a widow. Einstein remembered that his cousin Elsa as a young girl had often been in Munich and had impressed him as a friendly, happy person. The prospects of being able to enjoy the pleasant company of this cousin in Berlin made him think of the Prussian capital more favorably." This statement must be taken with some caution. Frank, who wrote his book in 1947, more than thirty years later, was an intimate of Einstein, and it is difficult not to believe that the source of the comment was Einstein himself. If this is so, and if the comment is correct, it implies considerable guile. It is true that Albert eventually married

Wilhelm II of Germany and King
Edward VII of Great Britain during
Edward's visit to Germany in 1906.
[The Mansell Collection]

Elsa Einstein; but when he moved to Berlin in April, 1914, he moved with Mileva and their two sons. The marriage had not yet broken up, and while there are indications that it was almost on the rocks, it seems overharsh to suggest that he accepted the Berlin appointment in the hope that it would eventually bring his marriage to an end. However, that is what happened.

Mileva Einstein's reaction to Berlin, very largely Slav dislike for all things Teuton, which for her contrasted so strongly with the casual happy atmosphere of Switzerland, had a counterpart in Einstein's own feelings. Seventeen years previously he had renounced not only German nationality but what he considered the essential Germanism: reverence for obedience, regimentation of the body, and a rigidity of the spirit that forced minds narrowly upward like the pinetrunks of the dark German forests. Now, as a man, he would be walking back into the environment from which he had escaped as a boy. Yet throwing down an intellectual gauntlet, taking a calculated risk, were actions that not only had led to Einstein's fame but were typical of his mental makeup; accepting a post in the Kaiser Wilhelm would enable him to do both things. In Berlin, moreover, under the conditions provided by Planck and Nernst, he would be unencumbered by money worries, would avoid the disturbing conflicts of a teaching routine. More than one friend, more than one colleague, has stressed how he was in some ways more of an artist than a scientist—or at least "an artist in science." And "the true artist will let his wife starve, his children go barefoot, his mother drudge for his living at seventy, sooner than work at anything but his art." Einstein would even put himself in pawn to the Prussians.

The problem of nationality, raised when the question of going to Berlin had first been discussed, at last appeared settled. Haber had pointed out that membership in the Prussian Academy of Sciences would automatically make Einstein a Prussian citizen— and two decades later Professor Dr. Ernst Heyman, perpetual secretary of the Academy, wrote of Einstein's "Prussian nationality which he acquired in 1913 simply by becoming a full member of the Academy." Einstein's version was that he made acceptance of a possible appointment dependent on there being no change in his nationality, and that this was agreed to. Exactly what was finally done is not clear even today. But there had been a Professor Haguenin, a Frenchman in the Academy's Faculty of Letters, who had insisted on remaining French. The position was no doubt different in the case of a German who had renounced his German nationality, but Einstein was left with the impression that in Berlin he would not only retain his Swiss nationality but would avoid becoming a German once again. The Government, but not the Academy, later denied that this was so. If the Government was right, this did not necessarily mean that Planck

Berlin at the turn-of-the-century.
[German Information Center]

and Nernst had failed to keep their promise. The "agreement" may have first been discussed early in the summer. And it was only on July 13, 1913, that a new Nationality Law provided in its Section Fourteen that state employment in the service of the Reich, or in one of the federal states, gave German citizenship to the respective foreign employee, official, or civil servant.

Certainly, for a good deal of his life Einstein believed that he, as a Swiss, had gained professorial status in Berlin only by diplomatic sleight of hand. But it is typical of what his elder son has called his delight in making up good stories for good listeners that he should later give a different version. To Dr. Max Gottschalk, a prominent Belgian Jewish scholar and good friend, who asked how a Swiss had become a full German professor, Einstein explained that the Kaiser had visited the University one day. "He asked to be introduced to Professor Einstein and I was brought forward," he said. "After that, as the Kaiser had called me a professor I had to be a full professor."

Details were settled before the end of 1913, and it was arranged that he should take up his duties in Berlin on April 1, 1914.

In Zurich, Louis Kollros, his old colleague of E.T.H. days, organized a farewell supper for him in the Kronenhalle. "We all regretted his departure," Kollros has said. "He himself was delighted at the prospect of being able to devote all his time to research…delighted and a little anxious nevertheless; he did not know what the future held in store for him. When I accompanied him home that evening he turned to me and said: 'The gentlemen in Berlin are gambling on me as if I were a prize hen. As for myself I don't even know whether I'm going to lay another egg.'"

Einstein moved with his family from Zurich to Berlin on April 6, 1914. While events now moved on toward Freundlich's expedition to the Crimea, he traveled each morning to his office in the Academy, then housed in the Prussian State Library on the Unter den Linden. Here, he arranged with his new colleagues from the University how,

121

when, and about what, he would lecture during the coming autumn term. And here, he was visited by officials of the Kaiser Wilhelm Gesellschaft with whom he arranged details of the new institute. He has denied that when asked to outline his needs he said that these consisted only of pencils and paper, which he would supply himself. However, it is quite clear that he was determined to keep himself as clear as possible of the German bureaucratic machinery.

In Berlin Einstein was to see for the first time how the ramifications of science spread out not only into philosophy and metaphysics, but into politics and power and how they penetrated, like the metal rods in a ferroconcrete building, organizations on which the equilibrium of European peace still rested. At first, he was barely distressed by the new climate, although there were compensations. There was, above all, the new freedom to devote himself almost entirely to his work.

The most urgent thing now was the expedition to southern Russia to observe the eclipse in August, and from April onward Einstein and his family were in regular and close contact with the Freundlichs. As the date of the expedition's departure approached, Einstein withdrew more and more into his own scientific carapace; more frequently, he became the Einstein of the later newspaper caricatures, insulated from the normal contacts of life by his own interior problems. Thus there was the occasion when he pushed back the plates at the end of a meal with the Freundlichs. Before a word could be said, he began to cover a much-prized "party" tablecloth with equations as he talked with his host. "Had I kept it unwashed as my husband told me," said Frau Freundlich half a century afterward, "it would be worth a fortune." But this was typical. "I have seen him in his keenness," Lord Samuel once wrote, "when no table was handy, kneel down on the floor and scribble diagrams and equations on a scrap of paper on a chair."

There was also the complementary occasion when the Freundlichs arrived to dine with the Einsteins. After a long wait without their host, Mileva answered the telephone to discover her husband was calling from Dahlem. He had, he said, been waiting more than an hour at the railway station for Freundlich. As agreed Freundlich had kept the rendezvous at the Einstein apartment.

By this time Einstein was not only engrossed. He was also confident. Earlier doubts had been swept away, and even before coming to Berlin in the spring he had written in high spirits to Besso, saying he was confident of the theory whatever the results of the eclipse expedition might be. This is revealing. For Einstein was saying that if a man stood fast by his intuition, if he hung on in the face of difficulties, if he really felt from an inner sense of conviction that he were right, then an explanation for discrepancies would arrive; inconsistencies in the evidence would become explicable. It was, although he does not seem to have realized it himself, a final farewell to Mach and his deification of the sensations. It was also indulgence in an act of faith. Only Einstein the philosopher could have convinced Einstein the scientist that if the evidence did not agree with the theory then the evidence must be faulty.

Berlin crowds cheering the declaration of war on Russia on August 1, 1914. War was declared on France two days later. [Culver Pictures]

All these hopes were wrecked by Germany's declaration of war on Russia on August 1, 1914, her declaration of war on France two days later, and her invasion of Belgium, which brought Britain into the war on August 4. But Freundlich and the members of his team in southern Russia were luckier than they might have been, although their equipment was impounded and they themselves were arrested and taken to Odessa. By the end of the month their exchange for a number of high-ranking Russian officers had been arranged, and by September 2 Freundlich was back in Berlin. Here, he spent the rest of the war, mainly at the Observatory but giving part-time assistance to Einstein.

The war thus delayed the testing of the General Theory for five years, and it was to affect Einstein decisively in one other way: it was the instrument that finally brought his first marriage to an end.

His relations with Mileva had become increasingly fragile. Years later he complained that in Switzerland she had been jealous of all his friends, with the solitary

exception of Solovine, and inferred that her disposition had made life together impossible. But he looked back more in sorrow than in pain, accepting with resignation the fact that nothing could have made the marriage work properly and acquitting both his wife and himself of anything worse than bad luck. In 1914 he was far less equable about the matter.

It was at least reasonable that Mileva should return to Zurich with the two sons in the summer of 1914; it was even more reasonable that she should stay with them there when war broke out in August—at least until the immediate prospects had become clearer. By Christmas it was plain that something more was involved. Mileva remained in Switzerland with the children. Einstein, still a Swiss citizen, remained in Berlin, spending the holiday with Professor and Frau Nernst, a lonely but perhaps not entirely unhappy figure playing his violin to them on Christmas Eve.

Mileva did not return. Einstein did not care. In fact, there is a good deal of circumstantial evidence to suggest that he was heartily glad to remain on his own while he got down to the hard work of completing the General Theory. Not all his friends felt this was a satisfactory situation, and Haber in particular began a long series of kindly but unsuccessful attempts to bring the two together again. The slender hope of this is shown by a letter that Einstein wrote to Besso some months after the famous General Theory

Mobilized German reservists on their way to the railway station in Berlin, August, 1914. *[Culver Pictures]*

paper had been published and after he had experienced a stormy meeting with his wife in Switzerland. If he had not had the strength of mind to keep her at a distance, he would, he said, have been worn out.

Even by Christmas, 1914, one problem was evident—how to provide for Mileva and the two sons, one aged ten, the other four. Einstein had a qualified affection for the boys, as long as it did not take up too much of his time, and he was anxious that they should not suffer from the breakup of their parents' marriage. For the next few years, therefore, money—and the difficulty of getting it without loss from wartime Germany to neutral Switzerland—became one of Einstein's preoccupations.

If the First World War quickly put a temporary spoke in one of Einstein's scientific wheels and brought his private life to a climax, it also did something far more important: it brought him face to face, for the first time, with the interrelationships between science and world affairs. Until now he had looked on science as a vocation to be followed only by men of intelligence and moral integrity who were usually cut off from most other people.

This belief was ingenuous. Newton himself had been an adviser to the British Admiralty. Michael Faraday and Sir Frederick Abel were advisers to the British War Office. Dewar and Abel produced cordite, Nobel invented dynamite, and the studies on

125

Einstein and Fritz Haber (1868–1934), the German chemist whose method for producing ammonia was essential to the manufacture of explosives and fertilizers during the early years of the First World War. [AIP Niels Bohr Library]

the Stassfurt carried out by Van't Hoff, whose chair Einstein now filled, were of great use to Germany's wartime industry. Science had, in fact, been one of war's handmaidens since bronze replaced stone in prehistoric times. Yet the nature of Einstein's work on the fundamental problems of physics had tended to quarantine him away from this fact, and his self-imposed dedication to the task had aided the process. He was, therefore, shocked at what he witnessed in Berlin. For now his colleagues leapt to arms unbidden, as certain as Rupert Brooke where duty lay. His former assistant, Ludwig Hopf, joined the German Air Ministry and helped to develop military aircraft. Otto Stern was soon serving with the forces on the eastern front from which he maintained contact with Einstein by a series of brief letters and field postcards. The young Max Born, brought to the University of Berlin from Göttingen when Planck persuaded the Prussian Ministry of Education that he needed help, worked first for the German air force and then for a military board investigating the physics of sound-ranging. Schwarzschild the astronomer, whose calculations were to support the first confirmation of Einstein's General Theory, served as a mathematical expert with the German armies on the eastern front. Nernst became first a War Ministry consultant, advising on chemical agents for shells, and subsequently accepted a commission.

Above all there was Fritz Haber who had at once volunteered for service but had been rejected on medical grounds. "His resulting depression," says his biographer, "disappeared when he received a problem from the Ordnance Department. Request was made for gasoline with a low freezing point, since the army expected to fight through a Russian winter." Furthermore, it was not long before Haber was in uniform, and telling his wife that a scientist belonged to the world during times of peace but to his country during times of war. It had quickly become clear that his revolutionary method for producing ammonia—for which he was later awarded the Nobel Prize for Chemistry— was essential to the stockpiling of explosives and fertilizer without which the German war effort could hardly have continued. First, he was consulted on how this process could best be utilized. Next, he was brought in to advise on the practicability of gas warfare, first as a sergeant. "One of [his] great disappointments was lack of a higher military title," says his biographer. "As a full professor at a university, he had the feeling he was equivalent to a general; academy members had a comparable uniform for court occasions." Later, he was commissioned as a captain—but not before he compelled his hesitating colleague Richard Willstatter to join in gas mask research: "I am a sergeant" he said. "I command you to the task." Haber soon joined forces with Nernst, and within a few months was supervising production of enough chlorine for the first German gas attack in the spring of 1915. By the following year he had become the head of Germany's

Scrap metal being collected in Germany as the demands for it increased during the course of the First World War. [Culver Pictures]

chemical warfare service and, after experimenting with hundreds of substances, achieved a major technological success by introducing mustard gas in 1917. Einstein had no illusions. Reading a report of the Allied use of gas bombs, he remarked to his colleagues: "This is supposed to say that they stunk first, but we know better how to do it."

Even Einstein, critical of his own country since youth, had expected something different from what he now witnessed. Reaction from the universities reinforced all of Einstein's distaste for what he saw as the exlusively German characteristic of marching to the band. He looked askance at his own colleagues, and he later tended to overlook the fact that Lindemann risked his life testing service aircraft, that Madame Curie drove Red Cross ambulances, and that both Rutherford and Langevin worked as scientists on the inter-Allied anti-submarine committee that produced the first Asdic detectors. It might be wrong for Allied scientists to prostitute science; but, by Einstein's implication, it was worse for German scientists to do the same thing since Germany had been the aggressor. It was a plausible argument; but it should have destroyed any vestigial illusion that scientists could remain outside the battle.

The sight of the Berlin scientific establishment devoting itself to war with hardly a murmur of dissent drove Einstein toward a triple commitment to internationalism, pacifism, and socialism. These were all fine ideals, and all appealed to the best in him. Although there is little evidence that his support had any effect on the course of history, that support, the direct result of his wartime experiences in Berlin, led him after the war into waters where he was dangerously out of his depth. By that time he was a world figure. All his public actions were followed—either with reverence or amusement. The upshot was a worldwide belief that Einstein was fired by an almost saintly honesty of purpose and a less justifiable feeling that scientists almost inevitably lost their way in the corridors of power.

The war thus revolutionized Einstein's attitude to the world about him. He could no longer remain isolated. He had to play his part on the side of the angels. But physics still came first. It held him to Berlin, despite the fact that while he apparently hoped for an Allied victory, he was forced to turn a Nelsonian blind eye not only to the work of his colleagues but even to the sources of some of his own money. This came, at least in part, from Leopold Koppel who in 1916 created the Kaiser Wilhelm Foundation for Military Technical Sciences. The full details of Einstein's links with Koppel are not known, but in a letter to Freundlich in December, 1913, Einstein named Koppel as the man providing his Academy salary. According to the Max Planck Gesellschaft into which the Kaiser Wilhelm Institute was transformed in 1946, Einstein's Institute for Physics received regular sums—twenty-five thousand marks from October 1, 1917 to March 31,

1918—from the Koppel donation that set up the military foundation. Einstein himself wrote to Hedwig Born in 1919 saying that his academic pay depended on Herr Koppel, while Professor Jens of Tübingen University has stated that Einstein "was first given the opportunity for undisturbed research by a Prussian banker who undertook to pay Einstein a supplementary salary of four thousand Reichsmarks from April 1, 1914 onwards for a period of twelve years," and names the banker as Koppel. "Einstein," he sums up, "knew that the sumptuous bed in which he lay swarmed with bugs."

Whatever the exact figure, it is clear that Einstein at the height of his powers was being supported by the very people he was soon condemning and exhibiting a surprising ability to prevent his left hand from knowing what his right hand was doing. But physics came first; so much so that even had he troubled to think about the matter there would have been no contradiction in declaiming against the war while using for science the money of those who supported the war. Like Major Barbara, Einstein would no doubt have reflected that the money was better in his hands than theirs.

Einstein's ingrained distrust of all things military and of all things Prussian was first revealed clearly by his reaction to the "Manifesto to the Civilized World." This manifesto was a fulsome and pained expression of surprise that the world should have objected to the German invasion of Belgium. Issued early in October, 1914, it disclaimed Germany's war guilt, justified the violation of Belgium on the grounds that it would have been suicide to have done anything else, spoke of "Russian hordes…unleashed against the white race" in the tones of Dr. Goebbels twenty years later, and claimed that "were it not for German militarism, German culture would have been wiped off the face of the earth." The Manifesto gained ninety-three supporters from the upper echelons of the intellectual world where it was circulated. Wilhelm Röntgen, the discoverer of X-rays, signed it. So did Ernst Haeckel, the evolutionist. So did Paul Ehrlich, the biologist. And so did Max Planck.

A reaction to "The Manifesto of the 93," as it was to be known, came within days from George Nicolai, professor of physiology in the University of Berlin, soon to be the author of *The Biology of War*, and the conscript-turned-pacifist who during the closing months of the war made a sensational escape from Germany by plane. The exact part that Einstein played in Nicolai's "Manifesto to Europeans" is not clear, but Nicolai himself gives him credit for being coauthor. Even though the counter-manifesto was a joint effort, its wording is extraordinarily reminiscent of the statements, announcements, messages, and exhortations for international cooperation that were to come in a stream from Einstein throughout the next forty years.

Drawn up in the University of Berlin, it was circulated among the professors. It was signed by Nicolai and by Einstein. It was signed by Wilhelm Forster, the eighty-year-old head of the Berlin Observatory who had already signed the Manifesto of the 93, and by Otto Buek. That was all.

Einstein no doubt felt its ineffectiveness, and a month later was drawn for the first time into membership of a political party. This was the Bund Neues Vaterland, established on November 16, 1914, and included among its founder-members the banker Hugo Simon who in 1919 became Prussian minister of finance, and Ernst Reuter who became a famous burgomaster of Berlin after the Second World War. The main object of the group was to bring about an early peace. The second was the creation of an international body that would make future wars impossible. Both were aims with which Einstein wholeheartedly sympathized, and he is reported to have been "very active, attending meetings and delivering speeches." The Bund, struggling for existence in a nation not only at war but enthusiastically supporting the war, was obviously doomed to an early death. Einstein's support, however, was open, something very different from the support that he was to give, through connections in Holland and Switzerland, to the forces striving for an early end to the war, even if this involved Germany's defeat.

It has been said with some justice that "to work in any open way for peace under the Kaiser's regime in 1914 was equivalent to treason," and if Einstein is taken to be a German, some of his actions have more than a touch of it. Had all of them been publicly known in the immediate aftermath of the Armistice, his trials and tribulations during the early 1920s would have been that much greater. For he appears to have hoped not only for an end to the war but, more specifically, for German defeat. The attitude linked him loosely with at least part of the "German resistance" of thirty years later, although with one difference. In the Europe of 1914-18 he was not only able to continue his life's work from his privileged position in Berlin, he was also able to carry on his "resistance" work of pleading peace in both Holland and Switzerland with the minimum of personal risk since in any trouble he could always claim the protection of his Swiss passport. There is nothing shameful in the fact that circumstance thus enabled him to have the best of both worlds; yet it tended to widen the gap that already separated him from most other men.

Einstein's first wartime contacts outside Germany—with the exception of personal letters to his wife—were with Ehrenfest and Lorentz in Holland. To both he wrote with a mixture of resignation, pity, and disgust. How was it possible for sane men to behave like this? Especially, how was it possible for some of the great men of science to support war, doing in the name of the state what had once been done in the name of religion? Surely, something could be done to unite men of science in the various "Fatherlands?" Surely, scholars and intellectuals were not helpless? This was the tenor of his writings for the first year of the war. He seems, despite everything, to have gone on hoping that peace would break out.

Then, in September, 1915, he left Berlin for Switzerland. With his Swiss passport, his wife still living in Zurich, and his numerous friends in both Zurich and Berne, this was on the face of it an acceptable journey to make. Its main object, however, was to visit Romain Rolland, the famous author and pacifist then living in Vevey on the shores of Lake Geneva. Einstein had written to Rolland in March, telling him that he had heard through the Bund Neues Vaterland of Rolland's efforts to remove the differences

Left: Romain Rolland (1866–1944), the French writer and Nobel Prize winner whose essays published in 1915 urging Germany and France to act humanely during the First World War brought protests from both countries. *[The Mansell Collection]*

Right: American troops moving up to the front in France during the First World War. *[The Mansell Collection]*

between the French and the German people. He was, he went on, anxious to help in any way possible.

It is not quite clear how he thought he could help, but Rolland in neutral Switzerland subsequently received a letter from Berlin saying that there was much good news about their work that could be given by a man close to them—the scholar Einstein, who would be visiting him shortly.

Now, in mid-September, Einstein arrived at Vevey from Zurich, accompanied by Dr. Zangger from the E.T.H., who had helped get him back there in 1912. With Rolland, Einstein laid the blame for the war unequivocally on what he saw as the essential German spirit, but the intensity of his feeling shocked Rolland. Their meeting over, the two men exchanged a few more words, standing on the station platform at Vevey as the train prepared to leave for Berne. "In looking at Einstein," wrote Rolland, "I noted how he, one of the very few men whose spirit had remained free among the general servility, had been led, as a reaction, to see the worst side of his own nation and to judge her almost with the severity of her enemies. I know certain men in the French camp who, for the same reason, would shake hands with him. (Incidentally, Einstein is a Jew which explains his international outlook and the mocking character of his criticism)." The strength of Einstein's feeling was remarkable; and he must have questioned even the scientific benefits of life in Berlin when he considered that his patrons included the creator and financial supporter of the Kaiser Wilhelm Foundation for Military Technical Sciences.

In neutral Switzerland his views could be declared without fear of serious contradiction. In Germany he put a slightly different emphasis on reasons for the war. Asked by the Berlin Goethe Association a few months after his return for a short article outlining his feelings, he made no mention of the German guilt he had stressed so strongly to Rolland, but bluntly laid the cause of war on the aggressive nature of Homo sapiens.

This was a good deal more cautious than the opinions he had voiced to Rolland. By the end of 1915 prospects of a quick victory had faded and with them went the comparative freedom of the first year of war. Not even Einstein would have survived expression of open hope "for a victory by the Allies which will ruin the power of Prussia and the dynasty." Indeed, he seems to have compartmentalized his feelings with surprising ease. He remained on the friendliest of terms with Haber, the poison gas expert, and with his help was able to squeeze from the German General Staff a travel permit for a colleague. He was also, according to Max Born, one of the Berlin intellectuals who in midwar met high officials in the German Foreign Office to dissuade them from starting

unrestricted U-boat warfare "as it would be bound to bring the United States into the war and thus lead to final defeat."

It can be claimed, however, that Einstein was supporting such humanitarian pleas on moral grounds under the cover of expediency, for as hopes of a quick victory faded, any suggestion of limiting operations had a defeatist ring that could no longer be tolerated. The Bund Neues Vaterland was outlawed, and while hints of a negotiated peace might be made privately, they produced in public the same vilification that comparable ideas produced in Britain. There is little evidence that this tightening of the official attitude had much effect on Einstein's privately expressed views, and his correspondence with Lorentz, largely concerned with scientific work, continued to be sprinkled with the strongest pacifist sentiments that could have been noted by the censor. Luckily he was not involved in work where indiscretion would have been more dangerous to friends than to foes.

He retained the privileged position of a critic whose presence would be tolerated although his views were disliked. This position was the result partly of the renown that the General Theory had brought him in 1915, partly of his legal status as a Swiss. It nevertheless rankled with more than one Allied scientist when the war was over.

As a Swiss Einstein retained advantages in Berlin, not the least being freedom to visit neutral countries with less bureaucratic interference than most Germans, and he made use of this at Easter, 1916, to visit his wife in Zurich. The meeting was disastrous. Einstein, according to his correspondence with Besso, made an irrevocable decision not to see Mileva again. Hans stopped writing to his father when Einstein returned to Berlin. And when, Mileva being ill, the question of another visit to Zurich was raised in the summer, Einstein poured out his troubles in a long letter to Besso who henceforth was to act as honest broker between the couple. If he came to Zurich, he said, Mileva would demand to see him, and he would have to refuse, partly because of his earlier decision, partly to avoid emotional scenes. If his wife had to go to the hospital that would be different. Then he would visit her—and see the children on neutral ground. Otherwise, "No."

With the worsening war situation, even travel abroad became complicated. In the autumn of 1916 Einstein visited Holland, but was able to do so only after Lorentz had sent him an official invitation and he had obtained his original Swiss naturalization papers from Zurich.

The following year he experienced a serious breakdown, partly nervous collapse, partly long-standing stomach upset, the latter no doubt exacerbated by the trials of wartime Berlin and a bachelor existence. The illness was hardly surprising. For years he

Left: Gas warfare was introduced by the Germans during the First World War in the spring of 1915. Einstein's former colleagues Walther Nernst and Fritz Haber worked on its development. *[Culver Pictures]*

Right: Dawn at Passchaendale, also known as the Third Battle of Ypres, which lasted from the end of July until November 10, 1917. *[The Mansell Collection]*

had been deeply immersed in scientific work which has been described as the greatest intellectual effort of any single human brain. His views on the war were different from those of the men and women around him. In addition, he was living a makeshift existence that gave full rein to the inclination summed up by his doctor-friend Janos Plesch. "As his mind knows no limits, so his body follows no set rules," he wrote; "he sleeps until he is wakened; he stays awake until he is told to go to bed; he will go hungry until he is given something to eat; and then he eats until he is stopped."

During the first two months he lost over fifty pounds. Although he wrote to Lorentz in April that he was getting better, it was summer before he was out and about, and August before he was able to recuperate in Switzerland.

While he was ill, Hedwig Born, the young wife of Max Born, became a frequent visitor. "His utter independence and objectivity, and his serene outlook, enabled me to ride up over the awful darkness of those days and to look far beyond the desperate day-to-day conditions," she has said of the years in the German capital.

Independence from the hopes and fears of ordinary men included independence from the fear of death itself. "No," Einstein told Frau Born when on one visit during his illness she asked whether he was afraid of dying. "I feel myself so much a part of all life that I am not in the least concerned with the beginning or the end of the concrete existence of any particular person in this unending stream." This, she says, was typical of the unity which he looked for in all nature:

> It is probably not surprising that it was he who helped me to be an objective scientist, and to avoid feeling that the whole thing was impersonal. Modern physics left me standing. Here was only objective truth, which unhappily meant nothing to me, and perhaps the possibility that in the future everything would be expressed scientifically. So I asked Einstein one day "Do you believe that absolutely everything can be expressed scientifically?" "Yes," he replied, "it would be possible, but it would make no sense. It would be description without meaning—as if you described a Beethoven symphony as a variation of wave pressure." This was a great solace to me.

There was certainly a flaw in this attempt to regard all human life—even one's own—as merely a bubble on the cosmic stream. To Freundlich, Einstein once confided that there was no one in the world whose death would worry him. "I thought how terrible it was for a man with a wife and two children to believe and say such a thing," says Frau Freundlich. "Then, a year or so afterwards, Einstein's mother died in Berlin, where she had come to spend the last few months of her life with him. In a way I was glad. For Einstein wept, like other men, and I knew that he could really care for someone." And many years later his friend Gustav Bucky wrote: "He believed that nothing really touched him inwardly. But this man who never wanted to show emotion wrote just one sentence to me after my bad illness: 'From now on, I will be thankful every hour of my life that we are left together.'" Always, despite himself, humanity kept breaking in.

Einstein's illness of 1917 had a more important result than stomach trouble. For

Einstein and his wife, Elsa. *[The Bett-mann Archive]*

it at last brought him under the wing, first mothering and eventually matrimonial, of his cousin Elsa. At what point they renewed their youthful acquaintance is vague, but it was almost inevitable that he should meet, if only on a family basis, the cousin he remembered from his childhood days in Munich.

Elsa's mother was the sister of Pauline Koch, which meant that both Elsa and Albert could claim Cäsar Koch as an uncle, while both were also related farther back along the family tree. By 1917 Elsa had become Elsa Lowenthal, a pleasant widow with two daughters, Ilse aged twenty and Margot aged eighteen. In appearance she was comfortable rather than beautiful, but she lacked the curiosity that had at times made Mileva so mentally importunate. "I'm glad my wife doesn't know any science," Einstein later said to a colleague. "My first wife did."

Nearsighted and slightly provincial, Elsa was an easy butt for the enemies that her protectiveness readily made during her husband's triumphal progress through the world. But she was careful, conscientious, undemanding, and suitably awed by fame—in

The home at Haberlandstrasse 5 (marked X), where Einstein and his second wife lived for many years after the First World War. [Hebrew University of Jerusalem]

many ways the ideal wife for the absentminded genius of which Einstein was the epitome. Her character was unconsciously described by Einstein himself when he made a remark to his friend Philipp Frank "based," as Frank says, "on many years of experience." Said Einstein: "When women are in their homes, they are attached to their furniture. They run round it all day long and are always fussing over it. But when I am with a woman on a journey, I am the only piece of furniture that she has available, and she cannot refrain from moving round me all day long and improving something about me."

It is not true that from 1917 onward Einstein allowed Elsa to make up his mind for him on everything except science, pacifism, and politics. Even outside the three interests of his life, only Einstein made up Einstein's mind. But when he had done so, he allowed Elsa to organize details, to implement decisions, to handle the minutiae, and thus allow him to get on with his work.

During his illness Elsa, not surprisingly, looked after him. In the later stages of his convalescence he was taken to her Haberlandstrasse apartment. Given the context, it was a not unexpected outcome that in 1919, after finally obtaining a divorce from Mileva, he should marry cousin Elsa.

As he slowly recovered in 1917 he decided to finish his recuperation in Switzerland; the Swiss citizen thus exchanged the growing austerity of wartime Berlin for the comparative luxury of a neutral country. He had intended to take the cure at Tarasp in the Lower Engadine but, as he explained to Besso, lack of funds forced him to content himself with a rest at his mother's in Lucerne.

In Switzerland he had hoped to meet Rolland again. When this proved impossible, he wrote instead. His letter was long and pessimistic, although he claimed that he was not more depressed than he had been two years previously. He criticized Germany's religion of power, stressed that it would be dangerous to come to terms with her and emphasized that she must be made to realize that neither force nor treachery would work any longer.

The vigor of the anti-German sentiments that Einstein expressed struck Rolland forcefully. In his diary he pointed out that the policy of crushing Germany had no greater supporters than some prominent Germans. "I note once again," he added, "the extreme injustice, through an excess of justice, to which the most liberal spirits come, vis-à-vis their own country."

Bearing all this in mind, it is at first strange that Einstein should have returned to Berlin as quickly as he did. Zangger wrote to Rolland urging him to induce the visitor to remain in Switzerland. Other friends did the same. But after spending a week with his two sons in Arosa, he returned from the country that he loved to the country he detested.

The unfortunate meeting with Mileva at Easter, 1916, had not been repeated. He had no intention that it should be, and any hint that he was making more than a brief visit to Switzerland might well have brought his wife to his door. He had continued to support

Einstein and his wife, Elsa, in their
Berlin home at Haberlandstrasse 5,
about 1927. [Ruth Jacobi]

her; but now more than ever he had no wish to be brought personally into the negotiations, so far mainly conducted through Besso, the ever-faithful go-between. In a letter written to him on May 15, he confided that he was increasingly hard pressed financially. Of his total income of about thirteen thousand marks a year, roughly seven thousand was being sent regularly for the upkeep of his wife and children. Another six hundred marks a year went to his mother in Lucerne, and some of his customary additional fees were now disappearing. He had perilously little left to maintain the status of a professor, let alone anything for luxuries or reserves. He had, after all, been obliged to abandon fashionable Tarasp for homely Lucerne.

Soon, however, there was hope of a change. Shortly after his return to Berlin, he told Besso that his address would in future be Haberlandstrasse 5, adding that his move seemed to have taken place already—a turn of phrase that suggests that Elsa was the initiator of the marriage that was to take place in eighteen months' time.

This was to have little effect on the course of Einstein's purely scientific career, which had reached its climax before 1919. It did, however, affect crucially his impact on the world, as father figure, as oracle, as the man whose support was for years a useful weapon in the hands of any group ingenious enough to win it. For without the care and protecting intervention of this kindly figure, placid and housewifely, of no intellectual pretensions but with a practiced mothering ability that made her the ideal organizer of genius, two things would almost certainly have happened: he would have cracked under the strain of unrelenting publicity and public demands, and withdrawn from pacifism, Zionism, and socialism, into the shell where he carried on his scientific work. He would also have made a fool of himself more often than he did, have issued more statements that he had to retract, signed more documents without reading them properly, and been used more frequently by men of ill-will.

It was part of his genius that he could isolate himself from his surroundings, and this was never more necessary than in the apartment at Haberlandstrasse 5. On the dark

green wallpaper of the main sitting room there hung the expected portrait of Frederick the Great, looking down without a smile on the heavy immobility of the Biedermeier furniture; on the corner cabinets stocked with porcelain; on the huge round central table with the starched white tablecloth edged with crochet; on Schiller and Goethe, the white eyes of their white busts firmly fixed on each other from opposite sides of the room. Beyond lay the library, its walls soon to be ornamented by a large framed picture of Michael Faraday. Into this epitome of all things that were proper came Albert Einstein, unchangeable by the pleas of Elsa, happy to be shepherded by her through the mundane necessities of everyday life, grateful for the protecting shield that she was to interpose between himself and the overcurious world, yet quite determined to go his own way in the things that mattered.

Before the situation could be regularized, however, Mileva had to agree to a divorce. This she did within less than a year. Negotiations were under way by the early summer of 1918 when Einstein sent through Besso details of how he would be prepared to support her and the children. During these negotiations the question of the Nobel Prize was raised. It is not quite certain who first suggested that the interest from the Prize, then some thirty thousand Swedish kroner, would be sufficient to keep Einstein's family in at least modest circumstances, but it appears to have been Mileva. If so, it is a striking tribute to her faith in him.

Early in July Einstein received the first divorce papers. Then he had to give evidence before a tribunal in Berlin. And after that an ever-growing dossier had to be returned to Zurich. All this he took lightly enough, acknowledging receipt of the first papers with the exclamation "Till Eulenspiegel!" and later noting to Besso that the divorce was entertaining all those in Berlin who were in the know.

As the legal moves continued and as Einstein heard from friends in Holland that the British were planning to carry out a test of his theory during the eclipse of 1919, the war situation began to change dramatically. After the failure of the great German offensive in the spring, the influence of the United States began decisively to affect the balance of forces. On the Western Front preparations continued for the Allied offensive, which in August 1918 ruptured the German front for the first time in four years. On November 9 the Kaiser abdicated. Karl Ebert, the staunch imperturbable saddler's son, was handed the chancellorship, and at 2 P.M. the Republic was proclaimed from the steps of the Reichstag.

The Reichstag, Berlin, which was burned to the ground on February 27, 1933, shortly after Hitler's rise to power. The Nazis denounced the act, claiming it was the result of a Communist plot. [The Mansell Collection]

For Einstein, as for other Germans of like mind, the Republic and the Armistice were twin trumpets heralding the millennium. Now, they fondly imagined, they would have help in the task of leading their misguided countrymen back into the peaceful ways from which they had been diverted half a century earlier. Perhaps so. But even Einstein, optimistic as ever, might have thought twice as he considered his old friend Planck. A few weeks before the fall of the Kaiser, the Bund Neues Vaterland, which had continued an underground existence since being banned by the authorities in February, 1916, came into the open once more. Einstein sent Planck a copy of the opening declaration and asked for his support. But this would mean a demand for the Kaiser's abdication; Planck replied that his oath to the Emperor made support impossible. No such problems worried Albert Einstein, who threw himself wholeheartedly on the side of the Republic.

With the formation of workers' and soldiers' councils, which followed the disintegration of law and order on November 11, there had come a similar move in the University of Berlin. Here, one of the first actions of the student council was to depose and lock up the rector and other members of the staff. The remaining members of the administration knew Einstein's left-wing views and turned to him for help. Would he intervene on their behalf with the students?

Einstein telephoned Max Born and another colleague, the psychologist Max Wertheimer. The three men made their way to the Reichstag where the student council was meeting.

As soon as Einstein was recognized all doors were opened, and the trio was escorted to a room where the student council was in session. The chairman, before dealing with their business, asked Einstein what he thought of the new regulations for students. He did not think very much of them, a reaction that caused the council to decide that the problem presented by the three professors was not one for them but, instead, for the new government.

In the Reich Chancellor's Palace, amid a contradiction of imperial footmen and delegations from the new workers' and soldiers' councils, the three men were received by Chancellor Ebert. The fate of the Reich itself still hung in the balance, and he could spare them little time. But he wrote a few words for them to the appropriate minister.

At the time, November, 1918, Einstein was, within the comparatively small world of physicists, a creature of extraordinary power and imagination. Outside it, he was still unknown. This situation was to be dramatically altered within a year.

8.

THE SENSORIUM OF GOD

The autumn of 1918, which brought Germany bitter and apparently irretrievable defeat, also brought the Republic. To Einstein this was a gleam of hope in the darkness, the only one that held out a promise for the future as the Empire dissolved between the hammer of the Allied armies on the west and the anvil of emergent communism to the east. Just as he now believed there was political hope for a country he had so long considered beyond hope, so was there at last the prospect of proof or disproof for the General Theory of Relativity over whose difficulties he had triumphed while the war went on.

In Berlin, four years earlier, he had settled down to work in earnest. First, he had expectantly looked forward to the results that Freundlich and his party would bring back from the Crimea. Yet even had their efforts not been snuffed out by the war, they would have provided experimental confirmation only for a theory that was incomplete. Although Einstein was now convinced of the revolutionary idea that gravity was not force but a property of space itself, he had not yet been able to construct the mathematical framework within which it could be described. He continued to wrestle with this task as his colleagues went to war, Haber struggled with his poison-gas production, and his English friend Lindemann reported at the Royal Aircraft Factory, Farnborough, as a temporary technical assistant at £3 a week.

After the failure of the Russian expedition to the Crimea and Freundlich's return to Berlin, Einstein pressed on with the theoretical work for every available minute, letting slide everything that would slide. During this period Freundlich, entering Einstein's study, saw hanging from the ceiling a large meat-hook end bearing a thick sheaf of letters. These, Einstein explained, he had no time to answer. Freundlich, asking what he did when the hook was filled up, was answered by two words: "Burn them."

The agony continued into the summer of 1915 and into the autumn. In November, 1915, he wrote to Sommerfeld saying that he had lived through the most exacting and the most fruitful period of his life. He had at last realized what was wrong with his field equations for gravitation. He had tackled the problem from a different point and had finally succeeded. Sommerfeld was not impressed at first—causing Einstein to send him a postcard saying that he would be convinced once he had studied the General Theory, which was about to be published.

Sommerfeld did not have long to wait. There soon appeared Volume 49 of the *Annalen der Physik*. It contained, on pages 769 to 822, "Die Grundlage der allgemeinen Relativitätstheorie" ("The Foundation of the General Theory of Relativity"). "The theory appeared to me then, and it still does," said Born, "the greatest feat of human thinking about Nature, the most amazing combination of philosophical penetration, physical intuition and mathematical skill. But its connections with experience were slender. It appealed to me like a great work of art, to be enjoyed and admired from a distance."

The General Theory, which brought the first realization "that space is not merely a background for events, but possesses an autonomous structure," was to be the starting point for an even larger collection of papers and developments than the Special Theory. Einstein wrote some of them, and for another forty years he was, necessarily, deeply involved in the arguments about the universe that the General Theory unleashed. In some ways he saw this as the cornerstone of the arch he had started to build more than a decade previously and he himself as now free for other things. From now onward, according to Wolfgang Pauli—aged only sixteen in 1916 but within five years to be writing one of the classic expositions of the General Theory—Einstein was often to comment: "For the rest of my life I want to reflect on what light is."

Whereas Special Relativity had brought under one set of laws the electromagnetic world of Maxwell and Newtonian mechanics as far as they applied to bodies in uniform relative motion, the General Theory did the same thing for bodies with the accelerated relative motion epitomized in the acceleration of gravity. But first it had been necessary for Einstein to develop the true nature of gravity from his Principle of Equivalence. Newton had seen it as a force operating instantaneously over limitless distances; Einstein's conception was very different, even though in practice most of his results approximated very closely to those of Newton. Basically, he proposed that gravity was a function of matter itself and that its effects were transmitted between contiguous portions of space-time, rather as the effects of a shunting engine are transmitted down a line of stationary railway cars. Where matter exists, so does energy; the greater the mass of matter involved, the greater the effect of the energy that can be transmitted.

In addition, gravity, as he had postulated as far back as 1911, affected light—the arbiter of straight lines and the wave-emanation whose passage over a unit of distance gives a unit of time—exactly as it affected material particles. Thus the universe that Newton had seen, and for which he had constructed his apparently impeccable mechanical laws, was not the real universe but only what he had seen through the misleading spectacles produced by gravity. The law that appeared to have worked out so well had been drawn up for a universe that did not exist, as though a tailor had made a suit for a man he had seen only in a distorting mirror. This was the logical follow-on from the Principle of Equivalence and from Einstein's assumption that gravity was basically a field-characteristic of matter. That Newton's suit fitted the real man tolerably well was hardly the point.

Einstein's paper gave not only a corrected picture of the universe but also a

German aircraft handed over to the Allies and then destroyed following the end of the First World War in November, 1918. [Culver Pictures]

fresh set of mathematical laws by which its details could be described. These were of two kinds. There were the structural laws, which dealt with the relationships between the mass of a gravitating body and the gravitational field, with the very existence of the mass automatically created; and there were the laws of motion, which could be used to describe the paths taken by moving bodies in gravitational fields. These laws utilized Riemannian geometry, the need for which had been the direct result of the assumption that light would be deflected by a gravitational field and that the shortest distance between two points in such a field would not, when viewed from outside it, be coincident with a straight line. For there were certain consequences of assuming that what appeared as a straight line-of-sight to anywhere in the universe, as ramrod true as any sergeant major could wish, was, in fact, as curved as the route followed by a ship steaming around the world on the shortest path from A to B—and that the exact curvature would depend on the gravitational field, and, therefore, the mass of matter, which was involved.

One consequence is evident from the simple consideration of a globe. It is that Euclidean geometry, in which the angles in a triangle always add up to two right angles, is not relevant for a triangle formed by the equator and two lines of longitude. Those running from the equator to the North Pole through Greenwich and New Orleans, for instance, enclose with the equator not two but three right angles—even though equator and lines of longitude follow the shortest route from point to point. As Einstein allegedly explained to his younger son, Eduard: "When the blind beetle crawls over the surface of a globe, he doesn't notice that the track he has covered is curved. I was lucky enough to have spotted it."

Einstein had seen that his assumption of a curvature of light in a gravitational field meant that Euclidean geometry, satisfactory enough when coping with the small distances of everyday life, had to be replaced by something more sophisticated when dealing with the universe. The geographer and the surveyor have a comparable problem, selecting one projection that is satisfactory for the small areas of topographical maps and another projection for the vastly larger areas of regional or national maps. Einstein searched about for some time before he found something to help him. In Prague, on George Pick's advice, he had studied the work of Ricci and Levi-Civita. Back in Zurich he had worked with Marcel Grossmann to make the preliminary sketch of the General Theory that appeared in 1913. But it was only when he turned back to Riemann, the young German who had died almost half a century earlier, that he found what he wanted.

Riemann was the mathematician whose masterpiece, *Über die Hypothesen, welche der Geometrie zugrunde liegen* (*On the Hypotheses Which Determine the*

Foundations of Geometry) Einstein had studied a decade earlier with his companions of the Olympia Academy in Berne. Handicapped by a shy character, dogged by bad luck and the bad health that killed him at forty, Riemann had been a brilliant product of nineteenth century Göttingen, who at the age of twenty-four had speculated that "a complete, well-rounded mathematical theory can be established which progresses from the elementary laws for individual points to the processes given to us in the plenum ('continuously filled space') of reality, without distinction between gravitation, electricity, magnetism, or thermostatics." This apparent rejection of "action at a distance" in favor of the field theory was dramatically in advance of its time. Yet it was merely a prelude to the construction of a non-Euclidean geometry that, in the words of the late E. T. Bell, "taught mathematicians to disbelieve in *any* geometry, or in *any* space, as a *necessary* mode of human perception. It was the last nail in the coffin of absolute space, and the first in that of the 'absolutes' of nineteenth-century physics."

In Riemann's geometry, parallel lines do not exist, the angles of a triangle do not add up to 180°, and perpendiculars to the same line converge, a conception that is easier to understand in an age of worldwide air travel than when the University of Göttingen was the intellectual pride of the Kingdom of Hanover. In Riemann's world the shortest lines joining any two points are not straight lines but geodesics and, a corollary self-evident even to nonmathematicians, the length of the shortest distance between any two points on such a curved surface is determined by a formula different from that determining the length of a line on a plane surface.

Einstein used Riemannian geometry to create equations by which the movements of the stars in their courses and the structure of the universe itself could be described. But this was followed by the introduction of a phrase well enough understood by mathematicians but almost as confusing to the layman as the definition of time as the fourth "dimension." This was "curvature of space," part of the terminology that Sir Edmund Whittaker later described as "so well established that we can never hope to change it, regrettable though it is, and which has been responsible for a great deal of popular misconception." Mathematicians apply the word "curved" to any space whose geometry was not Euclidean:

> It is an unfortunate custom [Whittaker went on] because curvature, in the sense of bending, is a meaningless term except when the space is immersed in another space, whereas the property of being non-Euclidean is an intrinsic property which has nothing to do with immersion. However, nothing can be done but to utter a warning that what mathematicians understand by the term "curvature" is not what the word connotes in ordinary speech; what the mathematician means is simply that the relations

between the mutual distances of the points are different from the relations which obtain in Euclidean geometry. Curvature (in the mathematical sense) has nothing to do with the *shape* of the space—whether it is bent or not—but is defined solely by the metric, that is to say, the way in which "distance" is defined. It is not the space that is curved, but the geometry of the space.

"Space-curvature," the renewed claim that light did not go straight, the idea that the universe could only be viewed from the earth through the distorting spectacles of gravity, would all have combined to create an immediate sensation had Europe been at peace. As it was, only a narrow path led through the minefields of the war from Einstein in the Berlin of 1916 to the shattering first proof of the theory in 1919.

Einstein himself was well aware that proof would not be easy. Two and a half centuries earlier Newton, pressed on the question of whether gravity was or was not exercised instantaneously, admitted that he could see no way of experimentally solving the problem. To do so would require, he commented, "the sensorium of God." Einstein, if challenged, would no doubt have been torn between modesty and a full awareness of what he was accomplishing. Despite the fundamentally different concepts of gravity put forward by Newton and himself, the differences in experimental results would in most cases be slight and thus difficult to detect.

One prospect seemed to be offered by the planet Mercury. In the two hundred years that had followed Newton, the discoveries of science had revealed a succession of facts that had each fallen into place in his grand design. Not only the passage of the moon around the earth and the curving flight of the cricket ball, but the flow of the tides and the fiery trails of the comets were shown to follow the orderly paths that his universal scheme demanded. One feature of this had been the repetition of the planetary circuits around the sun; Venus and Mercury, Mars, Jupiter, and Uranus, together with their orbiting colleagues, followed their same elliptical paths with only insignificant change, tracing out through the heavens circuits that appeared to remain the same throughout the centuries.

The first man to suspect that this might not be so was Dominique Arago, the fiery French republican from whom not even Louis Napoleon could extract an oath of allegiance. In the early 1840s Arago proposed to Urbain Jean Joseph Leverrier, a young French astronomer, that he should carefully analyze the motions of Mercury. The result was surprising. For Leverrier's figures showed clearly that the perihelion of Mercury—the point on its elliptical path that is nearest to the sun—advanced by a specific amount each year. The rate was extremely small, but even after the effects of the other planets had been taken into account, the advance remained about forty-three seconds of arc each century. Thus the path of Mercury around the sun was not a static closed ellipse, but a nearly closed circuit, slowly gyrating and coming back to its original position once every three million years.

This lack of coincidence with the path planned out for it by Newton in his grand

Opposite: Portrait of Einstein.
[Private Collection]

143

scheme profoundly distressed astronomers, and some desperate expedients were put forward in an effort to correlate fact and theory. Leverrier himself decided that the anomaly would be accounted for if there existed an as yet unseen planet only one thousand miles across and circling the sun at a distance of nineteen million miles. In anticipation of discovery, this was named Vulcan; but despite careful searching of the skies at each subsequent eclipse, no such planet could be located. From Asaph Hall, the discoverer of the satellites of Mars, there came an even more ingenious proposal: that in the Newtonian formula concerned the exponent two might be altered to 2,0000001612. The suggested trick had something in common with that of the "scientist," armed with chisel and tape measure, who was found by Flinders Petrie to be "adjusting" a side of the Great Pyramid "which did not quite conform to the length required by his theory." As Einstein was to comment, the discrepancy in Mercury's orbit "could be explained by means of classical mechanics only on the assumption of hypotheses which have little probability, and which were devised solely for this purpose." So much was true even after fullest consideration had been given to the various influences that the planets as a group exercised on each individual in the group, the astronomical problem of "perturbations," as it was called.

The discrepancy had worried Einstein as far back as 1907 when he had told his colleague Conrad Habicht that he was working on a theory that he hoped would account for the changes in the perihelion movement of Mercury. Now with Riemannian geometry the perihelion of a planet moving around a central attracting body in a nearly circular orbit would advance. The amount would not be great, but Mercury's enormous speed, comparatively small size, and closeness to the intense gravitational field of the sun might yield a significant figure. Einstein applied the equations from the General Theory to the motion of Mercury. The results showed that the perihelion should advance about 0.1″ for each complete orbital revolution of the planet. Roughly 420 such revolutions were made in a century. Thus the secular advance of Mercury's perihelion each century as deduced from the General Theory was some 42″—almost exactly the figure provided by Leverrier's observations. The theory thus, as Einstein said to the daughter of Simon Newcomb, who spent much of his life in producing more accurate orbital tables for the moon and the planets, brought about a full agreement between theory and experience.

Einstein announced this result before he had completed his General Theory, reading two papers on it to the Prussian Academy of Sciences in the autumn of 1915. He was immensely excited with his success but it was not the excitement of surprise. Asked whether he had been worried about the outcome of the calculations, he replied: "Such questions did not lie in my path. The result could not be otherwise than correct. I was only concerned with putting the answer into a lucid form. I did not for one second doubt that it would agree with observation. There was no sense in getting excited about what was self-evident." However confident he may have been, he was delighted when shortly after the publication of his own Mercury paper the astronomer K. Schwarzschild published a description of how to obtain the same results in a far more elegant manner.

Opposite: Einstein and the famous Dutch astronomer Dr. Willem de Sitter (1872–1934), meeting at the Mount Wilson Observatory in the summer of 1932. De Sitter brought Einstein's General Theory to the notice of British scientists and subsequently postulated an expanding universe based on the theory. [Wide World]

145

The use of the field equations of the General Theory to supply figures that were unlikely to be coincidental, and that solved one of the most stubborn riddles of astronomy, was cited by Einstein in his paper of 1916. The figures certainly supported his theory, but they did not exactly give proof; the Mercury anomaly had been known for years; the General Theory had merely provided one satisfactory explanation and there might be others. The two remaining possibilities for a test put forward by Einstein in 1911 both concerned the behavior of light in a gravitational field, and both had one thing in common. They concerned phenomena that had never been either known or suspected; and if they could be shown to exist, they would, therefore, be in a totally different class. They would, in fact, be comparable to the prediction of a new planet in the sky just where Neptune was later discovered, or to Mendeleyev's forecast of the undiscovered elements in the periodic table. They would by implication give substantial proof that in the General Theory there was to be found a more accurate description of the universe.

The more esoteric of the two tests concerned the effect of gravity on the frequency of light. The mathematical route followed by Einstein led him to assume that an atom radiating in a strong gravitational field would vibrate more slowly than in a weak gravitational field. For if time as well as space was inevitably altered by the deflection of gravity, then the vibration of atoms, those impeccable timepieces of the universe, would also be affected. But the frequency of vibration governs the color of light radiated and an atom radiating in a strong gravitational field would emit light a little closer to the red end of the spectrum than when it was radiating a weaker gravitational field. Such displacements had already been noted by L. F. Jewell in 1897 and by other workers early in the twentieth century, but they had been explained as entirely due to "pressure effects." These did indeed exist, and their presence increased the difficulty of isolating as a separate characteristic "the Einstein shift" as it was unlikely to be observed even if the gravitational field of the sun were used as a test-bench. However, there are bodies in the universe producing immensely stronger fields than the sun, and a decade after Einstein's prediction the huge gravitational field of the "white dwarf" star near Sirius—so dense that a cubic inch of it would weigh more than half a ton on earth—was utilized. And almost half a century after Einstein's paper, Robert Oppenheimer was able to write of the Einstein shift: "The most precise and, I think, by far the most beautiful example of this is a recent experiment conducted at Harvard in which light was simply allowed to fall down from the third floor to the basement of the Physics Building. One could see how much bluer it had become; one part in 10^{14}; not very much."

No such possibilities existed in 1916, and readers of Einstein's paper turned naturally to the other proposed method of testing the theory. This was the method that Freundlich had been going to adopt in the Crimea in August 1914: the observation of light from the stars during an eclipse to discover whether it was deflected when passing through the gravitational field of the sun.

The summer of 1916 was hardly a propitious period for devoting men, money,

At the Leiden Observatory, September 26, 1923. Front row (left to right): Arthur S. Eddington and Hendrik A. Lorentz; back row (left to right): Einstein, Paul Ehrenfest, and Willem de Sitter. [AIP Niels Bohr Library]

materials, and thought to any scientific subject unless it seemed likely to help the war effort. Britain and Germany were locked in a struggle whose outcome no one could yet foresee, and American entry into the war was still nearly a year away. All effort was harnessed to the task of winning; in Germany the Kaiser Wilhelm Institutes and the University of Berlin were on national service, and elsewhere the situation was similar. Rutherford from Britain and Langevin from France were deeply engaged on anti-submarine work. Pure science, it seemed, must await the coming of peace.

In these circumstances, one of Einstein's acts was to be of crucial importance. On receiving copies of *Annalen der Physik* containing his paper on the General Theory, he sent one to Willem de Sitter, professor of astronomy in the University of Leiden and a foreign correspondent of the Royal Astronomical Society in London. De Sitter passed on his copy to the Society's secretary, Arthur Eddington, who was now drawn into a developing drama.

Eddington was in 1916 Plumian Professor of Astronomy at Cambridge, and director of the university observatory. A Quaker, with the Friends' typical mixture of bold humanity and mystic faith, he had been a Senior Wrangler, and his *Stellar Movements and the Structure of the Universe*, published in 1914, had created the new subject of stellar dynamics. As secretary of the Royal Astronomical Society, Eddington had the task of producing the Society's *Monthly Notices*, and this involved close scrutiny of Einstein's paper which arrived from Holland, a scrutiny that soon convinced him of its significance to his own cosmological investigations.

The important factor in 1916 was Eddington's superb mathematical ability, which "enabled him not only to grasp the argument, but very soon to master the absolute differential calculus of Ricci and Levi-Civita, and to use tensors as a tool in developing contributions of his own." One result was that Eddington asked De Sitter to write for the Royal Astronomical Society's *Monthly Notices* three long articles explaining the General Theory. These articles, the second produced after Einstein had held several conversations with De Sitter in Leiden, introduced Einstein's new theory to the non-German-speaking world. Their importance in what was to follow cannot be overestimated:

147

Even if Einstein has not explained the origin of inertia [concluded the second article] his theory represents an enormous progress over the physics of yesterday. Perceiving the irrelevance of the representation by co-ordinates in which our science is clothed, he has penetrated to the deeper realities which lay hidden behind it and not only has he entirely explained the exception and universal nature of gravitation by the principle of the identity of gravitation and inertia, but he has laid bare intimate connections between branches of science which up to now were considered as entirely independent from each other, and has thus made an important step towards the unity of nature. Finally his theory not only explains all that the old theory of relativity could explain (experiment of Michelson, etc.), but *without any new hypothesis or empirical constant*, it explains the anomalous motion of the perihelion of Mercury, and it predicts a number of phenomena which have not yet been observed. It has thus at once proved to be a very powerful instrument of discovery.

Even in the gloomy concentration of the war, scientists were soon speculating on how to investigate the "number of phenomena which have not yet been observed." Sir Frank Dyson, the astronomer royal, ordered a study to be made of photographs taken during the eclipse of 1905 in the hope that something might be discovered from them, but the search was unsuccessful. Lindemann and his father contributed a paper to the *Monthly Notices* on the daylight photography of stars and concluded: "It is suggested that experiments…be undertaken by some observatory possessing a suitable instrument, and enjoying a fine climate, with a view to testing Einstein's theory." The possibility had been rejected as impracticable by Hale before the 1914 eclipse, and even if a suitable observatory could have been found and persuaded to do the work, it seems unlikely that current technology could have produced useful results. There were other suggestions, but none that seemed likely to be successful.

Help was at hand, however. Another solar eclipse would take place on a day when the stellar background would be ideal. If the problem of testing the General Theory "had been put forward at some other period of history," as Eddington later pointed out, "it might have been necessary to wait some thousands of years for a total eclipse of the sun to happen on the lucky date."

That this opportunity was seized by the British was due not only to Eddington's personal enthusiasm for relativity but to his influence on Dyson. Sir Frank was to become a firm friend of Einstein, and the latter's portrait by Rothenstein for long hung in a place of honor in Flamsteed House, the astronomer royal's official home at Greenwich. Throughout his career he had shown a special interest in solar eclipses, and despite the uncertainties of war he was anxious to make full use of the opportunities provided by 1919. But it was, nevertheless, largely due to Eddington's influence that Dyson so quickly emphasized the opportunities for testing the General Theory that the eclipse would offer. De Sitter's articles, which had whetted the scientific appetite, had been published largely as a result of Eddington's initiative, and soon afterward he was commissioned by the Physical Society to prepare his own account of what the General Theory was and signified. The *Report on the Relativity Theory of Gravitation* that followed was published in 1918 and later expanded as *The Mathematical Theory of Relativity*. Long before this, however, Dyson had moved into action.

On May 29, 1919, the sun would be seen in a field of stars of quite exceptional brightness, part of the Hyades group that lies at the head of the Taurus constellation. In a note from Greenwich dated March 2, 1917, and printed in the *Monthly Notices*, Dyson drew attention to "the unique opportunities" that this would offer. "There are an unusual number of bright stars, and with weather conditions as good as those at Sfax in 1905—which were by no means perfect—no less than thirteen stars might be obtained," he wrote, adding that these "should serve for an ample verification, or the contrary," of Einstein's theory. The track of the eclipse would unfortunately cross the Atlantic, but he had been in touch with the secretary of the Royal Geographical Society, who would tell him how many observing stations might be used, and he had "brought the matter forward so that arrangements for observing at as many stations as possible may be made at the earliest possible moment."

These plans were made as the U-boat blockade was tightening on Britain and the Russian front collapsing, as American entry into the war was still problematical, and peace remained below any visible horizon. Yet they typified not so much British isolation from reality as a somewhat lofty confidence equaled a quarter of a century later when, with the Germans hammering at the gates of Stalingrad and the Eighth Army with its back to the Nile, the Allied ministers of education in exile met in London to plan what eventually became UNESCO.

During 1917, as British plans for the eclipse expeditions went ahead, Einstein published two more important papers. In one of them he returned to the radiation problem that had occupied him intermittently since 1905; in the other he used the General Theory to give a picture of the universe that was not only important in its own scientific right, but added a spectacular significance to the theory itself.

In the radiation paper, "Zur Quantentheorie der Strahlung," in which he derived Planck's original quantum law from a different starting point, he suggested that as well as spontaneous emission and absorption there could also take place the process of stimulated emission. In 1917 this seemed mainly of theoretical interest; forty years later it was utilized to provide the maser and laser of modern technology. In addition to postulating this fresh process, Einstein also stressed that the momentum transfer that took place with emission was directional. The importance of this, as far as Einstein was concerned, lay in the admission that had to be made at the same time—that the direction was "in the present state of the theory…determined only by 'chance.'" It is significant that Einstein put quotation marks around "chance." He still believed that what had to be attributed to chance in the current state of knowledge would one day be explicable on causal grounds. How strongly he continued to feel about this was shown when he wrote to Born seven years later, saying how intolerable he found the idea of an electron,

149

exposed to radiation, being able to choose, of its own free will, not only the moment at which it jumped off but also its direction. Yet it was his paper of 1917 that provided chapter and verse for just such an idea.

Meanwhile, his development of the General Theory continued. Just how great were the demands made on him is indicated in a letter to Ehrenfest in February in which he jokingly complained that his work was producing the risk of his being placed in a madhouse.

The paper that occasioned this outburst was shorter than the final outline of the General Theory but was in some ways almost as important. For while the details of the General Theory were to remain in dispute over the years, and the first rapture created by the results of the British expeditions was to be qualified by later observations, the importance of Einstein's potentially explosive paper of 1917 was to remain undisputed—even though its suppositions were to be questioned with a brusqueness that has not affected the General Theory itself. The paper was called, quite simply, "Kosmologische Betrachtungen zur allgemeinen Relativitätstheorie" ("Cosmological Considerations Arising from the General Theory of Relativity"). What it did was to utilize the equations of the General Theory to speculate on the physical extent of the universe; and, in so doing, it is generally accepted, to found the study of modern cosmology. Even for Einstein, this was playing for high stakes.

His reason for starting on this controversial game was a very practical one. The idea that the system of fixed stars should ultimately determine the existence of centrifugal force was an important part of the conceptual background to the Theory of General Relativity. This was not a new idea and had been put forward in general terms by both Berkeley and Mach. However, with his field equations Einstein had given a numerical quantity to account for this action of the surrounding stars.

He had linked the distant twinkle of the night sky with the homely gravity of everyday life, and one question quickly followed: were there enough stars in the universe to produce the centrifugal force that could be observed and recorded? The need to answer this question inexorably drew Einstein into thinking about a specific extension of the question to which he was devoting his life. He now needed to know not merely how God had made the world but also about its actual extent. Thus the relativistic cosmology that Einstein now initiated was, as Hubble later described it, a natural offshoot of the General Theory, a "superstructure including other principles." If it was subsequently found to be wanting, it did not necessarily invalidate the General Theory itself.

The comfortable idea of a finite universe with the earth at its center had been suspect from the beginning of the scientific renaissance and had finally been abandoned with the coming of Newton. For with Newton it had seemed clear that a finite material universe would tend to collapse in upon itself much as it had been suspected, before Bohr's prescribed electron orbits, that particles circling an atomic nucleus would inevitably be drawn down toward it. The new universe of Newton's day was something nobler if more impersonal, an infinitude of stars scattered through infinite Euclidean space, an idea that survived against only sporadic objections, usually overcome by special pleading. With the nineteenth century and the growing interest in astronomy, an alternative was put forward: a finite universe that existed, island-like, in the immensities of infinite and "empty" space. But all such blueprints had one thing in common; each represented a static universe whose size and contents remained unchanging in quantity throughout the endless passage of time.

As Einstein wrestled with the cosmological implications of the General Theory, the first of these alternatives—the world-centered universe of the Middle Ages—was effectively ruled out; but both the others were considered. Both were rejected. The reasons for rejecting the Newtonian universe can be simply understood, although in the light of current knowledge about the recession of the galaxies they appear rather dated. For it seemed mathematically clear that the effect of an infinite number of stars would, even at infinite distances, produce an infinitely strong force whose effect would be to give the stars a high velocity through the universe. But observation indicated that compared with the speed of light the velocities of stars were small. Thus it was essential that the stars should be finite in number.

The possibility of a finite "island-universe" in an infinitude of empty space was ruled out for slightly more complex reasons. One reason was based on a theory of the way in which particles—or stars—would distribute themselves in random movement, and which appeared to make an island-universe impossible. Another reason sprang from the fact that since the curvature of space was dependent on the distribution of matter, space would be curved in the vicinity of the island-universe but Euclidean in the empty space of infinity beyond. This, in turn, meant that bodies beyond the island-universe would move in straight lines, according to Newton's law of inertia, since inertia was itself equivalent to gravitational force, which would not be present.

Einstein was forced, therefore, to consider whether it was possible to conceive of a universe that would contain a finite number of stars distributed equally through unbounded space. His answer to the apparent contradiction lay in the idea that matter itself produced the curvature of space. For in the "Einstein world," as it soon became known, the curvature produced by matter turned space back on itself so that a ray of light, moving in a straight line in terrestrial terms, would return to its starting point after circling the universe, a universe whose three dimensions contained as finite a number of stars as the number of names on the two-dimensional surface of a globe, but whose surface was itself as unbounded as that of the same globe. These stars were, moreover, distributed equally, as though the names were spread out equally across the surface of a globe. This was an essential if the "Einstein world" was to conform to Einstein's own inner intuition that just as the laws of nature must be the same for all observers, so must the view of the universe. "There must be no favoured location in the universe, no centre, no boundary; all must see the universe alike," as Hubble put it. "And, in order to ensure this situation, the cosmologist postulates spatial isotropy and spatial homogeneity, which is his way of saying that the universe must be pretty much alike everywhere and in all directions." This universe included local irregularities of curvature, comparable to the hills and valleys on a world globe built in relief; yet it also had an overall curvature, like the overall curvature of the earth itself, which produces a terrestrial world with a radius of some four thousand miles.

With the help of the General Theory, two equations could be obtained that included only two unknowns—the curvature of space and the total mass of the particles making up the universe. It was a relatively simple matter to provide estimates from these for the mass; thus the universe of the "Cosmological Considerations" of 1917 was a universe to which a size might be given, however rough an estimate this was:

> The whole universe [Einstein said to his friend Alexander Moszkowski in Berlin] has a diameter of about 100 million light years, in round numbers. That amounts to about 700 trillion miles. It follows from the mathematical calculations which I have presented in "Cosmological Considerations arising from the General Theory of Relativity," in which the figure I have just quoted is not given. The exact figure is a minor question. What is important is to recognize that the universe may be regarded as a closed continuum as far as distance-measurements are concerned.

Einstein had achieved a plausible result. But he had done so only by a piece of mathematical juggling that was to have an interesting history: the introduction of a fresh term into the field equations of the General Theory, the "cosmological constant" representing a repulsive force that, contrary to ordinary gravitational attraction, increases with the distance between objects. The value given to this term determines the character of the universe that is produced, and from the first it was a matter of controversy. Einstein justified its use when he gave "the theoretical view of the actual universe" at the end of his 1917 paper.

The Einstein world with its "quasi-static distribution of matter" was quickly challenged by De Sitter who maintained that while the General Theory indicated a curved space, this curvature was continually decreasing. Thus the De Sitter world built on the General Theory was steadily increasing in size; space was constantly straightening itself out, becoming less curved and more Euclidean. This idea of an expanding universe had as yet no observational support, and for some time the ideas of both Einstein and De Sitter on the structure of the universe were considered as equally comparable possibilities between which it was difficult to make a choice. Only in the 1920s, as the work of Hubble and others at Mount Wilson verified the recession of the galaxies and the continual expansion of the universe, was the position drastically altered. And only in 1930 did Einstein withdraw the "cosmological constant."

Long before this, however, the terms had come under attack for totally different reasons from Professor Friedmann, a Russian astronomer who had begun to study Einstein's publications from a purely mathematical standpoint. George Gamow, who was working under Friedmann at the time, has described what happened:

Einstein in the 150–foot solar tower telescope at the Mount Wilson Observatory, Pasadena, California, in 1931. He is with staff member Dr. St. John. [© Carnegie Institution of Washington; courtesy Mt. Wilson Observatory]

Friedmann noticed that Einstein had made a mistake in his alleged proof that the universe must necessarily be stable and unchangeable in time [he says]. It is well known to students of high-school algebra that it is permissible to divide both sides of an equation by any quantity, provided that this quantity is not zero. However, in the course of his proof, Einstein had divided both sides of one of his intermediate equations by a complicated expression which, in certain circumstances, could become zero.

In the case, however, when this expression becomes equal to zero, Einstein's proof does not hold, and Friedmann realized that this opened an entire new world of time-dependent universes: expanding, collapsing and pulsating ones. Thus Einstein's original gravity equation was correct, and changing it was a mistake. Much later, when I was discussing cosmological problems with Einstein, he remarked that the introduction of the cosmological term was the biggest blunder he ever made in his life. But the "blunder," rejected by Einstein, and the cosmological constant denoted by the Greek letter λ, rears its ugly head again and again.

Despite Gamow's well-justified comments, Einstein's entry into the cosmological arena was important both for science and for Einstein:

This suggestion of a finite, but unbounded space is one of the greatest ideas about the nature of the world which ever has been conceived [as Max Born put it]. It solved the mysterious fact why the system of stars did not disperse and thin out which it would do if space were infinite; it gave a physical meaning to Mach's principle which postulated that the law of inertia should not be regarded as a property of empty space but as an effect of the total system of stars, and it opened the way to the modern concept of the expanding universe.

Furthermore, the idea was put forward at a significant moment, just as observational astronomy was preparing to give practical muscle to the theoretical flesh.

At a different level, Einstein's direct use of the General Theory to present a picture of the universe gave him an almost mystic significance for the layman. A scientist who could give a fresh, and apparently more reliable, explanation for the movements of the stars in their courses was an important enough figure. A physicist who could apparently show that light did not always run straight had at his command an almost conjuring-trick attraction. But a man who could talk in familiar terms of curved space, and with a friendly gesture from the blackboard explain how the universe was both finite and boundless, had stretched out to touch untouchable things in a way that made him part magician and part messiah.

That is, if the General Theory were right. As Einstein, Born, and Wertheimer intervened with the students in Berlin in November, 1918, as the Empire went down in defeat and De Sitter in Holland constructed his own blueprint of the universe, final plans were being made in Britain to discover whether this was so.

9.

THE FABRIC OF THE UNIVERSE

The first turning point in Einstein's life had come with the publication of his paper on the electrodynamics of moving bodies, an event whose significance, like the thunder of the guns at Valmy, was recognized at first by only a few. The second was of a totally different order—and not only because the implications of the General Theory were more important. This of itself would have ended his normal life as a Berlin professor, well enough known in his own field but still comparatively obscure outside it. But the circumstances in which the General Theory was tested brought Einstein a worldwide scientific fame that arrived almost literally overnight and swept him away from his scientific moorings into the stream of public events. Between the Armistice of November, 1918, and the end of the following year, he became the most famous scientist in the world.

This was not all. Scientific renown came just as events in Germany and elsewhere pushed him into a political activity for which he had little aptitude. He instinctively supported the left-wing movements set free by defeat and became a devoted if muddled supporter both of pacifism and of a world government that could only be maintained by force. He revealed his zealous and perhaps ingenuous belief that Germany's good name would be restored if her war crimes were publicly investigated and, if necessary, admitted. And he became emotionally committed to the cause of Zionism. These actions were enough to make his name disliked by German nationalists while he remained obscure, and detested once he became famous. As a result, his scientific fame became during 1919 inextricably entangled with political controversies. All this was further complicated at a personal level by his divorce from Mileva, his marriage to Elsa, and the death of his mother, who spent her final days with him in a Berlin threatened equally by starvation, inflation, and revolution.

Within a few months of Germany's defeat Einstein's opinion of his own countrymen had begun to change. Up until now he had tended to forget—or to try to forget—that he himself was a German and to submerge what remained of the thought in the reality of his Swiss passport. He had looked upon the majority of his compatriots with almost unqualified distaste, regarding them as the people who supported an aggressive war with only minor protest and who condoned barbarous activities that he did not shrink from calling war crimes. But as the defeat of November 1918 merged into the starvation of 1919, so the differences between the Germans he had detested and the Allies whom he had so hoped would win tended to disappear. During the war he had thought that an Allied victory would be a lesser evil than a German victory. He now believed that the difference was not as great as he had imagined. In a similar way he now began to feel that, in general, mankind's moral qualities were the same in most countries. He held these opinions for little more than a decade between the anti-Prussian hatred of his youth and the more understandable anti-German paranoia of his later years. But during this decade Einstein's native Germanism rose to the surface once again, and he was no longer so worried about being what he was.

Einstein's attempt to exculpate the German academics, much as the "stab-in-the-back" theory attempted to exculpate the German armed forces, was partly the result of his being knocked off balance during the immediate postwar months. Einstein, and others, trustingly expected that they would have Allied cooperation in rebuilding a new and democratic Germany; that they would now be helped in the task of putting their house in order. The fact that the Reichswehr could boast of a formidable army still in being, that there remained a considerable danger that the Armistice would not easily be enforced, did not dampen their hopes. But instead of the hand stretched out, in cooperation if not in friendship, they met the rigor of the Allied blockade, whose only effect, other than the starvation of civilians, was to make the task of the Republican Government even more difficult.

All this quickly prodded Einstein into the political activity for which he had little liking and less competence, and when the Bund Neues Vaterland, illegally revived in September, was formally refounded on November 10, 1918, after an open-air meeting at the foot of Bismarck's statue in front of the Reichstag, Professor Albert Einstein appeared not only as a member but among those who sat on the Working Committee. He was one of the hundred intellectuals from Europe and the United States who in December signed the Petition du Comité de la Fédération des Peuples, addressed to the heads of state about to meet in Versailles for the peace conference and prophetically asking them to "make a peace that does not conceal a future war." And in December, 1918, he hoped that he would shortly be visiting Paris to plead with the Allies for food for the German population.

Einstein's changed attitude cannot be accounted for entirely by bitterness at the Allied blockade. With the exception of pacifism—for which he had an honorable blind spot and on whose behalf he would usually sign the most specious of propaganda manifestos—he was not abnormally gullible. His enthusiasms were rarely of the ephemeral sort, which justified the claim made of Lloyd George that he was a pillow, always bearing the imprint of the last head that had rested on it. His changing and sometimes contradictory views on the Germans, and on the need for political action, often sprang from his belief that different situations demanded different attitudes. Circumstances, he felt, really did alter cases, and in fields other than science. Just as there were no absolutes in time and space, so was there nothing immutable about the attitudes that men should take up when dealing with the kaleidoscopic, irrational, and

Einstein and Hendrik A. Lorentz
(1853–1928). Photograph believed to
have been taken in Leiden shortly
after the end of the First World War.
[Museum Boerhaave, Leiden]

infinitely complicated actions of their fellow men. The point of view was logical enough. But it gave his enemies useful weapons.

Einstein did not go to Paris at the turn of the year. Instead he went to Zurich, where he had some months earlier been offered a chair to be held jointly at the University and the E.T.H. He had turned down the offer but had agreed, instead, to visit the city for a month or six weeks, twice a year, and on each occasion give a series of a dozen conferences.

The arrangement was convenient since his divorce was at last in its final stages. The thing would be settled within the first few weeks of 1919, and it would be useful, if not essential, for him to be in Switzerland.

He left Berlin during the last week of January, 1919, arrived in Zurich on the 27th, and stayed at the Sternwarte boarding house in Hochstrasse. The General Theory of Relativity had in academic circles become as great a subject of discussion as the Special Theory, but it was still a subject for specialists alone, and its author was known in Zurich as a former professor rather than as a man about to shake the world. This is illustrated by an incident recalled by Hermann Weyl. Due to the coal shortage that was an aftermath of the European war, the authorities had to "ration" entry to the lectures, which could only be attended by those who bought an invitation card for a few francs. On this occasion Einstein appeared with Professor Weyl and the latter's wife. But Frau Weyl had forgotten her invitation card, and a steward stopped her. Einstein became as angry as Einstein ever could become and said that if Frau Weyl was not allowed in, then there would be no lecture. The steward gave way, under protest. But shortly afterward, Einstein received a letter from the rector in which he was politely but firmly asked not to interfere with the authorities' regulations.

The divorce was settled in Zurich on February 14, 1919. Simultaneously, he awarded to Mileva any money that might come from a Nobel Prize. When it came, three years later, the cash was passed on from Sweden, via Berlin, to Zurich. Some was lost in movement through the foreign exchanges and more by bad management. With what was left Mileva bought a pleasant house on the Zurichberg. The following year she formally obtained permission to retain the name of Einstein; and, as Mileva Einstein, she lived for another quarter of a century, overshadowed by illness and the worry of a schizophrenic younger son.

Einstein did not lose touch with her. Once the final break had been agreed upon, mutual animosities loosened and dislike dissolved, if not into affection at least into mutual understanding. Even before the divorce had gone through, Mileva was advising him on his projected marriage to Elsa; what her advice was can be inferred from his reply—that if he ever wished to leave his second wife, no power on earth would stop him.

As soon as his lecture series in Zurich was completed in the spring of 1919, Einstein returned to Berlin. And here, on June 2, he married Elsa in the registry office at Berlin-Wilmersdorf, traveling back to Zurich shortly afterward, apparently to discuss the

Food scarcity in Berlin, 1920. *[Culver Pictures]*

future of his sons with Mileva. He remained in Zurich until June 25 when he appeared again in Berlin, leaving for Zurich once more on the 28th and remaining in Switzerland for another three months until, on September 21 he returned to Berlin again.

While thus settling his personal affairs, Einstein was also being swept up by the rising tide of Zionism. Here, it is only necessary to note that during his Berlin visits of the spring and summer of 1919, he was approached by the Zionists and won over to their cause. They were gratified. But as they saw it, their "catch" was merely that of a prominent Jewish scientist. Before the year was out, their minnow was to grow into a leviathan.

Espousal of the Zionist cause greatly affected Einstein's position in Germany during the next decade and increased his nonscientific notoriety. This was augmented by the fervor with which he now began to discuss German war crimes. He had first raised the subject with Lorentz in 1915, and he returned to it now in the hope that investigation would help to create an understanding among the Germans of how non-Germans felt.

It is doubtful whether the crimes that most countries commit in the heat of war can satisfactorily be examined afterward either by their own nationals or by the victors—let alone on the instigation of anyone who had hated his own country from his youth. Even among those who believe that the Nuremburg trials were not only necessary but just, many would have preferred to see the work carried out with the visible impartiality of neutrals. In this light, Einstein's revival of the subject was well-intentioned but unfortunate. It was doubly so since he was still apparently a renegade German who preferred to travel on a Swiss passport and whose ignorance of international machinery was equaled by his lack of any personal contact with the machinery of war.

This much was clear to Lorentz, to whom Einstein wrote on April 26, 1919, saying that with five other private citizens he had formed a commission to examine the charges that were considered as proven. Would Lorentz join the commission as one of the neutrals who would help to get documentary evidence?

Lorentz' reply was a cautious masterpiece of tact. He was an internationalist. He was visibly a man of goodwill. More than most he understood Einstein, and a few months earlier he had written to Ernest Solvay, when future congresses were being discussed, noting that "a man such as Einstein, that great physicist, is in no way 'German' in the way that one often uses the word nowadays; his opinion of events in recent years is no different from yours and mine." But Lorentz had also a far clearer idea of the possible, and of the likely, reactions of fallible men. While willing to help Einstein through second parties, he himself deftly sidestepped the invitation to serve on the proposed commission. "You must not deceive yourself that your task will be an easy one," he replied. "The

The second Solvay Congress was held in Brussels in October, 1913. Seated (left to right): Walther H. Nernst, Ernest Rutherford, Wilhelm Wien, J. J. Thomson, Emil Warburg, Hendrik A. Lorentz, Léon M. Brillouin, Barlow, Heike Kamerlingh Onnes, R. W. Wood, M. Gouy, and Pierre Weiss; standing (left to right): Franz Hasenöhrl, E. Verschaffelt, James Jeans, William L. Bragg, Max von Laue, Heinrich Rubens, Madame Curie, Goldschmidt, Arnold Sommerfeld, E. Herzen, Einstein, Frederick A. Lindemann, Maurice de Broglie, W. J. Pope, Gruneisen, M. H. C. Knudsen, Hostelet, and Paul Langevin. [AIP Niels Bohr Library]

main difficulty, of course, is that this first step has only just been taken; it would have been more successful if it had been taken when Germany was still winning." Moreover, he pointed out, it was extremely urgent that the Germans officially support the move. "You must be absolutely certain," he went on, "that the Government will allow you full discussion and publication and not put obstacles in your way. It seems to me that you must obtain this assurance before you make any contact with the Belgians or the French because if they discover, after they have heard of your intentions, that you are not completely free to speak out, then you will have lost more than you have won." Lorentz, however, was about to visit Paris and Brussels. He would make what inquiries he could, arranging with a colleague in Holland to pass on news from Einstein while he, Lorentz, was traveling. The results were hardly satisfactory. Lorentz, willing to help, was obliged to inform Einstein of the detestation felt for Germans "good" and "bad" alike, inside the countries that had been occupied.

This detestation was underlined shortly afterward when he discussed prospects for the next Solvay Congress. "It is clear that at the moment Germans will not be invited (there is difficulty in their coming to Brussels)," he said, "even though there is no mention of their formal exclusion; the door will be held open to you, so that in future it will be possible for everybody to work together again. Unfortunately, however, this will have to wait for many years." There was, in fact, some doubt whether the door would be held open even for Einstein. M. Tassel, the Congress secretary, had to deal particularly with Professor Brillouin, who had attended the 1911 Congress and who on June 1, 1919, wrote from the Collège de France about "the pro-German neutrals, whatever their scientific value," as well as about the problem of Germans. "I am thinking, for example," he went on, "of Debye, the Dutchman of great merit, who spent all the war as a professor in Göttingen. Naturally, also of Einstein who, whatever his genius, however great his anti-militarist sentiments, nevertheless spent the whole war in Berlin and is in the same position. It is only afterwards that they have made the necessary political effort to throw light on their German colleagues and dispute the abominable and lying Manifesto of the 93."

Einstein's relations with the Congress were to complement his weathercock attitude to his own countrymen. He had attended the Second Congress in 1913, although he read no paper there and, as forecast by Lorentz, he was invited in the summer of 1920 to the Third Congress, to be held the following April. Germans as such were still not to be invited. But as the Secretary wrote, "an exception [had] been made for Einstein, of ill-defined nationality, Swiss I believe, who was roundly abused in Berlin during the war because of his pacifist sentiments which have never varied for a moment." Rutherford put it slightly differently: "The only German invited is Einstein who is considered for this purpose to be international," he wrote. Einstein accepted with great pleasure and later in the year Lorentz informed Rutherford that he would be speaking at the April, 1921, Congress on "L'Électron et la Magnétisme; effets gyroscopiques." Only in February, two months before the Congress was to be held, was he told that Einstein would not be present. The reason was the request for him to speak for the Zionists in the United States in March and April. Nevertheless, Einstein wished the Congress every success.

Two years later, when the Fourth Congress was being planned for 1924, the situation was different. Once again Einstein was to be invited. But on August 16 he wrote to Lorentz from Lautrach in southern Germany. He was staying with Sommerfeld, who said that it would not be right for Einstein to take part in the Solvay Congress if his German colleagues were excluded. And Einstein himself felt that politics should not have come into the matter at all and that if he went to Brussels, he would be condoning a situation that he believed was wrong.

Only in 1926, after Germany had joined the League of Nations and the international relations of science were returning to normal, did the position alter. "Now," Lorentz noted on the telegram that told him of the new situation, "I am able to write to Einstein." But in 1926 there was still one more formality to be observed—and in view of Einstein's subsequent links with the Royal Palace in Brussels it has some significance. It was thought proper that the approval of King Albert of the Belgians should be sought, and on April 2, 1926, Lorentz was given an audience at which His Majesty specifically approved the nomination of Einstein to the scientific committee of the coming Congress and the proposal to invite Planck and other ex-enemy scientists. "His Majesty," Lorentz subsequently reported, "expressed the opinion that, seven years after the war, the feelings which they aroused should be gradually damped down, that a better understanding between peoples was absolutely necessary for the future, and that science could help to bring this about. He also felt it necessary to stress that in view of all that the Germans had done for physics, it would be very difficult to pass them over." This sweet reasonableness was just as well. By 1926 physics was in the ferment of the new quantum mechanics, and the 1927 Congress would have been meaningless without the presence of Heisenberg, Born, Planck, and Einstein.

Eight years earlier, as in the summer of 1919 Einstein tried to conscript Lorentz into an investigation of German war crimes, things were not like that. Just what degree of help Lorentz finally gave is not clear, either from the correspondence in the Algemeen Rijksarchiv in The Hague or from the complementary letters in the Museum of Science in Leiden. But at the end of the summer the commission on whose behalf Einstein was working produced its first publication. This was a small booklet dealing with alleged atrocities in Lille, which startled Einstein when he saw it. The preface was "tactless" and—partly at Einstein's instigation one suspects—the whole edition was eventually withdrawn for correction, amendment, and reissue early in 1920.

It is at this point in 1919 that Einstein, facing what seemed to be the Allied condemnation of a whole nation, further qualified his previous rabid anti-Germanism and rejected an extraordinarily tempting offer from Leiden. The reason may have been partly a wish to give "the new Germany" a chance to pull herself up by her moral

Instruments used by the British eclipse expedition of 1919, which supported Einstein's General Theory of Relativity. [Cambridge University Press]

bootstraps, partly the fear that a "thirst for power" might be growing up in an "elsewhere" that Einstein—like many other Germans—identified with France.

The offer came from Ehrenfest. He had not yet got the approval of the authorities, but there seemed little doubt that he would get it—even for the terms that he outlined on September 2, 1919. What he suggested was that Einstein should come to Leiden University, where the normal maximum salary of seven thousand five hundred guilders would be Einstein's minimum. There would be no lecturing duties, and the only obligation would be for him to make his base in or near the city.

A fortnight after Einstein replied to Ehrenfest, turning down the Leiden offer, he received a historic telegram sent by Lorentz from Leiden five days earlier. It was dated September 27, 1919, and ran: "Eddington found star displacement at rim of sun, preliminary measurement between nine-tenths of a second and twice that value." The words were to mark a turning point in the life of Einstein and in the history of science.

In Britain the Royal Astronomical Society had noted of the Special Theory in 1917 that "experimental confirmation has been ample, and no serious doubt of its truth is entertained, criticism being confined to questions of its exact scope and philosophical implications." But confirmation was the result of physicists laboring in their laboratories. Something on a different scale was required to test the General Theory, and it says much for Sir Frank Dyson that in March, 1917, he had drawn "attention to the unique opportunities afforded by the eclipse of 1919" to test Einstein's theory.

In March, 1917, Britain's darkest weeks of the war still lay ahead, and the prospect of sending expeditions to South America and to Africa, where the eclipse could best be seen, could not be viewed without misgiving. Despite this, Dyson was given £1,000 from the Government, for use by the Joint Permanent Eclipse Committee of the Royal Society and the Royal Astronomical Society under his chairmanship. In the spring of 1918, as the Germans broke through to the Marne and once again brought the issue of the war into doubt, plans went steadily ahead for British expeditions to Sobral in northern Brazil and to Principe on the Gulf of Guinea.

Early the following year, in January 1919, a series of test photographs, showing the Hyades against a reference frame of other stars, was taken at Greenwich Observatory. Two months later Eddington and E. T. Cottingham, who were to make the eclipse observations in Principe, and C. D. Crommelin and C. R. Davidson, who were to do the same at Sobral, met for a final briefing in Flamsteed House, Greenwich. Next morning both parties left for Funchal, Crommelin and Davidson traveling on to Brazil, while Eddington and Cottingham sailed to Principe, where they arrived on April 23. One month of hard work followed.

May 29 began with a heavy rain that stopped only about noon. Not until 1:30 P.M., when the eclipse had already begun, did the party get its first glimpse of the sun:

160

Eclipse of the sun, May 29, 1919.

We had to carry out our programme of photographs on faith [wrote Eddington in his diary]. I did not see the eclipse, being too busy changing plates, except for one glance to make sure it had begun and another half-way through to see how much cloud there was. We took sixteen photographs. They are all good of the sun, showing a very remarkable prominence; but the cloud has interfered with the star images. The last six photographs show a few images which I hope will give us what we need.

It looked as though the effort, so far as the Principe expedition was concerned, might have been abortive. Only on June 3 was the issue settled. "We developed the photographs, two each night for six nights after the eclipse," Eddington wrote, "and I spent the whole day measuring. The cloudy weather upset my plans and I had to treat the measures in a different way from what I intended, consequently I have not been able to make any preliminary announcement of the result. But one plate that I measured gave a result agreeing with Einstein."

"This," says Eddington's biographer, "was a moment which Eddington never forgot. On one occasion in later years he referred to it as the greatest moment of his life."

At a dinner of the Royal Astronomical Society following Eddington's return to Britain, he described the trials and tribulations of Principe in a parody of the *Rubaiyat*, whose final verses went thus:

> The Clock no question makes of Fasts or Slows,
> But steadily and with a constant Rate it goes.
> And Lo! the clouds are parting and the Sun
> A crescent glimmering on the screen—It shows!—It shows!!
>
> Five minutes, not a moment left to waste,
> Five minutes, for the picture to be traced—
> The Stars are shining, and coronal light
> Streams from the Orb of Darkness—Oh make haste!
>
> For in and out, above, about, below
> 'Tis nothing but a magic *Shadow* show
> Played in a Box, whose Candle is the Sun
> Round which we phantom figures come and go.
>
> Oh leave the Wise our measures to collate.
> One thing at least is certain, LIGHT has WEIGHT.
> One thing is certain, and the rest debate—
> Light-rays, when near the Sun, DO NOT GO STRAIGHT.

Despite Eddington's moment of drama at Principe, full confirmation did not come all at once. While the Principe photographs had been developed and measured in West Africa, those of the Sobral expedition were brought to Britain before being processed. The first were disappointing. Then came the main set of seven. "They gave a final verdict," wrote Eddington, "definitely confirming Einstein's value of the deflection, in agreement with the results obtained at Principe."

Only on September 27, 1919, did there come Lorentz' telegram: "Eddington found star displacement at rim of sun." Einstein's first reaction was to pass on the good news to his mother in Lucerne.

Looking back, both Einstein and his colleagues were apt to harp on his inner certainty. But this was not the certainty of hindsight; all along he had believed that the theory would be confirmed. Nevertheless, he was glad enough now to begin preparations for a trip to Holland.

Before he left Berlin he received further news from Lorentz. "I have not yet written to you about the observation of the rays glancing off the edge of the sun, as I thought that one of the English journals, *Nature* for instance, would have written fully about it," Lorentz explained on October 7:

> This has not yet happened so I do not wish to wait any longer. I have heard of Eddington's results through Mr. Van der Pohl, the conservator of this laboratory. He visited the British Association meeting at Bournemouth and told me on his return what Eddington spoke about. As the plates are still being measured he cannot give exact values, but according to Eddington's opinion the thing is certain and one can say with certainty that the deflection (at the edge of the sun) lies between 0.87″ and 1′74″.

So far, the warnings that a major change in man's ideas of the physical world was at hand had seeped out only gradually. No results had been publicly available when the British expeditions had returned to London. The accounts given at the British Association meeting had stressed that vital measurements and comparisons still had to be completed. Even Lorentz' telegram to Einstein had given a general rather than a specific indication of success. Thus the reports had hardened slowly, over the weeks, lacking the suddenness that alone could give headline quality in a Europe grappling with the problems of postwar chaos. There was, moreover, to be a final twist before the news finally broke on the world.

This was given in Leiden, where Einstein arrived in the latter half of October. The vital results of the British expeditions were known here, privately at least, by October 23. But even now, only a small handful of professors were in the know. Two days later, on the evening of Saturday, October 25, the situation changed dramatically. The Dutch Royal Academy met in Amsterdam. Einstein was there. So was Lorentz and so was Ehrenfest. First, the routine business was disposed of. Next, Einstein was formally welcomed. Then, in the words of the Academy's official report, "Mr. H. A. Lorentz communicated the most recent confirmation of Professor Einstein's General Theory of Relativity." But, as the agenda put it, the communication would "not be printed in the report." No press representatives appear to have been present. For another ten days the rest of the world remained in ignorance of the fact that Newton's view of the universe had received an amendment from which it would never totally recover.

It was not until the afternoon of Thursday, November 6, 1919, that the Fellows of the Royal and the Royal Astronomical Societies met in Burlington House to hear the official results of the two eclipse expeditions. Here, if nowhere else, men were aware that an age was ending, and the main hall of the Society was crowded. J. J. Thomson, now president of the Royal Society, James Jeans, and Lindemann were present. So were Sir Oliver Lodge and the mathematician and philosopher Alfred Whitehead. All were agitated by the same question. Were the ideas upon which they had relied for so long at last to be found wanting?

> The whole atmosphere of tense interest was exactly that of the Greek drama [wrote Whitehead later]. We were the chorus commenting on the decree of destiny as disclosed in the development of a supreme incident. There was dramatic quality in the very staging—the traditional ceremonial, and in the background the picture of Newton to remind us that the greatest of scientific generalizations was now, after more than two centuries, to receive its first modification. Nor was the personal interest wanting; a great adventure in thought had at length come safe to shore.

Thomson rose to address the meeting, speakng of Einstein's theory as "one of the greatest achievements in the history of human thought" and then pushing home the full measure of what relativity meant. "It is not the discovery of an outlying island but of a whole continent of new scientific ideas," he said. "It is the greatest discovery in connection with gravitation since Newton enunciated his principles." As *The Times* put it, Einstein's Theory dealt with the fabric of the universe.

Then Dyson read the body of his report, giving the figures provided by the photographs and describing their significance. "Thus the results of the expeditions to Sobral and Principe," he concluded, "leave little doubt that a deflection of light takes place in the neighbourhood of the sun and that it is of the amount demanded by Einstein's generalized theory of relativity as attributable to the sun's gravitational field."

The discussion that followed brought out one thing: that while the results of the eclipse expedition had yielded a convincing key piece of evidence, the new theory was acceptable on entirely different grounds. Eddington was to emphasize the point nearly twenty years later when there had been further astronomical support. The theory, he said, was primarily concerned with phenomena, which, without it, might have seemed mildly puzzling:

> But we do not need to observe an eclipse of the sun to ascertain whether a man is talking coherently or incoherently. The Newtonian framework, as was natural after 250 years, had been found too crude to accommodate the new observational knowledge which was being acquired. In default of a better framework, it was still used, but definitions were strained to purposes for which they were never intended. We were in the position of a librarian whose books were still being arranged according to a subject-scheme drawn up a hundred years ago, trying to find the right place for books on Hollywood, the Air Force, and detective novels.

Einstein had altered all that.

10. THE NEW MESSIAH

Einstein on the cover of *Berliner Illustrated Magazine*, December 14, 1919: "A new great figure in world history...." *[Ullstein]*

Einstein awoke in Berlin on the morning of November 7, 1919, to find himself famous. It was an awkward morning for fame, with the Wilhelmstrasse barricaded, all traffic stopped on the orders of Gustav Noske, the Republican minister of defense, and warning leaflets from the Citizens Defense Force being handed out to passersby. On the second anniversary of the Russian Revolution it seemed that Berlin was to be torn apart by a struggle between the workers who believed that the German Government had not moved far enough to the left and the army who believed that it had moved too far.

Einstein was, of course, already known to the equivalent of today's science correspondents. In addition, the esoteric quality of his work had combined with his own individuality to produce a local notoriety. Now, on the morning of November 7, the situation was dramatically changed. Even a month later he could write to Born that the publicity was so bad that he could hardly get down to work. Any journalist who felt that the newsworthiness of the British expeditions had ended with their safe return to England learned better as accounts of the previous afternoon's meeting in Burlington House, and the subsequent leading article in *The Times*, arrived in the German capital. Under "The Fabric of the Universe," *The Times* stated that "the scientific conception of the fabric of the Universe must be changed." And after an account of the British expeditions and their purpose, it concluded thus: "But it is confidently believed by the greatest experts that enough has been done to overthrow the certainty of ages, and to require a new philosophy of the universe, a philosophy that will sweep away nearly all that has hitherto been accepted as the axiomatic basis of physical thought."

This was strong meat. Its effect was not lessened by accounts in other papers, which with few exceptions agreed that the world would never be the same again. Attention turned to the man responsible. Throughout the day Einstein was visited by an almost continuous stream of reporters. He genuinely did not like it. But he soon realized that there is a time for compromise as well as a time for standing firm. There was, moreover, one way in which the distasteful interest could be turned to good use. So there were no free photographs of Einstein; as one reporter later noted, "these, his wife told me, are sold for the benefit of the starving children of Vienna." It was not only photographs that could coax money into the channels through which he thought it should flow, and before the end of the month he was in touch with a young correspondent for *Nature* and had agreed to contribute an article to *The Times*.

The *Nature* correspondent was Robert Lawson, the young physicist who had attended his lecture in Vienna six years previously. Interned at the outbreak of war, but nevertheless allowed to continue his scientific work at the Radium Institute, Lawson returned to the University of Sheffield at the end of 1919, and now, as well as writing to Einstein himself, gave Arnold Berliner, the editor of *Naturwissenschaften*, an account of the situation in Britain:

> The talk here is of almost nothing but Einstein [he said], and if he were to come here now I think he would be welcomed like a victorious general. The fact that a theory formulated by a German has been confirmed by observations on the part of Englishmen has brought the possibility of co-operation between these two scientifically-minded nations much closer. Quite apart from the great scientific value of his brilliant theory, Einstein has done mankind an incalculable service.

Berliner passed the letter on to Einstein who in acknowledging Lawson's direct request for material for *Nature* mentioned the article he was writing for *The Times*. This appeared on the 28th, but the paper had already renewed its efforts to explain to readers how important the confirmation of the General Theory really was. It was becoming clear that the announcement at the Burlington House meeting was not just a nine days' wonder. Although some scientists were reluctant to accept all that Einstein had claimed, and although others, like Sir Oliver Lodge, were still gruffly skeptical, the ablest minds in science realized, and publicly acknowledged, that this was not an end but a beginning. On November 15 *The Times* added its weight in a leading article headed "The Revolution in Science."

> The ideals of Aristotle and Euclid and Newton which are the basis of all our present conceptions prove in fact not to correspond with what can be observed in the fabric of the universe [it concluded]. Space is merely a relation between two sets of data, and an infinite number of times may co-exist. Here and there, past and present, are relative, not absolute, and change according to the ordinates and co-ordinates selected. Observational science has in fact led back to the purest subjective idealism, if without Berkeley's major premise, itself an abstraction of Aristotelian notions of infinity, to take it out of chaos.

A fortnight later came Einstein's own article. Using the opportunity to deplore the war, he began with a typical Einsteinian flourish by saying: "After the lamentable breach in the former international relations existing among men of science, it is with joy and gratefulness that I accept this opportunity of communication with English astronomers and physicists." He went on to outline the basic principles of relativity, special and general, displaying in what was his first popular exposition all those abilities that still make Einstein on relativity a good deal clearer than most other writers.

At the end of the same article he lightly commented on the status that the English had given him, tossing a joke into the future that was to be thrust back in his face within a decade. "The description of me and my circumstances in *The Times* show an amusing feat of imagination on the part of the writer," he said. "By an application of the theory of relativity to the taste of readers, today in Germany I am called a German man of science and in England I am represented as a Swiss Jew. If I come to be regarded as a '*bête noire*' the description will be reversed, and I shall become a Swiss Jew for the Germans and a German man of science for the English." Unwilling to censor the comment, *The Times* was equally unwilling to let it pass. "We conceded him his little jest," an editorial admitted. "But we note that, in accordance with the general tenor of his theory, Dr. Einstein does not supply any absolute description of himself."

The comment was indicative of an undertow of feeling in some conservative circles, both scientific and lay. Thomson, Eddington, Jeans, and many other bright Fellows of the Royal Society, appeared to have accepted the extraordinary ideas of this Jew of whose nationality no one appeared to be certain. But could the thing really be true? Was there not somewhere, in some fashion, a more reasonable explanation to which sane men would wake up one morning? Some distinguished men thought so. Among them was Sir Oliver Lodge, who had left before the end of the famous meeting of November 6, even though expected to speak in the discussion—and who later explained this on the grounds of a previous engagement and the need to catch the six o'clock train. On the 24th, Lodge, whose *The Ether of Space* well qualified him for leading the skeptics, addressed an impressive if polyglot company that included the Bishop of London, Lord Lytton, Lord Haldane, Sir Francis Younghusband, H. A. L. Fisher, and Sir Martin Conway. Newton, Lodge affirmed, had not understood what gravitation was. "We do not understand it now," he went on. "Einstein's theory would not help us to understand it. If Einstein's third prediction were verified, Einstein's theory would dominate all physics and the next generation of mathematical physicists would have a terrible time." Indeed, they did.

This third prediction, the Einstein shift, still exercised Einstein himself, as he revealed in a letter to Eddington that shows vestigial doubt as well as gratitude, courtesy, and humility. He congratulated Eddington on his work and said how amazed he was at the English interest in the theory.

Einstein was not alone. In addition to the doubters headed by Lodge there were others who feared that relativity might be beyond them, or who had doubts as to whether the results of the eclipse expeditions were, scientifically speaking, a good thing.

The archives reveal some surprising names in both camps. In the first there is Dyson, who wrote to Hale at the Mount Wilson Observatory on December 29. "I was myself a skeptic, and expected a different result," he said. "Now I am trying to understand the principle of relativity and am gradually getting to think I do." Hale was less optimistic. "I congratulate you again on the splendid results you have obtained," he wrote to Dyson on February 9, 1920, "though I confess that the complications of the theory of relativity are altogether too much for my comprehension. If I were a good mathematician

I might have some hope of forming a feeble conception of the principle, but as it is I fear it will always remain beyond my grasp. However, this does not decrease my interest in the problem, to which we will try to contribute to the best of our ability." His doubts were repeated to Rutherford to whom he wrote that relativity seemed "to complicate matters a good deal."

Rutherford's own qualifications and doubts were unlike those of Dyson and Hale. He noted that the interest of the general public was very remarkable and almost without precedent, the reason being, he felt, that no one was able to give an intelligent explanation of relativity to the average man. He himself did not have much doubt about the accuracy of Einstein's conclusions and considered it a great bit of work. However, he feared that it might tend to draw scientific men away from experiments toward broad metaphysical conceptions. There were already many like that in Britain, he went on, and no more were needed if science was to continue advancing.

This was a typical Rutherford attitude, illustrating his built-in belief that the only worthwhile experiments were those whose results he could personally repeat and check. So far as the work of Einstein was relative to Newton, he said in 1923, it was simply "a generalization and broadening of its basis, in fact a typical case of mathematical and physical development." But nine years later the balance had altered. "The theory of relativity by Einstein, quite apart from any question of its validity," he agreed, "cannot but be regarded as a magnificent work of art." This qualification, however deeply rooted in scientific intuition, may have reflected the slight allergy to Einstein himself, which comes out at times in Rutherford's comments. Certainly, he showed no wish to have him in Cambridge when the idea was debated in 1920, or even when Einstein was a refugee from Germany in 1933.

Much the same lukewarm view appears beneath the surface in J. J. Thomson. "[He] accepted these results (1919) and the interpretation put upon them, but he never seemed particularly enthusiastic on the subject nor did he attempt to develop it, either theoretically or by experiment," said his biographer, Lord Rayleigh, some years later. "I believe, from a conversation which I can recall, that he thought attention was being too much concentrated on it by ordinary scientific workers, with the neglect of other subjects to which they were more likely to be able to make a useful contribution. His attitude to relativity was that of a looker-on. Probably the same was true of nearly all his contemporaries. It was the creation of a younger generation." And when it came to cosmology, Thomson's patience ran out. "We have Einstein's space, De Sitter's space, expanding universes, contracting universes, vibrating universes, mysterious universes," he noted in his memoirs. "In fact the pure mathematician may create universes just by writing down an equation, and indeed if he is an individualist he can have a universe of his own."

A semiquizzical note can be heard in many of the repercussions that followed the November meeting at Burlington House. Eddington, speaking in support of relativity

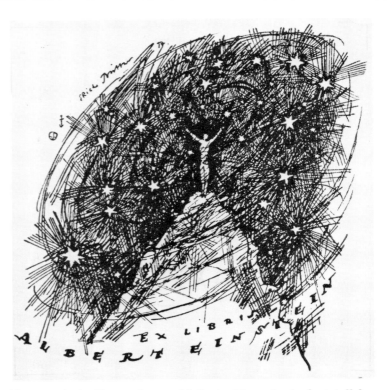

Einstein's bookplate, 1922, which he used while living on Haberland-strasse, Berlin. [Ullstein]

in Trinity College, Cambridge, early in December, said that although six feet tall he would, if moving vertically at 161,000 miles a second, shrink to a height of only three feet. J. J. Thomson, adopting the same line, remarked that "the tutor who preferred rooms on the ground floor to the attic would hardly be consoled to know that the higher he was up, the more Euclidean his space became because it was further from the effects of gravitation." A good deal of the light-headedness that took hold of so many serious men when they began to discuss relativity no doubt sprang from Eddington's example. As his biographer has said in writing of *Space, Time and Gravitation*, the relativist could, like the Mad Hatter, experience time standing still. In later books Alice herself moved mystifyingly across his stage, the living embodiment of the Fitzgerald contraction; and the Red Queen, "that ardent relativist," proclaimed the relativity even of nonsense.

The trend was spurred on by the simultaneous fame of Jacob Epstein and produced the following verse:

> Einstein and Epstein are wonderful men,
>   Bringing new miracles into our ken.
> Einstein upset the Newtonian rule;
>   Epstein demolished the Pheidian School.
> Einstein gave fits to the Royal Society;
>   Epstein delighted in loud notoriety.
> Einstein made parallels meet in infinity;
>   Epstein remodelled the form of divinity.

Anti-Germanism, understandably enough after the long haul that victory had demanded, also showed itself in diverse reactions, and from Rutherford's Cavendish Laboratory there came a typical poem from A. A. Robb. One of the few English physicists who had given more than passing attention to the Special Theory, Robb had written as early as 1914 that "although generally associated with the names of Einstein and Minkowski, the really essential physical considerations underlying the theories are due to Larmor and Lorentz." His allergy to Einstein was increased by General Relativity, and in the introduction to *The Absolute Relations of Time and Space* he caustically wrote of Einstein's theory of simultaneity that "this seemed to destroy all sense of the reality of the external world and to leave the physical universe no better than a dream, or rather a nightmare."

168

The acclaim that surged up at the end of 1919 naturally presented too good an opportunity to miss; the result was Robb's "Hymn to Einstein," to be sung to the tune of "Deutschland Über Alles":

> Scientists so unbelieving
>   Have completely changed their ways;
> Now they humbly sing to Einstein
>   Everlasting hymns of praise.
> Journalists in search of copy
>   First request an interview;
> Then they boost him, boost him, boost him;
>   Boost him until all is blue.
>
> He the universe created;
>   Spoke the word and it was there.
> Now he reigns in radiant glory
>   On his professorial chair.
> Editions of daily papers,
>   Yellow red and every hue
> Boost him, boost him, boost him, boost him;
>   Boost him until all is blue.
>
> Philosophic speculators
>   Stand in awe around his throne.
> University professors
>   Blow upon his loud trombone.
> Praise him on the Riemann symbols
>   On Christoffel symbols too
> They boost him, boost him, boost him;
>   Boost him until all is blue.
>
> Other scientists neglected
>   May be feeling somewhat sick;
> And imagine that the butter
>   Is laid on a trifle thick.
> Heed not such considerations
>   Be they false, or be they true;
> Boost him, boost him, boost him, boost him;
>   Boost him until all is blue.

Einstein himself also seems to have been affected. Thus he started, early in December, one hare that was to run through decades of books about relativity, naturally enough ignored by science but enjoyed by many simple souls. Interviewed by the *New York Times*, he was asked how he had come to start work on the General Theory. He had been triggered off, he replied, by seeing a man falling from a Berlin roof. The man had survived with little injury. Einstein had run from his house. The man said that he had not felt the effects of gravity—a pronouncement that had led to a new view of the universe. Here is perhaps a link with Planck's illustration of energy—his story of a workman carrying bricks to the top of a house and piling up energy that remained there until the bricks slipped and fell on his head weeks later. Here, too, is another illustration of Hans Einstein's statement that his father was always willing to exaggerate in order to explain, and would at times delight in making up a story to please an audience.

All this, however, was froth on the top of the argument. Beneath the humor, the Alice in Wonderland analogies, the limericks concerning the young lady called Bright, whose speed was much faster than light, there lay an almost universal agreement that Einstein's view of gravitation was more consistent with the available facts than Newton's. There might be debate over details, the third proof had not yet been obtained, and there were to be several attempts—all either unsuccessful or inconclusive—to show that the outcome of the Michelson-Morley experiment itself could be faulted. But the band of responsible critics was comparatively small, and it was clear that Einstein had, in fact, cast fresh light not only on the subject of gravitation but on the whole question of how scientific knowledge might be acquired. For Newton's theory had been founded on the most detailed observational evidence; each twinkling pinpoint in the heavens appeared to support the belief that the accumulation of evidence, and the induction from it of general laws, could lead to the ultimate truth. Now it has been shown that by starting with a purely speculative idea, it was possible to construct a theory that would not only be supported by the mass of observational evidence with which Newton had worked, but that would also explain evidence that Newton could not explain. By the opening weeks of 1920 it was clear that Einstein held the field.

But to some people he had yet to live down his presence in Berlin throughout the war, however pacifist his sentiments might be. M. Brillouin had his counterparts in England, as Eddington was forced to make clear early in the New Year.

As keen as Einstein himself for the restoration of scientific cooperation between the belligerent countries, Eddington had stressed this point in his first letter, when on December 1, 1919, he had written to Einstein from Cambridge saying that since November 6 "all England has been talking about your theory.... It is the best possible thing that could have happened for scientific relations between England and Germany," he went on. "I do not anticipate rapid progress toward official reunion, but there is a big advance toward a more reasonable frame of mind among scientific men, and that is even more important than the renewal of formal associations.... Although it seems unfair that Dr. Freundlich, who was first in the field, should not have had the satisfaction of accomplishing the experimental test of your theory, one feels that things have turned out very fortunately in giving this object lesson of the solidarity of German and British science even in time of war."

So far so good. Eddington's liberal sentiments were held by many men of science, possibly a majority. When, later in December, three names were proposed for the Royal Astronomical Society's Gold Medal, Einstein was voted for the award by an overwhelming majority. He was duly informed, and writing to Born on January 27 about the peace treaty noted that he would be going to England in the spring to receive the Medal.

A few days later he received an apologetic letter from Eddington and was disabused. Eddington said that the officials of the Royal Astronomical Society had met to vote on the Gold Medal award. But a purely chauvinistic lobby had been mustered at the last minute and had successfully stopped its being made to Einstein. For the first time in thirty years, no Gold Medal would be awarded. "I am sure," wrote Eddington, "that your disappointment will not be in any way personal and that you will share with me the regret that this promising opening of a better international spirit has had a rebuff from reaction. Nevertheless, I am sure the better spirit is making progress."

As with Solvay, Einstein had to wait for a change in the political climate. Then, at last allowed to join in the game, he scooped the pool. In 1925 he was awarded the Royal Society's Copley Medal; and, the following year, the Royal Astronomical Society's Gold Medal.

Whatever the difficulties in making formal British awards to a German, Einstein had by the first months of 1920 gained not only success but notoriety.

The speed with which his fame spread across the world, down through the intellectual layers to the man in the street, the mixture of semireligious awe and near-hysteria that his figure aroused, created a phenomenon that has never been fully explained, but is well described by Alexander Moszkowski, a Berlin littérateur and critic who moved on the fringe of the Einstein circle. Moszkowski's book, *Einstein the Searcher*, caused Einstein's friends a great deal of misgiving, and the Borns felt so strongly about it that they persuaded him to try and stop publication. The outcome of a long series of conversations, during which Einstein had spoken about his work quite freely and in simple terms, the book was an overpopularization of science more unusual then than it would be today. It also had considerable, and somewhat dramatic pre-publication publicity, and it was this, more than the substance of the book itself, which angered Einstein's would-be protectors. He himself appears to have cared very little about the temporary furore that the book created:

> Everything sank away in the face of this universal theme which had taken possession of humanity [Moszkowski wrote of the huge public interest in relativity]. The converse of educated people circled about this pole, and could not escape from it, continually reverted to the same theme pressed aside by necessity or accident. Newspapers entered on a chase for contributors who could furnish them with short or long, technical or nontechnical, notices about Einstein's theory. In all nooks and corners, social evenings of instruction sprang up, and wondering universities appeared with errant professors that led people out of the three-dimensional misery of daily life into the more hospitable Elysian fields of four-dimensionality. Women lost sight of domestic worries and discussed co-ordinate systems, the principle of simultaneity, and negatively-charged electrons. All contemporary questions had gained a fixed centre from which threads could be spun to each. Relativity had become the sovereign password.

Exaggerated as it sounds, this account is more than the truth even if the truth in fancy dress. The attitude was, moreover, not confined to the uninitiated:

> To those who have the vision, the world of physics will take on a new and wonderful life [wrote the reviewer in *Nature* of Einstein's own book on relativity]. The commonest phenomena become organic parts of the great plan. The rationality of the universe becomes an exciting romance, not a cold dogma. The thrill of a comprehensive understanding runs through us, and yet we find ourselves on the shores of the unknown. For this new doctrine, after all, is but a touchstone of truth. We must submit all our theories to the test of it; we must allow our deepest thoughts to be gauged by it. The metaphysician and he who speculates over the meaning of life cannot be indifferent.

It was, therefore, predictable that learned societies should hold many meetings at which the special and the general theories were discussed; that *The Times Educational Supplement* should devote three full-page articles to interpretations of relativity by Professor Lindemann, Dr. Herbert Carr, and Alfred Whitehead; and that an Einstein Society should be started in the House of Commons in 1920. "Its formation was due more to the curiosity of those of us who had unexpectedly survived the First World War than to any profound scientific search," says one of its members, Colin Coote.

Within a year there were more than a hundred books on relativity, and intellectual interest was being shown not only in the world's capitals but in the provinces. "At this time," writes Leopold Infeld, later one of Einstein's collaborators, "I was a school teacher in a small Polish town, and I did what hundreds of others did all over the world. I gave a public lecture on the Relativity Theory, and the crowd that queued up on a cold winter's night was so great that it could not be accommodated in the largest hall in the town." When Eddington had lectured in Cambridge on a similar night in December, in his own words, "hundreds were turned away, unable to get near the room." In Paris the American Eugene Higgins presented five thousand dollars through the *Scientific American* for the best three-thousand-word exposition of relativity. "I am the only one in my entire circle of friends who is not entering," observed Einstein. "I don't believe I could do it." The prize, fittingly enough in view of Einstein's Berne background, was won by Lyndon Bolton, a senior examiner of the British Patent Office.

If all this was explicable in terms of an important new scientific theory that had become the common coin of intelligent conversation, Einstein was also raised to the far less comprehensible position of a popular celebrity. From London, the Palladium music hall asked whether he would appear, virtually at his own figure, for a three-week "performance." The "Einstein cigar" appeared on the market. Children were blessed, or otherwise, with his name. The cartoonists took him to their hearts. In Germany, he was shown in company with French President Millerand, who was advocating the heaviest possible reparations from the country. "Can't you persuade the simpleminded Bôche that even with an absolute deficit of 67,000,000,000 marks he is still *relatively* well off?" In Britain, a detective shown catching a bank thief with the help of a flashlight whose light rays turned corners, laconically remarked: "Elementary, my dear Einstein." He had, in fact, been hoisted into position by the same mob that hoists film stars. Reason had little to do with the matter. But in one way the treatment of Einstein was different in its results. Film stars pontificating on the future of the world, boxers dogmatizing on politics, can be good entertainment, and few people take them more seriously than this. Einstein was in another category.

The sheer audacity of his theory helped. "Light caught bending" was an affront to common sense that few could in their heart of hearts take seriously; there was, if nothing else, a curiosity value about the man who had apparently shown that it did. Yet to attribute Einstein's popularity to this alone is to rate the inner awareness of the common people too low. Some weight must be given to Infeld's view:

> It was just after the end of the war. People were weary of hatred, of killing and international intrigues. The trenches, bombs and murder had left a bitter taste. Books about war did not sell. Everyone looked for a new era of peace, and wanted to forget the war. Here was something which captured the imagination; human eyes looking from an earth covered with graves and blood to the heavens covered with the stars. Abstract thought carrying the human mind far away from the sad and disappointing reality. The mystery of the sun's eclipse and of the penetrating power of the human mind. Romantic scenery, a strange glimpse of the eclipsed sun, an imaginary picture of bending light rays, all removed from the oppressive reality of life. One further reason, perhaps even more important; a new event was predicted by a *German* scientist, Einstein, and confirmed by *English* astronomers. Scientists belonging to two warring nations had collaborated again. It seemed the beginning of a new era.

Even this was only part of the story. Quite as important was the intuitive realization that the new light cast on the physical world struck at the very vitals of what they had always believed. Few could understand the implications, let alone the complex intellectual structure from which these implications sprang; even so, deep within there lay a sensitive sounding board, developed since the days when man had first stood up on two feet out of four. Erwin Schrödinger, who six years later was to become a standard-bearer in the new cause of wave mechanics, hinted at the underlying reason for the Einstein phenomemon in his Tarner Lectures of 1956:

> I have sometimes wondered why they made such a great stir both among the general public and among philosophers [he said of the transformations of time and space produced by relativity]. I suppose it is this, that it meant the dethronement of time as a rigid tyrant imposed on us from outside, a liberation from the unbreakable rule of "before and after." For indeed time is our most severe master by ostensibly restricting the existence of each of us to narrow limits—seventy or eighty years, as the Pentateuch has it. To be allowed to play about with such a master's programme believed unassailable until then, to play about with it albeit in a small way, seems to be a great relief, it seems to encourage the thought that the whole "timetable" is probably not quite as serious as it appears at first sight. And this thought is a religious thought, nay I should call it *the* religious thought.

Erwin Schrödinger (1887–1961), the Austrian physicist who, with Paul Adrien Maurice Dirac (b. 1902), was awarded the Nobel Prize for Physics in 1933 "for the discovery of new fruitful forms of atomic theory." It was Schrödinger who erected the basic structure of wave mechanics in which the electron particle was envisaged as a standing electron wave. Heretofore considered a wave-controlled corpuscle, it was now recognized as a corpuscular wave. [Ullstein]

173

Einstein and Max Planck, the originator of the quantum theory, which played a key part in the development of Einstein's theories. [Bundesarchiv]

The Einstein mythology also began to flourish, the complex structure of story and half-story, half-truth, quarter-truth, adorned exaggeration, and plain lie, which from now onward increasingly surrounded his activities. All men caught in the white-hot glare of public interest discover—sometimes with amusement, sometimes with resignation, often with resentment—that their smallest doings are memorialized, embroidered, and explained away in a continuous flow of anecdote whose connection with the truth is frequently marginal. Einstein was to suffer more than most from such attentions and soon learned to regard them with amusement—as must any biographer who meets the same quasi-documented story appearing in different decades, from different continents, and being retailed in all good faith, to illustrate one or more of Einstein's extraordinary, endearing, or unconventional attitudes.

There were many reasons for the mythology that developed from 1920 onward. One was that inventions had good ground to grow in. Immersed in his work in Berlin, Einstein did on one occasion use a check as a bookmark; it was, therefore, pardonable that the story should surface as the account of how he had placed a fifteen-hundred-dollar check into a book and then lost the book. His character was kindly and gentle, and he was at least once asked by a neighbor's small girl to help with her sums; after that, small girls all over the world had Einstein doing their homework—despite the fact that he had refused the request on the grounds that it would not be fair. The legends themselves, melting in the harsh light of investigation, show not so much what sort of man he really was as what kind of man the world thought him. Behind his confidence, Einstein was genuinely humble—and legend made him forbear comment when a female graduate, failing to recognize him, voiced surprise that he should still be studying physics with the words: "I finished physics when I was twenty-five." Only Einstein, out of time with his fellow musicians at an amateur recital, would receive the criticism: "Einstein, can't you count?" Only Einstein, unable to find his glasses and asking the dining-car attendant to read the menu, would be met with the comment: "Sorry sir, I ain't had education either." And only Einstein, looking like an untidy middle-class nonentity, could go unrecognized by officialdom in a score of stories, pottering his way through the crowd, a Chaplinesque figure somehow embodying all the human virtues of "us" against "them." Thus he became, as the forces of left and right jockeyed for position in the postwar Germany of the Weimar Republic, a new sort of international image, the scientist with the touch of a saint, a man from whom an awed public expected not only research but revelation.

From outside Germany there came adulation—and in 1921 the much-prized Foreign Fellowship of the Royal Society. Inside, opinion was mixed. Planck and Sommer-

Niels Bohr and Einstein in Paul Ehrenfest's home. Photograph by Paul
Ehrenfest. [AIP Niels Bohr Library]

feld, Von Laue and Rubens, Nernst and Haber, were among those who knew what Einstein had accomplished, while some Weimar politicians mentally seized upon him as typifying the new Germany, which they hoped could now be presented to the world. Yet there were many others to whom his success was deeply offensive, uniting in one man all that they detested—the success of an intellectual left-wing pacifist Jew.

This feeling counterbalanced the adulation in many ways. In Ulm, for instance, the authorities at first intended to make him a freeman of the city. "But before I approach our collegium," wrote Herr Dr. Schemberger, Stadtvorstand, to the Faculty of Philosophy in Tübingen University, "I would like to find out whether it is true that Einstein's work is really of such outstanding merit." The answer was an unqualified "Yes," which concluded: "What Newton did for mechanics, Einstein has done for physics." But when Dr. Schemberger wrote to Einstein on March 22, it was not the freedom of the city that was offered, but merely congratulations and the assurance that the town was glad to have him as one of its sons. Einstein's thanks were read out at the next council meeting. Two years later, when the award of the Nobel Prize for Physics put the seal on his work, the authorities settled for a street to be named after him. Perhaps it was only coincidence that it lay on the outskirts of the city and in a poorish area. More than a quarter of a century later, in 1949, he was asked to become an honorary citizen. He refused.

The honors from outside Germany increased throughout 1920. The first came from Leiden. Lorentz had telegraphed him as soon as he had heard of the Royal Society's meeting in November, 1919, and there soon followed the proposal of Kamerlingh Onnes that he be appointed *byzondere Hoogleerarden*, or Special Professor, for three years at an annual salary of two thousand guilders. Einstein accepted, after receiving a plea to do so from Ehrenfest, and having been told by Lorentz that Kamerlingh Onnes, who just twenty years earlier had ignored Einstein's appeal for work, "would regard it as a high honour if you would discuss with him the researches being carried out in his cryogenic laboratory."

There were numerous delays, and although Einstein visited his friends in

Leiden in May, 1920, it was not until five months later that he made his first formal visit as a Special Professor. Between these two visits he met Niels Bohr for the first time. Bohr, who had just started the Institute of Theoretical Physics in Copenhagen, had been invited by Planck to lecture to the Physikalische Gesellschaft, and on his arrival both Planck and Einstein came forward to meet him.

Something was sparked off between Bohr and Einstein at this meeting, the first of a long series of mental collisions whose succession through the years was to have a quality quite separate from the impact of genius on genius. For it was Einstein who, fifteen years earlier, had first brought an air of unexpected respectability to the idea that light might conceivably consist both of wave and of particle and to the implication that Planck's quantum theory might be applied not only to radiation but to matter itself. It was Bohr who was to bring scientific plausibility to the first of these ideas with his principle of complementarity, and substance to the second with his explanation of Rutherford's nuclear atom. Yet these very ideas were to create not a unity between the two men but a chasm. From the early 1920s, as Bohr and those of like mind followed them on to what they saw as inevitable conclusions, Einstein drew back in steadily growing disagreement, withdrawing himself from the mainstream of physics and giving to his later years a tragic air that not even the staunchest of his friends could argue away.

Immediately after this first meeting with Bohr, Einstein wrote to Ehrenfest saying how much he had enjoyed it. Bohr was quite as impressed with Einstein. "The discussions, to which I have often reverted in my thoughts," he later wrote, "added to all my admiration for Einstein a deep impression of his detached attitude. Certainly his favoured use of such picturesque phrases as 'ghost waves *[Gespensterfelder]* guiding the photons' implied no tendency to mysticism but illuminated a rather profound humour behind his piercing remarks." And on July 27 he wrote to Rutherford, saying that his visit had been "a very interesting experience, it being the first time I had the opportunity of meeting Planck and Einstein personally, and I spend [sic] the days discussing theoretical problems from morning till night."

Later, he gave some details of these discussions. "What do you hope to achieve?" he had asked, when Einstein had doubted whether it was necessary to give up causality and continuity. "You, the man who introduced the idea of light as particles! If you are so concerned with the situation in physics in which the nature of light allows for a dual interpretation, then ask the German Government to ban the use of photo-electric cells if you think that light is waves, or the use of diffraction gratings if light is corpuscular."

Einstein remarked: "There you are: a man like you comes and one would expect that two like-minded persons had met, yet we are unable to find a common language. Maybe we physicists ought to agree on certain general fundamentals, on certain general propositions which we would regard as positive before embarking on discussions."

A machine gun in the streets of Berlin during the Spartacist revolt of January, 1919. [Culver Pictures]

But Bohr objected: "No, never! I would regard it as the greatest treachery on my part if, in embarking on a new domain of knowledge, I accepted any foregone conclusions." This "certain difference in attitude and outlook" between the two men, as Bohr described it, was clear from the first day. It was sharpened and increased during long discussions over more than three decades. But it was the difference between the sides in a great game in which both men strove "To set the cause beyond renown/ To love the game beyond the prize/ To honour, while you strike him down,/ The foe that comes with fearless eyes."

Something of their mutual admiration shines out from their first letters:

For me [wrote Bohr as he learned that Einstein would be visiting Copenhagen] it is one of the great experiences of life that I can be near you and talk to you, and I cannot say how grateful I am for all the friendliness which you showed to me on my visit to Berlin, and for your letter which I am ashamed not to have answered before. You do not know how great a stimulus it was for me to have the long-awaited opportunity of hearing from you personally your views on the very question with which I myself have been busy. I will never forget our conversation on the way from Dahlem to your house, and I very much hope that during your visit here an opportunity will arise of continuing it.

Einstein was by the midsummer of 1920 making numerous lecture-visits of the sort that Bohr referred to. After each he returned to Berlin, and after each he found opposition to himself, and to all that he stood for, ominously growing. Now, he decided to straighten out the anomalous question of his nationality. He had renounced his German citizenship and as far as he knew was merely a German-born Swiss, an awkward situation that made him a sitting target for his enemies. There was one simple way of coming into the body of the Kirk: he could take up German civic rights again, an action that might underline his support for the Republic and would at least suggest that he was no longer ashamed of his country.

On July 1, 1920, Einstein was sworn into the Weimar constitution and some nine months later, on March 15, 1921, into the Prussian constitution.

If Einstein hated Germany, a portion of Germany certainly hated him. The reasons for this, given the situation in the country July and August, 1920, are simple to explain, if difficult to excuse: patriotic passion, born of defeat, distrusted pacifist leanings, and international connections; and if anti-Semitism was a convenient though dishonorable weapon, desperate times demanded desperate measures. Such feelings

177

were epitomized by the new symbol of General von Luttwitz' Erhardt Brigade, which had marched into Berlin from the Baltic to support the abortive Kapp putsch a few months earlier. On their helmets they wore a reverse of the swastika, a religious symbol usually associated with the worship of the Aryan sun-gods Apollo and Odin.

In the ferment of postwar Germany, where internal divisions were lessened by what appeared to be the vindictive brutality of the Allied blockade, there was more than one group willing to direct rising passions against Einstein, a ready-made target for hatred. There were those scientists who genuinely did not believe in the theories that had brought him a fame unique in their scientific experience. There were others who, whatever they believed, could not bear the thought of such acclaim being lavished on a man who had spent the hard-fought war burrowing away in the University of Berlin. It was bad enough that an unknown professor should have declaimed against the war, held out a welcoming hand to the enemy across the French frontier, and failed even to bend his energies to the commonweal like other scientists such as Haber and Nernst; it was intolerable that the same line should be followed by the man now that he had been jerked to fame overnight.

The attacks started before the end of 1919, and there was soon formed the Study Group of German Natural Philosophers, the Arbeitsgemeinschaft Deutscher Naturforscher, which had at its disposal large sums of money, and offered fees to those who would write or speak against Einstein. Leader of this so-called study group was Paul Weyland, a man entirely unknown in scientific circles and of whom, over the years, nothing was discovered. Much of his support came from assorted riffraff; some of it came from more scientifically respectable sources. The physicist Ernst Gehrcke joined the association and so did a number of other men who could genuinely claim to be classed as bona fide even if undistinguished scientists.

Above all there was Philipp Lenard, whose work on the photoelectric effect had been the forerunner of Einstein's and whose achievements had been stressed by Einstein in his letters to Jakob Johann Laub. Lenard had been considered something of an oddity by many of his colleagues at Heidelberg, but before the war he had not been an anti-Semite. He read the ultra-respectable *Frankfurter Zeitung* and, according to Laub, held a high opinion of Einstein's photoelectric paper. One thing that did rankle was Einstein's implied dismissal of the ether as an unnecessary complication in the universe; this, in turn, although rather irrelevantly, led Lenard to denigrate the theory of relativity. And in 1920 he reappears as the Nobel Prize winner enthusiastically providing scientific respectability for the Weyland organization, which described relativity as part of a vast Semitic plot to corrupt the world in general and Germany in particular.

In August the "Anti-Relativity Company," as Einstein called it, announced twenty meetings to be held in Germany's biggest towns. Berlin was its headquarters, and it hired the Berlin Philharmonic Hall for a set piece demonstration against both relativity and Einstein to be held on August 27.

178

Philipp Lenard (1862–1947), German physicist, who strongly attacked Einstein's theory of relativity. [Bundesarchiv]

In some ways the packed meeting had an air of farce as much as of high drama. On to the stage came Weyland, apparently the "handsome dark-haired man of about thirty who wore a frockcoat and spoke with enthusiasm about interesting things" later described by Einstein's colleague Leopold Infeld. "He said that uproar about the theory of relativity was hostile to the German spirit. Then there came a university lecturer who had a little beard, was small, who also wore a frockcoat, and who read out his speech from a brochure which had been sold before the lecture. He raised objections about understanding the theory of relativity."

This second spokesman seems to have been Gehrcke, and as he dived into some rudimentary technicalities, there was a murmur of "Einstein, Einstein" in the audience. For Einstein had arrived to see what it was all about. There he was, sitting in a box, obviously enjoying himself. As the speakers went on, attacking relativity, omitting, distorting, unbalancing, appealing to the good Aryan common sense of their audience and invoking its members not to take such stuff seriously, the clown that lies not far below genius began to show itself. At the more absurd statements about relativity Einstein could be seen bursting into laughter and clapping his hands in mock applause. When the meeting had ended, he greeted his friends: "That was most amusing."

However, the so-called Study Group was a symptom of something more sinister than scientific absurdity, and Einstein replied in the columns of the *Berliner Tageblatt*, the first time that he had come down into the marketplace to face his accusers. His statement was headed: "My Answer to the Anti-Relativity Theory Company Ltd." Opponents, he said, had relied on such devices as quoting results from one British eclipse station, already known to be incorrect due to a technical defect, and omitting all reference to the British announcement that the theory had been proved. Thus his demolition task was easy.

Von Laue, Rubens, and Nernst had sent their own short letter of protest against the activities of the association to the leading Berlin newspapers. This, published in the *Berliner Tageblatt*, read as follows:

> We cannot presume in this place to utter our opinion on the profound, exemplary intellectual work which Einstein has brought to his relativity theory. Surprising successes have already been achieved, and further proof must naturally lie in future research. On the other hand, we must stress that apart from Einstein's researches into relativity, his work has assured him a permanent place in the history of science. In this respect his influence on the scientific life not only of Berlin but of the whole of Germany can hardly be over-estimated. Whoever is fortunate enough to be close to Einstein knows that he will never be surpassed in his respect for the cultural values of others, in personal modesty and dislike of all publicity.

Sommerfeld himself had been deeply aroused, particularly in view of fresh rumors that Einstein was planning to leave Germany. As president of the German Physics Society he felt it necessary to come to the rescue:

179

Dear Einstein [he wrote on September 3], You must not leave Germany! Your whole work is rooted in German (and Dutch) science; nowhere will you find so much understanding as in Germany. It is not in your character to leave Germany now, when she is being so dreadfully misinterpreted by everyone. Just one more point: had you, with your views, lived during the war in France, England or America, you would certainly have been locked up, had you turned your back on the Entente and its false system as I do not doubt you would have done (as were Jaurés, Russell, Caillaus, etc.).

In emphasizing that Einstein should stand his ground Sommerfeld was appealing, ironically enough, to Einstein's feelings for Germany, the nation cast off in 1896 whose actions he had bitterly criticized throughout the war. To retire to Holland, or even Switzerland, would be desertion, desertion not only of his scientific colleagues but of that Germany "whose trials are everywhere so apparent."

At the end of August, 1920, Einstein was, therefore, once again being pulled in two directions—away from Berlin by the threat of anti-Semitism and the friendships of Lorentz and Ehrenfest; toward Berlin by his loyalty to University colleagues and his newfound hope for a Republican Germany. He knew that a permanent post at Leiden University could be his for the asking, and the same was no doubt still true of Zurich. His thoughts were already turning to England, and to a young British visitor, who called on him to discuss German requests for periodicals from British universities; he "referred to his lecturing at Oxford and expressed the pleasure that it would be for him to do so some time." Lindemann, recently made head of the Clarendon Laboratory, Oxford, had also called on him in Berlin. They had recalled their last meeting at the Solvay Congress, agreed to exchange future papers, and it is more than likely—especially in the light of future events—that Lindemann put the idea of an Oxford visit into Einstein's head. Something more substantial had already been suggested to Rutherford, who had taken J. J. Thomson's place at the Cavendish the previous year. For on September 1, Jeans had written to Rutherford from Zermatt, sending what was probably a report of Einstein's statement in the *Berliner Tageblatt*, and suggesting Einstein for a post in Cambridge.

There is no record of Rutherford's reply, but it seems likely that he was still slightly allergic to Einstein. Nevertheless, for a man of such unique reputation almost all options were open, and it would not have been surprising had Einstein now left Germany for a permanent post outside the Reich. But by the time he replied to Sommerfeld on September 6, he had decided otherwise.

For a couple of days he had really thought of leaving Berlin. But then he realized that he had taken the attacks too seriously—and that it would, in any case, be wrong to leave his friends. But he had felt it impossible to say nothing in his own defense as the attacks had continued. Nevertheless, it was clear that he would be staying with the Academy.

Yet if he had agreed not to leave Germany, the decision could be changed. The agents of the German Republic now acted to prevent such a catastrophe. One was

Planck, the other was Haenisch, the German minister for education; both were determined that for the sake of German science Einstein should be discouraged from having second thoughts.

Planck wrote to Einstein on September 5, from Gmund am Tegernsee in the south Tyrol. He could scarcely believe reports of the meeting in the Berlin Philharmonic Hall and found it impossible to understand what was going on. But one thing was much more important. He was, he went on, tormented by the thought that Einstein might eventually lose patience and take a step that would punish both German science and his friends. He was able to write not only from his Olympian height but also from a position of long friendship.

He was, moreover, now supported by the minister, Haenisch:

Most respected professor [Haenisch wrote to Einstein] with sorrow and shame I see by the Press that the theory represented by you has become a public object of spiteful attacks which go far beyond the limits of pertinent criticism, and that even your own scientific personality has not been spared from defamation and slanders.

It is of special satisfaction to me to know in connection with this affair that scholars of recognized repute, among whom are prominent representatives of the University of Berlin, are supporting you, are denouncing the contemptible attacks upon your person, and are drawing attention to the fact that your scientific work has assured you a unique place in the history of science. Where the best people are defending you, it will be the easier for you to pay no further attention to such ugly actions. Therefore, I may well allow myself to express the definite hope that there is no truth in the rumours that, because of these vicious attacks, you wished to leave Berlin which always was, and always will be, proud to count you, most respected professor, among the first ornaments of the scientific world.

Einstein appears to have delayed his reply, although he no doubt acknowledged the minister's appeal. He had good reason to be cautious, for it seemed possible that the "Anti-Relativity Company" might muster considerable support, from rabble-rousers if not from scientists. And in the volatile atmosphere of early Weimar Germany there was a genuine danger of violence at Bad Nauheim, where the meeting of the Gesellschaft Deutscher Naturforscher und Ärzte was to start on September 25.

The spa is a leisurely place in the foothills of the Taunus, lying among the pines, accustomed to conferences and old people, and on the morning of September 25 its inhabitants were surprised to find the Badehaus guarded by armed police with fixed bayonets, an indication both of the extent to which anti-Semitism had already been aroused and of Weimar's wish to avoid trouble. The Badehalle was packed for the discussion on relativity.

Lenard's style can be judged from his opening words: "I have much pleasure in today taking part in a discussion on the gravitation theory of the ether. But I must say that as soon as one passes from the theory of gravitation to those of the powers of mass-proportion, the simple understanding of the scientist must take exception to the theory." One could, he went on, express the result of observations through equations; or one could explain equations in terms of observations. "I would very much favour the second idea whereas Einstein favours the first."

Einstein now rose to reply. No verbatim account appears to have survived. Dr. Friedrich Dessauer, who was sitting on Einstein's left, says that the argument was not quite as grim as was feared, and the report in the *Physikalische Zeitschrift* gives the impression of a decorous exchange and counterexchange. Born later commented, however, that Einstein "was provoked into making a caustic reply," while Einstein himself later wrote to Born saying that he would not allow himself to get excited again, as he had in Nauheim. According to Felix Ehrenhaft, he was "interrupted repeatedly by exclamations and uproar. It was obviously an organised interruption. Planck understood this and was pale as death as he raised his voice and told those making the row to be quiet."

When Einstein had finished, Lenard rose to say that he had not heard anything new. "I believe," he added, "that the fields of gravitation which have been spoken of must correspond to examples, and such examples have not yet appeared in practice." Instead of the obvious retort that the British expeditions had provided them, Einstein replied more soothingly: "I would like to say that what seems obvious to people and what does not seem obvious, has changed. Opinions about obviousness are to a certain extent a function of time. I believe that physics is abstract and not obvious, and as an example of the changing views of what is clear, and what is not, I recommend you to consider the clarity with which Galilean mechanics has been interpreted at different times."

The argument was continued at this level, and it was then discovered, no doubt to Planck's relief, that time was up. "Since the relativity theory unfortunately has not yet made it possible to extend the absolute time interval that is available for the meeting," he announced, "our session must be adjourned."

The dangerous corner had been turned. Einstein went home to Berlin, comforted. Early in October it was formally announced that he would be remaining there.

If this decision had been made solely on the same ground as his original decision to join the Kaiser Wilhelm Institute—the wish to remain in closest possible contact with the men who were investigating the nature of the physical world—this would have been understandable enough. But by 1920 it was no longer necessary for Einstein to move toward the center of interest; by now, the mountain would come to Mahomet. Einstein thus stayed on in Berlin for a tangle of motives almost as complex as those that had brought him there six years earlier. According to Frank, his reassuring letter to Haenisch, saying that he would not be leaving, had stated: "Berlin is the place to which I am bound by the closest human and scientific ties." But there was more to it than that. He believed that the Weimar Republic held out a new hope for Europe in general as well as for Germany in particular; and also, according to Frank, he felt that "it was now important for all progressively-minded elements to do everything possible to increase the prestige of the German Republic."

Einstein at home in Berlin, about 1920.
[Ullstein]

Basically, he still wanted a quiet life. He still half-believed, as he had hopefully said to Elsa toward the end of December, 1919, that "it will soon all die down." But Lenard and the "Anti-Relativity Company" had kicked him into full awareness of what anti-Semitism could really be like. Thus there was a compensation for the objectionable limelight that now burned down on him. If he had to live within its glare, he would at least make use of it, he would use the ridiculous acclaim that he was now being given to good, nonridiculous purpose. He would ensure that his fellow Jews were given all possible support in their efforts to preserve their culture, in a homeland of their own if necessary. He would fight the good fight against militarism and nationalism with all the logic and reason that he still expected other men to appreciate. And Berlin was a better place for that task than Leiden or Cambridge or Zurich.

11.

AMBASSADOR-AT-LARGE

Einstein at about the time he was to assume a new role of ambassador-at-large. [Ullstein]

By the time the Berlin church bells were ringing in 1921, it was clear that Einstein had weathered the first of the nationalist, anti-Jewish storms for which he was to act as lightning rod. It was also clear that his fame was to be neither nine-days' nor nine-months' wonder; the blaze of public interest that had flared up throughout the world showed every sign of continuing into the foreseeable future.

He, therefore, faced a series of foreign engagements and tours, which he could hardly avoid. He faced them with mixed feelings, well aware that in spite of what he had done, he was in some ways like the men on Everest, metaphorically standing on the shoulders of predecessors. "I've had good ideas," he would say, "and so have other men. But it's been my good fortune that my ideas have been accepted." He was never in any doubt about his own worth; he had no cause to be. But in general he hated the hubbub created around him by those ignorant of the very language of science that he spoke.

There were compensations; for Einstein could now dispense his favors much as he had signed photographs during the first flush of fame at the end of 1919. Then the publicity had been made bearable by contributions that he exacted for the poor. Now the rigmarole of tours and public lectures was counterbalanced in the United States by aid to the Zionist cause, in Britain and France by the help he could bring to the forces that wanted to rebuild a new Europe, including Germany, on a basis of mutual trust. In science he had achieved almost transcendental success by paring problems down to their simplest terms. Surely, the same process would work in national politics and international affairs? Einstein walked into the lion's den devoutly believing this was so.

The first of his major tours—the thorns in the side of his colleagues at the Academy as he called them—was to the United States, primarily in support of the Zionist cause, even though he also lectured at Columbia and Princeton Universities. Before this, however, early in 1921, he visited both Prague and Vienna, returning to the former city's university as the man who had unexpectedly become its most famous professor.

In Prague he stayed with his old friend Philipp Frank, who has left a vivid account of how Einstein spoke to a crowded audience. When the clapping and cheering had died down, he said simply: "It will perhaps be pleasanter and more understandable if instead of making a speech I play a piece for you on the violin."

In two curious ways shadows from the future temporarily darkened this visit to the city where he had first sensed both the undercurrent of European anti-Semitism and the growl that he always believed to be the voice of Pan-Germanism. For despite his personal feelings he was now, for those Germans who found it convenient, a German hero. Thus a Sudeten paper could claim, on his arrival in the Czech capital, that "the whole world will now see that a race that has produced a man like Einstein, the Sudeten

German race, will never be suppressed." Here in Prague all his fears for the future, all the suspicions that the war had nurtured and that the Weimar Government had only partially subdued, rose to the surface once again. To Frank he confided one thing: his fear that he would be forced to leave Germany within ten years. He was wrong by only two years.

In Prague, also, a young man insisted on speaking to Einstein after his lecture. He had considered Einstein's mass-energy equation, and on its basis concluded it would be possible to use the energy locked within the atom for production of a new and immensely powerful explosive; furthermore, he had invented a machine which he claimed could help make such an explosive. "Calm yourself," Einstein replied. "You haven't lost anything if I don't discuss your work with you in detail. Its foolishness is evident at first glance. You cannot learn more from a longer discussion."

Einstein no doubt meant what he said. But one wonders whether the "foolishness" that he saw was purely technological, or whether his mind might not have harked back to the example of John Napier, the discoverer of logarithms, for whose work he had a profound respect. During Elizabethan times Napier invented a "tank" and the "burning mirrors" with which he hoped to destroy the Armada; but before his death he burned all records of his allegedly most deadly weapon—a device reputed to have wiped out a flock of Pentland sheep. One wonders, also, whether eighteen years later, writing his plea to Roosevelt that the Americans should investigate nuclear weapons, Einstein remembered Prague.

In Vienna, soon afterward, he gave his first big public lecture to an audience of three thousand in one of the city's largest concert halls. On realizing its size Einstein experienced a minor fit of agoraphobia, insisting that his host Felix Ehrenhaft walk with him to the hall and then sit near him:

> Einstein stayed in my house [Ehrenhaft recalled]. He came to Vienna with two coats, two pairs of trousers, two white shirts, but only one white collar. When my wife asked him if there was not something that he had left at home he answered "No." However, she found neither slippers nor toilet articles. She supplied everything including the necessary collars. However, when she met him in the hall in the morning he was barefooted, and she asked him if he didn't need slippers. He answered, "No. They are unnecessary ballast." Since his trousers were terribly crumpled, my wife pressed the second pair and put them in order so that he would be neat for the second lecture. When he stepped on to the stage she saw to her horror that he was wearing the unpressed pair.

This was the familiar Einstein *en voyage*, traveling with the minimum of baggage, forgetful of the mechanics of everyday life, and a constant worry to Elsa, who on occasion would pack a suitcase for his journeys only to find on his return that it had not been opened. The trait worried his hosts. It never worried Einstein, with his mind tied to the essentials. If the rest of the world wanted to fuss about such trivia as trousers and ties and toothbrushes, so much for the world.

From Vienna he returned to Germany. And here, during the next few months, he agreed to make a propaganda tour of the United States, during which he would speak specifically to raise money for the Hebrew University, already being built in Jerusalem.

Shortly after the trip had been settled, he received a letter from which great consequences were to flow. Dated February 14, 1921, it came from Sir Henry Miers, vice-chancellor of Manchester University, and invited Einstein to give the Adamson Lecture there at some date convenient to himself. Einstein accepted the invitation but implied that he would have to speak in German since his English was practically nonexistent and his French was imperfect. He could not settle a date, as he was already irrevocably committed to an American tour in March, but there was no doubt about his reason for acceptance: it was clear that he looked upon the invitation as evidence of a move to reestablish international links among scholars.

Einstein left Germany for the United States at the end of March, 1921. Meanwhile, Lindemann was involved in arrangements for the visit to England. He had received a letter from Freundlich and as a result wrote to Sir Henry: "Einstein would like [Freundlich] to be with him in England, if possible, to help him avoid any incidents when travelling. Freundlich's mother was English, in fact he proposes to stay with an aunt in Manchester, so that he should be able to look after the courier part of the visit." A special request to Lord Curzon, then foreign secretary, expedited the necessary visa, and Freundlich was waiting when the White Star liner *Celtic* docked at Liverpool on June 8. On board was Einstein, with his wife, somewhat exhausted after a marathon three-month tour of America but quite confident that he had helped Zionism toward a promising future.

The following day he began by addressing the members of the University Jewish Students Society on the needs of the Hebrew University, explaining what had made him "an international man," underlining the current anti-Semitism in German universities, and speaking of the Jerusalem plans as "not a question of taste but of necessity."

Later, in the main hall of the University, he came to the subject of relativity. He spoke in German throughout this first public appearance in Britain but, reported the *Manchester Guardian*—in the words of David Mitrany, a young Rumanian political scientist later to become Einstein's colleague and close personal friend at Princeton— "the excellence of his diction, together with the kindly twinkle which never ceased to shine in his eye even through the sternest run of the argument, did not fail to make their impression upon the audience." Subsequently, he was created a Doctor of Science, the first such honor to be bestowed upon a German in England since the outbreak of war

Viscount Haldane of Cloan (1856–1928), statesman, lawyer, and philosopher, with whom Einstein stayed during his visit to London in 1921. Haldane's *The Reign of Relativity* appeared in the same year. *[The Mansell Collection]*

seven years previously. Even when the objectivity of Einstein's work and nature is allowed for, his success in Britain is something of an achievement.

From Manchester, Einstein moved south to London, where Sir John Squire had added to Pope's epitaph on Newton, so that it now ran:

Nature and Nature's law lay hid in night.
God said "Let Newton be" and all was light.
It did not last: the Devil howling "Ho!
Let Einstein be!" restored the status quo.

There had been more than one change of plan in his departure from the United States and in the date of his arrival in London. "I recall...I had invitations to meet him in London and Manchester on the same night," Eddington wrote to Lindemann when he was due to see Einstein again a decade later. "This is doubtless explicable by the Principle of Indeterminacy; still I hope on this occasion you will have a more condensed distribution"—an Eddington remark comparable to his comment that Einstein had "taken Newton's plant, which had outgrown its pot, and transplanted it to a more open field."

In London the Einsteins' host was Viscount Haldane of Cloan, former secretary of state for war and former lord chancellor. Haldane had a special link both with Germany and with Einstein's philosophical outlook. He had studied at Göttingen before Einstein was born and had often returned to renew his friendships in the town; he had been sent by the British Government on an abortive mission to Germany in 1912 and had, subsequently, almost on the outbreak of war, been unwise enough to speak of Germany as his "spiritual home." Not unexpectedly, he had been hounded from office in 1915 after a propaganda campaign that alleged, among other things, that he was an illegitimate brother of the Kaiser, had a German wife—he was, in fact, a life-long bachelor—and had delayed the mobilization of the British Expeditionary Force in 1914. In a postwar Britain drained of most things except bitterness, Haldane was, therefore, in a delicate position vis-à-vis the Germans. It was certainly courageous of Einstein to have come so willingly to London; it was equally courageous of Haldane to be his host.

He had, in fact, a less than scientific interest in the visit. "Einstein arrives here in the early days of June," he wrote on May 12 to John Murray, his publisher, "and his advent will make a market for us which we must not lose." His foresight was well justified. In mid-June he was able to inform his mother that his *The Reign of Relativity*, which was to go into three editions in six weeks, was "being sold with Einstein's books in the bookshops." He had written to Einstein from his home in Queen Anne's Gate as soon as news of the proposed visit to England leaked out. "Will you do me the honour of being my guest at the above address during your London stay?" he asked. "I do not know whether you are coming alone or whether your wife will be with you. But it does not matter because the house is large enough." He followed the letter with a telegram, and

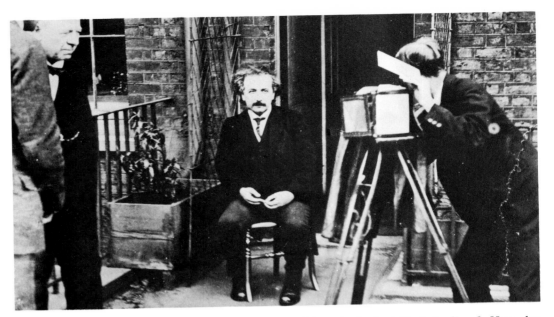

Einstein in the garden of Lord Haldane's house, Westminster, 1921. It was during this visit to England that, speaking on relativity at King's College, London, he became the first important German scientist to address a public audience in Britain after the First World War. [Ullstein]

the small *Absagen* written on it suggests that Einstein had at first declined. If so, he changed his mind—a wise course since there were few men better qualified than Haldane to convoy him through a Britain that was still uncertain whether it much wished to honor any German scientist, relativity or not.

In spite of this, "there was," Haldane wrote to his mother in Scotland on May 26, "much interest in the Einstein visit. Lord Stamfordham [private secretary to King George V] talked to me of it last night." Four days later he told her: "The social world is beginning to worry for invitations to meet Einstein, and I am sternly refusing two smart ladies—which I have no doubt they think rather brutal."

It was not only fashionable London that was anxious to meet this mystery man who had emerged from the shambles of a defeated Germany. From St. Pancras, where Haldane met the Einsteins at two o'clock on Friday the 10th, the visitors were taken directly to a meeting of the Royal Astronomical Society in Burlington House.

Here, Eddington, recently elected president, recalled how the first printed references to the General Theory had been published in England in the Society's *Monthly Notices*. He described the preliminaries to the two eclipse expeditions, and he indicated how one man's imaginative concept had changed the traditional view of the universe. Einstein, modestly smiling, accepted it all with the self-assured charm of a very bright boy.

Then the visitors were taken to Queen Anne's Gate, where a dinner party of quite exceptional nature was to be held for them that evening. Earlier, Haldane had planned a reception at which the Prime Minister was to be present. But Lloyd George had failed to meet Einstein.

The private dinner party that did duty for the reception was a glittering enough occasion. Heading the list of guests was the Archbishop of Canterbury. His apprehensions about the evening can be judged by a letter written to J. J. Thomson a few weeks earlier by Lord Sanderson, for many years a high Foreign Office official:

> The Archbishop…can make neither head nor tail of Einstein, and protests that the more he listens to Haldane, and the more newspaper articles he reads on the subject, the less he understands [Sanderson confided]. I am, or believe myself to be, in an intermediate stage, roaming the lawns and meadow leazes half way down. I therefore offered to write for the Archbishop a short sketch of what I imagined to be the pith of the theory in its more elementary form. I enclose it with his comment. It is of course very inadequate, but I fancy that as far as it goes it is not entirely at variance with Einstein's argument—some of his followers' critics seem to me to go further. But I should have been sorry to have misled the Archbishop. Do you think you could glance through it, or ask some expert to do so, and write a short note of any grosser errors?

Thomson obliged, thus helping to brief Archbishop Davidson for what seemed likely to be an intellectual tournament on the heroic scale. Also present in Queen Anne's Gate on the evening of the 10th were Eddington and Alfred Whitehead, who had been among the "chorus" at the Burlington House meeting two years earlier. Dr. Inge, the "gloomy Dean" of St. Paul's, was present with his wife. So was Bernard Shaw, Professor Harold Laski of the London School of Economics, and General Sir Ian Hamilton, the ill-starred leader from Gallipoli who had been a close friend of Haldane since the latter's days as Secretary of State for War. Over this formidable brain trust, a regiment that could have laid down an intellectual barrage sufficient to overcome most men, there presided Haldane and his sister Elizabeth, a distinguished woman in her own right and the translator of Descartes and Hegel.

The main outcome of the evening, disappointing to Haldane in some respects, must have been reassuring to the Archbishop. "I have never seen a more typical scientific lion in appearance—he might have been prepared for the role on the stage," he later wrote percipiently, "—a mass of long black hair tossed back, and a general appearance of scientific untidiness, but he was modest and quiet to talk to, and disclaimed a great deal of what is attributed to him."

Choosing his moment carefully, Davidson turned to Einstein and queried: "Lord Haldane tells us that your theory ought to make a great difference to our morale." But Einstein modestly replied: "Do not believe a word of it. It makes no difference. It is purely abstract science." This was only a brief version of his reply to an interviewer a few years later. "The meaning of relativity has been widely misunderstood," he said. "Philosophers play with the word, like a child with a doll. Relativity, as I see it, merely denotes that certain physical and mechanical facts which have been regarded as positive and permanent, are relative with regard to certain other facts in the sphere of physics and mechanics." He took the Archbishop's interest as natural, however, and noted later that more clergymen than physicists were interested in relativity. "Because," he explained when asked the reason, "clergymen are interested in the general laws of nature and physicists, very often, are not."

The Archbishop's wife fared little better than her husband. When, after dinner, she explained to Elsa how a friend had been talking about Professor Einstein's theory "especially in its mystical aspect," Mrs. Einstein broke into laughter with the words: "Mystical! Mystical! My husband mystical!" echoing his own reply to a Dutch lady, who in the German Embassy in The Hague said that she liked his mysticism. "Mysticism is in fact the only reproach that people cannot level at my theory," he had replied.

Saturday was a day of comparative rest; the following day the guests were taken

Einstein lecturing at the Collège de France, Paris, 1922. [Hebrew University of Jerusalem]

to lunch with the Rothschilds, where they met Lord Crewe and Lord Rayleigh, who had first seen Einstein at the Solvay Congress a decade earlier; and on Monday morning Einstein was taken by Haldane to Westminster Abbey where he placed a wreath on Newton's grave before being handed over to the Dean. After lunch he prepared for his first public appearance in London, at King's College in the Strand. All the tickets, sold in aid of a charity for distressed European students, were taken up well in advance, and when Haldane led Einstein on to the platform, even the gangways were filled with students. Among those in the audience were Whitehead, James Jeans, Professor Lindemann—and William Rothenstein, making notes for his remarkable portrait of Einstein, who is presented as a Struwelpeter character, smiling from an aureole of almost electrified hair.

Einstein had insisted on speaking in German—partly because of his almost nonexistent English; partly, it was reported, because he had complete confidence in English broadmindedness.

"Einstein had no notes, no hesitations and no repetitions," wrote the anonymous commentator of *The Nation*, "and the logical order in which he expounded his ideas was masterly beyond praise. One sat wondering how much of this exquisite performance was being wasted upon the audience; to how many was this carefully precise German an unintelligible noise?" As on other occasions, the objectivity of Einstein's demeanor, the other-worldliness of his dreamy eyes, and his shock of flowing hair disarmed potential critics. He talked for an hour, without interruption, somehow evoking an interest even among those who could understand little more than the occasional phrase. Then he paused and, still speaking in German, announced: "My lecture is already a little long." There was an unexpected storm of encouraging applause. "I shall take that as an invitation," he said. "But my further remarks will not be so easy to follow." Finally, he sat down. Then someone started clapping. The applause grew, and whole rows of men stood up, a spontaneous acclamation of courage as much as of relativity.

One interesting point in the lecture was Einstein's statement on the ancestry of Relativity. "I am anxious to draw attention to the fact that this theory is not speculative in origin," he said. "It owes its invention entirely to the desire to make physical theory fit observed facts as well as possible. We have here no revolutionary act, but the natural combination of a line that can be traced through centuries. The abandonment of certain notions connected with space, time, and motion, hitherto treated as fundamentals, must not be regarded as arbitrary, but only as conditioned by observed facts." Emphasis on observational experience compared with the exterior flash of intuition was really more true of the General than of the Special Theory. But it was more revealingly true of the earlier, "pro-Machian" philosophy that had so far supported Einstein than of the newer outlook that was already taking its place as his faith in sensation as the real yardstick of the physical world began to falter. When, later in life, he was asked by Hans Reichenbach, professor of philosophy in the University of California, how he had arrived at the theory of relativity, Einstein no longer mentioned observed facts. On that occasion his explanation was of a totally different kind: he had come to it, he said, because he had been "so firmly convinced of the harmony of the Universe."

There was no doubt about the success of the visit to England. As *The Nation* noted in an article headed "The Entente of the Intellectuals," the reception of the King's College lecture had marked "a definite turning-point in the post-war feeling" of Britain; the general welcome given to Einstein had gone "some way to restore the pre-war unity of culture for Europe and the civilized world." And, Haldane later wrote to Lindemann: "I think the German Ambassador was right when he told me on Monday evening that the reception of Einstein in England would do something toward making the way smoother for the approach to better international relations." Thus a main aim of the visit—a loosening of the pack ice that kept Britain and Germany apart—had been achieved.

One result of Einstein's journey was that he now felt there was a genuine hope of reopening scientific relations with Germany. It could be argued that the German aggression of 1914, and the excesses to which it led, had cleared the disease from a body politic that could now, more mature, more internationally oriented, play its part in creating a new and better Europe. Einstein, the new citizen of the Weimar Republic, sincerely hoped so.

France was a different proposition, as he realized when, early in 1922, he was invited to lecture in Paris. One impediment immediately arose. Many French scientists felt that such an invitation would imply that their hatred of the Germans was diminishing. They protested, and their protests might have succeeded had it not been for the support that Langevin obtained from Paul Painlevé. Powerful minister of war a few years earlier, and now premier and president of the Chamber of Deputies, Painlevé was a mathematician by profession, an amateur enthusiast of relativity, and he gladly gave unofficial blessing to Langevin's proposal.

In Berlin, Einstein was at first dubious: he tentatively refused the invitation. Then he mentioned it in passing to Walther Rathenau, the German minister of reconstruction. Rathenau was in many ways the antithesis of all that Einstein stood for. A German-Jewish industrialist, he had inherited control of the great Allgemeine Elektrizität-Gesellschaft and twice during the war had striven hard to save the Empire: first in

N.Y. PUBL.
PICTURE C.

Caricature of Einstein (left) and French mathematician and minister Paul Painlevé (1863–1933, right). *[AIP Niels Bohr Library]*

1916, when he had reorganized German economy to counter the effects of the British blockade; second in 1918 when, almost alone among responsible officials, he had proposed a *levée en masse* to meet the advancing Allies. With the coming of the Weimar Republic, Rathenau founded the new "Democratic Party" and rose swiftly to ministerial status. He first met Einstein in the house of a mutual friend, and Einstein invited him to the Haberlandstrasse home. The friendship ripened. Einstein was concerned by the effect that Rathenau's acceptance of a ministry might have on the position of the Jews in Germany; Rathenau, in turn, was interested in Einstein as a unique unofficial ambassador. There was no doubt about the advice he now gave. Einstein accepted.

In Paris there were fears that the visit would bring protests from French nationalists, and as arrangements for the occasion were completed, Langevin was careful to secure an apartment to which his guest could be taken in secret. Langevin himself remained uncertain of the reception to be expected and on the afternoon of March 28, 1922, traveled out from Paris to Juemont on the Belgian frontier. With him went Charles Nordmann, the astronomer of the Paris Observatory whose *Einstein and the Universe*, published in France the previous year, was a minor classic of popular description and interpretation.

At the frontier station they found their guest unassumingly sitting in the corner of a second-class compartment. Nordmann had never met him, and it is clear from his account that he was vastly impressed—not so much by the "creator of worlds," which would have been natural enough, as by the physical presence of the man:

192

The first impression that one gets is of astonishing youth [Nordmann wrote]. Einstein is big (he is about 1 m 76), with large shoulders and the back only very slightly bent. His head, the head where the world of science has been re-created, immediately attracts and fixes the attention. His skull is clearly, and to an extraordinary degree, brachycephalic, great in breadth and receding toward the nape of the neck without exceeding the vertical. Above all, the impression is one of disconcerting youth, strongly romantic, and at certain moments evoking in me the irrepressible idea of a young Beethoven, on which meditation had already left its mark, and who had once been beautiful. And then, suddenly, laughter breaks out and one sees a student. Thus appeared to us the man who has plumbed with his mind, deeper than any before him, the astonishing depths of the mysterious universe.

The three men faced a four-hour journey, from which Nordmann remembered some revealing remarks. When they began to talk of quantum problems, Einstein noted, significantly: "That is a wall before which one is stopped. The difficulties are terrible; for me, the theory of relativity was only a sort of respite which I gave myself during their examination." And, remarking that there was something crazy about it, he went on: "But there, physicists are all a bit crazy, aren't they. But it's just the same with racehorses: what one buys one has to sell!"

When they discussed the worldwide interest that his ideas had aroused, Einstein noted, as he repeatedly did with undisguised amazement: "It's unbelievable." Of the opposition to him and his ideas in Germany he commented, putting his hands on his chest: "So long as they don't get violent, I want to let everyone say what they wish, for I myself have always said exactly what pleased me." And, asked about the left-wing parties, he said, with a broad smile: "I don't know what to say about that since I believe that the Left is *une chose polydimensionelle*."

On the afternoon of Friday, March 31, he was driven to the Collège de France. Here, in the main hall, where Ernest Renan, Henri Bergson, and other giants of the French establishment had lectured, he explained the conflict between classical relativity and electrodynamics in a slow French to which his slight accent added a touch of mystery. Langevin sat immediately behind, ready to prompt him with the occasional word if he hesitated. Madame Curie was among the audience. So was Bergson. But the room was not packed as some had expected. Tickets had been sent only to a restricted number of scientists and students with a special interest in the subject. Paul Painlevé himself stood by the door, checking the formal invitations.

Einstein spoke to other selected audiences during the next few days, to the philosophical and mathematical sections of the Collège de France and, on April 6, to a session of the French Philosophical Society at the Sorbonne. Langevin was again present, as well as Bergson and Painlevé. His reception was kind if questioning, an attitude less critical than that of Emile Picard, permanent secretary of the French Academy of Sciences, who was quoted as saying: "On the subject of relativity I see red."

193

No-man's-land at Lens, one of the French towns destroyed during the fighting of the First World War. [The Mansell Collection]

As well as the French people, the French press was of two minds about the problem of how to regard members of the nation they had fought for more than four long years. "If a German were to discover a remedy for cancer or tuberculosis," asked one paper, "would these thirty academicians have to wait for the application of the remedy until Germany joined the League?" Among others that tried to edge their readers toward conciliation was the paper with the large headline: "Einstein in Paris! It is the victory of the archangel over the demon of the abyss."

During the journey into Paris Einstein had confided to Nordmann that he would like to see the battlefields, and on the last day of his visit he was collected from his apartment at six-thirty in the morning by Nordmann and Langevin. They were quickly among the ruins of war, a landscape of flattened villages, moldering trenches, and entire forests leveled by artillery barrage. Frequently, they stopped and dismounted. Einstein, visibly shaken, bewildered and almost uncomprehending that war could really have been like this, even worse than the propagandists claimed. At one point, among devastated farms and beside trees withered by gas, he turned to his friends. "All the students of Germany must be brought here," he said, "all the students of the world, so that they can see how ugly war really is. People often have a wrong idea because it comes from books. Thus most Germans have an image of Frenchmen that is purely literary; and many men have an equally literary idea of war and the ruins that it creates. How necessary it is that they should come and *see*."

They went through St. Quentin, where the Americans had first gone into action in strength, and then into the ruins of Rheims, Einstein stopping from time to time with the single word "Terrible." From Rheims they drove north across fifty miles of devastation, and Einstein was put on the train to Cologne. As it prepared to move off, he waved his broad-brimmed hat toward the German frontier: "I will describe all I have seen to the people over there."

Einstein was still concentrating on reconciliation. Some Frenchmen, it had been clear from his experiences in Paris, were ready to stretch out their hands. And it was with this fact very much in mind that on June 11 he addressed a meeting of the German Peace Federation on the floor of the Reichstag. He made a plea for European unity, deplored the differences created by language, and said that in future men of goodwill should ask, not "What can be done for my country?" but rather "What must my country do to make it possible for the greater entity to exist?"

Perhaps there was at last a chance to build a new world from the postwar chaos. Perhaps there was more than a glimmer of hope for Europe. Einstein thought so, and when he was invited by Sir Eric Drummond, secretary-general of the League of Nations,

First International Anti-War Museum in Berlin, opened by Ernest Friedrich, author of *War Against War*. [The Mansell Collection]

to join the newly formed International Committee on Intellectual Co-operation, he quickly agreed. The Weimar Republic was still threatened from within, a prickly bitterness still hampered Franco-German relations, and a sense of imminent chaos suffused Berlin itself. Even so, it did appear that the forces that stood for international reconstruction, for the slow painful business of recasting Germany in a less military mold so that she could live with her Continental neighbors, were at last gaining strength.

Then, on June 24, 1922, Walther Rathenau was assassinated by right-wing extremists as he left his home in the Berlin Grunewald.

The murder was part of a pattern. Earlier in the month two Nationalists had only just failed to kill Herr Scheidemann, the former prime minister, and a few days after Rathenau's death attackers seriously wounded another prominent Jew, the publicist Maximilian Harden.

Einstein saw Rathenau's murder as symbolic of a rising tide of anti-Semitism, which would soon be lapping around his own feet.

On July 4, he wrote to Geneva resigning from the International Committee. At the same time, he explained to Madame Curie, whom he had only recently recommended to accept, that he was doing so not only because of Rathenau's assassination but because of anti-Semitism among the people he was supposed to represent.

However, this was only a beginning, and two days later he canceled a lecture he had planned to give to the Natural Science Society in Berlin.

Madame Curie now wrote pleading with him to stay on the League of Nations Committee, saying that this would have been Rathenau's reaction. Einstein replied that she did not understand the situation in Germany and added that it was quite impossible for a Jew to serve both the Germans and an international intelligentsia.

By mid-July, 1922, he was thus yet again resigned to being driven from the country. He had lived there eight years, longer than he had lived anywhere since his youth. Now, once more, it seemed that he would be moving on. And now, as in 1919 and 1920, he was dissuaded from going at the last moment: from going possibly to Holland, possibly to Switzerland. This time he was dissuaded by Pierre Comert of the League of Nations, who appealed to him on much the same grounds as Madame Curie: to leave Germany now would be to abandon ship. Einstein decided to stay, for the moment, both in Germany and on the League Committee.

Some grounds for confidence were indeed provided the following month at the centennial meeting of the Gesellschaft Deutscher Naturforscher und Ärzte held in Leipzig. Einstein, still anxious not to provide too easy a target for the anti-Semites, had refused to attend as a key speaker. But the authorities had insisted on making relativity an important feature, and lectures on it were planned by Von Laue and others. As soon as this became known, the former members of the "Anti-Relativity Company" went into action, preparing a broadsheet that was sent to the papers and distributed in Leipzig as the conference opened. Those who signed it formed an even less impressive group than had been mustered at Bad Nauheim the previous year. It looked as though the anti-relativity plank in the anti-Semites' platform was cracking.

But Einstein was by this time alert enough to realize that the situation might change once again, just as significantly and just as quickly. Doubts remained beneath the brave front that he put on affairs—even though in the autumn of 1922 he was given one recognition that many felt he should have received earlier: the Nobel Prize for Physics.

However, it is possibly truer in the case of physics than in the other subjects for which the Prize is awarded—chemistry, physiology or medicine, literature, and peace—that considerable time must pass before achievements can be properly evaluated. The Prizes, moreover, were awarded for a "discovery"; furthermore, it should be one from which mankind had derived great use. Now it was questionable whether the Special Theory was, strictly speaking, a "discovery" at all; even if it were, it was still difficult to claim that by the early 1920s mankind had derived any great use from it. Relativity was already a commonplace tool in the laboratory when subatomic particles were being investigated, but this was not what Nobel had meant. During the autumn of 1922, however, the Academy decided that it could make the award and yet dodge the difficult relativity issues. The prize was awarded "independently of such value as may be ultimately attached to his theories of relativity and gravity, if these are confirmed, for his services to the theory of physics, and especially for discovery of the law of the photoelectric effect." Here, they were on safe ground; for the photoelectric law was not only a discovery revealing the quantitative relationship between light and the emission of electrons, but was even by the early 1920s being utilized in practical ways.

The announcement produced an anguished inquiry from the Swiss and German ambassadors in Stockholm, both of whom wanted to claim Einstein as their own. The result was a mixture of pathos and farce, which was not without international interest; for on the answer to the question depended the country whose ambassador could support Einstein at the elaborate Nobel Prize ceremony and at the state banquet given by the king of Sweden every year in honor of the prizewinners.

Einstein was traveling on a Swiss passport, a fact that the German Foreign Office immediately passed on to the German ambassador, Herr Nadolny, but which Nadolny, in the professional nature of things, was reluctant to take at its face value. He appears to have been justified. For when he telegraphed an inquiry to the Berlin

Einstein with his violin and Elsa Einstein at the piano, Imperial Hotel, Tokyo, 1922. *[Culver Pictures]*

Academy of Sciences at the beginning of December, he immediately received the reply: *"Einstein ist Reichsdeutscher."* "The Swiss ambassador was surprised when I told him this," Nadolny later wrote. "However, when I described the telegram to him he calmed down and accepted the situation with the comment that Einstein was generally looked upon as a German and probably now wished to be considered as a German." Nadolny, on his part, was equally gracious, suggesting to Berlin that Switzerland's part in Einstein's life and work should be stressed in any announcement to the papers and later proposing that the Swiss ambassador might, "as a worthwhile courtesy," be invited to the Nobel Lecture that Einstein was to give in Stockholm. The outcome was, in fact, a compromise. Einstein himself was unable to accept the award personally, being out of Europe on December 11, the anniversary of Nobel's death on which the prizes are awarded. This lucky chance enabled both the Germans and the Swiss to play parts in the act. In Stockholm the award was received by the German ambassador on Einstein's behalf, but in Berlin it was handed over to him, at his own request, not by the Swedish ambassador to Germany but by the Swiss. But in the Nobel records Einstein was recorded as "German."

One result of the imbroglio was that the Berlin Academy was instructed by the German minister of science, art, and popular education to elucidate once and for all the riddle of Einstein's nationality. Its report, made on January 13, 1923, merely stated that since all civil servants must be Germans and Einstein had in 1914 become a civil servant, "it must be inferred" that he was German, "even if he did not possess it [German nationality] from birth." The earlier Swiss nationality was not involved, it concluded, and the Academy, therefore, considered their man "chiefly Reichsdeutscher," the "chiefly" being a qualification that may have crept into the argument due either to caution or an inability to find the vital documents.

This, however, was not the end of the matter. When Einstein returned to Germany early in 1923, he was asked by the Academy to put forward his own views. He gave them on March 24, 1923, reiterating that when he had accepted the Berlin appointments in 1914, he had stipulated that he must be able to retain his Swiss nationality. In one way this was irrelevant. At issue was not his retention of Swiss nationality but whether he had, on moving to the University, automatically become German as well.

A group of German physicists and chemists in Berlin, 1920. Seated in front row (left to right): Hertha Sponer, Albert Einstein, Frau Franck, James Franck, Lise Meitner, Fritz Haber, and Otto Hahn; back row (left to right): Walther Grotrian, Wilhelm Westphal, Otto von Baeyer, Peter Pringsheim, and Gustav Hertz. [Bildarchiv Preussischer Kulturbesitz]

The German civil service would not easily let go—and it was supported by the German consul general in Barcelona, who reported to Berlin after Einstein's visit to Spain in 1923: "On the whole the local visit of Einstein, who, however, always appears as German not as Swiss, is reckoned a complete success, as much for himself and for German science as for German-Spanish cultural relations."

On May 14, 1923, the minister wrote to Einstein stating that there was nothing in the records concerning his nationality and advising that if he wished the matter to be finally settled he should get in touch with a senior civil servant, Dr. von Rothenburg. The interview took place six months later. Its result was a statement by Einstein, dated February 7, 1924, in which he accepted the situation. There the affair rested until, nine years later, Einstein gave up his passport in the German Embassy in Brussels and walked off German soil for the last time.

The Nobel Prize money went to Mileva. Even Einstein's closest friends did not know this, and Lorentz wrote happily that, quite apart from the honor, there was "a material side to the Nobel Prize and I trust that this will ease the cares of your daily life." By this time his financial position was, in fact, more reassuring. Requests to lecture came thick and fast, and it was the acceptance of one of these—arranged by a Japanese publisher—that had taken him from the country during the Nobel ceremonies. Acceptance of the Japanese invitation was very much a leap in the dark, and both his brief diary notes and the oblique references in several newspaper interviews suggest that in practice it turned out to be a disillusioning experience, even though he liked what he considered to be the simple, gentle Japanese. Little more might have been expected. He had been invited to lecture from one end of the country to the other, all expenses paid; he should not have been surprised if he was to be milked hard in the process.

He and Elsa arrived in Japan in mid-November. He held a press conference at the Imperial Hotel in Tokyo and then prepared for his first lecture. This was to be given in the main hall of Keio University, and by the time that he was due, the *Japan Weekly Chronicle* recorded, "the hall was filled with scholars, teachers and students. Some women were present, too." There was also Mr. Yamamoto Sanehiko, the proprietor of *Kaizosha*. Einstein began speaking at 1:30 P.M. and continued for three hours, a formidable effort even allowing time for translation. After this there was an hour's break, presumably for what might be called light refreshments. At 5:30 he was back at the rostrum once more. He started where he had left off, apparently delighted at having such attentive listeners and continued for another three hours. "The audience," it was reported, "were astonished at his staying power."

It was an auspicious start to what was on the whole an unsatisfactory tour. The Einsteins were introduced to the emperor and the empress, a singular honor, and Einstein later recorded how he had spoken with the empress in French. They attended the Feast of Chrysanthemums in the Imperial Gardens, and there were a number of other formal receptions before the start of the month-long tour. The audiences to which he now spoke were less serious than those in Tokyo, being attracted by his name as much as by the almost mystic significance that relativity had assumed for the Japanese. Not everyone welcomed its new status. "The excessive reliance on science and the contempt for faith have made a failure of the last century or so," noted the *Japan Weekly Chronicle*. "It is sad to reflect that the Japanese should nevertheless be so elated over a new scientific theory."

By the end of December Einstein was thankful to board ship for Europe. He arrived back in Berlin only a few weeks before an announcement in Washington gave further support to the General Theory. The previous September there had been another total eclipse of the sun, visible throughout a narrow belt stretching from Somaliland across the Indian Ocean to Australia, and a number of expeditions had been sent out to gather further evidence for or against the theory.

Seven months later it was revealed that their figures supported Einstein. Hundreds of star images were recorded on their four special phototelescopes, and some scores of these, shown on ten plates, had been selected for calculation and checking. On April 12, 1923, Professor W. W. Campbell of the Lick Observatory reported that the prints taken on September 21 and compared with those taken at Tahiti three months before the eclipse showed agreement with Einstein's prediction "as close as the most ardent proponent of the relativity theory could hope for."

Not everyone was pleased. "It is an interesting commentary on the reluctance of many leading men of science to accept the relativity theory," says Eddington's biographer, "that when Campbell was asked what he anticipated from the eclipse plates, he replied: 'I hoped it would not be true.' Undoubtedly some Fellows of the Royal Society and even a few in the Royal Astronomical Society felt the same way."

Back in Germany from Japan, Einstein must have felt that his travels were over, for the time being. His fears of the previous summer were evaporating, and he now looked forward to an untroubled continuation of work in Berlin.

But early in November he was suddenly jerked awake again to his position in Germany and to the dangerous situation of anyone who fraternized with communists. During the first days of the month he was visited by a prominent Jewish leader who appears to have advised him that his life was in danger. Just how serious the warning was is not known. But on November 7, Einstein wrote Planck a letter—no copy of which appears to have survived—saying that he was leaving the country for a few days and canceling a dinner date with Planck at his Haberlandstrasse home for the evening of the 9th.

Planck failed to receive the letter and arrived at the Einstein home on the 9th only to be received by Elsa with news of her husband's sudden departure for Leiden. Both had good cause for alarm. For between the writing of Einstein's letter on the 7th and Planck's arrival in the Haberlandstrasse, the National Socialists, led by Hitler and supported by General Ludendorff, had begun their attempt to take over the Bavarian Government in Munich as prelude to a march on Berlin. There had been fighting during the day, and what was to happen next was still uncertain.

Einstein's flight was not, in fact, linked with the Munich putsch. It was, rather, an indication of the anti-Semitic climate of the times; but on the night of the 9th it can hardly have looked fortuitous. But the rising was put down, and on November 10 Planck wrote to Einstein in Leiden, pleading with him yet again not to accept any of the offers which would no doubt be made to him.

There is no evidence whatever that Einstein suffered from personal fear; rather the reverse. But he wanted to get on with his work; he knew that there would be little chance of that under a National Socialist government, and it was in character that until he learned that the putsch had been crushed, he should seek the security of Leiden. It was equally in character that Planck should write to him in the name of German science and implore him to come back. He came. In 1923, as in 1914, Berlin still provided—as long as Weimar remained—the intellectual climate in which he could best get on with his work.

Einstein in Berlin, 1922. *[Ullstein]*

12. UNTER DEN LINDEN

Einstein returned from Holland to Berlin toward the end of November, 1923. For the next decade the city was his base for a central, consolidating period of his life. But what consolidated was not only the physicist with the international reputation, the man who had shown the universe to be built differently from accepted ideas. This absentminded scientist turning his huge, luminous, and inquiring eyes on visitors, behaving at times with an almost studied childlike simplicity, more an actor playing Einstein than the man himself, was only one facet. It was matched by another, by the man whom the President of the United States and the Emperor of Japan had been honored to meet, the Nobel Prize winner coaxed into helping the League of Nations, the physicist whose advice was constantly sought by the more formidable of the Jewish leaders. Moreover, this Swabian, whose triumphs in the realm of abstract thought had brought him the fame of an oracle and the veneration that goes with it, had during the transformation decided to use the reputation that chance had unexpectedly tossed him. He would campaign with the Zionists for a Jewish homeland in Palestine, and he would help build a new Europe—although whether it should be built on unarmed pacifist goodwill or beneath the umbrella of international arms was something that he found difficult to decide.

Yet Einstein was handicapped in all his efforts to implement his good intentions by the very qualities that made him the genius he was. First, and of overwhelming importance, was his determination to devote as much time as possible to discovering how the physical world was built. Kurt Blumenfeld, who recruited Einstein into the Zionist cause, shrewdly noted of him to Weizmann that "Zionism and Palestine were only peripheral concerns"; and in 1923 Einstein himself told Weizmann that he would give his name and talk to people in Berlin but would not "travel around or visit congresses." His dedication to the pacifist cause was equally unquestioned between 1919 and 1933. But his enthusiasm had perpetually to contend with the fact that there were scientific papers to be written or read, and men like Planck or Sommerfeld or Von Laue to discuss them with. Thus he was forced to overlook his homework, to skimp his practice in a game where there is always a watcher in the slips waiting to catch a man out.

Finally, there was his dislike of formalities and his sense of the ridiculous. He did not mind what he looked like, and he often did not mind what he said. He was, quite simply, too unconcerned to worry about trifles, even when circumstances began to push him more frequently than his scientific colleagues on to the public stage, where trifles matter more frequently. But they managed to look like figures from the great drama of public affairs; he too often evoked something less serious. It was thus inevitable that he should occupy a large place in human hearts and a small one in the corridors of power.

Albert Einstein in middle age, as Director of the Kaiser Wilhelm Institute, Berlin. *[The Bettmann Archive]*

In the capital Einstein not only occupied a unique position but lived under conditions more favorable than those he had previously been used to. For the first time in his life he had one home for more than a few years. To counteract the undertow of anti-Semitic nationalism, quiescent for a while but never very far below the surface, there was the respect of the university and the Kaiser Wilhelm Institute, which he knew was his due. In Leiden, where he delighted to stay with the Ehrenfests on his visits as professor extraordinary, he was enormously popular. Royalties from his book on relativity and his fees from Leiden helped to raise him from the rut of most professors; he had always been careless of money but now he could almost afford to be. He had his music, and he had his sailing—on a fine choice of lakes that ringed Berlin with the circlet of watery fingers that were to be marker points for the bombers in the Second World War whatever the camouflage experts could do. He had, moreover, an entree into the polyglot world of educated industrialists and civilized financiers, of artists and actors and designers, who during the first years of Weimar, appeared to have taken over the privileged position in the state so long occupied by the military. On the crest of the wave he became for a while almost as human as other men, expanding in the Weimar renaissance.

It was during this period that he walked one evening, as described by his doctor, Janos Plesch, to a favorite restaurant with the Russian physicist Joffé, with Plesch, and with a third companion. Einstein and Joffé, walking behind the other couple, were talking loudly, and Einstein burst out in a roar of enjoyment. When they caught up with their friends, Einstein explained: "Poor old Joffé can't make up his mind through which hole an electron will go if he fires it through a lead obstacle with a number of holes. An electron is indivisible, and therefore it must go through one hole only. But which hole? And the solution"—with a gust of Einstein laughter—"is really very simple; it goes through the fifth dimension." Physics was still, as yet, too important to be taken too seriously.

Einstein's base for operations was, of course, Haberlandstrasse 5, where his wife quietly helped to organize his life and where his stepdaughter Ilse often acted as secretary. The most important room in the apartment was Einstein's study in a corner turret of the block, reached by a small staircase and with a view only of rooftops and the sky. Here were the books, a round table in the small window alcove stacked with papers, notes, references, and an assortment of pamphlets. Here also, almost hidden on top of a bookcase, was the cigar box surreptitiously filled from time to time by Einstein's friends, who knew how Elsa tried to ration him to one a day for the sake of his health. The study was Einstein's absolute preserve. No cleaner was allowed in. Neither was Elsa.

Here, he worked on as the "relativity industry" continued to flood the Continent, as well as Britain and the United States with explanations that ranged from the

Left: Einstein in the study of his home on Haberlandstrasse in Berlin, 1926. [Bildarchiv Preussischer Kulturbesitz]

Right: Silhouettes of Einstein, his second wife, Elsa, and his stepdaughters, Ilse and Margot, made by Einstein. [Hebrew University of Jerusalem]

erudite to the simpleminded. "The stream continues," wrote E. Cunningham in *Nature* in June, 1922. "Here are seven more books on relativity." The previous year a bibliography prepared by the director of the International Catalogue of Scientific Literature included nearly six hundred and fifty papers, articles, and books dealing with the subject, and many score more had been added by the time that Dr. Cunningham settled down to his reviewing.

The study did not only see Einstein at work on those problems of the natural world that obsessed all physicists. Here, he dealt also as best he could with the torrent of appeals and begging letters, and requests for advice that poured down on him during these years of fame and notoriety. If Einstein could prove that light did not go straight, then he could do anything, however impossible it sounded. Such was a common belief.

He was much tried in other ways. The flat-earthers, the spiritualists, the inveterate believers, all latched on to the apparent enigma of relativity to bolster their own ideas. Sometimes they rolled many of them into one packet, like the author of *Spiritism: The Hidden Secret in Einstein's Theory of Relativity* for whom Hebrew words, the "uranium cubic diatonal," and mystic numbers all contributed to the secret.

To those in his own line of country, Einstein was always generous of time, money, and effort, a fact that quickly permeated the academic world. Thus the young foreign student who wished to study chemistry in Bonn, had been rejected by the Prussian Ministry of Education, and who knew it was against the law to make a second application, wrote as a matter of course to Einstein. He sent his entire biography, with every detail. "When you are twenty," he wrote years later, "you feel as important as I did. You are certain that the whole world appreciates this importance. Einstein did." Einstein not only recommended a second, albeit unlawful, application but produced for enclosure a letter from himself supporting the application and denouncing the injustice.

At one level, the physicist who technically headed the Kaiser Wilhelm Institute for Physics, still being developed, was the remote genius who had changed the human picture of the universe. At another level, he was the Einstein who delighted in taking control of the elevator in his Haberlandstrasse block and manipulating the buttons so that guests were whisked up, back, then up and down again past the floor at which they wished to alight. This was the Einstein who, when nagged about well-worn dress clothes, would say: "I will simply fasten a notice to it saying: 'This suit has just been cleaned.'" He retained the mixture of clown and small boy delighted with simple jokes, engrossed by absurdities. He was always ready to respond to the ridiculous challenge, and when a group of eminent friends called for him one evening, he accepted a bet to take off his vest without first removing his jacket. He was wearing his only dress suit, but immediately began a series of elaborate contortions. These continued for some time. It seemed he would have to pay up. Then, with a final tortuous twist he did the trick, triumphantly waving his crumpled vest and exploding into his long, deep belly laugh. This was not at all the thing for the quieter waters of Berlin academic society. It was not even the thing for

Einstein with his stepdaughter, Margot, and her husband, Dmitri Marianoff, in Berlin, 1927. [Bundesarchiv]

some of Einstein's friends, such as Haber with his perfectly run home. Ehrenhaft recalls how on one occasion he and his wife arrived at the Habers together with Einstein and Elsa, both men properly dinner-jacketed. As they sat down in the drawing room Elsa exclaimed: "But Albert, you haven't put your socks on." "Yes, yes," he replied, unblinkingly. "I have already disclosed the secret to Frau Ehrenhaft."

The stories of Einstein's reluctance to attend formal functions, to play the social lion in the expected way, are still numerous and must have been more so in the Berlin of half a century ago. Many are certainly apocryphal, but some ring true, as when he replied to a Berlin hostess who had described her list of guests: "So you would like me to serve as a table centre?" His frequent description of the more formal social functions was "Feeding time at the Zoo," while of academic dinners, he confessed to one of his sons-in-law: "On occasions like this I retire to the back of my mind and there I am happy." He genuinely hated it all—announcing to a companion as he joined one dinner party: "Now I go on the trapeze."

205

Einstein in 1921, standing at the entrance of the Einstein Tower solar observatory, Potsdam, Berlin, designed by Erich Mendelsohn. [Ullstein]

These newsworthy stigmata of the *enfant terrible*, like his frequent avowals of humility, sprang from deeply rooted convictions. And what often appeared to be awkwardness for awkwardness' sake was the natural action of a natural man. "I am happy because I want nothing from anyone," he once told an American correspondent. "I do not care for money. Decorations, titles, or distinctions mean nothing to me. I do not crave praise. The only thing that gives me pleasure, apart from my work, my violin and my sailboat, is the appreciation of my fellow-workers." Here is a hint of the bridge between the skylarking clown—the eccentric who at times gives the impression of acting with one eye on posterity—and the dedicated scientist.

It was this fierce dedication, as much as the revelations of the eclipse expeditions, that helped to set him apart from other scientists. At the lower levels, men said that only three physicists understood the riddles of the world—Einstein, Planck, and Lorentz. More to the point was Planck's reply to Freundlich, who one day presented him with a problem and hoped for an answer off the cuff. Freundlich's widow long recalled how her husband repeated to her what Planck had said: "I shall have to think about it and then I will write down the answer. I cannot provide it at once, just like that. Einstein could do so. I cannot."

Einstein was lucky in Berlin in having at least some support from industry. The prediction that light reaching the earth from the stars would be altered in frequency by the gravitational field through which it passed had interested Freundlich since his first contacts with Einstein. He had close connections with German business, and soon after the war persuaded a number of industrialists, notably Dr. Bosch, a director of I. G. Farben, to finance an institute that could investigate the phenomenon. This was the Einstein Institute in Potsdam, later to be amalgamated with the Royal Observatory there as the Institute for Solar Research. Throughout the 1920s a long series of observations was made from it. The results were inconclusive, a fact that may have played its part in the gradual estrangement between Einstein and Freundlich. Certainly, Planck took it that there had been a definite rupture in their relations—so much so that he wrote to Freundlich offering to intervene. Memories must be taken with caution; but Freundlich, with his Scots ancestry, was remarkably British in looks, sympathies, and demeanor. Einstein, in the early 1920s, had great hopes for Germany. "It was almost," said Frau Freundlich, thinking back with a pin-sharp perception that cannot be discounted, "as though my husband was too British, not Jewish enough."

The heart of the Institute was a long-focus telescope accommodated in a sixty-foot tower, surrounded by a second tower, built of stone. The sunlight reflected down this was turned through ninety degrees and taken along a forty-foot room, partly sunk in the

Einstein and Professor Ludendorf, chairman of the Congress of Astronomy, Potsdam, September 13, 1921. [United Press International]

ground. The demands made on the architect, Erich Mendelsohn, were considerable, and he satisfied them by designing a building in marked contrast to those standing nearby in the grounds of the Astro-Physical Observatory. They, built at the end of the previous century, were in the sober traditional Prussian style and utilized the red bricks of the Mark Brandenburg. Mendelsohn's "Einstein Tower," as it was soon known, was a concrete construction whose flowing white outlines were in some ways symbolic of the artistic renaissance already sweeping the Weimar Republic. It was even suggested that while the older buildings with their separate bricks epitomized the Euclidean concept of mathematics and atomic structure as understood at the turn of the century, Mendelsohn's long elegant curves epitomized post-Einsteinian physics. Certainly, the building became one of the things to be seen in Potsdam, and more than one tourist agency added the Einstein Tower to its tour of the Potsdam palaces.

Not everyone liked the new building. Photographs were taken to illustrate its slightly bizarre outline, and among the German papers that described it, there was one that called it "a cross between a New York skyscraper and an Egyptian pyramid."

The architecture of the Institute was, in fact, to play its own small part in the anti-Einstein campaign, which grew with the rise of the National Socialist party in the 1930s. For, it was asked, was it not in keeping that investigation of the absurd relativity theory should be carried out in a grotesque building that had no roots in German traditions? Was it not typical that the theory of the Jew Einstein should be investigated by the half-Jew Freundlich from a building that offended so deeply the decent nationalist traditions? A small point, but one not to be ignored by any competent rabble-rouser.

Einstein's observations with Freundlich were fitted into gaps between many other duties. He had an office in the Academy of Sciences, and his work at the Kaiser Wilhelm Institute took a good deal of time. Under his agreement with the university he did not have to lecture, but he nevertheless did so fairly frequently. On these occasions, as at most other Continental universities, attendance was not restricted to students taking specific courses. Some came more out of curiosity than scientific interest, and it was easy even for nonstudents to slip in as long as they did not cause trouble. On more than one occasion a ripple of anticipation passed through the listeners as a prostitute in full war paint came in, sat in one of the back rows to see for herself what the great man was like, and then left as silently as she had come. Einstein would continue unchecked; but it was clear from his quizzical half-smile that he noticed.

Every Thursday afternoon he attended the special students' physics seminar, watching for talent, listening to ideas, quite happy if even the youngest member of the group could suggest a line of thought worth following.

207

Left: Einstein with his violin and Paul Ehrenfest at the piano. Watercolor by Maryke Kamerlingh Onnes. [AIP Niels Bohr Library]

Right: Paul Ehrenfest (left), Ehrenfest's son, and Einstein, in Ehrenfest's home in Leiden, June, 1920. [Museum Boerhaave, Leiden]

There were also the seminars organized by Von Laue at which the latest scientific papers would be discussed by Planck, Nernst, Haber, Lise Meitner, or Einstein. These members of the university staff would occupy the front row of the old university building in which the meetings were held. Behind them there often sat physicists from the larger German industrial firms, invited men whose presence in the rarified upper atmosphere of the academic world was a sign of the cooperation that had strengthened the country's industrial sinews since the start of the century.

Then the talking started. "Sometimes he would step up to the blackboard," says Professor Cornelius Lanczos, who was his assistant for a while. "Then, all at once, what had seemed complicated seemed simple." The transformation was stimulating.

On one occasion there was present the young Hungarian who became the *deus ex machina* of Einstein's later years, an extraordinary character well meriting his soubriquet of "the grey eminence of physics." This was Leo Szilard, the man who on March 12, 1934—more than four years before Otto Hahn split the uranium atom, more than five years before Einstein's famous letter to Roosevelt—applied for a patent covering the laws of a nuclear chain reaction and later filed it as a secret Admiralty patent in London because of his "conviction that if a nuclear chain reaction can be made to work it can be used to set up violent explosions." In 1922, Szilard was only twenty-four. But he was a student in whom Einstein quickly saw one of those men, rich in ideas, who create intellectual and spiritual life wherever they are. He soon became a regular visitor to the Haberlandstrasse home.

Einstein's self-imposed duties at the university, his collaboration with Freundlich at the Potsdam Observatory, and his work at the Kaiser Wilhelm Institute would have been enough to occupy the mental energies of a normal man; to him, it was the background to more important things. What still concerned him most was any indication that he, or physicists elsewhere in the world, were touching things nearer the heart of nature. Thus he was a familiar figure at conferences, picking out the men he wanted to meet but dodging the social round. He conferred with Bohr in Denmark and was a frequent visitor to Holland, where he never missed a chance of seeing Lorentz.

In Leiden he usually stayed with the Ehrenfests, writing his name on the huge white wall of the study that did duty for a visitors' book and relaxing as he did in few other places.

He also wanted the company of children, although it was not in his nature to admit it. Therefore, he was a happy man when he took Ehrenfest's small children and their companions down to the seacoast dunes a few miles away and let them bury him up to the neck in the sands without a trace of concern. He was happy when he stood at the open windows of Ehrenfest's study on a summer evening, playing the violin in his shirtsleeves while Ehrenfest accompanied him on the grand piano in the book-lined room.

Even in Leiden he could be plucked out of his freedom. There is a record of one uproarious occasion on which Einstein and Ehrenfest were awakened by the telephone from an after-lunch siesta. Queen Wilhelmina, the Prince Regent, and Emma the Queen Mother, were visiting the Marine School in Leiden. They had heard that Einstein was "in residence," and they requested that he and his host should attend the reception being held later that same day. Einstein knew that his nearest black suit was five hundred miles away in Berlin. Ehrenfest knew that his solitary specimen was lying in a mothproofed trunk in the attic. Frau Ehrenfest rose to the occasion by telephoning several professors of Einstein's build and begging them to have their suits delivered as soon as possible. A few hours later the two men presented themselves to their Majesties, Einstein in a suit that fitted where it touched, Ehrenfest smelling strongly of mothballs.

This was only the beginning of a difficult evening. After a formal shaking of hands by the Queen, the two men tried to disappear in the crowd, duty done, honor satisfied—and now to get out of those clothes. They had not gone far when they were cut off by the Queen Mother's adjutant and asked to return. "I noticed that you tried to escape me, but I managed to catch you," she said according to the story that Einstein and his friend told their neighbor. "Surely you could offer your hand to an old lady too."

Einstein's regular visits to Leiden, the amiable round of work in Berlin, his interest in the affairs of Zionism in general and of the Hebrew University in particular, as well as a steadily increasing involvement in the problem of world peace, were all interrupted in 1925 by a lecture tour to South America. In itself, this was of little importance in his life. Indirectly, it was of great significance since it caused him to turn down an invitation to the California Institute of Technology later in the same year. Had he accepted, it is unlikely that he would have spent the last two decades of his life in Princeton.

There were many reasons why Einstein would have enjoyed a visit to the United States in 1925, not the least being that two quite separate but equally important confirmations of his "heuristic viewpoint" of 1905 had come from American scientists. The first was given by Robert Millikan who as a professor at the University of Chicago had in 1915 determined the size of the charge on a single electron. Eight years later Arthur Compton found that when X-rays were scattered by matter, the wavelength of some was lengthened; in other words, their energy was decreased.

Millikan had met Einstein briefly during 1921 in Chicago. Later in the year he moved to California as head of the Troop College of Technology at Pasadena, renamed the California Institute of Technology [Caltech], and by 1925 he was attracting to it not only a galaxy of brilliant staff but also as many distinguished visitors as could be encouraged into his orbit. There was one particular reason for thinking that Einstein might soon be among them, quite apart from any general desire to discuss physics at first hand with his American counterparts.

It was at Mount Wilson Observatory, high in the Sierras above Pasadena, that Dayton Miller had for years been carrying out a complex repetition of the Michelson-Morley experiment, whose verdict he still hoped to alter. In the spring of 1921 he announced results that at first glance appeared to do this. They broke down on investigation, but four years later he issued further figures. Einstein's reaction to the second announcement was shown by a letter to Millikan in June in which he inferred that if Miller's figures were correct, then his whole theory would collapse. Other scientists, to whom Miller announced his results at a special meeting, lacked Einstein's qualifications. "Not one of them thought for a moment of abandoning relativity," Michael Polanyi has commented. "Instead—as Sir Charles Darwin once described it—they sent Miller home to get his results right."

At Mount Wilson there was also Walter S. Adams, who had some years earlier shown the phenomenal density of the Companion to Sirius—the star later known as Sirius B. At the beginning of the century this density would have been considered impossible. But Rutherford, showing that the atom consisted largely of empty space, had thereby opened up the possibility of superdense stars in which subatomic particles were squeezed together in a concentration unknown on earth. Eddington pointed out soon after the success of the 1919 eclipse expeditions that such stars must have extremely intense gravitational fields. If Adams were correct, the "Einstein shift" exercised by Sirius B should be thirty times that exercised by the sun, and this would bring it well within the range of experimental test. Adams took up the challenge and by the beginning of 1925 was planning experiments that did eventually show a shift toward the red. Results were not precisely those predicted by the General Theory, but they were near enough to be considered as additional confirmation. If the presence of Millikan as head of Caltech and of Adams at Mount Wilson was not in itself enough to attract Einstein to Pasadena, there was also Edwin Hubble, now using the observatory's one-hundred-inch telescope to open up the study of the universe beyond the galaxy and raise fresh questions about the "Einstein world" of general relativity.

Pasadena's concern with relativity was certainly strong enough to augment Einstein's general interest in the work of American physicists, and early in 1925 he tentatively agreed to visit the institute later in the year. However, he had previously arranged to visit South America—partly to lecture at the Argentine State University, partly in the hope of coaxing money into Zionist funds from wealthy Jews. He loved South America but was slightly embarrassed by the fulsome welcome of the German colony, whose members metaphorically clasped him to their Teutonic bosom. As usual, he did not spare himself, and was forced to cancel the proposed visit to Pasadena.

In 1927 and in 1929 Millikan renewed the invitation. Again Einstein was forced to decline.

Thus the link with California—and with the work of Hubble and Hale at Mount Wilson, which was dramatically to affect Einstein's cosmological outlook—did not begin until 1930 and was to last a mere three years. He was then swept into the arms of Abraham Flexner and the Institute for Advanced Study at Princeton, a development that would probably not have taken place had his links with Pasadena been more permanent by that time. The result was that throughout the later 1920s Einstein remained in Europe, and for most of the time in Germany, ever more deeply involved in two major dramas. The first concerned postwar Germany's struggle first to pull herself back into European political respectability and then to hold her position, a struggle closely linked with her attitude to rearmament.

Yet this story of Germany between the wars was in some ways less important for Einstein than the scientific drama, which from now onward increasingly overshadowed his life. This concerned the riddle of the dual nature of things, by this time being extended from radiation to matter itself, and its solution by a method that led on to the dethronement of causality, up to now a cornerstone of physics. For as the physicists of the postwar world began to explain the duality of nature inherent in Einstein's conception of the photon, it eventually became difficult to fault one uncomfortable conclusion: that in the subatomic world, probabilities—rather than events—were all that could be forecast from any particular set of circumstances.

The story began during the early 1920s as it became evident that the great advances in physics started in the first decade of the century were losing their head of steam. They had solved individual problems but they had done nothing to replace the all-embracing pattern of classical physics, which they had first questioned, then shattered. Planck's quantum theory, and Einstein's photons; Rutherford's first ground plan of the nuclear atom and Bohr's disturbing explanation of it—these had each provided isolated answers to isolated problems. Yet in the process they seemed to have produced more riddles than they had solved. Within a few years, moreover, the confusions of this situation were to be drastically altered by a fresh picture of the subatomic world. This new conception, which came into being during the 1920s, has been considerably modified during the last forty years. But its fundamentals have stood the test and have tended to show it as a natural evolution from the ideas that started with the electron of Lorentz and J. J. Thomson and were altered and expanded by Planck, Einstein, Rutherford, and Bohr.

A fundamental premise of classical physics was that events followed each other in succession on a basis that could be predicted if only one understood the laws of nature and had sufficient facts. Laplace's belief that the positions and the velocities of all the objects of the universe would provide sufficient data for a prediction of the future might be an extravagant illustration of the idea. Yet this was little more than a grand if fantastic extrapolation of the idea that events could be determined not only in the laboratory but throughout the whole range of human experience. Certain factors in the quantum theory had first cast a ray of doubt upon this comfortable assumption; the electron in the Bohr atom, jumping from one orbit to another without obvious cause, tended to increase this doubt. Was there, perhaps, no real "cause" for such movements? Though they could be "predicted" in one sense of the word, must this forever be merely a statistical prediction, possible only because of the vast numbers involved? And if there were no identifiable "cause," if events at the subatomic level were governed solely by chance, might this not also be true at other levels? Might not the whole conception of causality in the universe be merely an illusion?

This possibility had already gravely disturbed Einstein. It had disturbed not only the remnants of his belief in classical physics but his sense of rightness in an ordered and orderly world, and as early as January 1920, he had voiced his doubts to Max Born, saying how very loath he would be to abandon complete causality.

Thus the new concept of the subatomic world was even by 1924 beginning to produce a gulf. Bohr, Born, and a number of Einstein's other contemporaries, as well as many of the younger men who were in great part responsible for the new idea, readily jumped the gap. Einstein stayed where he was. The scene in many ways, therefore, paralleled that into which he had launched his theory of relativity two decades earlier. But then he had been in the iconoclastic vanguard; now he took up station with the small conservative rearguard.

A chronological account of the story shows revealingly how the different groups of thinkers, starting to clear the confusion of the early 1920s from different points of attack, produced two different concepts of nature, which were quickly synthesized into one, a process that transformed the newly conceived wave mechanics into the more embracing quantum mechanics.

The first move came in 1923, and it was more directly linked with Einstein himself than is commonly realized. It was made by Louis de Broglie, younger brother of Maurice de Broglie who had been co-secretary of the first Solvay Congress. During his early studies before 1914 De Broglie had been captivated by relativity. "When, after a long absence, I returned to my studies with greater maturity at the end of World War I," he has written, "it was again the ideas of Einstein" that guided him. "I had a sudden inspiration," he says. "Einstein's wave particle dualism was an absolutely general phenomenon extending to all physical nature, and, that being the case, the motion of all particles, photons, electrons, protons, or any others, must be associated with the propagation of a wave."

De Broglie outlined this unconventional proposal—"the suggestion made...purely on grounds of intellectual beauty, to ascribe wave nature to ponderable particles" as it has been described—in three papers published in the Academie des Sciences' *Comptes Rendus* in 1923:

> In the months that followed [he says] I did my utmost to develop and extend my ideas still further in preparation of my doctoral thesis. Before doing so, I asked Paul Langevin, who was so well versed in the theory of relativity and in quantum theory, to examine my conclusions, and he saw fit to ask me for a second copy which he proposed to send to

Louis de Broglie (b. 1892), French physicist whose theory of wave mechanics, developed in the late 1920s, postulated the idea that the motion of all particles, whether photons, electrons, protons, or any others, must be associated with the propagation of a wave. [AIP Niels Bohr Library]

Einstein. Einstein quickly realized that my generalisation of his theory of light quanta was bound to open entirely new horizons to atomic physics, and wrote back to Langevin saying that I had lifted a corner of the great veil.

What was revealed behind the veil was more startling than the earlier idea that light might be considered as a collection of particles at one moment and as a series of waves at another. De Broglie's idea was not of the either/or variety; instead, he postulated that particles such as electrons were guided by what were soon to be called "de Broglie waves" or "matter waves." These waves produced the interference-effects that were familiar to scientists in their studies of light. Where the interference-effects added up, they produced the "preferred orbits," which Bohr had already postulated, and within these the movements of the particles were governed by the laws of wave propagation.

While De Broglie was developing this revolutionary idea for his doctoral thesis, Einstein again came into the picture. In the summer of 1924 he received from S. N. Bose, an Indian physicist of Dacca University, a short paper on "Planck's Law and the Hypothesis of Light Quanta," which considered radiation as a form of gas consisting of photons. Einstein was so impressed by the paper that he himself translated it into German and sent it to the editor of the *Zeitschrift für Physik*, who published it in July. The reason for his interest was simple. He had seen immediately that it was possible to extend Bose's statistical methods to ordinary atoms—"Bose-Einstein statistics" as they became known—if it were assumed, as De Broglie was assuming, that material particles had the simultaneous wave and particulate properties he himself had assumed for radiation two decades earlier. "His quick and immediate response…proved ultimately to be the turning point in my career as a scientist," says Bose. Einstein developed this theme in a two-part paper for the Prussian Academy. Before he read the second, he had received from his friend Langevin a draft of De Broglie's doctoral thesis, and he stressed in his paper how useful he had found De Broglie's ideas.

Einstein's comment on De Broglie's dissertation had also been noted by Erwin Schrödinger, a thirty-seven-year-old Viennese who was later to show a remarkable facility for riding across the frontiers between science and the humanities without noticing their existence, a man of two cultures who could claim ironically of later cosmic ray studies that they promised "the stepped-up realisation of the plan to exterminate mankind which is close to all our hearts." Schrödinger, in no doubt about the debt he owed to Einstein, now exhibited one of those brief spurts of concentrated genius that have more than once changed the face of physics. Within four months he erected the basic structure of what became known as wave mechanics. In this, the emphasis of the De Broglie waves on the electron particle was taken a step further. The particle itself now gave way to what was, in effect, a standing electron wave; instead of being a wave-controlled corpuscle, it became a corpuscular wave.

What had thus occurred within a very few years was a steady merging of the particle and wave concepts. The electron—and possibly the other particles about which

213

Niels Bohr (1885–1962) and his son Aage Bohr (b. 1922). From the first meeting of Niels Bohr and Einstein in 1920, their friendship was equaled only by their disagreements over some of the fundamentals of physics —notably, the significance of chance at subnuclear levels. [AIP Niels Bohr Library, Margrethe Bohr Collection]

physicists were still comparatively ignorant—had changed from being either a particle or a wave to being one under certain circumstances and the other under different circumstances. Now it appeared that it was both at the same time. Here, it seemed that science had run up not only against "common sense," which was already suspect when it began to deal with events in the subatomic world, but with rational logic. For could anything really be one thing and its opposite at one and the same time?

Waiting to provide the answer was Niels Bohr. His answer was an unqualified "Yes." He said so in the "principle of complementarity," which proposed that whether light or electrons were waves or moving particles depended entirely on the specific properties that were being investigated; the subject under study had dual characteristics, and whether it conformed to those we knew as wave-like properties or to those we knew as particulate depended solely on how we studied it. Bohr had his own characteristic way of explaining what he called the poetry of complementarity, and his disciple L. Rosenfeld describes how Bohr used a scene in Japan to illustrate it:

> At sunset the top of Fujiyama disappeared behind a curtain of gold-fringed clouds: the black mass of the mountain, surmounted by this fulgent crown, conveyed an impression of awe and majesty. On the next morning, it offered an entirely different spectacle: the pointed summit alone, covered with shining snow, emerged from the dense mist filling the valley; the landscape was radiating gladness and joy. So, Bohr mused, the two half-mountains together are not simply equal to a mountain: to each belongs a peculiar, individual impression, and the two are complementary.

Schrödinger's wave mechanics, which were quickly seen to provide a plausible explanation for much that had not previously been explicable, was thus credible on the grounds that reality is what you make it. This was disturbing enough to those who believed that all ignorance in science could be removed by an addition of knowledge. But more was to follow.

Even before De Broglie and Schrödinger had begun to explain the inner workings of the atom by what was essentially a physicist's combination of wave and particle ideas, a totally different approach was being made by Werner Heisenberg, a young German in his early twenties. Heisenberg started from Mach's assumption that theories should be based on physically verifiable phenomena, and in trying to discover the structure of the atom he seized upon the spectral lines that were the individual fingerprints of each element's atoms. The wave lengths for these could be determined by using a mathematical system called "matrix mechanics" or "quantum mechanics." Thus by 1927, the De Broglie-Schrödinger picture of the electron was being matched by a purely mathematical explanation of the atom, which used the spectral lines as a starting point but soon abandoned discrete pictorial representation for a discrete set of numbers.

214

Werner Karl Heisenberg (1901–1976), the German physicist whose uncertainty principle, indicating the limited accuracy with which the position of an electron and its simultaneous velocity can be measured, and his creation of quantum mechanics brought him the Nobel Prize for Physics in 1932. [Bildarchiv Preussischer Kulturbesitz]

These two advances had, in fact, been along parallel paths. And they were now brought together by arguments that effectively showed that both explanations were saying the same thing in different languages. Schrödinger made the first move in uniting the two ideas, and Born carried it further by providing a statistical interpretation of Schrödinger's wave conception; but he did so only by admitting that he was dealing with large numbers of random events and that his results dealt solely with their probability. The suggestion that a satisfactory picture of the physical world could consist not of a description of events but of their probabilities had already been made in Heisenberg's famous "uncertainty principle." This showed convincingly that at the subatomic level the mere act of observation affected what one was observing, and that the nearer one reached an accurate figure for either the position or the momentum of a particle, the less accurate became the figure for the other. Moreover, the uncertainty in the two factors was found to be linked, as though by a master craftsman, with a figure that had by this time become familiar: the Planck's constant of the quantum theory, discovered a quarter of a century earlier.

At this point, a stage in one of the great dramas of physics was brought to a satisfactory conclusion. De Broglie had played his part with Heisenberg. Schrödinger and Born had contributed in equal measure to the new conception, and both, forced to leave Germany a few years later, were to disagree on its implications. Planck with the magician's wand of his universal constant and Einstein with his power to influence men's minds by example, had played significant parts. Together they had produced "the new physics." Now they had to lie on the bed they had made.

The significant outcome of these events was, as De Broglie put it many years later, that quantum physics now appeared to be

> governed by statistical laws and not by any causal mechanisms, hidden or otherwise. The "wave" of wave mechanics ceased to be a physical reality and became a solution of partial differential equations of the classical type, and thus the means of representing the probability of phenomena taking place. The corpuscle, too, was turned into a mere phantom—we can no longer say "at such an instant a corpuscle will be found in such a place with such an energy or momentum," but only "at such an instant there will be such a probability that a corpuscle will be found at such and such a place." In other words, while a given experiment can either localise a corpuscle or ascertain its momentum, it cannot do both.

There were subtle differences in the manner in which the physicists involved regarded this central feature of indeterminacy, which occupied a key position in the new picture of the subatomic world. While Born, Heisenberg, and Bohr accepted it without qualification, Einstein and Planck accepted it only with the strongest qualifications. Yet these two were the very men who a quarter of a century earlier had pulled into physics the very ideas that they now thought of as its Trojan horse.

The break with the old world that this new concept epitomizes can be illustrated with a statement by Sir Basil Schonland, who describes the new world in *The Atomists*:

> It appeared experimentally proven [he says] that at the bottom of all phenomena there were to be discerned laws of chance which made it impossible to think of an ordered deterministic world; the basic laws of nature appeared to be fundamentally statistical and indeterminate, governed by the purest chance. On a large scale they could appear exactly the reverse but this was only because they involved such a vast number of events. They had the monumental stability of an enormous life insurance company though, like it, they rested on individual uncertainty.

At times Einstein was wryly humorous about his inability to accept the new world that his colleagues had created. Philipp Frank visited him in Berlin, apparently in 1932, and they began to talk of the new physics. Then, says Frank:

> Einstein said, partly as a joke, something like this: "A new fashion has now arisen in physics. By means of ingeniously formulated theoretical experiments it is proved that certain physical magnitudes cannot be measured, or, to put it more precisely, that according to accepted natural laws the investigated bodies behave in such a way as to baffle all attempts at measurement. From this the conclusion is drawn that it is completely meaningless to retain these magnitudes in the language of physics. To speak about them is pure metaphysics."

And when Frank pointed out to Einstein that he had invented the fashion in 1905, Einstein answered: "A good joke should not be repeated too often." More cogently, he explained to Infeld—the Pole who had visited him in Berlin and who was later to join him in the United States—"Yes, I may have started it, but I regarded these ideas as temporary. I never thought that others would take them so much more seriously than I did."

His feelings went deep, and were epitomized in the famous phrase—linked with his name as firmly as the equation $E = mc^2$—which he used in a letter to Max Born in December 1926. Quantum mechanics was very imposing, he said, but he was convinced that God did not throw dice. That remark was altered, repeated, paraphrased, and was to go around the world second and thirdhand. But the central meaning was clear and unqualified—that, in its usually repeated form, "God does not play dice with the world."

Thus he regarded the statistical laws necessary to explain the subatomic world as merely second-best; he could not accept them as the fundamental laws of physical reality—these, he believed, should determine events themselves rather than their probabilities. In time, when much more had been learned, it would be possible to throw overboard the current, purely statistical, explanations and replace them with something better. More satisfactory laws would be discovered. Eventually men would find out how a

216

non-dice-throwing God had made the world. This was the stance that he took up in the late 1920s. He retained it, almost unchanged, to the end of his life.

The formulation of this new idea of the subatomic world took place between the publication of De Broglie's papers in 1924 and the summer and autumn of 1927, which saw the publication of Heisenberg's uncertainty principle and the exposition of Bohr's complementarity principle. But most physicists still retained qualifications. Then, in October, they were forced to stand up and be counted. The occasion was the Fifth Solvay Congress in 1927. Together with the Sixth, which was held three years later in 1930, it marked a notable change in Einstein's position in the scientific world.

The general subject of discussion at the Fifth Congress was "Electrons and Photons" and the list of speakers and papers made it clear that differing views of the wave-like or corpuscular nature of matter would be hammered out energetically; so, it was equally clear, would the underlying riddle of causality versus indeterminacy, the ghost that European physicists had raised and that now looked over their shoulders wherever they went. Lorentz came from Holland, Sir William Bragg with his son, Lawrence, from England, Arthur Compton from the United States, Born and Heisenberg from Göttingen, Einstein from Berlin, Schrödinger from Stuttgart, and De Broglie from Paris. And from Copenhagen there came Bohr, anxious to explain his complementarity principle, strongly supported by Heisenberg. "At the Solvay meetings," he later wrote, "Einstein had from their beginning been a most prominent figure, and several of us came to the conference with great anticipation to learn his reactions to the latest stage of the development which, to our view, went far in clarifying the problems which he had himself from the outset elicited so ingeniously."

At the start of the conference, Bohr threw down the gauntlet with an account of the epistemological problems presented by the latest developments in physics. He agreed that certainty had been removed from the subatomic world, that there was now, as he put it elsewhere, "the impossibility of any sharp separation between the behaviour of atomic objects and the interaction with the measuring instruments which serve to define the conditions under which the phenomena appear." This meant that the wave or particle concept was determined by the type of experiment. Yet even when it had been decided to study the wave or the particle characteristics, Heisenberg's uncertainty principle still masked an exact picture of what nature was like. The trapdoor of indeterminacy had been opened, and those involved would have to make the best they could of it.

Einstein made very little. Strangely, perhaps, he read no paper at the Fifth Congress. But when those attending the Congress met after the sessions in the Fondation Universitaire, Einstein came out into the open. He still disliked uncertainty—and Bohr's complementarity—and he bluntly said so.

The fifth Solvay Congress was held in Brussels in October, 1927. Seated, front row (left to right): Irving Langmuir, Max Planck, Madame Curie, Hendrik A. Lorentz, Einstein, Paul Langevin, Charles E. Guye, Charles T. R. Wilson, and O. W. Richardson; seated, middle row (left to right): Peter Debye, M. H. C. Knudsen, William L. Bragg, Hendrick A. Kramers, Paul A. M. Dirac, Arthur H. Compton, Louis de Broglie, Max Born, and Niels Bohr; standing (left to right): Auguste Piccard, E. Henriot, Paul Ehrenfest, E. Herzen, Th. de Donder, Erwin Schrödinger, E. Verschaffelt, Wolfgang Pauli, Werner Heisenberg, Ralph H. Fowler, and Léon M. Brillouin. [AIP Niels Bohr Library]

Then the discussion opened out. Lorentz did his best to give the floor to only one speaker at a time. But everyone felt strongly. Everyone wanted to put forward his own view. There was the nearest thing to an uproar that could occur in such distinguished company, and in the near-confusion Ehrenfest moved up to the blackboard, which successive speakers had used, and wrote on it: "The Lord did there confound the language of all the earth."

Throughout all this Einstein remained Einstein:

> During a fairly long walk, he made a profound impression on me and fully confirmed my faith in him [writes De Broglie, whose papers had started the avalanche]. I was particularly won over by his sweet disposition, by his general kindness, by his simplicity and his friendliness. Occasionally, gaiety would gain the upper hand and he would strike a more personal note and even disclose some detail of his day-to-day life. Then again, reverting to his characteristic mood of reflection and meditation, he would launch into a profound and original discussion of a variety of scientific and other problems.

Having a final discussion with De Broglie, Einstein said "that all physical theories, their mathematical expressions apart, ought to lend themselves to so simple a description 'that even a child could understand them.'" And what could be less simple than the statistical interpretations of wave mechanics?

None of the protagonists was willing to let go this particular argument, and it was taken up with renewed vigor when the next Solvay Congress was held in 1930. The central problem still revolved around the one question: was it or was it not theoretically possible to ascertain the position of a particle and also its momentum at one specific moment?

In 1930 Einstein proposed a "thought-experiment," one that was theoretically possible even if ruled out by experimental limitations. The proposal was to enclose light within a mirror-lined box, which was weighed. One photon would then be automatically released by a time-control mechanism within the box, which would then be weighed again. From the change in mass it would be possible, using Einstein's equation, to calculate the energy or momentum of the photon, which was released at one specific moment. At first, and even at second glance, Einstein appeared to have an unbreakable case. Only the following day did Bohr realize that Einstein had overlooked one thing: the effect of the weighing on the clock.

There have been many explanations of the results of this exchange but none clearer than that given by Barbara Cline:

> Bohr's reasoning applied to any method of weighing, but to illustrate that reasoning most clearly he chose to imagine that Einstein's box of light was hung on a spring from a rigid scale. Thus when a photon was released the box would move in recoil. Its vertical position in relation to the earth's surface would change and therefore its position within

the earth's gravitational field. According to the General Theory of Relativity, this change in spatial position would mean a change in the rate of the clock, preset and attached to the box. The change would be extremely small but in this case crucial. For, due to a chain of inevitable uncertainties: the uncertainty of the escaping photon's direction, therefore of the box's recoil, therefore of its position within the earth's gravitational field, the precise time when the photon was released from the box could *not* be determined. It was indeed indeterminable to the extent given by Heisenberg's law—the cornerstone of the Copenhagen interpretation. This was the way Bohr answered the serious challenge of Einstein, who had forgotten to apply his own General Theory of Relativity.

The argument, which had really started seven years earlier and had changed the face of physics, involved two separate but linked questions: was matter as well as radiation wave-like and yet corpuscular as well, depending only on how it was considered; and were the laws of the subatomic world the indeterminate laws of statistics? The first of these problems had the greater practical effect on the scientific world, and Sir William Bragg, the director of the Royal Institution, who had been present at the 1927 Congress, had once commented: "On Mondays, Wednesdays and Fridays we teach the wave theory and on Tuesdays and Saturdays the corpuscular theory." Forty years later, the synthesis had been made. "Everything that has already happened is particles, everything in the future is waves," states Sir Lawrence Bragg, Sir William's son and, in turn, the director of the Royal Institution. "The advancing sieve of time coagulates waves into particles at the moment 'now.'" On this Einstein had moved in step, seeing the contradiction as one with which he could cope, a contradiction of common sense no less amenable to reason than the apparent contradictions of relativity.

Indeterminacy was a riddle at a different level, more fundamental and, as far as Einstein was concerned, more important. Here, his discomfiture—and it cannot be called less, however much his colleagues tried to soften the blow—ended the first series of battles in the long campaign he was to wage. They had altered his status in a small but certain way. To amend Snow's judgment that Einstein always remained in the Bradman class, he now appeared to have become a W. G. Grace in the Bradman era. His touch was as sure as ever, but it belonged to a previous age.

The gap remained throughout the years. At the height of the initial debate, early in 1927, Einstein showed his feelings at the end of a message to the Newton celebrations in England, concluding with the hope: "May the spirit of Newton's method give us the power to restore unison between physical reality and the profoundest characteristic of Newton's teaching—strict causality." Years afterward, he was just as hopeful.

A number of reasons can be adduced for the way in which Einstein began to slip from the mainstream of physics during the later 1920s. It can be claimed that the gem-like flame burned a little less gem-like as he diverted his energies into pacifism, the needs of the Hebrew University in Jerusalem, or the requirements of the Jewish Agency.

The post office at Davos early in the century. Einstein lectured in this town in 1928. [Swiss National Tourist Office, London]

Just as tenably, it can be argued that he spent more time in such pursuits because he felt his powers diminishing. More plausibly, it can be attributed to concentration on mathematics, so essential to his work on the unified field theory.

Yet the opposition that he maintained so stubbornly toward the indeterminacy of quantum mechanics was not based entirely on his inability to "see" it as he had "seen" many other innovations in physics. It was based on something more fundamental, upon an interior assumption about the world that had much more resemblance to religious faith than to the ever-questioning skepticism of science. Einstein believed that the universe had been designed so that its workings could be comprehensible; therefore, these workings must conform to discoverable laws; thus there was no room for chance and indeterminacy—God, after all, did not play the game that way.

Although he felt so strongly about the problem that was to cut him off from his colleagues, Einstein still laid the cards fairly on the table, sometimes with an objectivity that tended to mask his feelings. This was shown when, early in 1928, he lectured at Davos in Switzerland. He was very vulnerable to any call from that country and responded to an appeal that was to have important repercussions. The appeal came from the Davoser Hochschule, which was starting university courses for young men and women in the surrounding sanatoria. Treatment in these meant a break from regular studies, usually for months and often for years; but special courses could alter all that, and the Davos authorities appealed for specialist teachers to give their services for a few weeks late in March. Einstein responded readily.

His lecture was on "Grundbegriffe der Physik und ihre Entwicklung" ("Fundamental Concepts of Physics and Their Most Recent Changes"), and there was no doubt as to what he considered these were. "Today faith in unbroken causality is threatened precisely by those whose path it had illumined as their chief and unrestricted leader at the front, namely, by the representatives of physics," he noted. He went on to outline Newtonian mechanics and to describe how relativity had welded together both Newton's ideas and the more recent ideas of the field theory and had shaken the fundamental concepts of time and space. But now doubt had been thrown on the theory of strict causality, which had previously remained untouched. "We reach here," he went on, "a complication of questions with which the modern generation of physicists is struggling in a gigantic display of intellectual power."

While in Davos, Einstein suffered from an unexpected collapse, which revealed a delicate heart. The results were serious, and he had to be moved back to Berlin in easy stages. The details of the heart trouble remained unclear. Numerous remedies were sought. All were unsuccessful. Finally, Janos Plesch tried his hand.

Dr. Plesch was four years older than Einstein, a wealthy Hungarian who had built up in Berlin a successful and fashionable medical practice. With a fine town house in Berlin and an equally fine country estate at Gatow, with an intimate circle of acquaintances in the diplomatic and theatrical world, Plesch was in character the complete

Einstein with his doctor, Janos Plesch, on the grounds of Dr. Plesch's home at Gatow on the outskirts of Berlin. [United Press International]

opposite of Einstein. What united the two men was not only Plesch's diagnostic success, which dented Einstein's built-in skepticism of doctors; there was also his interest in the world of art and letters and his love for splendid living that had already touched Einstein's innate, if usually suppressed, love of good food and drink.

Plesch quickly diagnosed inflammation of the walls of the heart, put his patient on a salt-free diet, and eventually packed him off with Elsa and her two daughters, Ilse and Margot, to a small seaside resort on the Baltic coast north of Hamburg. Here, Einstein recuperated. But it was a slow business, not helped by the fact that he continued sailing until Plesch put a stop to it.

As a result of the illness he was deprived of his normal secretarial help at the Kaiser Wilhelm Institute and the University, and before he left Berlin to recuperate, he was obliged to engage a secretary for work at home. She was Helen Dukas, competent and diffident in almost equal parts. Her first task was to find a substitute for Einstein at the coming meeting in Geneva of the International Commission on Intellectual Co-operation. His work on this, like his work for the pacifist causes that he supported, and for the Zionists, was now to suffer a temporary interruption. He had already achieved mixed results in these fields when he began his fiftieth year. Meanwhile, Germany moved on toward the time, little more than a year away, when rising unemployment, the support of industrialists who feared communism, and the creation of a scapegoat in the shape of the Jews, would together transform Hitler's National Socialists into the second largest party in the country.

221

13.

THE CALL OF PEACE

Einstein's breakdown of 1928 put a rein on his activities for a time. But he was not a man to spare himself longer than necessary, and as soon as possible he was working once more in the pacifist cause, which he had vigorously supported since 1914. He had long been a staunch upholder of the German League for Human Rights, which the Bund Neues Vaterland had become, and from his sickbed was soon sending regular notes to its secretary-general, Kurt Grossmann, asking for information or giving advice. And shortly after his recovery, he was persuaded to make a gramophone record of "My Credo," in which his soft kindly voice outlined his pacifist beliefs as though they were something that any sensible man must agree with.

During the first postwar years pacifists had strong popular support, not only in Germany but throughout a continent exhausted by four years of blood-letting. Thus Einstein for once marched with the crowd rather than against it. But as the price of war became blurred by time and by the jollifications of regimental reunions, so did support for the martyrdom of pacifism ebb away. By contrast, Einstein's beliefs, explained whenever he found the opportunity in a plethora of interviews, statements, and articles, remained rock-hard through the 1920s.

In the immediate postwar years, it was the League of Nations on which the hopes of peace rested. Einstein, therefore, supported the League. Or, more accurately, he supported it until experience rubbed him up against it at close quarters. Then disillusion quickly set in. He was surprised that miracles were not worked overnight and shocked that when human beings began to manage great affairs of state they still behaved like human beings. After that, his support of the League had increasingly to be propped up by his friends.

He had returned to Berlin from the Collège de France only a few weeks when, on May 17, 1922, he was invited by Sir Eric Drummond to become a member of the International Committee on Intellectual Co-operation, then being formed by the League of Nations. In many ways it was an ancestor of UNESCO, which sprang from the United Nations after the Second World War, and its members were appointed, in the words of the under-secretary-general, "not as representatives of their respective countries but on account of their personal achievements. At the same time, the Council endeavoured as far as possible to give representation on the Committee to the big cultural groups of the world. In this sense, therefore, each member may be said to represent a certain culture, though he does not sit in the Committee as the official representative of any country in particular."

Einstein accepted Drummond's invitation by return, although he was not clear as to the kind of work to be done. However, the League was to pay a price for its acquisition. Einstein's "purity of heart," as Gilbert Murray described it, the fact that he was so "very reluctant to believe evil," his inability or unwillingness to admit that whatever the fine intentions of the League, it had to operate in the world of fallible men, combined to limit his usefulness.

In July, less than two months after his acceptance, Einstein wrote a brief letter to Pierre Comert, head of the Information Secretariat at the League, brusquely stating that he felt it necessary to resign from the Committee, whose first meeting was to be held later in the summer. No reason was given, although in an accompanying note Einstein expressed concern that the situation in Berlin was such that a Jew was well advised to exercise restraint about taking part in politics. In addition, he added, somewhat irrelevantly since his appointment was still on an international rather than a national basis, that he had no desire to represent people who would not have chosen him as their representative.

The officials of the League were thrown into despair, and desperate efforts to retrieve the situation were made by the secretary of the Committee. This was Inazo Nitobe, a Japanese Samurai, born with the right to wear two swords, whose philosophic journey was to lead him into the ranks of the Quakers. On receiving Einstein's resignation Nitobe had cabled to Murray: "Einstein resigns giving no reasons stop important to have him stop fear his resignation will have bad effect stop grateful if you can use your influence." He also appealed to Bergson, who said that he had no personal contacts with Einstein but made an ingenious suggestion. "It is my belief that since the Committee of Intellectual Co-operation is now properly constituted, the resignation of one of its members cannot become definitive until the Committee has accepted it. Therefore, before we meet you can ask Einstein to reconsider his decision." The League officials clutched gratefully at this straw, and Comert was dispatched to Berlin, where he met Einstein on July 27 and 28:

> I explained to you [he subsequently wrote to Einstein] that your sudden and motiveless retreat would gravely prejudice the Committee of Intellectual Co-operation since the public would be able to put a bad interpretation on your sudden decision to withdraw your collaboration.

> However, before my departure from Berlin, and with a spirit which I sincerely admire, you told me that you were giving up all thought of resignation. The work of the League of Nations, you told me, was so dear to your heart that for it you were ready to accept certain risks rather than compromise, by an inexplicable resignation, the task of the Committee. At one point during our interview I recall that concerning this you alluded to the eventuality, on your return from Japan, of a change in your domicile in order to ensure the peace and security of your work.

223

Delegates to a League of Nations meeting in London. Second from left at table is Dino Grandi (b. 1895), Italy. To his left, in order, are Pierre Étienne Flandin (1889–1958), France; President Stanley Melbourne Bruce (1883–1967), Australia; Secretary-General Joseph Louis Anne Avenol (1879–1952), France; Anthony Eden (1897–1977), United Kingdom; and Maxim Litvinov (1876–1951), Russia (reading a newspaper). [The Mansell Collection]

At the end of our conversations you wrote anew, on the 29th July, to the Secretary General. Your preparations for leaving for Japan prevented you from attending the first meeting of the Committee of Intellectual Co-operation but you declared that upon your return your collaboration would be even more zealous, thus making up, in some fashion, for the loss of time occasioned by your absence. It was with this friendly letter that you left us for the Far East.

The Committee held its first session in Geneva in August, and the official report explained that "Professor A. Einstein was prevented from assisting in the work of the Committee owing to his absence on a scientific mission to Japan."

In fact, Einstein did not leave for Japan until some months later, and at the end of August he was writing to Lord Haldane from Berlin in support of a solution to the reparations problem put forward in the *Berliner Tageblatt.*

Einstein's absence, extended by a visit to Palestine and a return to Germany by way of Madrid, continued until February, 1923, and it was only late in March that he returned to Berlin. He had not been in touch with the League. But, hearing indirectly that he was on his way home, its officials now expected that he would make preparations as promised for attending the session of the Committee due to start in July. They were to be startlingly disappointed.

On his way to Berlin, Einstein broke his journey in Zurich. And here, on March 21, he wrote to the League resigning from the Committee yet again. A copy of his letter was, moreover, immediately made available to the *Nouvelle Gazette de Zurich,* in whose columns the League officials were able to read it the following morning—while the letter itself was presumably still passing through their administrative machine.

"I have recently become convinced that the League of Nations has neither the force nor the goodwill [la bonne volonté] necessary for the accomplishment of its task," it said. "As a convinced pacifist it does not seem to me to be a good thing to have any relations whatsoever with it. I ask you to strike my name from the list of committee members."

Einstein's action—his second resignation from a Committee whose meetings he had not yet attended—had been caused by the French occupation of the Ruhr. Inflation in Germany had become unbearable, and at the end of 1922 the Weimar Government suspended payment of the German reparations agreed upon in April, 1921. The French, tried beyond endurance, in January, 1923, occupied the small oval heartland of industrial Germany in an effort to squeeze blood from a stone. The result was to bring Einstein in line with the protesting German nationalists, although for reasons very different from theirs. They felt that the League, and all it stood for, was too strong; Einstein's objections were the complete reverse.

Once again, however, he was coaxed back. One of the first developments after his return was the establishment of the International Institute of Intellectual Co-operation, in effect the Committee's executive organ. It was to be financed by the French

Einstein (fifth from left) and Professor Hendrik Lorentz (second from left) at a meeting of the International Committee on Intellectual Cooperation in Paris, October, 1927. [Ullstein]

Government and set up in Paris, and there was an unwritten agreement that its head should always be a Frenchman. After initially welcoming the idea, Einstein grew suspicious of possible French domination. He himself was unable to oppose the details due to absence in South America, but he tried to persuade Lorentz to protest in his name. Lorentz declined.

Einstein sat on subcommittees dealing with bibliography and with a proposed international meteorological bureau. He gave personal advice on the allocation among Russian emigre intellectuals of money donated by the Red Cross and he spent much time discussing how the prospects of peace in the future might be increased by means of school education in the present.

This interest in education led to one of the few concrete results of Einstein's cooperation with the League—"Why War?"—a slim publication containing Einstein's question to Freud asking how wars might be ended, and Freud's reply. It appeared only after Einstein had finally severed all connection with the League and had made a public and ill-judged protest against the disarmament conference being held under the League's auspices in Geneva.

Einstein, like most other men, was at times self-contradictory. But a great deal of the confusion that surrounds his pacifist attitude disappears once it is considered dispassionately and historically and once his somewhat tortuous self-justifications are ignored. The truth is that in 1920 he was an unqualified pacifist; that the logic of events added first one qualification and then another; and that with the coming to power of Hitler even Einstein was forced to realize that pacifism would not work. The evolution took place gradually but unevenly; at times it slipped back, and at times he himself does not seem to be clear what he really wanted to say. Furthermore, he continued to call himself a pacifist even while agreeing that the dictators could only be stopped by force of arms, an attitude that spread dismay through the pacifist camp.

But as late as 1928 his attitude was still uncomplicated and was underlined in many letters, messages, and appeals that he wrote or issued to such organizations as the Women's International League for Peace and Freedom, and the British No More War Movement. It was useless to discuss rules of war, or methods of war. Absolute refusal of military service was the only way. Thus Einstein was still holding out against the various ifs, buts, and compromises that were being put forward; the proposals that, in whatever form they were made, suggested that conscientious objectors might work their passage in society by carrying out alternative civilian duties in lieu of military service:

> On August 30th, 1930 [writes Harold Bing, the British pacifist leader], I was taken by Martha Steinitz [sometime Secretary of the Bund der Kriegdienstgegener and later Joint Secretary of the W.R.I.] to meet Einstein at his lakeside summer house near Potsdam…and, in reply to his questions, explained why I and others had refused alternative service because to accept such service was to recognise the state's right of conscription and to acquiesce in the conscription of others and because any work imposed upon us

225

Einstein, Robert A. Millikan (center), and Madame Curie (1867–1934) in Geneva, 1924. [California Institute of Technology]

by the state in wartime would be intended to assist the war effort. At the end of our conversation he declared that he now understood the absolutist position.

Understood maybe. But only three months later he gave little evidence of this in one of his most famous pacifist speeches. This was made in the Ritz-Carlton Hotel in New York on December 14, after he had broken his journey en route to Pasadena. "Even if only two per cent of those assigned to perform military service should announce their refusal to fight," he said, "…governments would be powerless, they would not dare send such a large number of people to jail." However, this phrase, which was to produce a rash of button-badges with the words "Two per cent" on them, was followed by a plea to countries that operate conscription to enact laws "permitting pacifists in place of military service to do some strenuous or dangerous work, in the interest of their country or of mankind as a whole."

His dedication to the pacifist movement tended increasingly to tug Einstein away from the over-cozy international atmosphere of the League. Always an instinctive outsider, he felt unhappy in the role of insider automatically conferred by membership of the Committee. In addition, there were problems within the organization itself. "National Committees" had been created, which by 1930 were acting as liaison groups between the central body in Geneva and the intellectual committees of individual countries. Einstein was a member of the German committee, created after Germany had joined the League in 1926, but his opinions were given only qualified support by fellow members, and their recommendations led him to criticize the system of national committees as such.

Then, in the spring of 1932, he wrote to M. Montenach, the Swiss secretary of the main Committee, suggesting that he should be replaced on it. The proposal was quickly followed in the League by an internal memorandum outlining various steps, which it was hoped would stave off Einstein's resignation. Gilbert Murray was again asked to intercede. M. Dufour-Feronce, who had once worked in the German Foreign Office and who knew Einstein personally, was to do the same.

All the blandishments failed. And Einstein, who found it "difficult to find the time" to attend Geneva for the July meeting, arrived there instead in May, and in circumstances that would certainly have made impossible any further connection with the League.

Einstein's distrust exploded in reaction to the Disarmament Conference, which opened in Geneva in February, 1932. It was a reaction that illustrated his bigness of heart but revealed the immense gap that divided the real world of nation-states and politicians from the world Einstein felt must exist because it should exist. It was a reaction that undermined those who believed he might be a useful ally in a practical struggle to avert war, and it was one that offered a useful weapon to those only waiting to claim that outside his own field Einstein was something between crank and buffoon. In almost every way it was one of his most disastrous interventions in public affairs.

On the morning of Monday, May 23, Einstein visited the League headquarters.

Einstein and Madame Curie walking near the Lake of Geneva after a meeting of the International Committee on Intellectual Cooperation, in the early 1930s. [AIP Niels Bohr Library]

As he entered the public gallery the Japanese and Russian delegates of the Air Commission were arguing that the mobility of aircraft carriers increased the offensiveness of the planes they carried; for the United States Allen Dulles and for Britain Captain J. T. Babington—who had won a hard-earned D.S.O. for the wartime bombing of the Friedrichshafen Airship Factory—were arguing the reverse. The speaker stopped for a moment, then continued, according to Konrad Bercovici, a young Rumanian-American journalist. "That brief second, however, was an acknowledgment, a more marked acknowledgment, of the greatness the man radiated than if all had stopped everything they were doing and applauded him," he wrote. "All eyes were turned toward Einstein. Where he was, the world was."

But Einstein had not come just to watch. That afternoon he held a press conference at the Bregues Hotel attended by about sixty correspondents. What he said, both here and elsewhere in Geneva, has been variously reported, but there is no doubt about the tenor of his statement, whose main points are given in a few key sentences in the "official" version: "One does not make wars less likely to occur by formulating rules of warfare." "War cannot be humanised. It can only be abolished." "People must be persuaded to refuse all military service."

It was not what he said, however, but the context of his opinions that tended to destroy his credibility for all except those who had already been converted to the conspiracy theory of war. This is made clear by Bercovici's account of the Geneva visit and by an interview with Einstein that he succeeded in obtaining before the press conference started. Its essential content consists of a long quoted statement, triggered off when Bercovici said that he had come to the city to watch the comedy of peace:

> This is not a comedy [Einstein replied] it is a tragedy. The greatest tragedy of modern times, despite the cap and bells and buffoonery. No one has any right to treat this tragedy lightly or to laugh when one should cry. We should be standing on rooftops, all of us, and denouncing this conference as a travesty!
>
> If you want peace in America then you must join us in Europe, and together we shall ask the workers to refuse to manufacture and transport any military weapons, and also to refuse to serve any military organisation. Then we will have no more conscriptions; we will have no more war! Governments could go on talking from now to doomsday. The militarists could lay any plans they wish.
>
> If the workers of this world, men and women, decide not to manufacture and transport ammunition, it would end war for all time. We must do that. Dedicate our lives to drying up the source of war: ammunition factories.

Einstein's attitude marks the high tide of his pacifism, which had been rising since the First World War. And with the reflection that within fourteen months he was to be encouraging men to take up arms, the only other nonscientific preoccupation of his life must now be considered: the support of Zionism, for which he showed the same white-hot idealism, a quality often producing results but which, here also, sometimes counterbalanced the value of his name.

14.

THE CALL OF ZION

Einstein playing his violin at a charity concert in a Berlin synagogue, 1930. [The Bettmann Archive]

The Zionists seized upon Einstein's fame from 1919 onward and exploited it to their advantage. No movement dedicated to so difficult a mission can let its tactics be too closely controlled by the principles of a gentlefolks' aid society; and with a genius of Weizmann's caliber in control, it was inevitable that the magnetism of Einstein, the incorruptible man of science, should be conscripted to the general task of implementing the Balfour Declaration, and to the special one of coaxing money from the pockets of American Jewry.

Einstein himself has stated that he did not become aware of his own Jewishness until after he went to Berlin in the spring of 1914. This is not as surprising as it sounds. The modern Zionist movement did not come into existence until 1897. The current for assimilation still continued to run swiftly through the Jewish community. Thus, despite the "nail from the Crucifix" brought into the Munich schoolroom, Einstein appears to have remembered no anti-Semitism from his student days, from his work in the Berne Patent Office, or from his years as a young professor in Zurich. "Different but equal" was the attitude of the liberal Swiss.

In Prague the Jewish community provided a power block in the struggle between the Czechs and the Germans into whose Austro-Hungarian Empire they had been brought. And here for the first time, it appears, Einstein became a member although certainly not a committed one, of a Jewish group. It met every Tuesday evening in the home of Bertha Fanta; but while almost every other member was an ardent Zionist, Einstein was completely uninterested.

One factor that changed his view was the transformation of Zionism from a pious hope to a practical possibility by the Balfour Declaration of 1917, the statement by the British foreign minister that "His Majesty's Government view with favour the establishment in Palestine of a national home for the Jewish people, and will use their best endeavours to facilitate the achievement of this object."

His recruitment into the Zionist cause has been described by the man who carried it out, Kurt Blumenfeld. "The method," says Blumenfeld, "found effective with him brought [other] friends and followers to Zionism: that is to say, the drawing out from a man of what is within him rather than the forcing from him of what is not truly within his nature."

Blumenfeld's account of his meetings with Einstein in February, 1919, is revealing both of Einstein and of the Zionist cause as it struggled into practical existence: "On this occasion," writes Blumenfeld of their second meeting, "he told me that Hermann Struck, the etcher, had tried to interest him in the Bible and the Jewish religion, but that he had refused to be drawn. 'I really don't know enough about my religious feelings,' he had said.... 'I have always known exactly what I should do, and I feel satisfied with that.'"

Shortly afterward, Blumenfeld noticed a change in Einstein's attitude. "I am against nationalism but in favour of Zionism," he said. "The reason has become clear to me today. When a man has both arms and he is always saying I have a right arm, then he is a Chauvinist. However, when the right arm is missing, then he must do something to make up for the missing limb. Therefore I am, as a human being, an opponent of nationalism. But as a Jew I am from today a supporter of the Jewish Zionist efforts."
The forces supporting assimilation were certainly strong, but so, too, were Einstein's contrary feelings once he had become seized of the Zionist cause, even though for him Zionism and Palestine were only peripheral concerns. Utilizing him for publicity purposes was thus a delicate matter and, said Blumenfeld, "was only successful if I was able to get under his skin in such a way that eventually he believed that words had not been put into his mouth but had come forth from him spontaneously."

If Einstein the Zionist thus found himself at odds with much of the Jewish community on matters of practical politics, he also had reservations about the character and methods of the key man in the Zionist movement. This was Chaim Weizmann, subsequently a good friend of Einstein but diametrically opposed to him in many ways. Weizmann was a Russian Jew who had emigrated to England before the war, became naturalized, and quickly achieved a position in the scientific world that owed nothing to his work as a propagandist for Zionism. In an ironic way Weizmann was the Allied counterpart of Fritz Haber. For while Haber found a method of supplying a blockaded Germany with unlimited explosives, Weizmann was a biochemist who discovered how one particular strain of bacterium could synthesize acetone, essential for the manufacture of cordite. On the outbreak of war he moved from Manchester University to government service. Subsequently, he became director of Admiralty Laboratories under A. J. Balfour, First Lord of the Admiralty.

Thus Weizmann soon found himself well placed for staking the Zionist claim to Palestine, and it was in the accepted order of things that he represented the Zionist Organization when this was given a hearing by the Council of Ten at the peace conference on February 27, 1919.

Positions of power usually demand a good deal of ruthless wire-pulling, a good deal of balancing and counterbalancing and not occasionally the bland reassurance on facts that are not facts at all. All these, the common coin of getting things done, are required even of a statesman with the moral integrity of Weizmann. But to a man of Einstein's temperament this element of wheeling and dealing was repugnant.

Late in 1920 Weizmann decided to visit the United States to raise funds for the

Left: Einstein and his wife Elsa en route to the United States on the S.S. *Rotterdam,* 1921. *[AIP Niels Bohr Library]*

Right: Einstein and Chaim Weizmann (1874–1952) arriving in the United States aboard the *S.S. Rotterdam,* April 2, 1921. Left to right: Menachem Mendel Ussishkin, Professor Chaim Weizmann, Mrs. Weizmann, Einstein, Elsa Einstein, and Ben-Zion Mossinsohn. *[United Press International]*

Keren Hayesod, to be formed in March, 1921, to take over from the Palestine Restoration Fund the main financial burden of constructive work. He quickly picked a strong party to accompany him while Blumenfeld received a detailed telegraphed directive:

> I was to stir up Einstein [he says], go with him to America, and there join in the propaganda for the Keren Hayesod. Einstein must be interested, above everything else, in the idea of the Hebrew University in Jerusalem.

> When I appeared before Einstein with this telegram he at first said No: "Do you think so much of the idea of a Hebrew University in Jerusalem?" It was unfortunate that I, for different reasons, was a bad advocate of the idea, and Einstein therefore said: "How is it that you are asking me to publicise an idea that you yourself do not whole-heartedly support? Besides, I consider that the role which is expected of me is an unworthy one. I am not an orator. I can contribute nothing convincing, and they only need my name which is now in the public eye."

> I did not reply, but read Weizmann's telegram aloud again. "It is irrelevant that we know what is necessary for Zionism today," I said. "We both know too little of all the factors involved. Weizmann represents Zionism. He alone can make decisions. He is the President of our organisation, and if you take your conversion to Zionism seriously, then I have the right to ask you, in Dr. Weizmann's name, to go with him to the United States and to do what he at the moment thinks is necessary."

"To my boundless astonishment," Blumenfeld writes, "Einstein answered: 'What you say now is right and convincing. With argument and counter-argument we get no further. To you Weizmann's telegram is a command. I realise that I myself am now part of the situation and that I must accept the invitation. Telegram Weizmann that I agree.'" Thus he prepared to take a major step toward the consolidation of his fame in America and of his notoriety in Germany as the focus of anti-Semitism.

The journey began on March 21, 1921, when the Einsteins left Berlin for Holland, where they were to embark on the *Rotterdam.* They were joined on board by the Weizmanns. "Einstein was young, gay and flirtatious," says Mrs. Weizmann. "His wife, I recall, told me that she did not mind her husband's flirting with me as 'intellectual women' did not attract him; out of pity he was attracted to women who did physical work"—a remark substantiated by more than one of his intimate friends. During the voyage across the Atlantic, says Weizmann, Einstein "explained his theory to me every day and on my arrival I was fully convinced that he understood it."

In New York he met reporters as the ship docked. One of the first questions had been a constant companion since November 1919: "Can you explain relativity in a few sentences?" Ever anxious not to disappoint, and in this case doubly so out of loyalty to

230

Einstein leaving New York's City Hall, April, 1921. [Brown Brothers]

Weizmann, Einstein had an answer that became a classic. "If you will not take the answer too seriously, and consider it only as a kind of joke, then I can explain it as follows," he said. "It was formerly believed that if all material things disappeared out of the universe, time and space would be left. According to the relativity theory, however, time and space disappear together with the things."

From then on he had their confidence, a smiling, tousle-haired figure in his high wing collar and knitted tie, anxious to assure them that his theory would not change the ideas of the man in the street, claiming that every physicist who studied relativity could easily understand it, and as confounded as were his interrogators by the extraordinary interest that his work had aroused. "Well, gentlemen," he concluded, "I hope I have passed my examination."

The ordeal over, they went ashore. Awaiting the Einsteins was more than the official reception committee. The Jewish areas of New York were gaily decorated, while Jewish Legionnaires, who had fought with the British to liberate Palestine from the Turks, were present in strength. Some of the crowds wore buttons with Zionist slogans, others waved the Jewish flag, then merely white and blue, without the Star of David that it bears today.

What the crowds saw at the top of the gangway was Weizmann, smiling but stiff, almost a model for Lenin in physical features as in singlemindedness, and beside him the shorter figure of Einstein. He wore a faded gray overcoat, by no means new, and a black hat. In one hand he carried a briar pipe and in the other his violin. "He looked like an artist, a musician," wrote one reporter. "He is of medium height with strongly-built shoulders, but an air of fragility and self-effacement." Under a broad, high forehead were the large and luminous eyes, almost childlike in their simplicity and unworldliness. Einstein, the public figure now emerged from the chrysalis of the professor, unconsciously dropped into the role of Einstein playing Einstein.

The two men and their wives were driven between a police escort to City Hall, whose public square was filled with more than five thousand Zionists. Here, they were formally received by New York, where there lived a third of all the Jews in the United States. And here, it had been tacitly arranged, Weizmann and Einstein would be given the freedom of the city.

231

Einstein and President Warren G. Harding in Washington, D.C., in 1921. The two men met when Einstein visited the President with a group from the National Academy of Sciences. [United Press International]

As a member of the Weizmann party, Einstein could not stand aside entirely from the arguments about Jewish development in Palestine. But Weizmann had not ignored Blumenfeld's warning about Einstein's propensity for saying "things out of naïveté which cause us trouble." He had given his colleague broad hints about when to stay quiet. Einstein, for his part, kept himself well in hand—although his feelings were shown privately during a big meeting in Madison Square Garden. While one Zionist orator was speaking with great heat, Einstein turned to the man next to him on the platform and whispered in German: "What an ass!"

The classic example of his wish to be good came on the evening of April 12, after Weizmann had spoken to eight thousand Jews at the 69th Regiment Armory.

Einstein then rose. "Your leader, Dr. Weizmann, has spoken, and he has spoken very well for us all," he said. "Follow him and you will do well. That is all I have to say."

Einstein's lectures on relativity, which were to broaden the knowledge of his work in the United States, began on April 15 at Columbia University, which had awarded him the Barnard Medal the previous year. It was the first time he had spoken on relativity—or on anything else it appears—to an English-speaking audience. He showed the same assured naturalness he used with allies and enemies, presidents and street sweepers, kings, queens, and custodians. "He several times brought chuckles and laughs from his audience by his references to the 'idiot' behaviour of certain bodies in accelerated systems," the *New York Times* noted. "Also he caused much amusement when he wished to erase some diagrams he had drawn on the blackboard and made futile motions in the air with his hand until Professor Pupin came to his rescue."

In Washington, Einstein and Weizmann visited President Harding with a group from the National Academy of Sciences, at whose annual dinner Einstein spoke. The formal speeches went on and on, and as one scientist after another accepted the Academy's annual awards Einstein turned to his neighbor, the secretary of the Netherlands Embassy, who was representing the physicist, Pieter Zeeman: "I have just got a new theory of Eternity," he confided.

Another visit was to Princeton, where on Monday, May 9, an honorary degree was conferred and where he gave a lecture a day for the rest of the week. It was after one of these, during an evening discussion, that he heard of D. C. Miller's first announcement, which appeared to refute the Michelson-Morley experiment. And here, believing that the truth did not lie in the convolutions demanded by Miller's results, he observed: "God is subtle but he is not malicious" ("*Raffiniert ist der Herrgott, aber boshaft ist er nicht*"). In Chicago, the next port of call, he made one contact that was greatly to affect his future.

Einstein (eighth from right), seen below the main telescope, at Yerkes Observatory, Williams Bay, Wisconsin, on May 6, 1921. [AIP Niels Bohr Library]

This was with Robert Millikan, who a few years previously had provided experimental evidence for Einstein's photoelectric equation.

Then, a few days before he was due to sail for Europe, leaving Weizmann to continue his Zionist work alone, the two men visited Cleveland. Most of the Jewish shops were closed for the occasion and the party was met at the Union Station by a two-hundred-car parade headed by the band of the Third Regiment of the National Guard.

The near-hysteria that had marked more than one phase of the visit was not entirely the result of the new-felt longing to be free, which surged through the Jewish world with the hopes of a National home raised by the Balfour Declaration, or of the intellectual cataclysm made by relativity. Both played their part. But both were reinforced by the extraordinary impact made by Einstein himself during what was for most practical purposes his first journey outside the academic world into the realm of the uninitiated. The curtains had parted, and behind them there was seen not the austere and aloof leader of science, but an untidy figure carrying his violin, the epitome of the world's little man immortalized in different ways by Charlie Chaplin, Hans Fallada, and H. G. Wells' Kipps. Astonishment increased as it became clear that however steely-keen Einstein's relentless dedication to science might be—and within the inner circle there was no doubt of that—here was the real article, genuinely humble, honestly surprised that so much fuss should be made of him.

After Einstein's return to Berlin he accepted the invitation to lecture in Japan. This was at the height of his use to the Zionist cause, and it was natural that he should be asked to visit Palestine on his way back to Europe from the Far East and to give the inaugural address at the Hebrew University.

He arrived with his wife at Tel Aviv on February 2, 1923, and was greeted by Colonel Frederick Kisch, who had retired from the British Army with a fine war record to join the Zionist Executive. "Found him rather tired as he had sat up all night," Kisch recorded in his diary, "but I later learned that this was his own fault, as he had insisted on travelling second-class in spite of every effort to persuade him to go into a *wagon-lit* which had been reserved for him." Three days later he was formally received by the Palestine Zionist Executive.

There was no doubt about Einstein's almost embarrassing enthusiasm for Palestine—or of Palestine's for him. This was shown the following day. That the most famous scientist in the world—if the most controversial one—should give such unqualified support to their efforts, genuinely roused the inhabitants and emboldened them to think that the reward would be equally unqualified. Einstein responded with an

233

answering enthusiasm. The interaction was shown when on February 6 he drove through streets lined with crowds of waving schoolchildren to a reception at the Lemel School organized by the Palestine Zionist Executive and the Jewish National Council. After he entered, there was, the *Palestine Weekly* reported, "no holding back the crowd who had assembled outside. The outer gates were stormed, and the crowd burst into the courtyard, and tried to force the inner gates which were stoutly held by three or four stalwarts."

Inside, Einstein was baring his soul. "I consider this the greatest day of my life," he said. "Hitherto I have always found something to regret in the Jewish soul, and that is the forgetfulness of its own people—forgetfulness of its being almost. Today I have been made happy by the sight of the Jewish people learning to recognise themselves and to make themselves recognised as a force in the world."

The following day he was to perform his main task in Palestine: delivery of the inaugural address at the Hebrew University, which had been founded five years earlier as the British and Turkish guns still faintly boomed away fifteen miles to the north. Before the ceremony he had a long talk with Kisch, which reveals the state of his mind.

"Interview with Deedes," Kisch recorded; "then a walk back from Mount Scopus to the city with Einstein to whom I explained the political situation and some of the intricacies of the Arab question. Einstein spoke of Ussishkin's attempt to persuade him to settle in Jerusalem*. He has no intention of doing so, not because he would sever himself from his work and friends, but because in Europe he is free and here he would always be a prisoner. He is not prepared to be merely an ornament in Jerusalem."

At four-thirty the same afternoon some hundreds of men and women, including members of the Consular Corps and the newly created Palestine Government and their wives, packed into the temporary building of the Hebrew University on Mount Scopus. The hall was hung with Zionist flags and the insignia of the twelve tribes. Above the platform hung the Union Jack with a portrait of the high commissioner and a Zionist flag with a portrait of Dr. Herzl, while from the ceiling descended a banner bearing the words *Orah ve Torah* (Light and Learning).

Ussishkin introduced Einstein with the announcement that two thousand years ago Titus and his avenging armies had stood where they now stood. But today they were inaugurating a temple of science. "Mount the platform which has been waiting for you for two thousand years," he concluded grandly.

Einstein did so, delighting those present by giving what Sir Herbert Samuel, the high commissioner with whom the Einsteins were staying, called "an opening sentence *pro forma* in a Hebrew that was evidently unfamiliar." Then he continued in French; and, at the end of the comparatively short address, repeated it in German.

During the next few days Einstein toured the country, planting a tree in the

*Menachem Ussishkin was president of the Zionist Executive and had been a member of the party which visited America in 1921.

garden on Mount Carmel outside Haifa and visiting the city's high school and technical college. He was impressed by what he saw, and said so to Weizmann on a leaf torn from his notebook.

His enthusiasm for the opportunities that Palestine would now be able to offer was stressed as he walked on the Mount of Olives with Norman Bentwich, attorney general to the Government. "The Jews had produced no genius of rank in the nineteenth century save a mathematician—Jacobi—and Heine," he said, according to Bentwich:

> The National Home in Palestine could release and foster their genius. For two thousand years their common bond had been the past, the carefully guarded tradition. Now they had a new bond, the active co-operation in building up a country. Then he went on to talk of other things. He delighted in the beauty of the Arab peasant dress and the Arab village growing out of the rock, and equally in the beauty of life in Japan and in their sense of corporate union. The Japanese dinner made you understand the meaning of eternity....On the journey from Japan, he had been thinking out a new theory of the relation of light to gravity. The ship gave the best conditions for thought; a regular life and no disturbing influence.

Palestine strengthened Einstein's Zionist sinews, and the memory of it helped him during the difficult decade that lay ahead. When he dined with the attorney general and his wife, borrowing a violin and making up a quartet with Bentwich and his two sisters, he not only played remarkably well, but "looked so happy while he was playing that I enjoyed watching as much as listening," Mrs. Bentwich remembered. "We talked of books, and of one he said, with a happy twinkle in his eye: 'It's not worth reading. The author writes just like a professor.' "

This was but one side of the coin. The other was represented by the formality of Government House, by the mounted troops that accompanied the high commissioner as he traveled with his guests, and by the boom of the cannon that echoed every time he left the official residence. All this worried Einstein, although he had already perfected a technique of behaving as if formality did not exist—a technique that was perfectly sincere but that at times gave a misleading impression of playing to the gallery or of being eccentric for eccentricity's sake.

Einstein and his wife left Palestine for Europe in mid-February. His parting advice was severely practical. Kisch records that as he said goodbye to his visitor in Jerusalem, he asked Einstein "to let us know if during his tour he had observed that we were doing anything which in his opinion we should not do, or if we were leaving undone things which should be done. He answered: 'Ramassez plus d'argent.' "

The journey to Palestine consolidated Einstein's feelings for Zionism, and these remained strong—despite its nationalism, which he mistrusted as he mistrusted all nationalisms, despite its cornerstone of a religion, which he could take no more seriously than he could take any other revealed religion. There were two other things that tended to make him qualify his support of Zionism. One was his belief that a first priority should be agreement with the Arabs. As Arab feelings hardened, as mandate policy appeared to be increasingly swayed by pro-Arab sentiment, and as practical Zionist aims were narrowed to nation-state or nothing, such internationalist and pacifist leanings began to make Einstein's position within the Zionist movement frequently difficult and sometimes anomalous.

There was also his guerrilla battle with the management of the Hebrew University, which continued from the University's formal opening in 1925 until the summer of 1934, a battle fought largely against the influence of Judah Magnes, the virtual ruler of the University, who exercised his power in line with the U.S. interests which had so largely financed it.

Einstein was elected one of the governors, and the board met under his chairmanship in Munich in September, 1925. Here, it was enlarged. An academic council was set up, and a "Palestine Executive" was created so that in future the University could almost be said to have two masters, one in London under the stern eye of Weizmann, who was to be chairman of the board for the rest of his life, the second in Jerusalem under the chancellor, who as the man on the spot always had the option of acting first and asking afterward. The chancellor was Judah Magnes. Weizmann supported Magnes. Einstein opposed the choice.

There were many difficulties, not the least delicate of which concerned the minutes of the Munich meeting. Einstein pointed out to Magnes on December 29, 1925, that he held the minutes and asked for the withdrawal of a second set, which Magnes had circulated. Magnes declined. He remained in possession of the field, and the best that Einstein could do was to write to him despairingly and admit that further correspondence between them was useless.

He still continued to work for the good of the University, however, visiting Paris in January, 1926, to lecture on it before the Franco-Palestine Society and sparing for Zionist activities whatever time he could squeeze from his work. But a man in Einstein's position, brought on to committees and governing boards for the prestige of his name rather than for what he was expected to do, could always threaten to play the strong card of resignation. This he now did, in the first of a series of actions that strangely mirrors his indecisive turnabout with the League Committee.

Early in the summer of 1926 Weizmann visited Berlin to discuss the unhappy University situation. Any ambiguity in Einstein's attitude was removed by a letter he wrote to Weizmann on July 6. Weizmann replied by reiterating his appeal that Einstein should not resign, an act that would only leave Magnes in undisputed control. Einstein acquiesced, at least for the time being. But eighteen months later, on January 8, 1928, he felt it necessary to complain in stronger terms.

As chairman of the board, Weizmann had mixed feelings. "Our income," he later stressed to Einstein, "is entirely from voluntary subscribers, and we had to depend on Magnes—as you yourself have admitted—because Magnes could secure at any rate a considerable proportion of the budget. The same argument covered even the choice of professors by the board of governors, who had to adopt the suggestions of those who controlled the purse of the University." To Weizmann, half a university was better than none. Einstein disagreed, and in his letter of January threatened to resign from the board unless action was taken within a year, since he felt it was better to delay the founding of a Hebrew University rather than create a second-class institution at once.

These were tough words. They were implemented a few months later, although Einstein's concern for the University forced him to conceal this from the world at large. Weizmann wrote in midsummer, proposing what Einstein subsequently described as compromises. He did not agree with them. And on June 14, 1928, he wrote that in the circumstances he had decided to retire completely from the University's affairs, although he would not officially resign. But six days later he decided to go.

Einstein's genuine concern for the University was a measure of his own individualistic Zionism, and he was among those invited to attend, and to speak at, the crucial Sixteenth Zionist Congress held in Zurich in August, 1929. In the words of Weizmann's invitation, the congress would be "of an unusually momentous character in view of the fact that it will be called upon to ratify the measures taken by the Zionist Executive for the enlargement of the Jewish Agency, so that it may be possible for the first meeting of the Council of the Agency to be held immediately after the Congress."

Einstein was, as always, only too happy to visit Zurich. He took the opportunity of visiting his children, telling Eduard, who asked why he had come, that he was attending a Jewish conference and adding: "I am the Jewish Saint." He visited Mileva and, although he appears to have put up at the Grand Dolder Hotel on the Zurichberg, was glad to shock Sir John and Lady Simon by telling them: "I am staying with my first wife." He visited the shop where he had bought "penny cigars" as a student. And he took the tram to visit his old landlady, Frau Markwalder, insisting that she should not be told of his coming since he "did not want to play the great man."

There had been bitter talk of "abdication" to the Jewish Agency, and it was claimed that the influential half of the new organization was concerned only with a much watered-down version of real Zionism. Little of this argument came through at the congress, although it is significant that in his speech Einstein, after speaking of "the brave and dedicated minority who call themselves Zionists," went on to say "we others."

The Zurich meeting marked a climax in Zionist endeavor and, for overlapping reasons, the end of one phase of Einstein's support. The enlarged Jewish Agency, with Weizmann at its head, had barely come into existence when serious anti-Jewish riots broke out in Palestine. On September 11, Louis Marshall, who had been a mainstay of the non-Zionist section of the Agency, died after an operation. The following month the Wall Street crash cut the hopes of major U.S. support and, at the same time, by triggering off the great depression in Europe, provided the cue for the nationalist, and largely anti-Semitic, forces waiting in the wings of the Weimar Republic.

15.

PREPARING FOR THE STORM

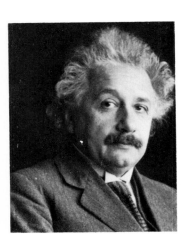

Einstein at the age of fifty. *[Ullstein]*

By the early months of 1929 Einstein was recovering from his collapse of the previous spring. He was by now past the age at which a scientist might be expected to produce original work; it was almost time to think of the administrative "plums" that academic life offered. He did nothing of the sort. He not only continued the good fight against indeterminacy in physics, where Born and Heisenberg could already claim substantial victories, but pressed vigorously on with what had for almost a decade been his main preoccupation, the construction of a field theory uniting the forces of electromagnetism and gravity. He had studied the forces of electromagnetism and produced the Special Theory, a new and more accurate yardstick for measuring the characteristics of the physical world. He had studied the force of gravity, found it to be not quite what men had believed it to be, and had produced the General Theory. Now he asked whether it would be possible to unite them.

Some men answered this question with an unqualified "No." Wolfgang Pauli, who believed that such a marriage of the laws of electromagnetism and of gravitation was impossible, summed it up: "What God hath put asunder no man shall ever join." Others were more optimistic, notably Hermann Weyl and Arthur Eddington, both of whom produced plausible but by no means satisfactory theories that attempted to unify the two fields.

Einstein set out on the formidable venture soon after he had completed the General Theory, and his correspondence of the immediate postwar years is spattered with references to it. In 1923 he published a preliminary paper on the subject based on an idea already put forward by Eddington; then, settling down after the return from his travels, gave the problem increasing attention. His efforts were soon given a further spur by the birth of quantum mechanics; for it was part of his lifelong, but unfulfilled hope that a unified field theory would help to remove the new, and for him, uncongenial statistical element that formed part of the new physics.

Even in the 1920s the prospects looked poor. Einstein himself knew this, and the explanation he gave late in life for devotion to this particular task was as relevant in 1929 as in 1949. "He agreed that the chance of success was very small," he told a colleague, Professor Taub of Berkeley, "but that the attempt must be made. He himself had established his name; his position was assured, and so he could afford to take the risk of failure. A young man with his way to make in the world could not afford to take a risk by which he might lose a great career, and so Einstein felt that in this matter he had a duty."

One paper giving the outline of a unified field was published in the *Proceedings* of the Prussian Academy of Sciences in 1928—probably the paper that caused Elsa to write of her husband to a friend: "He has solved the problem whose solution was the dream of his life." Then, on January 10, 1929, the Academy announced that Einstein had submitted a new paper on a unified field theory, which was being examined. This immediately aroused the interest of the world, and not only because the Academy appeared to be suggesting that something important was coming. Einstein was by this time approaching his fiftieth birthday, and the world was tickled by the fact that toward the end of his fiftieth year the man who had "caught light bending" might have perfected a set of equations that would, in the popular phrase, "solve the riddle of the universe."

It was announced that the paper would be published at the end of the month, and extensive, ingenious, but unsuccessful efforts were made by many of the world's newspapers to secure an advance copy. In an age when liaison between newspapers and leading scientists was less happy than today, distortions and absurdities were more apt to creep in, and these were particularly irksome to Einstein who knew that a real understanding of his work was beyond most laymen and many scientists. It was left to the chief Berlin correspondent of the *New York Times*, for which Einstein had developed a particular fondness, to explain that the spate of telephone calls and requests were solely the result of the theory whose publication was to be completed within a few days. Einstein could only murmur: "My God."

The paper for which the press had been waiting consisted of six pages covered by fairly large print and including thirty-three equations. "To the layman," commented *The Times'* correspondent, "the paper conveys next to nothing." This was not surprising since, as Eddington noted, "for the present, at any rate, a non-mathematical explanation is out of the question, and in any case would miss the main purpose of the theory, which is to weld a number of laws into a mathematical expression of formal simplicity." Einstein himself did the next best thing. He wrote a three-thousand-word, two-part article that was published in both the *New York Times* and *The Times*, and which outlined "the chain of discovery." The most important feature of the new theory was its hypothesis that the structure of four dimensional space could be described in terms of a synthesis of Riemannian and Euclidean geometry. On this rested the erection of unitary field laws for gravitation and electromagnetism. It was new, it was interesting, but during the next few years informed opinion tended to support the view of Eddington:

> For my part, I cannot readily give up the affine picture, where gravitational and electrical quantities supplement one another as belonging respectively to the symmetrical and antisymmetrical features of world measurement; it is difficult to imagine a neater dovetailing. Perhaps one who believes that Weyl's theory and its affine generalisation afford considerable enlightenment, may be excused for doubting whether the new theory offers sufficient inducement to make an exchange.

Left: Einstein and Wolfgang Pauli (1900–1958), Leiden, 1926. Photograph by Paul Ehrenfest. [AIP Niels Bohr Library]

Right: Einstein and H. G. Wells (third from left), meeting on the occasion of Wells' visit to Berlin in 1929 to lecture on "Understanding of Men." Also shown are Karl Heinrich Becker (second from left) and Dr. Paul Lobe (far right). [Wide World]

Einstein himself was soon dissatisfied and within a year was working on a fresh theory with a new assistant, Dr. Walther Mayer, an Austrian brought to see him in Berlin after publication of a book that Einstein greatly admired—*Lehrbuch der Differential-geometrie.* There was at first some difficulty in getting money for Mayer—possibly an indication of Kaiser Wilhelm's long memory of Einstein's attitude during the war—but eventually money for him was found by the Josiah Macy (Junior) Foundation of New York. He then moved from Vienna to Berlin for what was to be more than three years of collaboration.

The new attempt was announced when in October the Macy Foundation issued details of the new unified field theory from Einstein and Mayer. This, too, was eventually abandoned, as were the other attempts that Einstein continued to make for the rest of his life—most of them produced, as he wrote to an old friend, "in an agony of mathematical torment from which I am unable to escape."

The 1929 theory was published only a few weeks before his fiftieth birthday, an event that was to show that his ambivalence to the Germans was equaled by their ambivalence to him. On the one hand, there was such international fame that he was driven to the refuge of Janos Plesch's house at Gatow by journalists who wanted a birthday interview. The German chancellor described him as "Germany's great savant." The University of Paris conferred an honorary degree. The Zionists announced that they were to plant an "Einstein wood" near Jerusalem. To the apartment in Haberlandstrasse there came presents from great men and small men alike—the first that Einstein acknowledged being an ounce of tobacco sent by a German laborer with the apology that it was "a relatively small amount but gathered in a good field."

Yet these birthday celebrations took place beneath the shadow of a significant tragicomedy. Early in 1929 Dr. Plesch approached the Berlin authorities:

> I had to explain to Boess, the Mayor of Berlin, who and what Einstein was before I could convince him that his city numbered a really great man amongst its inhabitants and that it was his Council's obvious duty to show some recognition of the fact [he has written]. I am sure the worthy Boess was not entirely satisfied with what I told him, and pursued his inquiries further as to who this Einstein was. Apparently the result was satisfactory, for he finally agreed with me that it would be a good idea to acknowledge Einstein's birthday by presenting him with a house and garden as a mark of the deep esteem in which he was held by the Berlin Municipality.

Einstein's love of small boats had remained from the days when he had sailed the Zurichsee. What better, the Berlin Municipal Council therefore decided, than to choose for him a country villa on one of the Berlin lakes. Einstein was known to enjoy the Havel River, and it was announced that as a birthday gift he would be presented with a

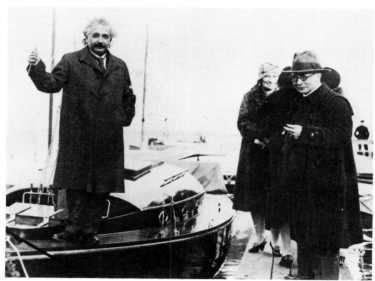

fine house on its banks, a little way upstream from its junction with the Wannsee. Only when Elsa visited the site to make domestic inquiries did she learn that the house was already occupied.

The Berlin Council changed its plans and hastily announced that a nearby plot would be presented to Einstein. But when other property on the estate had been leased, it had been agreed by the Council that no further building would be allowed to disturb the amenities or the view. Einstein might get his land; he would not be allowed to build on it. And when the Council selected yet a third plot, it discovered after the bequest was announced that the property was not theirs to present. Next, Einstein was asked to select his own site; the Council would pay for it. Elsa was not long in choosing a site in the village of Caputh, a few miles from Potsdam. Then a member of a leading nationalist party came into the open. Did Einstein deserve this municipal gift, he demanded? The Council, forced to the vote, did not know. The subject was moved forward for further discussion at the next meeting.

Einstein now acted with desperation but dignity, thanking the mayor for the Council's friendly intentions, noting that his birthday was now past. He declined the gift. By this time, however, he and Elsa had become fond of the plot they had chosen. So they bought it, and built their own house on it.

The new home had all the qualities of genuinely rural surroundings even though it lay only a few miles from the center of Berlin. Beyond Potsdam, on the road that led to Werder-on-the-Havel, Caputh was at that time little more than one straggling street and was rarely visited by the weekend crowds from the capital. North of it stretched the sandy heaths and pine forests, interspersed by lakes and streams, which continue for mile after mile to the Baltic. Just outside the village the ground rises to the edge of the trees, and here, only a few minutes from the Havelsee, on which white sails could usually be seen, the Einsteins built what was to be for a few years a good deal more than a weekend cottage.

The young architect who built the house ingeniously combined sophistication with a simple style that fitted the surroundings. From the exterior the impression was almost that of a log-built cabin; inside, the half-timbered construction concealed a comfortable roominess increased by smooth brown paneling and large windows giving on to the distant prospect of red Caputh roofs, the Havelsee, and the enclosing forest. This was also the view from the long first-floor room, which Einstein used as combined study and bedroom. Books lined the walls, the bed filled a recess, while in front of the tall French windows that opened on to a balcony there stood the large paper-cluttered desk at which he worked. And on the Havelsee there was berthed the *Tummler*, the small boat given him as a fiftieth birthday present by friends.

Left: Einstein outside his home at Caputh, a few miles from Berlin, which he acquired soon after his fiftieth birthday in 1929. *[The Mansell Collection]*

Right: Einstein with the sailing craft presented to him on his fiftieth birthday, March 14, 1929. He often took it on the lakes near his home at Caputh on the outskirts of Berlin. *[Wide World]*

Elsa and Einstein at Gatow, outside Berlin, 1928. *[Lotte Jacobi Collection]*

Opposite: Einstein at Caputh, walking down the path to his sailboat. *[© H. Landshoff]*

At Caputh, where he settled in during 1929, Einstein tried to isolate himself from unwanted visitors, newspaper correspondents, and the uncategorizable cranks who sought a few words with him. Contemplation of first principles progressively occupied his attention. One visitor, Dr. Chaim Tschernowitz, has given a vivid account of a summer trip with him on the Havelsee during which their discussions were often metaphysical: "The conversation drifted back and forth from profundities about the nature of God, the universe and man to questions of a lighter and more vivacious nature," he has written. "Suddenly [Einstein] lifted his head, looked upward at the clear skies, and said: 'We know nothing about it all. All our knowledge is but the knowledge of school-children.' 'Do you think,' I asked, 'that we shall ever probe the secret?' 'Possibly,' he said with a movement of his shoulders, 'we shall know a little more than we do now. But the real nature of things, that we shall never know, never.'" As Born said of Einstein after his death, "he knew, as did Socrates, that we know nothing."

Meanwhile, he worked on, at the unified field theory, at the problems posed by quantum mechanics, intrigued by the prospects being opened up in cosmology by the new telescopes of California, and in nuclear physics by the accumulating knowledge of the atom. In his own specialty he was lucky; in the days before computers he demanded no equipment, and as for helpers Dr. Mayer sufficed. "The kind of work I do can be done anywhere," he said when his friend Philipp Frank apologized that he might be late for a rendezvous near the Astrophysical Observatory. "Why should I be less capable of reflecting about my problems on the Potsdam Bridge than at home?"

It was natural that after mathematicians and scientists throughout the world had contributed to a special award that was to bear Max Planck's name, Einstein should be the first to receive it. The presentation was to take place at five in the afternoon, and after a morning's work Einstein visited Plesch for a lunch over which they discussed the crisis in the theory of causality. Then Einstein lay down on a couch and went to sleep. He woke at four, said: "They'll expect me to say something or the other," sat down at the doctor's writing desk, took a bootmaker's bill, which was the nearest piece of paper to hand, and scribbled away for twenty minutes. Half an hour later, in the packed hall of the Institute of Physics, Planck took the platform and after a conventional speech handed over the medal.

"Then Einstein spoke," writes Plesch: "'I knew that an honour of this sort would move me deeply' he began, 'and therefore I have put down on paper what I would like to say to you as thanks. I will read it.' And out of his waistcoat pocket came my bootmaker's bill with the scribble on the back, and he read out what he had written about the principle of causality. And because, as he said, no reasoning being could get on at all

Left: Einstein at a reception held by Reich Chancellor Dr. Heinrich Bruning in Berlin, 1931. Left to right: Max Planck, British Prime Minister Ramsay MacDonald, Einstein, German Finance Minister Dr. Dietrich (foreground), Geheimrat Schmitz of I. G. Farben, and Aussenminister Curtius (extreme right). [Ullstein]

Right: Einstein receiving the first Planck Medal from Max Planck in the hall of the Institute of Physics, Berlin, July, 1929. [AIP Niels Bohr Library]

without causality he established the principle of super-causality. The atmosphere was tense and most moving." Afterward, Plesch claimed his bootmaker's bill. Einstein also handed him the medal, of solid gold and with a relief of Planck. "It was still in the case," Plesch noted. "He never took it out or looked at it again."

This award and the stream of comparable honors and invitations from abroad were fair indications of the German position he still held in the scientific community. Outside, the situation was very different.

In the early 1930s Norman Bentwich, who as attorney general in Palestine had walked on Mount Scopus with Einstein seven years earlier, visited Berlin with his wife. "I was disturbed by grim signs of the rising anti-Semitic flood and the growing strength of the Nazi political party," he has written. "When we had spent a week there the previous year, on our tour through Europe, all seemed serene and hopeful. Now many Jewish shops had been sacked, and the Jews, who in 1929 were almost derisive about Hitler, were seriously alarmed. I visited Einstein in his sailing retreat on one of the lakes; and for all his serenity he was anxious."

He was well aware that he was seeing merely the tip of the anti-Semitic iceberg. More than once he spoke to his wife of taking a post abroad, of renouncing German nationality for the second time, and of holding up for public examination the attitude of Germany toward the Jews. Perhaps it would have been better for the Jews had he done so. But he hesitated. The magnet provided by the society of the Berlin physicists proved too powerful.

Yet as the 1930s started their disastrous course downhill, Einstein's faith in the future of Europe in general and of Germany in particular began to wane. This was revealed not only by his increasingly pessimistic utterances, publicly on platforms and privately to friends, in magazine and newspaper articles, but also in the new pattern of life soon produced by acceptance of two different sets of engagements. One was with the California Institute of Technology, which he agreed to visit for a few weeks early in 1931 on what was mutually if loosely expected to be the start of a long-term regular engagement. The other was at Christ Church, Oxford, where he accepted a research fellowship that allowed him to spend one term a year in the university. His work in Berlin would, of course, continue as before; but it would dovetail conveniently into an annual program that would involve departure from Germany for the United States in December, return during the late winter or early spring, then summer in Oxford before a return to Berlin in the early autumn. This plan had the advantage of retaining his links with Planck, Von Laue, and his other colleagues while providing two alternative refuges against the rise of anti-Semitism or the outbreak of war. Meanwhile, adding to the luster of German science, he continued to feed the hand that bit him.

244

"Branded" Jewish shops in Germany in the 1930s. *[The Mansell Collection]*

Before the start of these series of visits to California and to Oxford, which developed under the increasingly sinister pressure of events in Germany, Einstein made three other significant journeys abroad, one to Holland and Belgium, two to Britain. The first, which began in 1929 as one of his regular trips to Leiden, was the most important. He called as usual on his Uncle Cäsar in Antwerp, just across the frontier. And here, he received an invitation to visit the queen of the Belgians at Laeken on Monday, May 20. King Albert, epitome of the liberal-minded constitutional monarch, still a symbolic figure from the First World War, a trenchcoated king defying the German invaders in Flanders fields, had a genuine interest in science and was absent only because of an appointment in Switzerland. Queen Elizabeth, formerly Princess Elizabeth of Bavaria, was unconventional and artistic, and on May 20 Einstein and his violin spent the first of many musical afternoons at the Palace, Her Majesty "playing second fiddle." There followed, according to the Queen's own notes in her agenda book, tea under the chestnuts and a walk in the grounds, followed by dinner at seven-thirty.

The meeting marked the start of an unusual friendship. During the next four years—as long as Einstein remained in Europe—he would rarely visit Belgium without being invited to the palace at Laeken. He was the usual Einstein, being missed at the railway station by the royal chauffeur, who failed to recognize the drably dressed figure with the violin case; alarming a small cafe by requesting the use of a telephone and then asking direct for the Queen, and generally behaving in the simple unpremeditated way of a man with his mind on other things.

In 1930 Einstein made two visits to England. Berfore he left Berlin for the first, he received a request from Professor Veblen, whom he had met in Princeton nine years previously. A new faculty lounge was being built in the university for the mathematics and physics department. Could they have permission to use on it his phrase, which had lodged in Veblen's memory—"God is subtle but he is not malicious"? Einstein consented,

Einstein, Lord Rothschild (believed at the time to be the world's wealthiest man), and George Bernard Shaw (far right) at a dinner in London in August, 1930, of the O.R.T.-Ozl, an organization for helping Jews in Eastern Europe. *[United Press International]*

adding that what he had meant was that nature concealed her mysteries by means of her essential grandeur, not by her cunning, and the original phrase was carved on the room's marble fireplace.

Shortly afterward, he left for England, going first to Nottingham, where he gave to the university a general survey of relativity and the unified field theory. Then he traveled on to Cambridge to accept an honorary degree, a happy occasion since it enabled him to meet Eddington, whose knighthood was announced in the King's Birthday Honors during the visit. In the autumn he came to London for a special dinner of the O.R.T.—an organization for helping Jews in Eastern Europe—staying with Lord Samuel in Porchester Terrace, where, as he later described it, he played a "star-guest role." But he skillfully evaded a further invitation "to meet...many prominent men," pleading that he had a prior appointment in Switzerland, where he was anxious to discuss the health of his younger son.

Samuel's notes of Einstein's visit, written a few hours after his guest's departure, cast an interesting sidelight on Einstein at the age of fifty. During the meal he mentioned that he was still frequently being attacked in Germany—"*parce que je suis Rouge et Juif.*" Samuel, knowing that Einstein's politics were pink rather than red, commented: "*Mais pas très Rouge.*" "*Et pas très Juif,*" added Einstein.

Soon after he arrived back in Berlin, he was visited by Arthur Fleming, the chairman of the board of trustees of the California Institute of Technology. The visit appears to have been made on the suggestion of Richard Chase Tolman, the Institute's professor of physical chemistry and mathematical physics, for reasons that were soon to be self-evident. "The result was better than Tolman expected," Fleming wrote to a colleague, "so that when I first met Einstein at his home in the country, and invited him to come to us with the money provided by Mr. Thomas Cochran, his first question was, 'You have a man named Tolman at your institution?' I said we had, and he then asked if Tolman were a visitor or one of our men. I informed him that he was one of ours."

Tolman was handling much of the theoretical work at Mount Wilson Observatory concerning the nature and size of the universe. Einstein was anxious to discuss this firsthand with the men concerned, and he quickly agreed to visit the Institute as a research associate early in 1931.

When the news was announced, he was soon brought up once more against the interest of the United States in all he said and did. Before the end of the week, fifty cables a day were arriving from across the Atlantic. U.S. mail began to outnumber German letters. Elsa, who was left to handle the welter of invitations, stated firmly that the professor would be traveling purely on holiday; that he wished to be left alone; and, finally, that she would not allow him to land in New York, but would insist that he

246

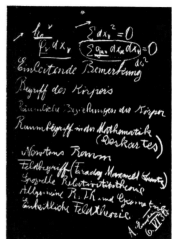

Left: Einstein at Oxford University in May, 1931, when the honorary degree of Doctor of Science was conferred on him. He is shown here walking in the procession during the ceremony. *[United Press International]*

Right: The blackboard used by Einstein when he lectured at the University of Nottingham, England, on June 6, 1930. *[The University of Nottingham, England]*

remained on board while their Belgian ship continued its journey south, through the Panama Canal, and up to California.

At Antwerp he repeated that this was merely a holiday trip, although agreeing that he would be visiting El Paso Observatory and would discuss with his American friends questions in which they were mutually interested. "If you really want to send a message to the press," he told reporters, "let it be that I want to be left alone. Personally I consider it indecent to delve into people's private affairs, and the world would certainly fare better if newspapers cared more for things that really matter instead of dealing with trifles."

As the liner pulled out into the Atlantic, Einstein was left comparatively at peace in the three flower-filled staterooms that had been allotted him. Here, he was to work throughout much of the voyage with Dr. Mayer, permanently guarded from intrusion by a member of the crew stationed outside the door to his suite.

But the radio-telephone continued to bring news: of the *Völkischer Beobachter*, which was violently attacking him for traveling on a Belgian ship instead of the German *Europa*, due to arrive in New York the same day (but not sailing on to the West Coast); and of the National German Jewish Union, taking up the old stick that Einstein was using his scientific fame to propagate Zionism, a charge that it would have been difficult to deny.

During the voyage, a working one for Einstein and Dr. Mayer, Elsa was persuaded that it would, after all, be better for them to go ashore in New York. Einstein himself agreed that it would be simpler for him to meet the press when the ship came into the harbor. The occasion, when it came, had an air of comedy. Fifty reporters and fifty photographers swooped on their victim. Einstein, good-natured but bewildered, was called upon "within the brief quarter of an hour to define the fourth dimension in one word, state his theory of relativity in one sentence, give his views on prohibition, comment on politics and religion, and discuss the virtues of his violin." He proved remarkably adroit at handling his questioners, answering the scientific conundrums so that the replies were comprehensible, sidestepping the more irrelevant demands, and interspersing his remarks with the occasional debating point or colorful phrase. Asked whether there was any relation between science and metaphysics, he declared that science itself was metaphysics. And asked what he thought of Hitler, he replied: "I do not enjoy Mr. Hitler's acquaintance. Hitler is living on the empty stomach of Germany. As soon as economic conditions in Germany improve he will cease to be important."

Then Einstein went ashore, for five crowded days of speechmaking and sightseeing, returning every night to the *Belgenland*, where he could be protected from the hundreds of visitors who wished to invoke his personal aid. He received the keys of New York at a ceremony attended by Mayor Walker and President Butler of Columbia University. He saw his statue adorning Riverside Church overlooking the Hudson River—the only statue of a living man among the thinkers who had changed the world from the days of Socrates and Plato. He celebrated the Jewish festival of Hanukkah at a crowded meeting in Madison Square Garden, and on the 14th he gave his famous "two per cent" pacifist speech to the New History Society at the Ritz-Carlton Hotel. He visited the *New York Times*, and he visited the Metropolitan Opera, where he was spontaneously cheered when the audience noticed him sitting quietly in a box. Here, he was handed a slip of paper on which the Metropolitan's publicity director had written: "Relativity: There is no hitching post in the universe—so far as we know." Einstein studied it carefully, added "Read, and found correct," and then signed it. And here, spying the press photographers who were awaiting him, he nimbly aboutfaced and escaped from them— a Marx Brothers incident in which the publicity director was seen running after the world's most famous scientist plaintively calling: "Mr. Einstein, Mr. Einstein."

The dislike of publicity was usually genuine, even if it at times gave the impression of a Lawrence of Arabia backing into the limelight. He continued to evade the trail of autograph-hunters, although those who wrote got a strictly business treatment. "If the autograph is wanted very badly, if the letter brings, say, three dollars for the Berlin poor," Elsa said, "the doctor will be happy. And with pictures for autograph with, say, five dollars, the doctor will be happy."

The Einsteins sailed from New York on December 16, touched at Havana three days later, then passed through the Panama Canal before turning northward up the coast of California. The autograph business was flourishing. He was reported to be charging a dollar a time for charity.

At the end of the month the *Belgenland* reached San Diego. Einstein gave a New Year's broadcast over the local radio, attended local festivities including one public reception at which local Jews presented him with an inscribed gold *Mezuzah* containing a Hebrew prayer, and another at which he was given a floral float.

From San Diego the Einsteins were driven to Pasadena. Here, they soon chose a small bungalow, the "shingled gingerbread house," as Einstein called it, where they were to live for their two-month stay at the Institute. As a celebrity Einstein was much sought after even in a land of celebrities. Upton Sinclair, who took him to see Eisenstein's famous film about life in Mexico, later claimed a local millionairess had contributed ten thousand dollars to Caltech on the promise of meeting him. He and Elsa dined with Charlie Chaplin "as a result of expressions of mutual desire on the part of himself and the professor to meet each other." And during a visit to Hollywood he was given a special showing of Remarque's *All Quiet on the Western Front*, already banned in Germany. "I thank you for all the things you have said of me," he said at the special dinner that followed. "If I believed them I would not be sane, and since I know I am sane, I do not believe them."

All this, however, was the froth on an important working tour. The purpose of Einstein's visit, he announced on arriving, "would be to fit into the life of the California Institute of Technology and discuss problems with noted scientists more intimately than is possible by correspondence." The day after his arrival he gave a further clue to the reason for his visit. "New observations by Hubble and Humason"—both workers at the Mount Wilson Observatory above Pasadena—"concerning the red shift of light in distant nebulae make it appear likely that the general structure of the universe is not static," he said. "Theoretical investigations made by Lemaître and Tolman fit well into the General Theory of Relativity." Einstein had, in fact, traveled halfway around the world to see whether it was really necessary to revise the picture of the universe with which he had virtually founded modern cosmology in 1917; and, if so, in what way.

Only thirteen years separated his "Cosmological Implications" from 1930, but within that period a revolution had taken place in cosmology quite as shattering as the revolution in physics that separated the work of Lorentz and J. J. Thomson in the last years of the nineteenth century from that of Planck and Einstein in the first years of the twentieth. In 1917 the mathematical projections of the universe provided by Einstein and De Sitter were given due consideration, even though astronomers had not entirely abandoned a belief that the Milky Way, the galaxy that contains the sun and its solar system amongst millions of other stars, formed the entire universe. However, it was not denied that some of the faint mysterious patches of light scattered across the night sky might be other galaxies lying unimagined distances away. V. M. Slipher at Lowell Observatory certainly thought so and suggested that at least some of them were receding from the Milky Way.

After the end of the war, evidence began to accumulate with the advance of technology, in this case with the use of ever more powerful telescopes, notably the one-hundred-inch instrument on Mount Wilson above Pasadena. Here, Edwin Hubble had from 1920 been probing into Jeans' "mysterious universe." It seemed clear to him that some of the light patches in the sky were merely clouds of gas illuminated from stars that lay within the galaxy of the Milky Way. But about others there was doubt that slowly began to be removed. In 1924 he was able to observe individual stars within the Andromeda M 31 nebula. Shortly afterward, it became evident that such stars were some eight hundred thousand light-years away—eight times the distance of the farthest star in the Milky Way. Thus the galaxy of which the solar system formed part was but a portion of the universe.

These discoveries were dramatically supported within two years, by both theoretical cosmology and observational astronomy. Listening to Hubble's account of his Andromeda discoveries at a meeting of the National Academy of Sciences in Washington had been a young Belgian priest, who after studying astrophysics in Cambridge, had moved to the Massachusetts Institute of Technology. He was Abbé Lemaître, "the mathematician for whom symmetry was nearly as important as truth." Shortly afterward, Lemaître returned to Belgium, and in a paper published in 1927 showed not only that the Einstein world would have to be unstable, but that it would, in fact, expand along the lines of De Sitter's world. A unique feature of Lemaître's cosmology was that his presupposed world had started as a "primeval atom" or "cosmic egg," which had initially contained all the matter in the universe and whose disintegration had marked the beginning of time and space. Thus the contemporary universe was merely one phase in an evolving universe. This could have started as a greatly modified "Einstein world" before turning into a continuously expanding De Sitter world in which the galaxies were moving ever farther away from one another and in which the density of matter was becoming less while its amount remained static. Lemaître's paper passed virtually unnoticed at the time. But two years later Hubble, at Mount Wilson, made the sensational announcement that the galaxies were receding at a speed proportional to their distance—receding not only from the Milky Way but also from each other. All intergalactic distances were, in fact, increasing simultaneously, and the entire universe was expanding at a rate that doubled its dimensions roughly every 1,300 million years.

Einstein on the streets of Berlin, about 1930. [Ullstein]

Spurred on by these revelations, Eddington began an inquiry with one of his research students into whether or not the "Einstein world" was stable. They soon received a copy of Lemaître's paper. This helped to convince them that the answer was "No." Thus by the middle of 1930 Hubble the astronomer, Lemaître the unknown theoretician, and Eddington the astrophysicist, agreed that Einstein's formula for a stable universe could not be valid.

There was an ironic corollary to this. The "Einstein world" had been produced with the aid of the cosmological constant, and this had been necessary, in Einstein's own words, "only for the purpose of making possible a quasi-static distribution of matter, as required by the fact of the small velocities of the stars." But now Hubble's discoveries were revealing that at least some of the galaxies, and, of course, the stars within them, were moving at speeds that were sizable proportions of the speed of light. Thus there had been no need for the cosmological constant in the first place.

One other point was that Lemaître had included in his paper an equation that gave a term for the rate of recession of the galaxies. Hubble had put a figure to this term, and with its aid the Lemaître equation could be used to provide a radius for the initial Einstein world. This given, Einstein's original work could still give a figure for the total mass of the universe. What it could no longer do was give a picture of what was happening to that mass, for this depended on the character of the cosmological constant. If this were zero, it was possible to postulate a universe that had begun some ten

Top: Einstein playing the violin on the S.S. *Belgenland* in 1931 during his voyage to the United States. *[Brown Brothers]*

Top right: Einstein and relatives leaving Europe for the United States, December 9, 1930. The photograph includes Margot Marianoff, Einstein's stepdaughter (extreme left); her husband, Dr. Dmitri Marianoff; Einstein; and Elsa Einstein (extreme right). *[United Press International]*

Right: Einstein at the California Institute of Technology with A. A. Michelson (left), of the famous Michelson-Morley experiment, and Robert A. Millikan (right), the head of the Institute, in the winter of 1930–31. Walter Mayer, Einstein's collaborator, is in the middle of the back row. *[California Institute of Technology]*

Bottom: Einstein broadcasting from the organ pavilion at Balboa Park, San Diego, California, after arriving on the S.S. *Belgenland,* early in 1931. *[United Press International]*

Top left: Einstein and his wife Elsa with Charles Chaplin (center), arriving at the première of a new Chaplin film in California in 1931. *[United Press International]*

Top right: Einstein and his wife being photographed in a process shot at the Warner Brothers First National Studios. *[Culver Pictures]*

Left: Einstein in Los Angeles, 1933, with Abbé Georges Lemaître (1894–1966), the Belgian priest and scientist whose theory of the expanding universe became a focus of cosmological controversy in the early 1930s. On the left is Dr. Robert Millikan, head of the California Institute of Technology, who had invited Einstein to the United States. *[United Press International]*

Bottom left: Dr. Walter S. Adams (1876–1956; left), Sir James Jeans (1877–1946; center), and Edwin P. Hubble (1889–1953; right), at the Mount Wilson Observatory, Pasadena, California. In the early 1930s, all three men were correlating the new cosmology with the implications of the General Theory. *[AIP Niels Bohr Library]*

Bottom center: Einstein lecturing to scientists in California, January, 1931. *[United Press International]*

Bottom right: Einstein and his assistant Dr. Walther Mayer in front of their Pasadena residence in 1931, where they lived while Einstein was working at the California Institute of Technology. *[United Press International]*

thousand million years ago with a "big bang" and that had been expanding uniformly ever since. If it were positive, as Lemaître had envisaged, then his primeval atom had begun to disintegrate some sixty thousand million years ago, and the result had begun to stabilize itself after some fifty thousand million, the contemporary expansion being caused by an upsetting of that stabilization and not by the initial "big bang." While both these theories envisage the evolution of the universe as arising from a unique situation, use of a negative value for the cosmological constant provides a third blueprint: that of the alternately expanding and contracting universe. These possibilities—to which that of a universe constantly expanding, but kept in a steady state by the continuous creation of fresh matter, had not yet been added—formed the highlights of a development that had been going on since 1920. They were still under constant and sometimes acrimonious discussion in the scientific world when Einstein arrived in Pasadena.

He remained based there throughout January and February, meeting the aged Dr. Michelson of the Michelson-Morley experiment at a dinner given in honor of them both. He was taken for short "rest" visits to a number of Californian ranches—and he cruised off Long Beach with Millikan.

Real work started when he met Tolman and Dr. Paul Epstein, professor of theoretical physics. Following this he was driven up the long circuitous road that winds out above Pasadena and then back to the top of the Sierra Madre, from one of whose summits the Mount Wilson Observatory looks down upon the town. Here, Elsa, when told that the giant telescope was required for establishing the structure of the universe, is claimed to have made a reply that may be apocryphal but is in true Elsa style: "Well, well, my husband does that on the back of an old envelope." Here, Einstein conferred with Hubble and early in February officially announced that he had abandoned the idea of a closed spherical universe. Later, he was to agree with the more complex theory of an alternately expanding and contracting universe.

In mid-February, a fortnight before he was to leave Pasadena, Einstein addressed several hundred students. His speech must have been surprising to many members of the faculty, particularly to Millikan, whose natural inclination was to believe that all was for the best in the best of all possible worlds. For instead of singing the praises of scientific progress, Einstein asked why it had brought such little happiness. In war it had enabled men to mutilate one another more efficiently, and in peace it had enslaved man to the machine.

Millikan, who was to receive angry protests about the "two per cent" speech that Einstein had made in New York on his way to Pasadena, was worried about what would happen during his guest's overland return to the East Coast. But nothing sensa-

Einstein (fourth from right, front row), Robert A. Millikan (front row, fifth from right) and members of the Physics/ Mathematical Faculty, California Institute of Technology. [California Institute of Technology]

tional did happen. On March 3 Einstein broke his journey in Chicago, where he was welcomed by a peace group and spoke from the rear platform of his train. In New York he found a waiting delegation from the War Resisters League, but the chance of an explosive after-dinner speech whose sentiments might brush off on to Caltech and discourage its wealthy supporters—and which would, in any case, have offended Millikan's conservative soul—was fortuitously removed by Weizmann.

The Jewish leader had cabled an urgent appeal for help, which Einstein received before he left Pasadena:

> Financial position movement and work Palestine extremely difficult in danger of immediate collapse especially harmful now that political situation much improved through satisfactory conclusion negotiations Government. We are making all efforts here but as you know resources Europe limited. I am urged come America help drive. Serious work here and necessity going Palestine for negotiations with Arab friends prevents my undertaking trip now must be postponed till April. You are the only man to render real assistance this critical moment by responding invitation our American friends and attending very few banquets in States. I know this imposes heavy burden but having done so much for Palestine I hope you won't refuse come to its assistance at this anxious time.

Einstein did not refuse. He rarely did. And the whole of his evening in New York was spent in preparation for, and at, a fund-raising dinner organized by the American Palestine Campaign at the Astor Hotel.

When he returned to the docks, he found banner-bearing pacifist groups awaiting him, and he subsequently cabled the leaders a message of goodwill. Two years later he was urging that only resistance to the pacifist movement would bring success against Hitler.

In mid-March he arrived back in Berlin. Less than two months later he left Germany again, this time for Oxford to receive an honorary degree and give the Rhodes Lectures.

On arrival in Oxford, Einstein was taken under Lindemann's wing and given the services of the latter's indefatigable servant and general factotum, James Harvey.

His first lecture was on relativity, the second on cosmological theory, and the third on the unified field theory. While the first and last were largely syntheses of views that Einstein had already expounded on at length, the second dealt with his recent abandoning of the cosmological constant. He admitted that this presented two problems. It would be difficult to know from what the expansion of the universe had started: and while its age worked out at about 10^{10} years, there was already considerable evidence that the earth itself was older than this. Another point was that his theory now limited the radius of the universe to 10^8 light-years, a distance to which the Mount Wilson telescope had already almost penetrated. As he said, if they went further, this would "put the varnish on" his theory.

In Oxford he saw an England very different from the formality of Lord Haldane's London residence, an England where his Jewishness, his German ancestry, and his stature as a scientist all tended to be taken for granted and then passed over so that he could be weighed and considered as a human being. He liked the experience; he enjoyed Lindemann's friends, he soaked up the atmosphere of an Oxford that has largely disappeared in the last fifty years; and whenever he wished he broke through the screens raised to ensure him privacy.

On May 23 he received an honorary doctorate of science. He spent a few days making final courtesy calls. Then he left for home, arriving in Berlin during the first days of June, and immediately giving Lindemann a graphic and pessimistic account of the developing situation in Germany. "…I have hopes," Lindemann was soon writing, "that this period as Rhodes Lecturer may initiate more permanent connections with this university which can only prove fertile and advantageous in every respect."

The first move came quickly. It was proposed that Einstein should be made a "Research Student," the most honorific post to which the college could elect him. Einstein accepted without delay, delighted at being able to keep in touch with Oxford and with Lindemann. As events turned out, he was to appear as a Student at Christ Church during only two years of his appointment.

The Christ Church offer had formally come as Einstein was completing arrangements for a second visit to the California Institute of Technology. Earlier in the year Fleming had proposed that he should come to Pasadena on a regular basis, and Einstein had tentatively accepted. Fleming appears to have acted largely on his own initiative, a circumstance common to his later years and one that added an air of chaos to some of the Institute's proceedings, and details of the offer are not clear. His version was described in a long letter to Hale from A. A. Noyes, director of chemical research at Caltech:

> Fleming read *not* his own letters to Einstein, but two replies he had received from Einstein, the second one written in July stating that he (Einstein) had definitely accepted the permanent appointment, with $5,000 annually plus $15,000 in any year when he comes for ten weeks to the Institute, plus a $3,000 annuity to his widow. Einstein himself proposed reducing the annual payment from the $25,000 proposed by Fleming to $20,000, and the proposed annuity from some larger sum to $3,000. Fleming said that Einstein cabled him in August asking to know whether the arrangement was definite, as his plans for the present year must be consummated, but we have never

been able to get out of Fleming just what reply he made to that last cablegram of Einstein, though I made two attempts. It seems *probable*, however, that Fleming told Einstein that the arrangement was definite for this year, but that the permanent plan must await action by the trustees.

This, in fact, was what happened. Millikan, who would shortly be in Europe, was given the job of ensuring that the Institute netted Einstein for the coming season but that any offer of a permanent post was evaded for the time being. In addition, he was given an even more delicate task. "Board is of opinion commitment of $20,000 all inclusive has been made for coming year," he was informed soon after reaching Europe by E. C. Barrett, the Institute's Secretary. "If Einstein thinks so, board will carry out this commitment. If Einstein does not feel we have such commitment board voted that you offer $15,000 or thereabouts all inclusive."

However, Millikan the faithful servant of the Institute, took a worldly view of Einstein's vagueness about money:

> Now the 7,000 dollar figure which we talked about for a ten or twelve weeks' annual stay in Pasadena [he wrote on October 11] was one which I had already suggested to some of my financial friends as a dignified and suitable one for such a service as Professor Einstein would there render, and I hope soon to be in a position to suggest such an arrangement as a continuing one—and that too without putting a strain upon the finances of the Institute....For the present year, in view of some previous correspondence which I believe has already been had, I am sure the Trustees expect us to decide upon a considerably larger figure and they are prepared to meet it whatever it is that we have determined upon. In other words, they want you, and we all want you very much to come.

Despite Einstein's apparent otherworldliness, despite the fact that he once used a check as a bookmarker instead of depositing it into the bank, his character yet contained a strong streak of peasant awareness that quickly noted any attempt at financial sleight of hand.

His reply to Millikan, written from Caputh on October 19, 1931, was not, therefore, as surprising as it probably appeared to Millikan. Einstein thanked his American friend but said that he had decided to remain in Germany for the winter. He had told Fleming so, and for Millikan's information he enclosed a copy of his letter to Fleming.

So far so good. But this was not the end of the encounter. What happened next is not entirely clear. But the outcome was revealed when Elsa wrote to Millikan about a month later, enclosing the contract, signed by her husband.

The sudden change on Einstein's part may well have been due to a further

Einstein and his wife at a function in Pasadena during one of his visits to the California Institute of Technology. [Culver Pictures]

appeal on the part of Fleming. It is certainly true that when the Einsteins arrived in Pasadena at the end of 1931, they were accommodated not in private quarters but in the splendid premises of the Athenaeum, the faculty club, where Fleming had given up his own apartment for the occasion.

Einstein's second journey to Pasadena was thus made in the same one-visit circumstances as the first. But the question of a journey each year had now been raised. He had been led by Millikan to assume that this was still a distinct possibility if not a likelihood, and with this in his mind he arrived in Pasadena for the second time, a significant situation in view of one meeting that was shortly to come.

This was with Abraham Flexner, the American educationalist then preparing to set up a new kind of educational institute, made possible when Louis Bamberger and Mrs. Felix Fulds had two years previously provided five million dollars for what Flexner called a "haven where scholars and scientists may regard the world and its phenomena as their laboratory without being carried off in the maelstrom of the immediate."

It had been agreed that the organization, whose location had not yet been decided, would first concentrate on mathematical studies, and early in 1932 Flexner visited Pasadena to get the advice of Millikan. There was one obvious suggestion—why not have a word with Einstein? "I drove over to the Athenaeum where he and Mrs. Einstein were staying and met him for the first time," Flexner has written. Before they parted Flexner said that he would be in Europe later in the year. Einstein would be spending the spring term at Oxford with Lindemann, and it was agreed that they would meet again. "I had no idea," Flexner later recorded, "that he would be interested in being concerned with the Institute for Advanced Study, as the organisation became, but he gave me the best of reasons for thinking that an informal organisation such as I had in mind would be much more important at this stage of our development and at the stage of the world's development than another organised university." This then was Flexner's story: that at this point he entertained no idea of attracting Einstein from Caltech to his new institute. Nevertheless, he left Pasadena having carefully made his arrangements for a further meeting.

Einstein returned to Berlin in the spring, and early in May he set out for England once again, first to deliver the Rouse Ball Lecture on Mathematics in Cambridge and then to make his first visit to Oxford as a research student. He was given rooms in Christ Church and dined at high table most evenings:

> He was a charming person [says Sir Roy Harrod] and we entered into relations of easy intimacy with him. He divided his time between his mathematics and playing the violin; as one crossed the quad, one was privileged to hear the strains coming from his rooms. In our Governing Body I sat next to him; we had a green baize tablecloth; under cover of this he held a wad of paper on his knee, and I observed that all through our meetings his pencil was in incessant progress, covering sheet after sheeet with equations. His general conversation was not stimulating, like that of the Prof [Professor Lindemann]. I am afraid I did not have the sense that, so far as human affairs were concerned, I was in the presence of a wise man or a deep thinker. Rather I had the idea that he was a very good man, a simple soul and rather naive about worldly matters.

Before Einstein left Oxford, Flexner arrived. They met in Christ Church. "As it dawned on me during our conversation," Flexner has written, "that perhaps he might be interested in attaching himself to an institute of the proposed kind, before we parted I said to him: 'Professor Einstein, I would not presume to offer you a post in this new institute, but if on reflection you decide that it would afford you the opportunities which you value, you would be welcome on your own terms.'" Einstein was apparently noncommittal; but he agreed that as Flexner was visiting Berlin later in the year they could well meet again.

He returned from England at the end of May, 1932. Berlin was already ominously different from the city of even a few months previously. In April there had taken place what was, on the face of it, an encouraging presidential election. The octogenarian Field Marshal Hindenburg, representing the Democrats and Socialists, had been reelected, defeating the leader of the National Socialist Party, Adolf Hitler. However, the president soon showed where his sympathies lay. In May he forced Brüning, the Reich chancellor, on whose support he had largely won the election, to give way to Von Papen, a man determined to end the Weimar Republic. Von Papen's ostensibly nonparty but, in fact, ultra-right-wing cabinet was formed a few days later. It quickly expelled the Socialist-Center Prussian cabinet under a form of martial law and dissolved the Reichstag. Rule by bayonet had arrived.

It was against this background that Abraham Flexner made his promised visit to Einstein in Caputh. "We sat on the veranda and talked until evening, when Einstein invited me to stay to supper," he has written. "After supper we talked until almost eleven. By that time it was perfectly clear that Einstein and his wife were prepared to come to America. I told him to name his own terms and he promised me to write within a few days."

Einstein accompanied his guest back to the bus for Berlin, walking through the rain hatless and in an old sweater. "I am full of enthusiasm" ("*Ich bin Feuer und Flamme darüf*"), he said as they parted.

The following Monday Flexner prepared a memorandum covering the details of what was to become Einstein's official appointment for virtually the rest of his life. These included, in Flexner's words, location of the new Institute "contiguous to Princeton University, residence from autumn until about the middle of April, salary, pension, etc. and an independent appointment for Professor Mayer."

When the question of salary had first been raised, Einstein said that he wanted three thousand dollars a year. "Could I live on less?" he asked, according to Flexner's later recollections. "You couldn't live on that," he had replied. "Let Mrs. Einstein and me arrange it." The result was a salary of sixteen thousand dollars a year, to be continued after retirement.

It is clear that acceptance of Flexner's offer was a significant change of emphasis from the old Caltech to the new Institute. That Millikan himself saw it in this light is obvious from the disgruntled letter that he wrote to Flexner. He was not, he implied, thinking of his own Institute, but of more important things. "Whether the progress of science in the United States would be advanced by such a move, or whether Professor Einstein's productivity will be increased by such a transfer, is at least debatable," he went on. "The work in which his interest and his activity lies is certainly much more strongly developed here than it is at Princeton, and I am inclined to think that with the astrophysical advances that are in prospect here this will continue to be the case." He concluded with the hope that Flexner might still collaborate with his own Institute in some joint venture and that, even if this were not possible, Einstein might be able to "spend half the time which he would normally be in this country in Princeton and half the time here."

Flexner, with the Einstein contract safely in his pocket, could afford the lofty reply. After noting that "altogether by accident" he had been in Oxford at the same time as Einstein, he defended himself in slightly injured terms. "I cannot believe that annual residence for brief periods at several places is sound or wholesome. Looking at the entire matter from Professor Einstein's point of view, I believe that you and all his friends will rejoice that it has been possible to create for him a permanent post of the character above indicated."

The question of the coming autumn visit was soon resolved: Millikan would be as glad as ever to see Einstein—not least, one must feel, because this would strengthen his hand against whatever blandishments Flexner was offering. What was to happen after Einstein had begun to visit Princeton—"maybe a solution will be found so that he can from time to time come to Pasadena," Elsa wrote to Millikan on August 13—was left in the air. But Einstein never visited Pasadena after the winter of 1932-33.

The appointment at Princeton was still only a part-time winter affair. This feature of the contract was made clear in a statement Einstein issued in Berlin. "I have received leave of absence from the Prussian Academy for five months of the year for five years," this explained. "Those five months I expect to spend at Princeton. I am not abandoning Germany. My permanent home will still be in Berlin."

Einstein sailing on Princeton's Carnegie Lake, 1936. *[AIP Niels Bohr Library]*

Then, unexpectedly, he was asked by Weizmann to rejoin the board of governors of the Hebrew University,

a request which I know would be backed by everyone who really has the University at heart. I remind you of a promise you gave me, that you would do so under my leadership. All those who have fought for reforms, which now look like being successfully carried through, would see a great moral boost in your return, quite apart from the other good it would do. We cannot lose you, although we cannot offer you a "scientific home" as Princeton can. But who knows! Now that I shall be spending a longer time in Jerusalem I have every intention of improving the Physics, and Chemistry, and perhaps you will then visit us.

Einstein replied that he was delighted to hear the news. He added that he would be glad to rejoin the board if there were university reforms, but he made it clear that he did not take Weizmann's assurances entirely at their face value.

Then, in the late autumn, he prepared for Pasadena again. Early in December he and Elsa completed their preparations. Despite the earlier statement that he intended to keep a permanent home in Berlin, despite his unwavering hope and brave front, he was under no illusions as he spent the final days of November in the house at Caputh that he had come to love. As he left it for Berlin and the train to Antwerp where he and his wife were to board ship for the United States, he turned to her with the warning: "Before you leave our villa this time, take a good look at it." When she asked why, he replied: "You will never see it again." Elsa, says Philipp Frank, thought he was being rather foolish.

261

16.

GOODBYE TO BERLIN

Cartoon by C. R. Macauley for *The Brooklyn Eagle*, 1933. Published after Einstein had said that in some circumstances he would not reject military service. *[Library of Congress]*

Einstein and Elsa arrived in California early in January, 1933. It was the third time he had visited Caltech in three successive years, and it now looked as though this might be a regular thing, even though the summer months were securely earmarked for Princeton and commitments in Berlin would further limit his free time. Millikan certainly hoped so, and had gone to great lengths to land his catch for the third visit at a time when it seemed that the Institute might not find the necessary money.

Salvation eventually came from the Oberlaender Trust of Philadelphia, set up "to enable American men and women without regard to race, creed or color, who are actively engaged in work that affects the public welfare, to become better acquainted with similar activities in German-speaking countries." In 1932, the Trust voted "to appropriate the sum of seven thousand dollars to cover the expenses of Professor Einstein in America some time during the academic year 1932-33. The money to be forwarded through Professor Millikan as a grant to Professor Einstein, exclusively for scientific work." There was a rider to the exclusivity, however. For while Millikan was completing arrangements with Einstein, he wrote to the Trust agreeing that his guest should make "one broadcast which will be helpful to German-American relations."

Dourly conservative, faintly militarist, and with more than a touch of right-wing enthusiasm, Millikan had cause for worry. Einstein's persistence in advocating his pacifist ideals during earlier visits had done much to foster the undercurrent of objection that flowed through the American scene and that not even the general adulation could entirely conceal.

Millikan did what he could. He stood up in honorable fashion to defend what he had no particular wish to defend. But underneath his confident exterior he was seriously worried that his guest might make another "two per cent" speech that would invalidate the coming broadcast or affect the flow of money into the Institute from rich patrons. This much is clear from his private comments to the Trust after Einstein had met reporters on arrival in Pasadena. He "handled himself," wrote Millikan, "with a skill which, I am sure if your trustees had seen, would help to relieve their minds as to any possible adverse influence which he might exert in the way of furnishing additional ammunition to those who have been spreading these grotesquely foolish reports about his connection with influences aimed at the undermining of American Institutions and ideals."

The broadcast to "help German-American relations" was to be made on January 23, and until then Millikan's security measures worked, although only at the cost of revealing to Einstein how limited his freedom of action really was.

The broadcast, "On German-American Agreement," was the one-shot success that everyone had hoped it would be. It was preceded by a full-dress dinner at the Athenaeum, and here Einstein first met Leon Watters, a wealthy Jewish biochemist who was to become an intimate friend for the last two decades of his life. Watters, a New Yorker, had the previous month begun to finance work at the Institute and as a result found himself and his wife placed by Millikan at the top table, separated from Einstein only by a woman of considerable wealth, who was also supporting the Institute financially.

In some ways Watters, with his chauffeur-driven car and his apartment on Fifth Avenue, with his dilettante approach to science, was the antithesis of all that Einstein believed in. Yet an interior practical kindness was enough to bind him both to Einstein and to Elsa, as the long and deeply personal correspondence between them was later to show. The foundations for it were laid that evening as Watters and the rest of the carefully picked guests followed Einstein to the Pasadena Civic Auditorium. Here, the program, entitled "Symposium on America and the World," sponsored by the Southern California College Student Body President's Association, was to be broadcast by the National Broadcasting Company.

Einstein remained in Pasadena for another seven weeks, obeying Millikan's injunction to hold his tongue. But early in February, Millikan's fears were realized. Einstein was to return east by train. Moreover, he was to make one address in Chicago and another in New York. In view "of the near slips which we have been fortunate enough to avoid making," Millikan wondered what the Trust in Philadelphia could do.

The answer was that it could do very little. The secretary, Mr. Thomas, wrote from the Trust to Einstein, noting that he had had no reply to earlier letters, stating that he had heard of plans to make addresses, and saying rather plaintively that he would like to know about them as soon as possible. The scanty evidence suggests that if Einstein gave Mr. Thomas's letters any attention at all he stuffed them into his pocket determined that on leaving Pasadena he would make up for the silence so far forced upon him. As it turned out, other events were to dominate his thoughts. For while Einstein was again discussing the riddle of the universe with Hubble and Tolman at Mount Wilson, events in Germany had rolled forward with ominous inevitability. During the last month of 1932 Kurt von Schleicher had become chancellor; for some weeks he had desperately tried to form a stable government. He failed, the third man to do so in as many years. On January 30, President Hindenburg turned to the one leader he felt might at last square the circle—Adolf Hitler.

Einstein's first action was to cancel the lecture due to be given at the Prussian Academy on his return to Berlin. A few hours later the Reichstag was in flames, set alight by the subnormal Dutchman Van der Lubbe. Within a few days the incident had been

A Nazi demonstration in Munich of young supporters during the 1930s. [The Mansell Collection]

exploited by the new Nazi government to rush through emergency decrees that gave them totalitarian powers. And on March 2 any remaining doubts that Einstein's unique position might guard him from the government's growing anti-Jewish wrath were dispelled by a leading article in the *Völkischer Beobachter* on "cultural internationalism," "international treason," and "pacifist excesses." In it, Einstein was singled out for attack, together with Heinrich and Thomas Mann, Arnold Zweig, and a short list of Germany's leading intellectuals, academics, and artists.

On March 10 Einstein made his decision public. In a long interview with Evelyn Seeley of the *New York World Telegram* on the eve of his departure from Pasadena he said: "As long as I have any choice in the matter, I shall live only in a country where civil liberty, tolerance and equality of all citizens before the law prevail. Civil liberty implies freedom to express one's political convictions, in speech and in writing; tolerance implies respect for the convictions of others whatever they may be. These conditions do not exist in Germany at the present time."

Thus in mid-March, 1933, Einstein arrived at the position he had correctly forecast to Infeld little more than a decade previously. He was no longer able to live in what was both the country of his birth and, since 1919, the country of his voluntary adoption. As in 1920, there were no doubt elements in Germany that were rational, civilized, and libertarian; as in 1920, they formed a minority, helpless and silent. Einstein's disillusion was thus compounded. For the rest of his life he felt a double grudge against Germany: first that he had been born there and, worse still, that he had been misguided enough to take German nationality again when he might have remained simply a Swiss.

He and Elsa left Pasadena on March 11, traveling overland to New York by way of Chicago, as expected. The repercussions were less than Millikan had feared, partly because he had agreed to attend a birthday luncheon arranged by a local committee in aid of the Hebrew University and his time for other matters was, therefore, limited.

But he did what he could, and finally agreed to attend a pacifist meeting on the morning of the 14th. Thus far there appears to have been no crack in his pacifist armor. "His firm faith in the decent impulses of the human heart is evident and inspiring," wrote Mrs. Lloyd who had helped organize the meeting. "The peace campaign must go on. Let the Youth Peace Council whose representatives sit with us note his plain teaching. Let all pacifists take courage and be as extreme as they like. Einstein will never abandon the peace movement because it is too bold." Only thirteen weeks later the plain teaching was to be different. Were he a Belgian, Einstein then declared, he would give military service cheerfully, in the belief that he would be helping to save European civilization.

From Chicago he traveled on to New York where he arrived shortly after Weizmann had left for Palestine—one of those missed meetings that might have altered history. In New York he spoke at a function to be held for the joint good of the Jewish Telegraph Agency and the Hebrew University. Dr. Rosenbach, the noted American

264

Left: A Nazi demonstration in Germany during the 1930s. [The Mansell Collection]

Right: The Reichstag, Berlin, in flames on February 27, 1933, allegedly as a result of a Communist plot. [Culver Pictures]

bibliophile, was in charge and had organized a dinner for more than six hundred at the Commodore Hotel. It was on a dignified level; Einstein's Zionism was quickly submerged in physics and Rosenbach's lost in the world of books. Congressman Sol Bloom had given up his seat beside Einstein to Harlow Shapley, and the two scientists were soon absorbed in the universe, Einstein using his body to illustrate a point, the ribs being the heavens and his backbone the Milky Way.

The following day Einstein squeezed in a visit to Princeton, conferred there with Oswald Veblen, and went on a preliminary round of house hunting in preparation for his return in the autumn. So far, his only public reaction to the news from Germany had been his measured statement that he would not be returning. This was reasonable enough; and it gave no weapons to his enemies. Now, with only a few hours to go before sailing for Europe, he attended a reception at the Waldorf-Astoria to launch *The Fight Against War*, an anthology of his pacifist writings to be published later in the year. So far, he had spoken openly only of his own personal position in relation to the new German government; he had given the world no other reaction of the world's most famous Jew to the rise of the world's most famous Jew-baiter. That was the way he wanted it.

Now, at the Waldorf-Astoria, he stepped into the ring, attacking the German Academy of Arts, pointing out that in Germany pacifists were considered enemies of the state, and saying that the world should be made aware of the dangers of Hitlerism. All this made it easier for the German authorities to attack him. They would, of course, have done so anyway. But his honesty in speaking out, without reserve and while on a "mission of molding public opinion to better German-American relations," as Millikan had put it to the Oberlaender Trust—made their task that much simpler. He issued no plea for U.S. intervention, and he was not atrocity-mongering; but by the time reports reached Germany via the New York correspondents, his action could easily enough be distorted into such, and it was fuel for the virulent anti-Einstein campaign exemplified by the *Berliner Lokal-Anzeiger*. "Good news from Einstein—he's not coming back," this said. "…Relativity is in little demand by us now. On the contrary. The ideals of national honour and love of country which Herr Einstein wanted to abolish, have become absolute values to us. So the outlook for Einstein here is very bad."

It was in this atmosphere that he and his wife left for Europe. As the *Belgenland* crossed the Atlantic, Einstein playing the violin at benefit concerts for refugee musicians, there came more reports from Germany. In mid-ocean, he learned that his home in Caputh had been searched, the pretext being that an arms cache might be found there. "The raid…by an armed crowd is but one example of the arbitrary acts of violence now taking place throughout Germany," said Einstein in a statement issued on the ship. "These acts are the result of the government's overnight transfer of police powers to a raw and rabid mob of the Nazi militia. My summer home has often in the past been honoured by the presence of guests. They were always welcome. No one had any reason to break in."

SHOPPING FOR EINSTEIN

Between the spring and the autumn of 1933 Einstein was driven to action in three different fields. Virtually barred from Germany, he had to decide where to settle. Faced with a Third Reich under Hitler, he had to reconsider his pacifist beliefs. And as the future of the Jewish scholars driven from Germany grew into a major issue, he felt forced to bring into the open his long-standing argument with the Hebrew University. These climaxes in his life, all the direct result of Hitler's rise to the chancellorship, developed simultaneously as he continued with his work, amiably agreed to lecture to all and sundry, and was reluctantly transformed into a symbol of the anti-Nazi forces that began to form throughout the Continent. They give to his life a muddled and incoherent pattern paralleled by Europe as it reacted in its own way to the rise of the National Socialist Party.

One of Einstein's first actions after reaching Antwerp revealed how the events of the previous few weeks had hardened his opinions. In Pasadena, talking to Evelyn Seeley of the *New York World Telegram*, he had remarked that his citizenship of Germany was "a strange affair" but had gone on to say that "for an internationally-minded man, citizenship of a specific country is not important. Humanity is more important than national citizenship."

Now he was convinced that the Nazi actions satisfied some urge in the Prussian character and, once again, decided to renounce his German citizenship.

He was driven to Brussels, and there in the German embassy he formally surrendered the rights of full German citizenship he had taken with such determination after the war. He retained his Swiss nationality, so he could hand in his German passport. Descending the steps of the German embassy, Albert Einstein, the Swabian from Ulm, left German territory for the last time.

His immediate problem was to decide where to go. A return to Switzerland seemed likely. His personal feeling for the country and its people remained strong, and Zurich would have welcomed him back. Yet he had firm links with Holland, where Lorentz had died only five years previously, and the ties with Switzerland were tangled by the fact that Mileva was still living in Zurich. For the moment, therefore, he remained in Belgium.

Here, in the last days of March, he received a letter that was to have considerable repercussions later in the year. It came from one of the more colorful characters who was to cross Einstein's path. This was Commander Locker-Lampson, English barrister and journalist. Member of Parliament for the Handsworth Division of Birmingham, he was the younger son of Frederick Locker, the Victorian poet, and in the First World War had pursued an adventurous career, first in the Royal Naval Air Service and then in armored cars, which he commanded in Belgium, Lapland, Prussia, Austrian Galacia, and Russia. It was in character that Locker-Lampson should have served under the Grand Duke Nicholas and later been invited to murder Rasputin by one of the men who eventually carried out the assassination.

On the face of it, the mutual attraction of Einstein, the natural-born pacifist, and Locker-Lampson, the natural-born fighter who had "Combative" as the first word of his telegraphic address, seems almost absurd. The simplest explanation of their friendship is probably the most accurate: mutual support for the underdog, which had produced in Locker-Lampson a hatred of the Nazi government equaled only by his hatred of the Communists. In addition, the commander must fully have appreciated that association with Einstein would bring his name into the news, where he was not averse to seeing it. This fact, though too plain in the record to be smudged, should not hide the genuine feeling with which he acted.

Locker-Lampson, writing from the House of Commons, began by recalling a chance meeting with Einstein at Oxford a few years previously and offered him the hospitality of his London home.

Einstein politely declined the offer and moved with his wife to Le Coq-sur-Mer, a small resort near Ostend. From here he severed his link with the Prussian Academy, the magnet whose distinguished company had first drawn him to Berlin almost exactly two decades earlier.

This act—closely followed by his expulsion from the Bavarian Academy of Science—drew a sharp line across Einstein's life.

Thirteen years earlier the anti-Jewish movement of which Einstein became the focal point had brought nodding acquiescence, if not downright approval, from a sizable percentage of the German people. They had not changed. And on May 10 in Berlin—even Berlin, where cosmopolitanism and culture have always been a little higher up the scale than elsewhere in Germany—here in Berlin forty thousand inhabitants watched and cheered what William Shirer has called "a scene which had not been witnessed in the Western world since the late Middle Ages": the sight of five thousand swastika-bearing students burning in a massive pile before the Opera House two thousand volumes that included the works of Einstein and Freud; Thomas Mann, Remarque, and Stefan Zweig; and of Americans such as Helen Keller and Upton Sinclair. After the flames had leapt upward, wrote one observer later, there was a sudden silence. Perhaps it was not only conscience. Perhaps some among the crowd caught a psychic glimpse of the flames that exactly a decade later would be sweeping through far larger parts of Berlin.

However, it was not only the mob that acquiesced. Thirteen days later, on May

Einstein (center) at a reunion in May, 1933, of the Aarau graduating class of 1896, during Einstein's last year in Europe. *[Hebrew University of Jerusalem]*

23, Professor Ernst Krieck asserted during his investiture as the new rector of the University of Frankfurt, that the German universities could never have struggled from their paralysis without a folk renascence. "The chief characteristic of this renascence is the replacement of the humanistic ideal by the national and political," he said. "Nowadays the task of the universities is not to cultivate objective science but soldierlike militant science, and their foremost task is to form the will and character of their students."

Nor was Krieck alone among the academics in such sentiments. On the day that he spoke in Frankfurt, the twenty-second annual meeting of the Kaiser Wilhelm Society was held in Berlin. Planck presided. No one in Germany could be permitted to stand aside, "rifle at rest," he said. There should be only one ideal—"the consolidation of all available forces for the reconstruction of the Fatherland." And he then read the following message sent by the Society to Chancellor Hitler: "The Kaiser Wilhelm Society for the Advancement of the Sciences begs leave to tender reverential greetings to the Chancellor, and its solemn pledge that German science is also ready to co-operate joyously in the reconstruction of the new national state."

In this climate the Nazi attack on Einstein gathered weight. On April 2 his Berlin bank account was taken over by the authorities, and cash and securities totaling thirty thousand marks were confiscated on the grounds that they would otherwise be used for treasonable purposes. His Haberlandstrasse apartment was formally closed and a lock put on the door. Shortly afterward, his summer house at Caputh was seized. On April 12 his two stepdaughters left Germany for France, and on the same day Dr. Walther Mayer arrived at Le Coq. Dr. Plesch, the man who had discovered the real cause of Einstein's heart trouble a few years earlier, also left. And in Le Coq there arrived a special album published in Germany and containing photographs of leading opponents of the Nazi government. On the first page was a portrait of Einstein. Underneath it were the words: "Discovered a much-contested theory of relativity. Was greatly honoured by the Jewish Press and the unsuspecting German people. Showed his gratitude by lying atrocity propaganda against Adolf Hitler abroad." And then, in brackets, there were the words *"Noch ungehangt"*—"not yet hanged." But his reaction was disdainful. As with so many other human problems, he was the outsider looking in. He could afford to be dispassionate; so long, that is, as he was able to get on with his work.

As he sat on the Belgian dunes with Dr. Mayer in the spring of 1933, doggedly searching for an answer to the riddle of a unified field theory, the question of where he was to work in future was still the one that mattered most. There were many ways of answering it, since the news that Einstein would not be returning to Germany had been quickly followed by a flood of academic offers.

He agreed to lecture to the Fondation Universitaire in Brussels, a week later

268

Oliver Locker-Lampson (left), Einstein, Ernest Rutherford, and Sir Austen Chamberlain at the meeting of the Academic Assistance Council, Royal Albert Hall, London, October 3, 1933. *[Library of Congress]*

accepted the offer of a chair at the University of Madrid and agreed to move to Spain in April, 1934—an acceptance from which he withdrew following an attack by the Spanish Catholic Press. Both his perplexity with the present, and his plans for the future, were expressed in a letter to his old friend Solovine, in which he deplored the hatred spreading across Germany and revealed that he wanted to start a refugee university for Jewish professors, possibly in England.

But his interest soon evaporated. There were many reasons for this, including pressure of other work and, probably more influential, the fact that in both England and the United States academic aid organizations sprang up and showed every sign of being able to handle the worst of the problem.

He might also have done more had his guerrilla war with the administration of the Hebrew University not suddenly erupted into a major engagement. For now, as the situation in Germany made it essential for the Jews to form a united front, he brought his breach with the University into the open with an unthinking timing that had the quality of Greek drama.

In August, 1932, the board of governors, meeting in London, had elected a committee for the purpose, in Weizmann's words, "of drawing up a constitution for the University, and of introducing into that constitution as many practical reforms as possible, with a view to making the young and struggling university into an institution rather more worthy of the name." Sir Herbert Samuel, Professor Norman Bentwich, Sir Philip Hartog, and Weizmann himself were members. Despite the cautious description by Weizmann, the committee represented a first step toward dealing with Einstein's criticism of the way Magnes was running the University; and when Weizmann met Einstein in Berlin in the autumn of 1932, shortly before he was to leave for the United States, Einstein tentatively agreed that on certain conditions he might rejoin the board of governors. But these had not yet been brought about.

This was the situation when, soon after his arrival in Belgium in the spring of 1933, Einstein received a cable from Weizmann in Jerusalem that invited him to join the University. Weizmann had received no reply when he left Palestine on April 19. "But on my arrival in Cairo the following day," he wrote to Einstein on reaching London, "I was met by a statement in the press to the effect that you had considered this invitation and had refused it because you were dissatisfied with the management of the University." Only half-believing, Weizmann telephoned Dr. Magnes in Jerusalem. "He read out to me, over the telephone," Weizmann continued, "the letter just received from you in which you state that you are refusing our invitation because you have been informed from four different and independent sources that the position of the University is so deplorable that it is undesirable for you to allow your name to be associated with it."

Einstein did not withdraw his charges in detail. Neither did he back them up.

269

Einstein working in September, 1933, with his secretary, Helen Dukas, at Le Coq-sur-Mer, Belgium, where he had taken refuge from the Nazis who reportedly had offered a reward for his murder. Shortly afterward, he left Europe for the United States, where he was to spend the rest of his life.
[United Press International]

The only informant he named was Professor Yahuda, the scholar who had brought the Spanish offer from Madrid, who had been refused a chair at the Hebrew University by Magnes, and who can hardly be considered an impartial witness. Furthermore, in his reply to Weizmann on May 7, he reaffirmed his action. For good measure he suggested that Weizmann had committed a breach of faith by not resigning from the university board when he himself had done so.

As Weizmann grappled with realities, as the Jewish exodus continued to France and to the temporary security of Austria and Czechoslovakia, and as Hitler prepared the Third Reich for its thousand years of power, Einstein, his future still undecided, began to get ready for his visit as a research student to Christ Church.

He arrived on June 1st. Despite the disagreement that had prefaced his election to the Research Fellowship, he was extremely popular, and an ambitious program had been prepared for him. The first day after his arrival he attended the Boyle Memorial Lecture, given to the Junior Scientific Society in the University Museum by Rutherford, and proposed the vote of thanks. It was an impressive occasion, Rutherford the big booming extrovert who had searched the interior of the atom contrasting once again with the smaller figure of Einstein whose mind had grappled with the immensities of space:

> I can almost see Einstein now [writes one of the undergraduates who attended the meeting], a poor forlorn little figure, obviously disappointed at the way in which he had just been expelled from Germany by the Nazis. As he delivered his speech, it seemed to me that he was more than a little doubtful about the way in which he would be received in a British University. However, the moment he sat down he was greeted by a thunderous outburst of applause from us all. Never in all my life shall I forget the wonderful change which took place in Einstein's face at that moment. The light came back into his eyes, and his whole face seemed transfigured with joy and delight when it came home to him in this way that, no matter how badly he had been treated by the Nazis, both he himself and his undoubted genius were at any rate greatly appreciated at Oxford.

On May 10, 1933, two thousand books by Einstein, Freud, Thomas Mann, and other authors were burned by Nazi sympathizers in front of the Opera House in Berlin. [Culver Pictures]

Three days later he received a letter from Weizmann, about to leave Britain for an important visit to the United States but suggesting that Einstein and he should meet. Einstein, preparing the Herbert Spencer Lecture; the Deneke Lecture, which was to follow; and the first George Gibson Lecture, which he was to give in Glasgow on the 20th, replied that he could not spare the time. He did not wish to be wooed away from his better judgment by oratory and personal pleas.

Weizmann replied with a three-page letter that is a minor masterpiece and offered Einstein the chance of building a new department of physics in the Hebrew University. If anything could have drawn Einstein to Palestine it was probably this. Yet its failure was inevitable. The Hebrew University was important; but to Einstein it was less important than physics. And as far as physics was concerned, his present arrangements with Flexner had two great advantages over anything dangled by Weizmann. Einstein was not a political animal, and he had no wish to become entangled in the skein of diplomatic maneuvers, which would inevitably hamper the scientific work of a man building a new department in such conditions. In addition, he was not by nature the teamworker, the man who excelled in directing the energies of younger men. He did not want to direct; he wanted to get on with his thinks.

He replied by return, firmly standing his ground. The letter was as decisive as Einstein could make it, and the upshot was as anticipated. With Einstein's attitude openly criticized by Weizmann, an investigation would now be favored. Later in the month Sir Philip Hartog wrote that he was willing to chair a committee or commission that would specifically inquire into conditions in the University. Weizmann agreed, and the tactfully named Survey Committee was set up in the autumn. Its members visited Jerusalem at the end of 1933 to investigate "with a view as to such reform as may be found desirable, and to the framing of plans for the development of the University." In the words of Magnes' biographer, Norman Bentwich, the Committee "proposed radical changes in the administration and in his position. Action was shelved for a year; but things could never be the same to him thereafter, and he accepted a change in his functions."

On September 23, 1935, Rabbi Stephen Wise, returning from Palestine, reported to Einstein the outcome of the crucial meeting of the University's board of governors. "It retired Magnes from the academic direction of things and made him the President, which means that he becomes a more or less decorative figure," he said. In his place there was appointed as rector Professor Hugo Bergmann, whom Einstein had, quite coincidentally, known in Prague two decades earlier. Doing a vice-chancellor's job, Magnes had been known as chancellor; now, ostensibly upgraded to a presidency, he was to have powers comparable to a chancellor at a British university. These powers were in some ways considerable, and he remained a trusted link with the British administration; yet effectively the move gave game, set, and match to Einstein, who had proposed almost this very thing a decade previously.

OF NO ADDRESS

The end of the long disagreement about the Hebrew University still lay two years ahead as Einstein dissuaded Weizmann from visiting him at Oxford and prepared to put the finishing touches to his Herbert Spencer Lecture, "On the Method of Theoretical Physics."

Two days later he gave the Deneke Lecture to a packed audience in Lady Margaret Hall, dealing with the inner meaning of physics and apparently concluding with the comment: "The deeper we search, the more we find there is to know, and as long as human life exists I believe it will always be so." The qualification is necessary. On this occasion Einstein spoke only from notes and no script of the lecture survives.

From Oxford he traveled north to Glasgow to give the first George Gibson Lecture. He arrived in the city unexpectedly and found himself, apparently unrecognized, in the center of a huge crowd that had gathered to welcome the film star Thelma Todd. Luckily, he was soon seen by a local reporter, who telephoned the University. A rescue operation soon brought Einstein safely home to port. Thelma Todd, speaking of the incident later, was contrite: "I wish I had known," she said. "I'd have lent Einstein some of my crowd."

That afternoon he spoke for twenty minutes in the University's Bute Hall, addressing the attentive audience in English on "The Origins of the General Theory of Relativity." His exposition was one of the clearest ever given of the process that led from the Special to the General Theory and that, after numerous errors, led Einstein "penitently to the Riemann curvature, which enabled [him] to find the relation to the empirical facts of astronomy."

A few days later, after receiving the by now customary honorary degree, he returned to Belgium, apparently turning down the offer of a stay in Canterbury, which had come from Hewlett Johnson, the "Red Dean," who recalled that twelve years earlier he had listened to Einstein's lecture in Manchester.

Einstein's refusal is significant. In his invitation, Johnson stressed Einstein's labors for peace, a hint of his own long-term efforts for the communist version of pacifism. But at this particular moment in his life, Einstein was both anxious to dissociate himself from the smear of communism and worried about his own pacifism.

For now, to the alarm of his friends and the dismay of his supporters, he crossed the great divide between pacifism and nonpacifism, renouncing his earlier conviction that the use of force was never justified; implying in the words of his former colleagues that he lined himself up with those who would "save European civilisation by means of fire bombs, poison gas and bacteria"; announcing without a flicker, like the cool customer he was, that the change was not in himself but in the European situation, and that nonviolence was no longer enough.

Einstein's rejection of the pacifist cause did not come suddenly. The blunt statement that he issued in the late summer of 1933 may give this impression, but the truth is more complex, and he was already moving away from his unqualified pacifism when he returned to Le Coq from Britain late in June. This is apparent in a letter he wrote on July 1 to the Reverend J. B. Th. Hugenholtz who had visited him the previous summer at Caputh, and who now revived his idea of an International Peace House in The Hague. He felt that the times were out of joint for the further advocacy of certain pacifist ideas, he said. And he asked whether one was justified in advising Frenchmen or Belgians to refuse military service in view of the German policy for rearmament. His answer was "No." Instead, what was required was a supra-national force rather than the end of all armed forces.

He sent a statement along the same lines to the *Biosophical Review* in New York, but this was not published until the autumn. Outwardly, therefore, the attitude of Albert Einstein, the most famous of those who had expelled themselves from Germany on the rise of Hitler, was still that of the confirmed pacifist. The revelation came before the end of the month.

While he had been lecturing in Oxford, two Belgians had been arrested for refusing to undertake military service. Their case had been taken up by Alfred Nahon, a young French pacifist living in Belgium who now appealed to Einstein to appear for the defense.

Before Einstein had time to reply, intervention came from an unexpected quarter. "The husband of the second fiddler," said a letter delivered to Einstein at Le Coq, "would like to see you on an urgent matter." The second fiddler was Queen Elizabeth, with whom Einstein had been playing quartets on at least three occasions during May.

Einstein traveled to Brussels and met King Albert in the palace at Laeken. The audience was handled circumspectly, and for good reason. For in some quarters Einstein's continued presence in Belgium was regarded as a distinctly mixed blessing. It would be unfair to suggest that the country harbored any sizable pro-German party, yet there existed—as indeed there existed in England—an overall wish to mollify rather than to criticize dictators. Nowhere in Belgium was much more than three hours' drive from the German frontier, and if threats that Einstein might be kidnapped or assassinated were exaggerated, this was not certain at the time.

In this climate, intervention by a constitutional monarch in a matter involving military service had to be handled with care, and the King appears to have kept no record of the views that he put to Einstein, or of Einstein's reaction. The latter is, however, clearly implied in the exchange of letters that followed the audience.

On July 14 Einstein wrote to the king. The crux of his letter was that he had decided not to intervene as Nahon had proposed. It was a letter typical of Einstein; humane and courteous, thoughtful of the wider services that men might render to one another. Yet it was still a letter written on the brink of decision; it burked the entire issue of whether mine labor, stoking furnaces aboard ships, and such services, might not be quite as essential to a country's war effort as service in the armed forces.

The king's reply, dated from Ostende on the 24th, was friendly but noncommittal, and to avoid the accusation of being unconstitutional he was careful to speak of anonymous "Belgian Governments" rather than the specific current administration:

> My dear Professor, I have received with great pleasure the letter you have so kindly written me, and I send you my warmest thanks. I am most responsive to what you say about Belgium and the sincerity of its foreign policy.
>
> Belgian Governments intend to stay out of the conflicts that are taking place in or among its neighbour countries; under no circumstances will they consent to discriminatory practices which the great majority of Belgians consider unacceptable. As you have said it so well, our army is defensive in character. To serve in it means to serve the will of a free people intent on maintaining the place which is legitimately theirs in the society of nations.
>
> We are delighted that you have set foot on our soil. There are men who by their work and intellectual stature belong to mankind rather than to any one country, yet the country they choose as their asylum takes keen pride in that fact.
> The Queen joins me in sending you best wishes for a pleasant stay in Belgium. Please accept my expression of high esteem. Albert.

There is an air of fencing about the exchange, and it seems likely that the king was still not certain of what Einstein would do next.

However, Einstein's mind had already been made up. On July 20 he wrote to Nahon. He asked that the contents of his letter should be publicized—a letter in which Albert Einstein, who had once declared that "he would rather be hacked in pieces than take part in such an abominable business as war," said that if he were now a Belgian, he would cheerfully accept military service.

On August 18 Einstein's letter was published in *La Patrie Humaine.* Protests were pained and vociferous. Three days later, Lord Ponsonby, a leading British pacifist, wrote expressing his "deep disappointment." H. Runham Brown, secretary of the War Resisters International, declared Einstein's letter to be "a great blow to our cause," while the press service of the International Antimilitaristic Commission claimed that "The apostasy of Einstein is a great victory for German National Socialism," a statement whose line of reasoning is perverse rather than obscure. To all, he replied in much the same terms: Germany was now a threat to the peace of Europe and could only be resisted by force. Circumstances altered cases.

Einstein and Winston Churchill, in the grounds of Churchill's country home, Chartwell, in Kent, 1933. [Hebrew University of Jerusalem]

As the protests continued to arrive, Einstein felt forced to issue a general statement:

> My ideal remains the settlement of all international disputes by arbitration [he proclaimed]. Until a year and a half ago, I considered refusal to do military service one of the most effective steps to the achievement of that goal. At that time, throughout the civilised world there was not a single nation which actually intended to overwhelm any other nation by force. I remain wholeheartedly devoted to the idea that belligerent actions must be avoided and improved relations among nations must be accomplished. For that very reason I believe nothing should be done that is likely to weaken the organised power of those European countries which today represent the best hope of realising that idea.

There are two other significant points that should not be smudged. Despite his readiness to abandon pacifism at the very point when it was put to the test, and despite his support for an international force, Einstein continued to regard himself as a pacifist, an attitude to which many of his former friends not unnaturally took exception. In addition, it is notable that he concentrated his new-found belief in military defense against Germany in particular rather than against dictators in general. Certainly it was Germany that in 1933 represented the major threat to the peace of the world. Yet even in later years his admission that tyranny must be met by force only rarely flowed over to deal with the cases of Italy or Japan, let alone Russia. His vigor was concentrated to the exclusion of almost all else against the Germany whose evils he saw as a natural extension of his experiences at the Luitpold Gymnasium. His honesty, his international standing, his Jewishness, all helped to reinforce the anti-Nazi figurehead into which this vigor had turned him. As such he had his uses. But after 1933 not only Zionists and members of the League but also pacifists could plainly see his limitations as well.

Einstein's position as a symbol of the anti-German forces now beginning to coalesce was emphasized while the affair of the two Belgian conscripts was still under way. For during the second half of July he became the centerpiece of what was essentially a political operation. The prime instigator is not known, but on July 20 the indefatigable Locker-Lampson wrote to Lindemann, whom he had first met during his time as private secretary to Winston Churchill. "My dear Prof," he said, "Someone has seen Einstein and is bringing him to England and has asked me to put him up at my cottage this weekend. I have therefore arranged to do this and am taking him to Winston's on Saturday. I do hope you are likely to be there."

Einstein arrived a few days later and was taken first to Locker-Lampson's house at Esher, Surrey, a few miles from London. From here he was escorted not to one interview but to a trio. First, he met Churchill, with whom he was photographed in the

275

Einstein on Roughton Heath, near Cromer, Norfolk, in September, 1933. On horseback is Einstein's host, Commander Oliver Locker-Lampson. The other guests include the commander's secretaries, Miss M. Howard (left), and Miss B. Goodall (right). Einstein stayed in England as Locker-Lampson's guest for a month before leaving for the United States. [United Press International]

gardens of Chartwell. Next, he had lunch with Sir Austen Chamberlain, whom Locker-Lampson had accompanied to the peace conference in Paris fourteen years earlier. Finally, he was taken to Lloyd George's country home at Churt, and it was here that Einstein, signing the visitor's book in the rambling Surrey house before meeting the former prime minister, paused for a moment when he came to the column "Address." Then he wrote "Ohne"—"without any."

The following day Locker-Lampson made the most of the incident when he spoke in the House of Commons, seeking leave to introduce a bill "to promote and extend opportunities of citizenship for Jews resident outside the British Empire." Einstein, grave and silent in a white linen suit, looked on from the Distinguished Visitors' gallery. It was a moving incident, taking place at a time when Europe had reached a watershed of history, and oddly reflecting both the best and the worst in contemporary England—the eccentric outsider taking up arms for the downtrodden, and the House, which agreed in principle but quickly moved on to other things.

Locker-Lampson's private bill was the victim partly of apathy, partly of the British parliamentary system since there was no chance of a second reading before the session ended on November 17. This, in turn, meant the automatic lapsing of the bill.

Einstein now returned to Belgium, apparently accepting an open invitation from Locker-Lampson to visit him again before leaving Europe for his winter visit to Princeton. He had only a short time to wait before being thrust into a more glaring limelight.

On August 31, *The Brown Book of the Hitler Terror* was published by the World Committee for the Victims of German Fascism—by coincidence on the same day that Professor Theodor Lessing, a German who had fled to Czechoslovakia, was tracked down by Nazi thugs and murdered in Marienbad. The central core of the book was the allegation that the Nazis were solely responsible for the burning of the Reichstag, a claim that looked plausible enough in 1933 whatever doubts are thrown on it today. Einstein had given his name as head of the committee in his usual generous way. He now found himself saddled with part authorship and was forced to issue a retraction. "My name appeared in the French and English editions as if I had written it," he said. "That is not true. I did not write a word of it. The fact that I did not write it does not matter, and [sic] the truth has a certain importance. I was on the committee which authorised the book, but I certainly did not write any of it although I agree with the spirit of it. The cause of all this is that the regime in Germany is one of revenge; and I happen to be chosen as one of the victimised."

Naturally enough, this disclaimer had little effect on those who were baying for blood. "Einstein's Newest Infamy," a German newspaper banner underlined in red, was typical, and early in September it was reported that "Fehme," the extreme German nationalist organization, had earmarked £1,000 for the man who would kill Einstein. The news that this sum had been "put on his head" caused him to touch his white hair and remark smilingly: "I did not know it was worth so much."

Einstein's lofty disregard for his own safety was in the marrow of the man. All that worried him was the interference with his work that police surveillance often caused. Elsa was another matter, and it was Elsa who on Friday, September 8, asked a visiting reporter from England—Patrick Murphy of the *Sunday Express*—to telephone Locker-Lampson and ask whether Einstein could come back as a guest without delay. Locker-Lampson swung into action, eager to be host once more, especially in such dramatic circumstances, and on Saturday, Einstein was driven with Murphy to Ostend. In the cabin of the Channel boat he soon had his notebook out and was hard at work.

Arrived in London, he was taken for the night to a small boarding house in Earl's Court run by Locker-Lampson's former housekeeper, thankful that for once the hurried departure had enabled him to travel light. "If I travelled with two huge trunks my wife would still have a little paper parcel with excess luggage," he confided to Murphy.

The following morning he was driven by the commander's two female secretaries northeast from London, through Newmarket, where the three lunched, Einstein making himself understood as well as he could with his slight conversational English. He was taken to Roughton Heath, a sandy stretch of moorland three miles from Cromer where the commander owned a stretch of land. Here, he was installed in one of the holiday chalets. His stay was surrounded by a grotesque mixture of pseudosecrecy and publicity. "If any unauthorised person comes near they will get a charge of buckshot," threatened the commander. But the local Cromer photographer was allowed up to take pictures of Einstein in his sweater and sandals, while the female "guards," carrying sporting guns, posed for the agencies, whose pictures went around the world. Here, Einstein stated significantly to a reporter: "I shall become a naturalized Englishman as soon as it is possible for my papers to go through. Commander Locker-Lampson has already suggested to your Parliament that England should adopt me immediately instead of my having to wait the usual five years. Parliament will give us the answer when it reassembles. I cannot tell you yet whether I shall make England my home. I do not know where my future lies. I shall be here for a month, and then cross to America to fulfil engagements for a lecture tour.

"Professor Millikan the great American research worker, has invited me to make Pasadena University, in California, my home. They have there the finest obser-

Einstein and the bust sculpted by Jacob Epstein (right). The picture was taken at Oliver Locker-Lampson's property near Cromer in southeast England in October, 1933, where Einstein was living before finally emigrating to the United States. *[United Press International]*

vatory in the world. That is a temptation. But, although I try to be universal in thought, I am European by instinct and inclination. I shall want to return here."

Einstein spent about a month on Roughton Heath, living and eating in the small wooden building allocated to him, working with Dr. Mayer who soon joined him from Belgium, and sometimes walking for an hour or more over the rough heathlands, "talking to the goats," as he told one of the commander's secretaries.

His presence outside Cromer had become an open secret, and there were many visitors to the Locker-Lampson "encampment." To Roughton Heath there came Jacob Epstein, who was able to obtain three sittings for a bust. These took place in Einstein's small hut, which already contained a piano and was hardly the best place for the job. "I asked the girl attendants, of which there were several, secretaries of Commander Lampson, to remove the door, which they did," writes Epstein. "But they facetiously asked whether I would like the roof off next. I thought I should have liked that too, but I did not demand it, as the attendant angels seemed to resent a little my intrusion into the retreat of their professor. After the third day they thawed and I was offered beer at the end of the sitting."

Each session lasted two hours. At the first, Einstein was so surrounded with smoke that work was almost impossible. "At the second I asked him to smoke in the interval," says Epstein. "His manner was full of charm and *bonhomie*. He enjoyed a joke and had many a jibe at the Nazi professors, one hundred of whom in a book had condemned his theory. 'Were I wrong,' he said, 'one professor would have been quite enough.'"

278

During the golden month of September 1933 Einstein was a man beset from all sides: by the German establishment, by the "Hands off Hitler" movement in Britain, and by his former pacifist friends, with their accusations of betrayal. And now there came a more bitter personal blow: the news from Leiden that Paul Ehrenfest, perhaps after Lorentz the man for whom he had felt the deepest affection and respect, had committed suicide. The circumstances were tragic. He had first shot his young son, whom he only blinded, and then himself.

Einstein left Roughton Heath during the first days of October. He was bound for London, as star speaker at a mass meeting in the Royal Albert Hall, organized with typical thrust by Locker-Lampson. The initiative had come from the Academic Assistance Council, the prototype of so many rescue organizations that the Hitler purge brought into existence. It had met in June, but the Albert Hall meeting of October 3 was its first major attempt to reveal to the nonacademic public the size and scope of the movement now thrusting from Germany so many of the men who might have saved her in the war that lay only six years away. A meeting of some sort had been the idea of the Council's secretary, Walter Adams, then a lecturer in history at University College, London, and later director of the London School of Economics.

Adams drove out to Cromer a few days after Einstein had arrived. "First we were confronted by one beautiful girl with a gun," he says. "Then there was a second one, also with a gun. Finally we saw Einstein who was walking round inside what seemed to be a little hedged compound."

He quickly came to the point. Einstein as quickly agreed to speak on behalf of the Council. But it appears that neither then, nor for some while, did he fully appreciate what was involved. As he understood it, there would be a smallish meeting at which a number of well-known people would be asked to speak and would appeal for funds. But, in Adams' words, "once he had agreed Locker went away, picked up the telephone and hired the Albert Hall." Organization was then prodded forward by the commander and carried out by the Refugee Assistance Fund, an amalgamation of the Academic Assistance Council, the International Students Service, the Refugee Professionals Committee, and the German Emergency Committee of the Society of Friends.

On the evening of the 3rd Lord Rutherford was in the chair; others on the platform included not only Einstein but also Sir James Jeans, now at the height of his fame; Sir William Beveridge; and Sir Austen Chamberlain. The hall was packed; its ten thousand seats were all taken, and the overflow of hundreds sat or stood in the aisles. It was not only the famous names that had brought them; Locker-Lampson's carefully leaked story that an attempt might be made on Einstein's life had drawn those in search of drama.

The danger of trouble, if only local trouble, was real enough, and large numbers of police were stationed outside the hall to deal with protests from the British Union of Fascists. More than a thousand students, many from the University of London, acted as stewards—largely to handle the expected protests from Nazi sympathizers inside the hall. There were none.

Despite the big names on the platform, it was Einstein most of them wanted to hear. There is some disagreement about what he said, and the published versions differ considerably. A truncated text appears in Einstein's own *Out of My Later Years*, and the version printed in *Einstein on Peace*, revised by the editors from the German manuscript in Einstein's papers, omits the famous "scientists and lighthouse-keepers" statement, which he interpolated apparently on the spur of the moment.

"I lived in solitude in the country and noticed how the monotony of a quiet life stimulates the creative mind," he said of his stay on Roughton Heath. "There are certain callings in our modern organisation which entail such an isolated life without making a great claim on bodily and intellectual effort. I think of such occupations as services in lighthouses and lightships. Would it not be possible to fill such places with young people who wish to think out scientific problems especially of a mathematical or philosophical nature? In this way, perhaps, a greater number of creative individuals could be given an opportunity for mental development than is possible at present. In these times of economic depression and political upheaval such considerations seem to be worth attention."

Einstein's performance was direct, simple, and moving. He radiated the personal magnetism that typified the born actor and the natural politician. Like them, he believed what he said at the moment he said it, and he gained by contrast with the platitudinous comments of the other speakers. Only Sir James Jeans pushed through to the uncomfortable truth—that men such as Einstein—comparable to those whom the Council might help—"do not labour for private gain, neither for themselves, nor for their family, nor for their tribe, nor for their country."

Before Einstein sailed from England one possible meeting failed to materialize. It is tantalizing to speculate on what might have happened had it done so. On October 4 Lindemann drove to London from Oxford, telephoned Locker-Lampson, and made it clear that he hoped to meet Einstein the following day. With his firm intention of building up Oxford science in general and the Clarendon in particular with the help of refugee scientists, it is inconceivable that he was not now hopeful of strengthening the existing links with Einstein.

What happened next is not clear. But on the 5th Einstein wrote to Lindemann saying he had learned of the attempt to speak to him on the telephone, but had heard nothing more. He looked forward to their next meeting, and certainly implied that he expected to return to Oxford, as scheduled, in the summer of 1934.

Einstein talking to reporters before delivering a lecture to the American Association for the Advancement of Science in 1934. [Pittsburgh Post-Gazette, courtesy AIP Niels Bohr Library]

On the 7th he emphasized to reporters that he was only going to the United States for six months, although he did not know what he would do when he returned. Only a couple of months earlier he had prefaced his Herbert Spencer Lecture with the assurance that the links between himself and Oxford University were "becoming progressively stronger," and many at Oxford expected that he would soon be added to the select band already settling there under Lindemann's auspices. Lindemann himself, according to Christ Church legend, claimed for years afterward that "Locker-Lampson frightened Einstein from Europe."

Einstein left Southampton for New York on the evening of the 7th, joining the *Westernland*, on which Elsa had already embarked, at Antwerp. As the liner made its way down Southampton Water, past the clustered lights of the Isle of Wight, he apparently still believed that in due course he might be offered British nationality.

The voyage was uneventful. During its later stages plans were completed for disembarkation. In the months that had elapsed since the *Belgenland* sailed from New York, Einstein had learned a lot about avoiding publicity.

As the *Westernland* sailed up the approaches to New York Harbor, Einstein and his wife, Dr. Mayer and Miss Dukas, completed their preparations. At the Battery a tugboat came alongside. In it were two trustees of the Institute for Advanced Study, who now helped their visitor aboard. The *Westernland* continued on its way, and long before it docked Einstein and his party had been transferred to a car and were being driven to Princeton, unknown to those awaiting him at the 23rd Street pier in Manhattan.

He was taken to the temporary home rented for him. He changed into casual clothes and walked out alone to explore his new environment.

On Nassau Street, which runs the length of the town, there stood the Baltimore, an ice cream shop selling "The Balt," a special ice cream cone that was a favorite among students. "Einstein's boat was not yet at the pier in New York," says the Reverend John Lampe, then a divinity student at Princeton Seminary, who had just entered the Baltimore:

> Yet Einstein walked through the doorway just as the waitress behind the counter handed me my special ice-cream cone! The great man looked at the cone, smiled at me, turned to the girl, and pointed his thumb first at the cone and then at himself.
> I wish I could say that I had the generosity or presence of mind to pay for Einstein's first typically American treat. But that would not be the truth. When the waitress handed his cone over the counter, Einstein gave her a coin and she made change, muttering something like, "This one goes in my memory book."

Einstein had arrived in the United States for good.

19. LIVING WITH THE LEGEND

Einstein's immigration visa, dated May 28, 1935. [U.S. Immigration and Naturalization Service]

When Einstein came to Princeton he was still a Research Student of Christ Church, due to visit Oxford for some weeks during 1934, 1935, and 1936. The attractions of Europe were still great and nothing could quite replace the intellectual climate of the Berlin he had known, the closeness to Bohr in Copenhagen, the ease with which he could visit Leiden, Zurich, or Oxford. Years previously, Rutherford had told a friend that leaving England for Canada, after three years with J. J. Thomson at the Cavendish, had been leaving "the Physical World," meaning the world of physics. And when Einstein had first confided to Janos Plesch his plans to go to Princeton, the latter had asked: "Do you want to commit suicide?" Einstein always remembered the remark.

That he should finally have decided to settle permanently in New Jersey says much for the treatment he was accorded in Princeton, and for the quality of life there in the 1930s. Set conveniently midway between New York and Philadelphia, the town meanders along its one main street much as it did when Washington dated his farewell address to the army from the town. White-painted, wooden-frame houses stretch into undulating country that is not offensively North American. The nostalgic pseudo-English buildings of the University, in one respect a monument to architectural poverty, provide some solace to those who have crossed the Atlantic from necessity rather than choice. Einstein, never particularly partial to humans, had some feeling for places, preferring the quieter demonstrations of nature, the hills rather than the heights, the areas where the formal transition from winter through spring to summer, and from the blaze of the dying fall to winter came regularly and without commotion. Princeton satisfied these comparatively simple yearnings, and he settled down to the winter months as content as any refugee could expect to be.

The upheaval from Europe was not as great as it would have been for most people. "I have never known a place that to me was a homeland," he regretted a few years later to his New York friend Leon Watters, whom he had first met at Pasadena in January, 1933. "No country, no city has such a hold on me." Even Zurich, even Berlin, did not have quite that. Later, when he had lived in Princeton for two decades, as long as he had lived anywhere, he found that its tree-lined streets and quiet houses, each a comfortable island in its own garden, had almost begun to have the quality of home.

He and Elsa were soon established in 2 Library Place, a small rented house only a few hundred yards from the university campus. Around it, and the tousled head of Einstein, already haloed by the saintly white aureole that was to become his hallmark, there began to evolve a new set of legends. Within a few months he had been given a special place in American mythology, a place occupied not by the master of incomprehensible relativity but by the valiant David shaking his fist at Goliath-Hitler.

As Einstein became a part of the Princeton scene, he became also the great man to whom the small girl down the street was claimed to bring her "sums" regularly. He was the man to whom the local bus driver said in desperation as the stranger fumbled with his new money: "Bad at arithmetic." With his reputation for having changed man's ideas of the universe, his pervasive humility and his built-in ability to let the world make a fool of itself, he was tailor-made for apocrypha, and from the winter of 1933 onward this grew round him just as it had grown in Berlin in the 1920s. The stories are illuminating, not for their truth but for what Einstein was expected to be and to do. His kindliness was as well established as his physical presence, and if the small girl with her sums had not existed she would have been invented. He was a genuinely humble man, and it was natural that the earlier "Can't you count" story, almost certainly starting as a chance aside before embroidered into a score of variations that traveled wherever he played his violin, should be transferred from Europe across the Atlantic.

Sometimes nature apes art, sometimes the real man is more than any legend would dare claim. Churchill Eisenhart, son of the former dean of Princeton University's Graduate School, tells how a telephone call was taken in the dean's office shortly after Einstein's arrival. "May I speak with Dean Eisenhart, please?" the speaker asked. On being told that the dean was out, the caller said: "Perhaps *you* can tell me where Dr. Einstein lives." But it had been agreed that everything should be done to protect him from inquisitive callers, so the request was politely refused. "The voice on the telephone dropped to a near whisper," writes Eisenhart, "and continued: 'Please do not tell anybody, but I *am* Dr. Einstein. I am on my way home and have forgotten where my house is.'"

The absentmindedness was no more assumed than the untidiness. It did not have to be. What looked like caricature was the man himself, merely amused as the Princeton students, puzzled as well as honored by the settler in their midst, chanted: "The bright boys, they all study maths/And Albie Einstein points the paths./Although he seldom takes the air/We wish to God he'd cut his hair."

This was the sockless Einstein, who soon settled in, protected by the agreement that he should be left in peace to acclimatize. Both he and Elsa gradually became accepted, not least because he was always good company while Elsa, despite her obvious enjoyment of Princeton's "high society," had a naturalness that soon won confidence. Thus Einstein, asked at a dinner given by Dean Eisenhart which historical person he would most like to meet, was expected to choose Newton or Archimedes. But his choice was Moses—"I would like to ask him if he ever thought that his people would obey his

Left: Einstein on the day following his arrival at Princeton, October, 1933. Seen with him are Dean Eisenhart (left) and Dr. Walther Mayer (right), with whom he was to work at the Institute for Advanced Study in Princeton. *[United Press International]*

Right: In front of Einstein's home on Mercer Street, Princeton. Left to right: Helen Dukas, Dr. Thomas Bucky (rear), Margot Einstein (front), Einstein, Dr. Gustav Bucky, and Frida Bucky. *[Thomas Lee Bucky]*

law so long." And Elsa, invited to tea by the wife of the president of the University, took a long time to speak on finding that she was the guest of honor. But at last she was coaxed into a conversation with a group of faculty wives who were liberally quoting their husbands: "Well," said Elsa, "*my* husband always says…he's a physicist… and he always says…"

A hint of this new status they were being given in the United States came at the beginning of November when Roosevelt invited him to dine at the White House. The way this was handled by the Institute was a warning of things to come, and of the battle with Abraham Flexner that was only to end when the director was eased from office by the board and replaced by Dr. Frank Aydelotte.

Early in November, Colonel MacIntyre, President Roosevelt's secretary, telephoned the Institute, where Einstein's secretary accepted the President's invitation on his behalf. Shortly afterward, MacIntyre was surprised to receive a telephone call from Flexner. In the words of a memorandum from the White House Social Bureau, he "stated very strongly that appointments could not be made for Professor Einstein except through him." Lest there should be any doubt about the implication, Flexner followed up the call with a letter to the President:

> With genuine and profound reluctance I felt myself compelled this afternoon to explain to your secretary, Mr. [sic] MacIntyre that Professor Einstein had come to Princeton for the purpose of carrying on his scientific work in seclusion and that it was absolutely impossible to make any exception which would inevitably bring him into public notice. You are aware of the fact that there exists in New York an irresponsible group of Nazis. In addition, if the newspapers had access to him or if he accepted a single engagement or invitation that could possibly become public, it would be practically impossible for him to remain in the post which he has accepted in this Institute or in America at all. With his consent and at his desire I have declined on his behalf invitations from high officials and from scientific societies in whose work he is really interested.

The implication of Flexner's letter was that Einstein had personally agreed to refuse the President's invitation. Roosevelt himself might have continued to think this, had not Henry Morgenthau, then under-secretary of the treasury, written casually to Einstein mentioning the invitation that had been refused. Einstein, in reply, said he had not received it. A second invitation to the White House quickly followed Einstein's letter, and he and Elsa arrived in Washington on January 24. They dined with President and Mrs. Roosevelt and stayed the night, their long after-dinner conversations being in German, which, Einstein later recalled, the President spoke very well. There is indirect evidence of what they talked about in eight lines of doggerel, which Einstein wrote before

In Thomas Bucky's Model-A Ford in front of 5 East Seventy-sixth Street, New York City. Front seat (left to right): Maja Winteler, Einstein's sister, Frida Bucky, and Thomas Bucky; rumble seat: Dr. Gustav Bucky and Einstein. [Thomas Lee Bucky]

leaving, a copy of which is preserved in the White House archives. This says that there were cordial thoughts of an unidentified "you"—the indentification being revealed by the fact that the original of the doggerel was written on a postcard addressed to Her Majesty the Queen of the Belgians. It lies today in the Royal Library in Brussels.

The question of Einstein's nationality was publicly raised two months later. On Wednesday, March 28, Congressman Kenney of New Jersey proposed a joint resolution in the House of Representatives to admit Einstein to U.S. citizenship. The following day, presumably by coincidence, it was officially announced in Berlin that Einstein had been formally deprived of German citizenship.

He now decided to remain permanently in the United States and, soon afterward, began to search for a cottage away from Princeton, preferably where he could sail. Elsa handled the search, turning for help to Leon Watters. Early in 1934 plans were being made to celebrate the fiftieth anniversary of the Hebrew Technical Institute for Boys, which Watters ran in New York, and Watters induced Einstein to attend. The meeting sealed a friendship that quickly developed. Within three weeks the Einsteins had visited Watters' Institute, spent some time with him at his New York home, and accepted his offer of help in their search for a country cottage.

Watters himself soon became a minor Boswell in his recording of the extrovert Einstein. This is the Einstein arriving with his friend at what turned out to be a New York charity party and remarking of his host's floral exhibition: "One flower is beautiful, a surfeit of flowers is vulgar." It is the Einstein stopping Watters' chauffeur-driven car, jumping out to post his own letters, and replying to the obvious question with the answer that he "didn't wish to incommode us." It is also the Einstein who cannot or will not see that his own idea of equality can be embarrassing. "Just as we were all seated at the table," writes Watters in describing how they arrived back at the Einstein home after one Sunday drive, "Einstein rose from his chair, went outside, came back with my chauffeur and seated him at the table next to himself. [My driver,] a decidedly modest person, felt ill at ease, and just as soon as the meal was finished, he made the excuse that he had to do some work on the car and thus escaped. This was the second time that he had been an unwilling guest at their table."

Before the choice of a summer sailing retreat could be finally decided there came news from Europe that Ilse was seriously ill in Paris. Elsa announced that she must go at once to her daughter.

What would happen to Einstein? It was finally arranged that he should go after his wife's departure to "The Studio" at Watch Hill, Rhode Island, standing on the Sound just where it meets the sea. Here, he would share a rented cottage for the early summer with Dr. Gustav Bucky, a Leipzig radiologist whom Einstein had known in Berlin and who had moved to New York. Mrs. Bucky and the family's two sons would also be there, and Helen Dukas would keep house and deal with correspondence that would not wait.

At noon on May 19 Elsa sailed from New York on the French liner *Paris*. Her husband, having seen her off, was taken by Watters to his apartment and instructed to lie down before lunch. "I am not tired but I will not be insubordinate," he said, relaxing while Liszt's "Lorelei" was played on the Ampico. "Was it restful?" Watters asked as they went into lunch. "The sofa yes, the music not much—too sugary," Einstein replied.

While Einstein's friendship with Watters reflects his unwavering interest in Jewish causes, and the determined fight that American Zionists carried on for the use of his name, that with Bucky shows something different. The doctor was not only a radiologist and physician but also an inventor, and the correspondence shows that Einstein's intuition for seeing the strengths and weaknesses of a good idea, developed in the Patent Office thirty years earlier, had not left him. The two men patented a camera, discussed means of using gravitation to measure altitudes, and also of "obtaining a proportional description of sound waves by magnetic means."

Some of the father's ingenuity seems to have been shown by the Bucky boys. At "The Studio" they had, says Watters, "set up an excellent short-wave radio set with a directional antenna. On the porch was a signboard showing at what time each country would broadcast: England, France, Holland, Germany, etc. This was during the period when Hitler was occupying the centre of the world stage. When we heard his turgid, shrieking voice come over the air, we all agreed that his antics, had they not had tragic consequences, could have been rightly designated as comic."

At Watch Hill, Einstein spent most of his available time in the 17-foot boat that he kept at a small quay within walking distance of the cottage. His boat on the Havelsee outside Berlin had been, wrote Plesch, "perhaps the one thing that it hurt him to have to leave behind when the time came to shake the dust of Germany from his feet"; and until old age joined forces with ill-health, he continued to sail, not only on Princeton's Carnegie Lake but throughout the summer vacation. Sometimes his choice would be a hamlet on the eastern coast, sometimes it was one of the seaboard's inland lakes. Once he was persuaded by his friend to go to Florida instead. They had a hard time. Florida, as far as Einstein was concerned, was "too snobbish."

Sailing, like music, was for Einstein not so much a hobby as an extension of himself in which the essentials of his character and temperament were revealed. "The natural counterplay of wind and water delighted him most," says Bucky, who often sailed with him. "Speed, records, and above all competition were against his nature. He had a childlike delight when there was a calm and the boat came to a standstill, or when the boat ran aground."

He carried his passion for bare essentials to the point of refusing to have life jackets or belts on board—even though he never learned to swim. He never studied navigation and never looked at a compass when in a boat, making up for this with a good sense of direction—which he rarely showed on land—and what Watters called "the ability to forecast a storm with uncanny accuracy." Wind and weather had an obvious link with stress and strain, action and reaction, and the basis of physics and his long theoretical experience clearly gave him an intuitive knowledge of how to handle a boat. This was appreciated by the designer, W. Sterling Burgess, who some years later, when Einstein was on holiday at Newport, came to confer with him. "Burgess had made a number of drawings from which to determine the best configuration of the hull of the new American yacht, and he had several pages of computations and equations," says Watters. "Einstein patiently listened while Burgess read his notes; then he sat for a few minutes in thought, and taking pencil and paper, gave Burgess his answer."

Two other traits were revealed to friends who sailed with him. One was his indifference to danger or death, reflected in such fearlessness of rough weather that more than once he had to be towed in after his mast had been blown down. Another was his perverse delight in doing the unexpected. "Once when out sailing with him," writes Watters, "and while we were engaged in an interesting conversation, I suddenly cried out 'Achtung' for we were almost upon another boat. He veered away with excellent control and when I remarked what a close call we had had, he started to laugh and sailed directly toward one boat after another, much to my horror; but he always veered off in time, and then laughed like a naughty boy." On another occasion Watters pointed out that they had sailed too close to a group of projecting reefs. Einstein replied by skimming the boat across barely submerged rock. In his boat, as in physics, he sailed close to the wind.

At Watch Hill, as well as at other sailing resorts in later years, the Bucky boys were Einstein's regular companions, and as one of them has written, "While I never completely lost my awe of Einstein, he was never anything but natural and unpretentious with me. When together we simply were a man and a boy....During the summers we tramped together along the beaches of Rhode Island, Long Island, and Florida and the shore of Saranac Lake, New York. Often he stopped to gaze for many minutes at the sea, which held an endless fascination for him. Whenever in my private explorations I found an interesting inlet inhabited by crabs, starfish, and fish, or used by waterfowl, I reported my find to him, and we trudged to the spot to share the view in silence. We talked about geology, nature, my school studies."

Einstein enjoyed his first summer in America, even though the news, both from his wife in France and from friends who had succeeded in leaving Germany, grew steadily worse. Elsa had arrived in Paris to find her younger daughter, Margot, caring for a sister who was dying. Within a few weeks she was returning across the Atlantic with her elder daughter's ashes, to be kept in a casket in the Einstein home until it disappeared after her own death two years later. Elsa was to be followed to the United States from Europe by Margot and her husband and by Einstein's elder son, Hans Albert.

From his arrival in the United States until its entry into the war in 1941,

Left: German troops marching into the demilitarized zone of the Rhineland, March 7, 1936, in defiance of the Treaty of Versailles. *[Culver Pictures]*

Right: German children being taken by their mothers, on April 20, 1937, to a celebration in honor of Adolf Hitler's birthday. *[Culver Pictures]*

Einstein's research in Princeton was carried on against a background of extracurricular work. This ranged from fund raising to giving confidential advice on posts into which particular men might be fitted. He wrote letters, pulled strings, and unashamedly used all the considerable force of the small tidy "A. Einstein" at the foot of the page.

He disliked all that this work involved, and for several reasons. For instance, he disliked flanneling, epitomized when he pleaded with a friend to speak in his place. "You know I can't make speeches. I can't lie." But this did not mean that his colleague could do so. "Oh, no. You know how to be gracious."

As Hitler's hold on Germany was consolidated Einstein was increasingly worried by the absurd ideological division of physics into Aryan right and Jewish wrong. The first attempts at this, made in the backwash of the 1918 defeat, had been deepened by political propaganda during the decade that followed. But the straight condemnation of relativity as a Jewish theory seemed almost sane compared with the huge edifice of mumbo jumbo being created as Einstein settled into Princeton.

At one end of the German academic spectrum stood Professor Mueller of the Technical College of Aachen, seeing Einstein and his work as part of a Jewish plot to pollute science. "The theory was," he stated in *Jewry and Science*, "directed from beginning to end towards the goal of transforming the living—that is, the non-Jewish—world of living essence, born from a mother earth and bound up with blood, and bewitching it into a spectral abstraction in which all individual differences of people and nations, and all inner limits of the races, are lost in unreality, and in which only an unsubstantial diversity of geometric dimensions survives which produces all events out of the compulsion of its godless subjection to laws."

This grotesque Nazi interpretation of the new physical theories produced during the first third of the century, the expulsion of the Jews and the effect of this on the situation in Palestine, together with what seemed to be the inevitable approach of a new world war, formed the background against which Einstein settled into his work at the Institute for Advanced Study. He was much sought after. The prospect of a musical evening, or of some new development in science were baits most commonly used to draw him from the relative seclusion of Princeton. But he was not in demand solely because he was the most famous scientist in the world. He was in his mid-fifties, unsociable rather than the reverse, a dropper of bricks as much by intent as by accident. Yet in the true dictionary definition of "a favour specially vouchsafed by God," a charisma did not only set him apart but made almost any meeting with him a memorable occasion.

When Harvard wanted to confer an honorary degree on him, he was coaxed to the occasion by Harlow Shapley, who at Mount Wilson had laid the foundations for galactic astronomy, offering a private evening of chamber music at his house. Elsa, unable to come, gave her usual list of instructions. "He is a sensitive plant," she wrote. "He should smoke no cigar. He can have coffee for breakfast, but in the evening he must have Sanka; otherwise he will not sleep well." Einstein followed his instructions, says Shapley. "When we rose from the dinner table and the men went into the library, he said 'no' to the proffered cigar. Sadly he got out his pipe. Later I tempted him again. This time he took a cigar, saying softly, 'Ach, mein Weib.'"

Once he was induced to visit the Rockefeller Medical Center in New York, then run by Abraham Flexner's brother. Here Dr. Alexis Carrel, whose extracurricular interests were spiritualism and extrasensory perception, was working with Lindbergh on an apparatus for the perfusion of human organs, a device that helped open the way to the modern heart transplant. Carrel had invited Einstein to inspect the apparatus with its pulsating exhibits. Thirty years later Lindbergh still remembered Einstein coming into the room with Carrel. The latter, expounding his spiritualism, was saying: "But doctor, what would you say if you observed this phenomenon yourself?"

"I still would not believe it," Einstein replied.

By the start of 1935 he had become reconciled to the fact that Europe would never again be his home; even a sentimental visit would present problems. Three months later he arrived in Hamilton, Bermuda, with his stepdaughter, Margot, and Helen Dukas. He played the usual hide-and-seek with reporters, stayed long enough to make formal visa applications to the U.S. consul necessary under U.S. law since they still held only visitors' permits, and returned to Princeton at the end of a week. They now were able to take out the papers that eventually allowed naturalization.

Long before this, Einstein had put down his first real roots in the United States. In August, 1935, he bought 112 Mercer Street, the comfortable two-story house in its own piece of ground that was to become in time one of the most famous houses in the world—the "very old and beautiful house with a long garden," as Elsa described it in a letter to Uncle Cäsar in Belgium. Mercer Street is a rib that runs from the university site on Princeton's main backbone, a broad tree-lined avenue making for open parklike country in which the Institute for Advanced Study was built. Number 112, one hundred and twenty years old, quiet and comfortable behind its verandah and green shutters, had little to distinguish it from many similar white-painted houses. Tidy hedge, neat lawn, five-stepped approach to the porch, broad interior stairs leading up to the bedrooms—all these were the hallmarks of anonymity, as were the trees in the back and front, which enclosed the house in its own personal countryside.

Left: Fuld Hall, Princeton, home of the Institute for Advanced Study. *[Alan W. Richards]*

Right: Einstein's home at 112 Mercer Street, Princeton. *[Institute for Advanced Study, courtesy AIP Niels Bohr Library]*

The first change in the house came with the creation of Einstein's study, a first-floor room overlooking the back garden. Half the wall was replaced with a huge window that seemed to bring the trees into the room, so that Einstein could say it was hardly like being indoors. Two of the remaining walls were transformed into floor-to-ceiling bookshelves. The center of the room was almost filled with a large, low table, usually covered with a debris of pencils, pads, and pipes. In front of the window stood his desk. For ornaments there were portraits of Faraday, Maxwell and, soon afterward, of Gandhi. On the walls hung a simple diploma: that of his honorary membership of the Berner Naturforschenden Gesellschaft. In the rooms below, contrasting grotesquely with the colonial-style surroundings, was the bulky and outmoded furniture from Haberlandstrasse 5, surprisingly released by the Nazis and finally brought to the United States on Elsa's instructions. It seems that Einstein hated it.

With this home as headquarters, he became a familiar feature in Princeton. The tragedy that soon began was a human enough link with other men's lives. Only a few months after they had moved in, Elsa was affected by a swelling of the eye. Specialists confirmed that, as she had feared, this was a symptom of heart and kidney troubles. Hospital treatment in New York was proposed. But she soon came back to Mercer Street, to a drastic cure that involved complete immobilization.

At the start of their twenty years together, the Einsteins had achieved a working arrangement. While he devoted himself to discovering how God had made the world, she reduced to an absolute minimum the mundane problems of life. To an extent that offended the matriarchal society of the United States, he thought while she toiled, a division illustrated by a homely incident when they dined outdoors with two friends one summer night. As the air freshened, the hostess asked her husband to fetch her coat. Elsa was horrified: "I would never ask the professor to do that."

For his part the professor supported the family and irradiated genius from his own private world. "Your wife," Mrs. Eisenhart, wife of the dean of Princeton University's Graduate School said to him soon after his arrival, "seems to do absolutely everything for you. Just exactly what do you do for her?" Einstein replied: "I give her my understanding."

The understanding was tested in 1936. At first Elsa seemed to recover. When the summer came they both traveled to Saranac Lake, three hundred miles north of New York and high in the Adirondacks. But her condition failed to improve. To Watters, she confided a great deal, as was clear from his later comments. "Einstein," he wrote, "absorbed in his intellectual pursuits, found little time to fulfil the duties expected of a husband." It was true, he went on, that Elsa "enjoyed the sharing of the many honours which were bestowed on him, and the many travels with him, but she missed the sympathy and tenderness which she craved, and found herself much alone in these respects."

Back in Princeton, her condition continued to deteriorate. The ground floor of

Einstein and the German writer Thomas Mann (1875–1955) in Princeton, 1939. [Lotte Jacobi Collection]

the Mercer Street home began to resemble a hospital ward. Einstein, forsaking the Institute, worked on in his first-floor study. No more could be done, and Elsa died late in December, still grieving for the daughter she had lost in Paris two years previously, still proud of what Albert was accomplishing.

After her death he got down to it with even more self-centered concentration. From the beginning of 1937 he once more, and without distraction, devoted himself to the Institute. His attitude to quantum mechanics drew him further and further from the mainstream of theoretical physics. He himself was well aware of this. He told his old friend Infeld, who arrived in the United States in 1935, that "in Princeton they regard me as an old fool." Infeld, at first incredulous, later agreed. "Einstein, during my stay in Princeton, was regarded by most of the professors here more like a historic relic than as an active scientist," he wrote. The Princeton professors were not alone, and Max Born, noting that Einstein was unable to get him an invitation to the Institute, saw one obvious explanation: "Probably I was regarded there as a fossil, as he was himself, and two such relics from times past were too much for the modern masters of Princeton."

Thus Einstein's scientific position in Princeton, the aura of greatness that he radiated, and the extraordinary influence of his personality on the minds of his assistants and collaborators, continued in spite of his contemporary standing in theoretical physics rather than because of it. A decade and a half earlier, when he was at the height of his powers in Berlin, his idea of how scientific problems should be tackled, his facility for "making physics melt in his mouth," had created an overwhelming impression on his listeners. Now, even though many of his firmly held beliefs were fighting for their lives, the magic still remained.

When Elsa died, Einstein was only a few months from his fifty-eighth birthday. By all the rules of the game his creative life was finished. He had what lesser men could have regarded as a well-paid sinecure, beyond students, beyond competition, beyond the need to struggle upward. Yet the extraordinary thing was that now, at a time when most scientists were ready to drop into administration, and those with a dislike for it were happy enough to potter on, Einstein stuck to his last with the fierce determination of a master craftsman determined not to waste a minute of the waking day.

At the Institute until his retirement in 1945, and at Mercer Street until his death a decade later, he worked with a succession of colleagues and assistants on three different but closely interlocked areas of research. First, and certainly the most impor-

291

tant in his own view, was his persistent search for a unified field theory. His attitude to what even the comprehending scientist tended to see as a thankless task is highlighted by his reply after his accountant and friend, Leo Mattersdorf, had asked whether he felt he was nearing his goal. "He replied 'No,'" says Mattersdorf, "and he added: 'God never tells us in advance whether the course we are to follow is the correct one.' He had tried at least 99 solutions and none worked but he had learned a lot. 'At least,' he said, 'I know 99 ways that won't work.'"

Second only to the problems of a unified field was development of the General Theory of Relativity, particularly so that it could accommodate the new discoveries and speculations of cosmology. Here, Einstein was moving from the fringes of his own field into an area already being transformed by technological advance. Here, with his conception of the universe as he had first described it in 1917 and as he had later amended it, Einstein had much to offer. But he was now one man among many.

The third subject was the quantum theory as it had been developed a decade earlier, a theory that now seemed to satisfy the apparent duality of nature, but that in the process allowed indeterminacy to lord it over the universe. Here, Einstein obstinately stuck. He refused to accept the possibility that the new order was satisfactory, and over the years made successive efforts to demolish it.

One of the most important of these efforts came when, together with two colleagues, B. Podolsky and N. Rosen, he at first appeared to have struck a mortal blow at Heisenberg's Uncertainty Principle, the idea that had become if not the backbone at least an important item in the body of quantum mechanics. The paper that Einstein produced with his two fellow workers asked "Can Quantum-Mechanical Description of Physical Reality be Considered Complete?" When the article is stripped of its essential mathematics, it is easy to see how its simple statements constituted a major attack on the new ideas that had almost displaced those of Einstein's youth.

Heisenberg had claimed that in the study of very small objects, such as subatomic particles, their systems were inevitably disturbed in such a way that it was impossible to measure at the same time with equal accuracy two associated quantities. As measurement of position increased in accuracy, measurement of momentum became more uncertain; increasing certainty about the time of a subatomic event would inevitably be matched by increasing uncertainty about the energy involved.

Einstein and his colleagues began by pointing out that in judging the merits of any theory one had to consider both its agreement with human experience and the completeness that the description gave of the physical world. After this preliminary statement they went on to what was the nub of their ingenious exposition. They took a situation that could arise in quantum mechanics of two interacting systems, called for convenience system A and system B. After a while the interaction was allowed to stop. But by taking a measurement of one quantity in system A, it was still possible to get its value in system B; and by measuring an associated quantity in system A, it was possible to get its value in system B. But according to Heisenberg's Uncertainty Principle this was not possible; therefore, it was concluded, the description provided by quantum mechanics was incomplete.

The new physics had an answer to this. "I have used this opportunity to take up my old discussions with Einstein in the hope that we once may reach to an understanding regarding the actual position in atomic theory, which to my mind he does not quite realise," Bohr wrote to Rutherford. This attempt appeared in the next issue of the *Physical Review*, Bohr asking the same question as Einstein but providing a different answer. Einstein refused to be convinced, clinging to the attitude that he maintained to the end of his life: that the description of nature provided by quantum mechanics was not incorrect but incomplete, a temporary makeshift that would eventually be superseded.

His ability as a lecturer, together with his reputation as the most famous scientist of the century, made him a natural choice as guest speaker when the American Association for the Advancement of Science held its annual meeting at Pittsburgh, even though he was still dubious about addressing large public audiences in English. Leon Watters stagemanaged the occasion, organizing Einstein's stay with mutual friends in the city, taking him there by train, and later recording how Einstein, sitting in one train and watching another on a neighboring track, said that he had never before had the chance of watching how connecting rods worked.

The meeting was remembered for Einstein's Willard Gibbs Lecture on "Elementary Derivation of the Equivalence of Mass and Energy," given in English after a great deal of persuasion had been brought to bear. Legend claims that on the morning of the great day a notice appeared in the personal columns of the local paper, inserted by a well-wisher, and reading: "Don't be afraid, Albert, I am sure you can do it." Einstein did do it, speaking before two long blackboards that filled most of the stage. Watters and a colleague sat in the front row, ready to prompt if he stumbled over his English. It was not necessary. The only hitch came when he remarked that his line of reasoning was simple. He was greeted by shouts of "No."

The conference, with reporters providing the usual barrage of questions, was to produce one historic reply, repeated with various renderings over the years, and much quoted a decade later. "Do you think that it will be possible to release the enormous amount of energy shown by your equation, by bombardment of the atom?" he was asked.

"I feel that it will not be possible for practical purposes," he replied. "Splitting the atom by bombardment is like shooting at birds in the dark in a region where there are few birds."

Einstein's ability to think simply about physics and describe its essentials in terms that ordinary men and women could understand was further deployed in *The Evolution of Physics*, which he wrote in 1937 with Leo Infeld who, on Einstein's instigation, had been given a small grant that enabled him to work at Princeton, where he arrived early in 1936.

Infeld's grant at the Institute was for one year: it was not renewed, even though Einstein intervened on his friend's behalf. Having burned his bridges in Europe, Infeld was thus in danger of being left financially high and dry. He realized that there was one way out of his problem. He had been working for a year with Einstein. Why should they not collaborate in writing a popular book on science? There would obviously be no difficulty in finding a publisher, half of the advance might cover another year's stay in the United States, and who knew what might not turn up during that time? With a great deal of hesitation he put forward the idea, adding that it might possibly be a stupid proposition. Einstein knew that his colleague was desperate. "This is not at all a stupid idea. Not stupid at all," he replied. Then he got up, stretched out his hand to Infeld and said: "We shall do it."

The success of *The Evolution of Physics* in 1938 was a bright spot in a grim period. Einstein still had his science, but even a man bound up as tightly to his work as Einstein was to be until his last moments could not isolate himself entirely from the march of events in the outside world—particularly if he happened to be a German Jew.

To the sense of coming doom there was added, as his sixtieth birthday came and went, a feeling of personal limitation. This he confided to Watters, as he confided much else. After an introspective evening, his host jotted down what he remembered of their conversation. "I find my physical powers decreasing as I grow older," he remembers Einstein saying. "I find that I require more sleep now. I doubt if my mental capacity has diminished. I grasp things as quickly as I did when I was younger. My power, my particular ability, lies in visualising the effects, consequences, and possibilities, and the bearings on present thought of the discoveries of others. I grasp things in a broad way easily. I cannot do mathematical calculations easily. I do them not willingly and not readily. Others perform these details better."

He would go on with his work, of course. He would continue to help all and sundry, unknown Jewish refugees, disestablished professors whom he could guide into temporary positions, relatives such as his sister Maja who arrived in the United States from Florence, fearing the future too much to continue living under Mussolini. There seemed to be prospects of little else as the summer of 1939 approached.

The American Continental Club, whose purpose was to further European-American relations, visits Einstein in Princeton, June, 1941. *[Photographs by Trudi Dallos]*

EINSTEIN, THE BOMB, AND THE BOARD OF ORDNANCE

By the start of 1939 Einstein had spent more than five years in the United States. He had settled in satisfactorily, a self-styled bird of passage that had at last come to rest. He liked the openness and the natural generosity of the people. He liked their willingness to be lavish about research. At times he almost felt comfortable, a refugee in a nation of refugees.

But in Europe, as the Germans prepared to follow-up the Munich victory, things went from bad to worse, and the Wehrmacht prepared for the late summer's campaign across the plains of Poland. Meanwhile, scientists throughout the world debated the implications of an event that had taken place in the Kaiser Wilhelm during the last weeks of 1938. For here, Einstein's old friend Otto Hahn had split in two the nucleus of the uranium atom. The event not only ushered in the nuclear age and ended the age of innocence in physics, it also drew Einstein into the mainstream of world events with somber inevitability.

The importance of Hahn's discovery of nuclear fission in the long trail of events that led to atomic weapons is well known. So is Einstein's later involvement in that trail, even though its significance is often misunderstood. Less appreciated is the ironic way in which theoretical research produced the prospect of an ultimate weapon just as the world was preparing for war. No dramatist would have dared to arrange such events in such apparently contrived order.

The interpretation of Hahn's experiments early in 1939 by Lise Meitner and her nephew Otto Frisch led on to applications far more important than any others that sprang from that generation of investigators that included the Curies and J. J. Thomson, Planck, Rutherford, Bohr, and Einstein. The revolutionaries who had gathered in Brussels for the first Solvay Congress less than three decades earlier already had ample practical results to show for what had seemed, so recently, to be largely theoretical. Yet it was only now that physics began to touch with the tips of its fingers that most stupendous of possibilities: the use of the energy locked within the nucleus of the atom. It was not that this awesome prospect had lain beyond the imagination. As early as 1903 Rutherford had made what a correspondent, Sir William Dampier-Whetham, called his "playful suggestion that, could a proper detonator be found, it was just conceivable that a wave of atomic disintegration might be started through matter, which would indeed make this old world vanish in smoke." Planck, mulling over Einstein's $E = mc^2$, declared in 1908 of the atom's "latent energy" that "though the actual production of such a 'radical' process might have appeared extremely small only a decade ago, it is now in the range of the possible." They thought about the possibility often enough. Yet throughout the first part of the century, ignorance of the subnuclear world was a barrier stout enough to keep such projects within the realm of science fiction, or of those apparently impractical optimists who declared that a lump of fuel no bigger than a man's hand might one day drive a liner across the Atlantic.

The problem was transformed as knowledge increased: from being a theoretical conundrum it became a problem of practical technology. How would it be possible to penetrate the heart of the atomic nucleus with a bullet that would split the nucleus apart and release the energy that bound it together as one piece? How, moreover, could this be done not once or twice but on a vast multiplicity of occasions so that the immense number of atoms comprising the material under attack would release their energy in the minimum of time? The great steps forward in experimental physics made by Rutherford at Manchester in 1919 and by John Cockcroft and E.T.S. Walton in 1932 had little direct effect on this central and tantalizing problem. Rutherford bombarded nitrogen with the particles that were constantly being naturally ejected by radium. About one in every million of the ejected particles penetrated a nitrogen nucleus and transmuted it into the nucleus of an oxygen atom. But although the energy released by this transformation was greater than that of the bullet-particle, most particles missed the target and passed between the clouds of electrons encircling the nucleus. Much the same happened in Cambridge when Cockcroft and Walton used streams of hydrogen protons, artificially speeded up by the use of high voltages, to bombard targets of lithium. The "bullets" were not natural but artificially produced, and the "hits" were far more numerous than those that Rutherford had obtained; but the result still remained a net loss of energy. It was still true that more had to be put into the nuclear stockpot than could be obtained from it. Einstein's comment on the problem still held—"something like shooting birds in the dark in a country where there are only a few birds."

In public, Rutherford held much the same view, dismissing the use of nuclear energy as "moonshine" almost until his death in 1937. In private, he had doubts, warning Lord Hankey, then secretary of Britain's Committee of Imperial Defense, that the work of the Cavendish on nuclear transformations might one day have an important impact on defense and that someone should "keep an eye on the matter."

Rutherford's skepticism had something in common with Einstein's views on indeterminacy, and his reluctance to admit that God might "play dice with the world." Both men, investigating nature as they found it, had pushed science along particular paths; with the years, both became increasingly reluctant to follow that path to the end.

By the later 1930s, events were slowly moving toward the situation in which men like Einstein and Rutherford were to be faced with an agonizing choice. Only a few days before Cockcroft and Walton's experiments in Cambridge in 1932, the first perfor-

The apparatus with which Otto Hahn (1879–1968) split the uranium nucleus in Berlin in December, 1938. It is now in the Deutsches Museum, Munich. [Deutsches Museum, München]

mance of *Wings Over Europe* had taken place in London. Writing of the play—which asks but does not answer the questions posed by nuclear weapons—Desmond McCarthy set the scene for the main involvement of Einstein's later years. "The destiny of man," he said, "has slipped (we are all aware of it) from the hands of politicians into the hands of scientists, who know not what they do, but pass responsibility for results on to those whose sense of proportion and knowledge are inadequate to the situations created by science."

Not yet, maybe. But the following year of 1933, which was to mark a crisis in human affairs with the coming of Hitler, and in Einstein's with his final departure from Europe, was also to see a new turn given to physics by Leo Szilard. In England he noted a newspaper account of Rutherford's "moonshine" description of the prospects of liberating atomic energy. A few days later, he says, "It suddenly occurred to me that if we could find an element which is split by neutrons and which would emit *two* neutrons when it absorbed *one* neutron, such an element, if assembled in sufficiently large mass, could sustain a nuclear chain reaction."

Szilard's flash of inspiration was to have its consequences. One was the filing in the spring of 1934 of a patent that described the laws governing such a chain reaction. "I assigned this patent to the British Admiralty because in England a patent could at that time be kept secret only if it was assigned to the Government," he has said. "The reason for secrecy was my conviction that if a nuclear reaction can be made to work it can be used to set up violent explosions."

As important as Szilard among the figures now gathering in the wings was Enrico Fermi, a refugee from Fascist Italy. While Szilard had postulated the splitting of the nucleus but had failed to find experimental facilities in Britain for seeing if this could be done, Fermi had gone through a similar experience. In Italy he had used the chargeless neutrons discovered by Chadwick to bombard the heaviest known element, the metal uranium. The result had been a transformation of the uranium; but it was a transformation that took place in only a minute percentage of the atoms involved, and its true nature was missed by Fermi. What had happened, he believed, was the creation of a few atoms not found naturally on earth, the first of what came to be known as the transuranic elements.

Among those physicists not so sure about this was Lise Meitner, the young Austrian who had listened in rapt attention to Einstein in Salzburg almost three decades earlier, and Otto Hahn and Fritz Strassman, the two German chemists with whom she worked in the Kaiser Wilhelm Institute. All three began to repeat the Fermi experiments,

298

Left: Einstein with Irene Joliot-Curie, daughter of Pierre and Marie Curie, at his Princeton home in 1948. *[United Press International]*

Right: Enrico Fermi (1901–1954), who created the first self-sustaining chain reaction in uranium and worked on the atomic bomb at Los Alamos. *[U.S. Department of Energy]*

which had also been carried out by Irene and Frédéric Joliot-Curie in Paris with what appeared to be comparable results. Grotesquely, the operation was disturbed by the German invasion of Austria; for the Anschluss automatically brought Fräulein Meitner German citizenship. Since she was a Jewess it also brought the threat of the concentration camp. She moved on, first to Holland and then to Sweden.

Meanwhile, the work continued in Berlin under Hahn and Strassman. It finished a few days before Christmas, 1938, and Hahn immediately sent to Lise Meitner a copy of his paper describing the findings. By the first of a long series of coincidences that mark the release of nuclear energy, Lise Meitner's nephew, Otto Frisch, a worker in Niels Bohr's Copenhagen Institute, was spending the Christmas with her in Sweden.

Aunt and nephew discussed Hahn's paper during a long walk in the snow-covered woods outside Stockholm, a walk that was to help shape the future of the human race.

For Lise Meitner and her nephew discerned what Hahn had done: split the nucleus of the uranium atom into two roughly equal parts, with the release of a staggering amount of energy. "The picture," Frisch says, "was that of two fairly large nuclei flying apart with an energy of nearly two hundred million electron volts, more than ten times the energy involved in any other nuclear reaction." Bohr, about to leave Europe for the Fifth Washington Conference on Theoretical Physics, was immediately telephoned the news, which he took across the Atlantic. Within a few hours of his statement at the conference, Hahn's experiments were being repeated, notably by Szilard and by Fermi, who had both arrived in the United States by this time.

But an important uncertainty remained. The fission of a uranium nucleus in a microscopic specimen certainly released an immense amount of energy. But for the process to be developed into a weapon, such fissions would have to be repeated through a block of the metal. They had been produced in the Kaiser Wilhelm Institute by neutrons, and the crucial question was whether the fission process released other neutrons that would, in their turn, produce further fissions. Would the flicker of nuclear fire act as a detonator or would it merely peter out?

Only a few weeks after Bohr had spoken to the packed and excited meeting in Washington, this question was answered in Paris by a Collège de France team led by Joliot-Curie. For in Paris it was confirmed that the fission of the uranium nucleus with the resulting immense release of energy did unloose neutrons hitherto locked inside the nucleus. The number was not yet certain; but it appeared likely that in the right conditions it would be sufficient to cause yet further fissions. These, in turn, would create still more, feeding the nuclear fire until in a minute fraction of a second the release of energy would be indescribably more damaging than that of a chemical explosion.

Thus it seemed, in the early spring of 1939, as though the world might at last be at the start of a nuclear arms race. In the United States, George B. Pegram, dean of graduate faculties at Columbia University, urged on by Szilard and Fermi, wrote to Admiral Hooper of the U.S. Navy, warning him of "the possibility that uranium might be used as an explosive that would liberate a million times as much energy per pound as any known explosive." In France the members of the Collège de France team filed five patents covering the use of nuclear energy, number three being for the construction of a uranium bomb. In Holland the physicist Uhlenbeck informed his government of the situation and the minister of finance ordered fifty tons of uranium ore from Belgium's Union Minière, remarking: "Clever, these physicists." And in Britain, where in April research into the possibility of a nuclear weapon was officially brought under the charge of Sir Henry Tizard, both the treasury and the foreign office were approached by the Committee of Imperial Defense with one object in mind: to secure the necessary uranium for research and to ensure that, as far as was possible, stocks were kept from the Germans. In 1939 the greatest known supply lay in the Belgian Congo, where it was mined as ore by the Union Minière, and on May 10, 1939, Tizard met the company's president, M. Edgar Sengier, from whom he obtained certain assurances.

In Germany, Dr. Siegfried Flugge, one of Hahn's co-workers, produced a paper for *Naturwissenschaften* in which the building of a "uranium device" was considered. Shortly afterward, two separate groups, neither of whom acknowledged the existence of the other, began work in Germany on "the uranium problem." One was headed by Professor Erich Schumann, director of the research section of the German army's Ordnance Department, the other by Professor Abraham Esau, the official in charge of physics in the German Ministry of Education.

All this—the French patent, British earmarking of uranium stocks and German preparations—took place months before Einstein signed the famous letter to Roosevelt. Vannevar Bush, director of the U.S. Office of Scientific Research and Development, and later the key man in America's wartime defense science, has summed up the situation neatly: "The show was going on before that letter was even written." Nevertheless, Einstein's intervention was to be significant for reasons that have nothing to do with the chauvinism of priorities.

In January, 1939, Leo Szilard, who had been almost continuously at work in Columbia and had become even more convinced that a nuclear chain reaction was possible, discussed the situation with Eugene Wigner of Princeton University, also a physicist of note, also a refugee from Hungary:

> Both Wigner and I began to worry about what would happen if the Germans got hold of some of the vast quantities of the uranium which the Belgians had in the Congo

[Szilard has written]. So we began to think, through what channels we could approach the Belgian government and warn them against selling any uranium to Germany.

It occurred to me that Einstein knew the Queen of the Belgians [by now the Queen Mother], and I suggested to Wigner that we visit Einstein, tell him about the situation, and ask him whether he might not write to the Queen. We knew that Einstein was somewhere on Long Island but we didn't know precisely where, so I phoned his Princeton office and I was told he was staying at Dr. Moore's cabin at Peconic, Long Island. Wigner had a car and we drove out to Peconic and tried to find Dr. Moore's cabin.

Once in Dr. Moore's house, the two visitors explained their fears and their hopes, and Szilard described what Einstein later called "a specific system he [had] devised and which he thought would make it possible to set up a chain reaction." According to a letter written by Szilard to Carl Seelig, Einstein said that he "had not been aware of the possibility of a chain reaction in uranium." A few years later Einstein's statement was given by Szilard as "That never occurred to me" (*Daran habe ich gar nicht gedacht*).

Einstein's remark seems at first glance to have been an extraordinary one. Is it really possible that in the summer of 1939 he should never have considered the possibility of a chain reaction, even though the subject had been the nub of controversy in the physicists' world? The answer is that it is not only possible but likely. To think otherwise is to misjudge the extent to which Einstein had by this time isolated himself from the main stream of physics. The weekly copies of *Nature* and of *Science* arrived regularly at 112 Mercer Street, but they were usually filed away without Einstein glancing at them unless they contained some paper he had been specially recommended to read. He no longer joined in the seminars and discussions that his colleagues held. In some ways he was comparable to the Berne Patent Office clerk of 1905, whose strength lay partly in his isolation from the detail of current developments. Professor Aage Bohr, Niels Bohr's son, has said that Einstein "was deeply involved in his own work and I hardly think that he was following the current developments in nuclear physics." Furthermore, Professor Rosenfeld, working with Bohr in Princeton in the spring of 1939, believes that "during that visit Bohr and Einstein hardly discussed the matter of possible military implications of the nuclear developments."

Even had they done so, Einstein might still have been extremely skeptical about the practicability of nuclear weapons. As early as February 15, Bohr had put forward in the *Physical Review* the sobering proposal that only the U-235 nuclei could easily be split; and that the nuclei of the U-238—which comprised the overwhelming bulk of the element—would usually absorb any neutrons that hit them. If Bohr were right, it would be necessary to separate a substantial quantity of U-235 before a "nuclear fire" could be produced. This problem of isotope-separation—comparable to sorting a vast number of particulate sand grains from their identical companions on the seashore—looked totally insoluble in 1939. Indeed, it looked totally insoluble four years later, even to Bohr. When, in the spring of 1943, he was invited to England from German-occupied Denmark by James Chadwick, Bohr sent back a secret message through intelligence channels: "I have, to the best of my judgment, convinced myself that in spite of all future prospects any immediate use of the latest marvellous discoveries of atomic physics is impracticable."

The exact depth of Einstein's skepticism as he sat in the Long Island cottage with Szilard and Wigner on that summer afternoon is unknown. Yet he himself has gone on the record with one revealing statement about nuclear energy: "I did not, in fact, foresee that it would be released in my time. I only believed that it was theoretically possible." Scientific skepticism, however great or little it was, may well have been boosted by wishful thinking. Einstein's old friend Lindemann was so repelled by the idea of such destructive power being available to human hands that "he could scarcely believe that the universe was constructed in this way." Sir Henry Tizard, who had launched precautionary measures in England, had asked the same question to a colleague in surprisingly similar terms: "Do you really think that the universe was made in this way?"

There is no evidence to suggest that Einstein was any less skeptical about the chance of nuclear weapons in the summer of 1939 than Bohr was to be four years later; but if he could not genuinely share his visitors' scientific views, he could share their fears.

There was always the one-in-a-million chance that a bomb would prove feasible. Since nuclear fission had been discovered in the Kaiser Wilhelm Institute, it was wise to take precautions. If there were even a bare chance that nuclear weapons were possible, then the Americans should not lag behind the Germans.

Here, Einstein parted company with his old friend Max Born, who worked in Edinburgh throughout the war and took no part in the Allied nuclear effort since, as he has said, "my colleagues knew that I was opposed to taking part in war work of this character which seemed so horrible." Had his attitude convinced his colleagues, postwar history might have been different.

One day a young German working in his laboratory was asked to join the British nuclear team. "He was inclined to accept," Born has said. "I told him of my attitude to such kind of work, and tried to warn him not to involve himself in these things. But he was filled with tremendous hatred of the Nazis, and accepted." Thus Klaus Fuchs, who was to provide Russia—and possibly Britain—with details of the H-bomb left Edinburgh for Birmingham and Los Alamos.

At his meeting with Szilard and Wigner in July, 1939, Einstein agreed that Belgian stocks of uranium should not be allowed to fall into German hands. But the situation was delicate even for native-born Americans, let alone for two Hungarians and a German-born Swiss who had relinquished his first nationality but had not yet become American. Szilard, therefore, proposed a transitional step. "Before contacting the Belgian Government," he said, "it seemed desirable to advise the State Department of the step we proposed to take. Wigner suggested that we draft a letter to the Belgian government, send a copy to the State Department, and give the State Department two weeks in which to object if they are opposed to Professor Einstein's sending such a letter." Thus, as a first step, the Queen Mother was bypassed. Instead, Einstein dictated a letter to a Belgian cabinet minister, mentioning "the danger to the Belgian State" that seemed to be apparent, and it was agreed that a copy should be sent to the Belgian ambassador in Washington.

On his return to Columbia University, Szilard typed out a draft and put it in the mail to Einstein, together with the letter that he felt should be sent to the State Department.

Here, the process might have stuck. But now history nudged the project back on course: ironically using for its *deus ex machina* Dr. Gustav Stolper, not only a German refugee but a former member of the Reichstag:

> Somehow [says Szilard, referring to what had been arranged before he left Einstein] this procedure seemed to be an awkward one and so I decided to consult friends with more experience in things practical than we were. I went to see in New York Dr. Gustav Stolper and told him of our need to establish contact in this matter with the U.S. government. He recommended that I talk with Dr. Alexander Sachs. Dr. Sachs seemed very much interested and said that he would be willing to take a letter in person to President Roosevelt if Professor Einstein were willing to write such a letter.

Alexander Sachs, a well-known economist and an intimate of the President, was helpful. Szilard recognized a useful contact and on July 19 wrote again to Einstein saying that Sachs had recommended a direct approach to Roosevelt and that he himself would be willing to help. Enclosed, Szilard added, was a draft of the letter he felt should be sent to the White House. Would Einstein make any proposed corrections over the telephone, or did he think that a second meeting was necessary?

Einstein favored a meeting, and a few days later Szilard was at Peconic once again. This time his companion was Edward Teller of George Washington University, another of the brilliant Hungarians who had found refuge in the United States.

There is some difference in recollection about the details of this second meeting. According to Teller, "at the time [of the visit] Szilard had a final formulation of the letter with him. We had tea with Einstein. Einstein read the letter, made very little comment and signed it." Later Szilard wrote: "As I remember, Einstein dictated a letter in German which Teller took down and I used this German text as a guide in preparing two drafts of a letter to the President, a shorter one and a longer one, and left it up to Einstein to choose which he liked best. I wondered how many words we could expect the President to read. How many words does the fission of uranium rate?"

As far as they go, Szilard's recollections appear accurate on this point. But his papers reveal more. For when he sent the short and the long versions to Einstein on August 2—the date he put on both—he accompanied them with a note saying that Sachs

"Signing the Roosevelt Letter": A reconstruction, after the war, of the occasion in 1939 when, with the help of Leo S. Szilard (1898–1964), Einstein wrote to President Roosevelt warning of the dangerous possibilities of nuclear weapons. [AIP Niels Bohr Library]

now thought Bernard Baruch or Karl Compton might be the best man to get the letter to Roosevelt, but that he personally favored Colonel Lindbergh.

The last suggestion was unexpected, since it was felt in some quarters that Lindbergh was not particularly allergic to the Nazis. However, Einstein dutifully complied. He returned to Szilard not only his own choice of letters, but both of them signed. Szilard could make up his own mind which one to send, but Einstein's accompanying note urged him to curb his inner resistance and not "be too clever"—another indication that Einstein's views about the practicability of a bomb were different from Szilard's. At the same time, as requested, he wrote a note to Lindbergh, whom he had last met at the Rockefeller Center.

Szilard acknowledged Einstein's letters on August 9, saying he would note the "admonition" about not being too clever. Five days later he wrote to Lindbergh, enclosing Einstein's letter of introduction and suggesting that Lindbergh might approach Roosevelt. At the same time he sent to Sachs the longer of the two letters that Einstein had signed.

This was the famous and repeatedly quoted letter warning the President that a single bomb of the new type that might now be possible would be able to destroy a whole port together with some of the surrounding country.

Szilard now had two irons in the fire—the potential introduction to Lindbergh and the letter that reposed in Sach's office. Neither appeared to be getting hot. Lindbergh did not later recall the letter from Einstein. "If such a note was written and forwarded it may have been lost in the heavy mail that came in that year," he has said. The same presumably happened to the reminder that Szilard sent him on September 13. No record remains of what happened next, but on September 27, Szilard wrote to Einstein saying: "Lindbergh is not our man." By this time the Germans had not only invaded Poland but had effectively conquered most of it, and Szilard gloomily added that as Belgium would eventually be overrun, the Americans should try to buy fifty tons of uranium as soon as possible.

Six days later he wrote with equal gloom that "Sachs confessed that he is still sitting on the letter," and that it was "possible that Sachs was useless."

However, Sachs was merely biding his time. "Our system is such that national public figures...are, so to speak, punch-drunk with printer's ink," he has said. "So I thought there was no point in transmitting material which would be passed on to someone lower down." The outbreak of war, with Roosevelt's resulting involvement in the neutrality laws, caused initial delay, and it was not until October 11 that Sachs saw Roosevelt and handed over the Einstein letter with a memorandum prepared by Szilard.

304

Einstein with Dr. Lyman J. Briggs, director of the U.S. Bureau of Standards, in the summer of 1939. Briggs became head of the first United States committee charged with investigating the potentialities of nuclear fission. [Wide World]

This memorandum, rather oddly in view of all that preceded it, mentioned first the possibility that nuclear fission might be used to provide power; went on to suggest potential uses in medicine; and only then said that it might be utilized in a weapon. It mentioned also that in the previous March an unsuccessful attempt had been made to hold up publication of information on fission—an attempt frustrated by the French—and that a further attempt might now be made.

At the meeting with Roosevelt, Sachs, according to the official American history of events, "read aloud his covering letter, which emphasised the same ideas as the Einstein communication but was more pointed on the need for funds. As the interview drew to a close, Roosevelt remarked, 'Alex, what you are after is to see that the Nazis don't blow us up.' Then he called in Pa Watson"—General Edwin M. Watson, the President's secretary—"and announced 'This requires action.'" Sachs left the room with Watson, and by evening the Briggs Committee had been set up, a small group of men presided over by Dr. Lyman J. Briggs, director of the U.S. Bureau of Standards, charged with investigating the potentialities of nuclear fission.

The first meeting of the Committee was held ten days later and was attended by Szilard, Teller, and Wigner. A conspicuous absentee was Einstein. The official history of the U.S. bomb project implies that he had been invited but had declined to come; but it seems clear from Szilard's paper that no invitation had been issued. At the meeting it was decided to set up an expanded group to coordinate the research being carried out in American universities. Einstein was formally invited to become a member of this group. He as formally declined.

In the New Year, however, there was, as Sachs stated in his postwar evidence to the Senate, "pressure—by Einstein and the speaker—for a new framework and an accelerated tempo for the project....Dr. Einstein and myself were dissatisfied with the scope and the pace of the work and its progress." The pressure began after Sachs visited Einstein at Princeton in February. Here, they discussed, among other things, the report in a current issue of *Science* of the latest work of Joliot-Curie's team at the Collège de France in Paris. "While we felt that it was very important that...this exchange of ideas among free scientists should be carried on because they served as links and as stimuli to future work," says Sachs, "their accessibility through publications to Germany constituted an important problem."

The most significant outcome of this meeting, however, was the further nudge that it gave to the U.S. work. "Dr. Einstein said that he thought the work at Columbia was the more important," says Sachs. "He further said that conditions should be created for its extension and acceleration." There were further meetings between the two men

305

within the next few weeks, and Einstein then agreed to write another letter outlining the current situation.

The letter, written to Sachs for transmission to Roosevelt, and quoted by Sachs in hearings before the U.S. Senate Special Committee on Atomic Energy, was dated March 7, 1940, and reported increased work on nuclear research in Germany. It added that Szilard was about to publish fresh work in the *Physics Review*, and it is clear that the whole purpose of the letter was to give the administration a further prod.

The first reaction to the letter was tepid. The Briggs Committee recommended that until a report of the work going on at Columbia University had been received, "the matter should rest in abeyance." Sachs disagreed and finally persuaded Roosevelt to call another meeting between Briggs and army and navy representatives, at which the question of enlarging the project should be thrashed out. Roosevelt, writing to Sachs on April 5, and noting that Watson would fix "a time convenient to you and Dr. Einstein," took it for granted that Einstein was part of the organization. Watson himself, who noted that "perhaps Dr. Einstein would have some suggestions to offer as to the attendance of the other professors," apparently thought so as well.

Sachs again visited Einstein at Princeton. "It became clear," he subsequently told the Senate, "that indisposition on account of a cold, and the great shyness and humility of that really saintly scientist would make Dr. Einstein recoil from participating in large groups and would prevent his attendance. So he delegated me to report for him, too."

Precisely. "In case you wish to decline," Szilard had written to Einstein on April 19, "we shall prepare a polite letter of regret in English which you can use if you think it advisable." In the letter, the third that Einstein had signed in his efforts to get the U.S. nuclear effort under way, Einstein proposed the setting up of a board of trustees for a nonprofit organization that would be able to secure the necessary funds. It was to be implemented less than two months later. For then the drastically reorganized Briggs Committee was brought under the wing of the National Defense Research Committee—which Roosevelt created—and a special committee of the National Academy of Sciences set up to inform the government of any developments in nuclear fission that might affect defense.

By the summer of 1940, when the Briggs Committee was transformed, Hans Halban and Lew Kowarski, two important members of the French team that a year previously had shown a chain reaction to be possible, reached England and were contemplating going to America. In the United States itself Szilard and Fermi were only two of the workers at the head of research teams that owed comparatively little to official help. In Germany, research was known to be going ahead. In Britain, where Otto Frisch and Rudolf Peierls had made the astounding discovery that the separated uranium required for a bomb was measured in pounds rather than tons, numbers of physicists were at work on detailed studies of the time, money, labor, and raw materials required to make a specific nuclear weapon. All this would have carried the world into the nuclear age whether or not Einstein had signed a letter to Roosevelt.

There was also the specific impact of the Maud Report, the account of Britain's plans for building a bomb, which was completed in the summer of 1941. On October 3, copies were handed to Dr. Vannevar Bush. On the 9th, according to James Baxter, official historian of the Office of Scientific Research and Development, Bush "had a long conversation with the President and the Vice-President in which he reported the British view that a bomb could be constructed from U-235 produced by a diffusion plant." And two days later Roosevelt wrote to Churchill proposing that the British and the U.S. should work together. "Though the Americans were aware of this weapon as a possibility," Arthur Compton has written, "it was more than a year later before it became for us the focus of attention. In 1940 it was still difficult for us in America to concentrate our thought on war, while for the British it was their prime concern." And the official historians of the American effort, writing in *The New World* have this to say of the Maud Report: "[It] gave Bush and Dr. James Conant what they had been looking for: a promise that there was a reasonable chance for something militarily useful during the war in progress. The British did more than promise; they outlined a concrete programme. None of the recommendations Briggs had made and neither of the two National Academy reports had done as much."

All this fills out Bush's bare statement that "the show had been going long before Einstein's letter." But it does not relegate the letter to a place of no importance. Donald Fleming, writing in *An American Primer* of the British scientists who sat on the Maud Committee, and of the visit to England of George Pegram and Harold Urey in the autumn of 1941, puts the situation in perspective. "Their optimistic report of July, 1941, and the detailed case they made to American scientists who visited England in the fall, played a major, perhaps critical, part in the American decision to make a big push on the eve of Pearl Harbor rather than later. It does not follow that Einstein's letter of August, 1939, served no purpose. The decision of December 6, 1941, would have been comparatively empty if the Americans had no base to build upon." In other words, America would have built the bomb without Einstein. But they might not have had it ready for the war against Japan. Instead, the bomb would have been ready for Korea; by which time, without much doubt, the Russians would have had one too.

Einstein's letter of April, 1940, setting the U.S. administration along the road toward the Manhattan Project, ended the first phase of his wartime involvement with nuclear weapons. The second, which came a year and a half later, is one of extraordinary irony. It shows Einstein anxious to help the war effort—but kept from it as a security risk by men unaware that Einstein himself had set the whole U.S. machine moving two years earlier.

On December 6, 1941, a few hours before the Japanese attack on Pearl Harbor, the Office of Scientific Research and Development began a greatly expanded program of

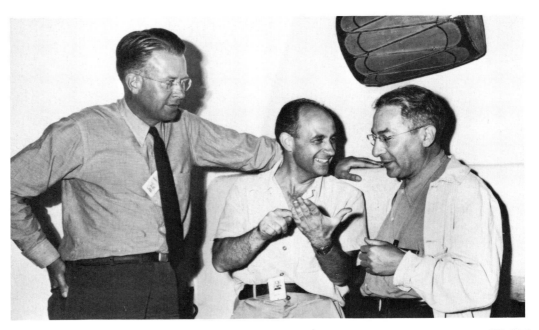

Ernest Orlando Lawrence (1901–1958), Enrico Fermi, and Isidor Isaac Rabi (b. 1898) at Los Alamos. *[Los Alamos National Laboratory]*

research into nuclear weapons. A key technological problem was the separation of U-235 from its chemically identical isotopes. One likely method was gaseous diffusion in which uranium in gaseous form is passed through an immense number of barriers pierced with extremely small holes. The U-235, with three fewer neutrons than the almost ubiquitous U-238, passes through more quickly, and the lighter isotope can eventually be concentrated. Many purely theoretical problems are associated with the barriers. They had to be solved without delay, and early in December, Bush turned to Einstein for help.

The request was made through Dr. Frank Aydelotte, by this time in Dr. Flexner's shoes as director of the Institute for Advanced Study. Einstein worked at the problem that Bush gave him, and on December 19, 1941, Aydelotte sent the handwritten solution to Bush at the Office of Scientific Research and Development in Washington:

> As I told you over the telephone [he said in his covering letter] Einstein was very much interested in your problem, has worked at it for a couple of days and produced the solution, which I enclose herewith. Einstein asks me to say that if there are other angles of the problem that you want him to develop or if you wish any parts of this amplified, you need only let him know and he will be glad to do anything in his power. I very much hope that you will make use of him in any way that occurs to you, because I know how deep is his satisfaction at doing anything which might be useful in the national effort. I hope you can read his handwriting. Neither he nor I felt free, in view of the necessary secrecy, to give the manuscript to anyone to copy. In this, as in all other respects, we shall be glad to do anything that will facilitate your work.

Bush passed on Einstein's calculations to Urey, head of the American gaseous-diffusion project, and Urey in due course discussed them with Bush. One thing quickly became clear: if Einstein's work was to be really useful, the problem would have to be presented to him in much more detail. But this was impossible. And it was impossible for reasons that Bush gave Aydelotte in a letter on December 30:

> I am not going to tell him any more than I have told him already, for a number of reasons. If my statement of the problem is not sufficient to make it clear, I will of course be very glad to make the statement as precise as possible, but I really believe that my statement placed the problem in its exact form. The reason that I am not going farther is that I am not at all sure that if I place Einstein in entire contact with his subject he would not discuss it in a way that it should not be discussed, and with this doubt in my mind I do not feel that I ought to take him into confidence on the subject to the extent of showing just where this thing fits into the defence picture, and what the military aspects of the matter might be. If I were to explain more than I already have, I feel sure that the rest of

Einstein, his stepdaughter, Margot (right), and Helen Dukas, his secretary (left), taking the oath of allegiance to the United States at Trenton, New Jersey, on October 1, 1940. *[United Press International]*

the story would immediately follow. I wish very much that I could place the whole thing before him and take him fully into confidence, but this is utterly impossible in view of the attitude of people here in Washington who have studied into his whole history.

So Einstein, who had put his name to a letter warning that a single nuclear weapon might destroy a whole port, was to be kept from knowing "where this thing fits into the defence picture"! The extraordinary contradiction is, in fact, simply explained. For as Bush has written of Einstein's letter, "in my many discussions with President Roosevelt on the subject he did not mention it."

Trying to get an answer from Einstein without telling him too much, unaware of his earlier involvement, Bush asked for help on a subject that was academic—even though it was clearly so secret that Einstein thought it unwise to have the answer copied. Thus it is not absolutely certain that when he produced the solution, and showed his "deep…satisfaction at doing anything which might be useful in the national effort," Einstein knew he was working toward a nuclear weapon. But it is a strong assumption.

The exclusion of Einstein from the inner councils of the scientists who drove the Manhattan Project to its conclusion was to have one important result in 1945. For it effectively prevented him from using his enormous prestige when the future of the bomb was being discussed. By that time he was the outsider, unable even to declare openly that he knew of the bomb's existence without betraying what his friends and acquaintances had let him know, consciously or unconsciously. Thus the prophet of $E = mc^2$ did not, in theory, know of the bomb's existence until it was dropped in anger. Sometimes, this has been too much for history to bear. One account mentions "Dr. Einstein" at Los Alamos—which Einstein never visited—without spoiling the story by adding that the name was a local soubriquet for someone else. And one biography has not only a drawn frontispiece showing Einstein "at the first test of the atomic bomb" but soberly has him speaking a farrago of nonsense there. In fact, Einstein remained officially—although not unofficially—unaware of America's nuclear effort until, on August 6, 1945, at Saranac Lake he heard the radio announcement of the Hiroshima bombing.

This period of Einstein's connection with nuclear weapons runs from July 1939 until, very approximately, the American entry into the war in December, 1941. Before the end of it he had taken U.S. citizenship, together with his stepdaughter Margot and Helen Dukas. Not every American was pleased. A letter in *The Tablet* complained of "Einstein the refugee Jewish Communist taking an oath of allegiance to the U.S. government," while a long article in *The Fifth Column in Our Schools* attacked Einstein's right to become a U.S. citizen at all.

309

Whatever the criticisms made of him, he was, inevitably, the much-sought-after distinguished guest for all manner of scientific gatherings, and he was drawn from the oasis of Princeton to attend the Carnegie Hall meeting celebrating the 400th anniversary of Copernicus' death. Since Copernicus was a revolutionary, a number of modern revolutionaries were invited. They included Einstein, T. H. Morgan the geneticist, Igor Sikorsky the helicopter designer, and Henry Ford. Einstein was one of the two who made brief speeches:

> It was in broken English, and Einstein's English had been pretty badly broken [says Harlow Shapley, who helped to organize the occasion]. He pointed out that it was not inappropriate for him to appear "because Copernicus was the great leader of scientists and he was our teacher"—or some such connection. It was a modest talk in pidgin English and the audience just roared. Carnegie Hall rattled with applause. In the front row were some of my friends from the Century Club. I had sent them tickets so they could come, and they did and applauded wildly. They are of course good Republicans and careful clubmen; that they would applaud this relativity man and his doings was a little surprising. That night I asked some of them about it and was told: "Well, I think the reason we applauded was that we'd always insisted that we couldn't understand one damn word of this relativity nonsense. And here we hear Relativity himself talking about it and still we couldn't understand it."

Anything that would aid the "fight against the Fascist pestilence" drew Einstein's immediate support. In 1943 he was asked by the Book and Author Committee of the Fourth War Loan drive to donate his original paper of 1905 for sale. Like many others, it had been destroyed when he received printed copies. However, he agreed to write it out once more in longhand.

He also handed over an unpublished manuscript on "The Bi-Vector Field," and the two manuscripts were auctioned in Kansas City on February 4, 1944, the Kansas City Insurance Company investing six and a half million dollars in war bonds for the relativity paper—and subsequently presenting it to the Library of Congress—while W. T. Kemper, Jr., a custodian of insurance funds, invested five million dollars of impounded funds to obtain the second paper.

By this time Einstein had again become directly involved in defense work and by August, 1943, had links with the navy and the Office of Scientific Research and Development in Washington. Vannevar Bush, the organization's director, writes: "Some friends of Einstein visited me and told me that he was disturbed because he was not active in the war effort. I accordingly appointed him a member of a committee where it seemed to me his particular skills would be most likely to be of service." What the committee was has never been discovered, but from internal evidence it is unlikely to have been concerned with nuclear research.

No such question mark hangs over Einstein's engagement with the U.S. Navy's Bureau of Ordnance. An announcement from Washington on June 24, 1943, stated that

Einstein in his study at Princeton, July 24, 1943, at the commencement of his work for the U.S. Navy's Bureau of Ordnance. With him are Captain Geoffrey E. Sage, U.S.N., and Lt. Cdr. Frederick L. Douthit, U.S.N.R. [National Archives]

"his naval assignment will be on a part-time contractual basis and he will continue his association with the Institute for Advanced Study, Princeton, N.J., where most of his studies on behalf of the Bureau of Ordnance will be undertaken." Records of the General Services Administration, St. Louis, Missouri, show that Einstein "was intermittently employed in Special Service Contract of the Department of the Navy, Washington, D.C., as a Scientist from May 31st, 1943, to June 30th, 1944. As a Technicist from July 1st, 1944, to June 30th, 1945, and also as a Consultant for Research on Explosives from July 1st, 1945, to June 30th, 1946." *Star Shell*, the Bureau of Ordnance publication, later stated that his work concerned "the theory of explosion, seeking to determine what laws govern the more obscure waves of detonation, why certain explosives have marked directional effect and other highly technical theories," while the St. Louis records further add that Einstein's service "was performed in the development of bombs and underwater weapons."

Einstein said, on accepting the consultantship, that he would be unable to travel to Washington regularly and that someone must come to him at Princeton:

> Since I happened to have known Einstein earlier, on nonmilitary grounds, I was selected to carry out this job [writes George Gamow]. Thus on every other Friday I took a morning train to Princeton, carrying a briefcase tightly packed with confidential and secret navy projects. There was a great variety of proposals, such as exploding a series of underwater mines placed along a parabolic path that would lead to the entrance of a Japanese naval base with follow-up aerial bombs to be dropped on the flight decks of Japanese aircraft carriers. Einstein would meet me in his study at home, wearing one of his famous soft sweaters, and we would go through all the proposals, one by one. He approved practically all of them, saying, "Oh yes, very interesting, very, very ingenious"; and the next day the admiral in charge of the bureau was very happy when I reported to him Einstein's comments.

One other idea was that of producing a certain effect by using a convergent detonation wave formed by combining two explosives with different propagation velocities. After Einstein had approved it, plans were made for a model test at Indian Head, the navy proving grounds on the Potomac River. But then, recalls Gamow, the high-explosives factory in Pittsburgh that was to make the device shied away from it. "On the next day my project was moved from the top of the priority list to the bottom," he says, "and I suddenly realised what was being worked on at a mysterious place in New Mexico with the address: P.O. Box 1663, Santa Fe. Years later, when I was fully cleared for work on the A-bomb and went to Los Alamos, I learned that my guess had been correct." Gamow

Einstein in his study at Princeton, 1943.
[National Archives]

gives no indication of whether he mentioned the incident, or passed on his guess, to Einstein. It seems likely.

Only part of Einstein's time was devoted to the navy, but there is no indication that he shirked it or shrank from that part. Indeed, there was no reason why he should. Events had taught him, in the words of his friend Max Born, "that the ultimate ethical values, on which all human existence is based, must, as a last resort, be defended even by force and with the sacrifice of human lives." Once that had been admitted, much followed, and any belief that Einstein deliberately tried to hold himself aloof from service matters has only the shakiest foundation in fact. Thomas Lee Bucky, one of the sons of his radiologist friend, recalls, for instance, how "during the early part of World War II when the Luftwaffe was bombing cities, Einstein and (his) father became engrossed in a discussion about a more accurate means of anti-aircraft fire. After toying with various ideas, they reached one possibility for a new method of fire that excited them." The writer later found them so full of enthusiasm for their new idea that they told him about it. Nothing came of the idea, but the fact that Einstein himself was so apparently eager to turn his mind to such matters emphasizes his change of stance from only a decade earlier. The reluctant admission that force was sometimes ethically respectable had first been made in the summer of 1933. Now "his satisfaction at doing anything which might be useful in the national effort" pressed his actions yet further against the grain of his normal inclinations. Circumstances altered cases; even in pacifism there were no absolutes. The war had to be won. All this was common sense enough. Many decent men did what they did in wartime only with reluctance, admitting ruefully that at times life offers only a choice between evils.

Yet the real tragedy of Einstein's situation can be judged not by the record of the war years, when his work for the services was openly acknowledged, but by the postwar period, when he banished the thought of what he had done as though it were a nightmare rather than the reality. After the war he disclaimed that he had been involved with applied science, or had worked with the military.

His reluctance in the later 1940s to think back to the war must also be seen in association with two other things. One was his natural, and later almost paranoic, distrust of the Germans, a distrust that he finally appreciated had paved the road to Hiroshima and that, when he considered the Japanese holocaust, must have filled him with mixed emotions. The other was his decision in December, 1944, when he had learned of the peril of nuclear weapons, to "abstain from any action" that might "complicate the delicate task of the statesmen."

For as the war rose to its climax, with the Allied invasion of Europe and the prospect of the Wehrmacht being driven back to Germany in defeat, the consequences of his action in July, 1939, became even more difficult to ignore. It is generally believed that Einstein was totally ignorant of the progress made by the Manhattan Project until the announcement that the first bomb had been dropped on Hiroshima. He himself never pushed such a claim—a fact adequately explained by the evidence now available.

He cannot have failed to note the disappearance from the academic scene of such men as Szilard, Fermi, Compton, Teller, Wigner, and a host of others who had been involved in uranium research during 1939 and 1940. He cannot fail to have noted the sudden dropping from academic discussion of all news about nuclear fission. And if he took more than a cursory interest in the subject of uranium itself—the very nub of his initial worry—he may even have noted the reference on page 828 of the *U.S. Minerals Yearbook* of 1943, which said: "The uranium industry in 1943 was greatly stimulated by a government program having materials priority over all other mineral procurement, but most of the facts were buried in War Department secrecy."

In addition, there was the case of his own Danish *alter ego*. In October, 1943, Neils Bohr had made one of the most spectacular escapes of the war, sailing with his son across the Kattegat to Sweden in a small boat and being taken first to England in a high-flying Mosquito and then to the United States. Bohr spent most of the summer of 1944 at Los Alamos, where he "instigated some of the most important experiments on the velocity selector…enlivened discussions on bomb assembly, and…participated very actively in the design of the initiator."

Bohr also visited Einstein in Princeton. He arrived while other friends were there, and only as these friends were leaving did Einstein hurry downstairs and warn them that on no account must they mention that Bohr was in the United States. His presence in America was officially secret since he was traveling in the name of John Baker, and had even been given a British passport for the purpose—reportedly the only foreigner ever to have been granted one.

Bohr was a man of honor. He kept confidences. He no doubt denied himself the pleasure of describing to Einstein the technological successes with which he had been brought face to face at Los Alamos. But he now knew that two years previously Fermi had succeeded in producing the first self-sustaining chain reaction in the famous Fives Court in Chicago. He knew that the forecast he had made in his secret message to Chadwick a year earlier was incorrect. And it is clear from subsequent correspondence that he discussed with Einstein the postwar control of new and vastly more destructive weapons—which, in the context of their talks, can only have been atomic bombs.

It is unlikely that Einstein knew much of the technological details involved in

Otto Stern (1888–1969), the Silesian physicist who became a pupil of Einstein's in Prague and in Zurich. He emigrated to America in the 1930s and became associated with the war-time Manhattan Project, whose members built the world's first nuclear bombs. He had a dramatic effect on Einstein when, in mid-December, 1944, he visited and discussed with him the dangers of such weapons. *[Bildarchiv Preussischer Kulturbesitz]*

313

the Manhattan Project. For one thing, General Groves' policy of compartmentalization made it difficult for any one man to know more than the necessary minimum—or to impart it, even if he wished to do so. More important, Einstein would not have been interested in purely technological detail. However, by the winter of 1944 he had talked on many occasions with an adviser to the Manhattan Project, had discussed with him the need to prevent a postwar arms race for weapons, and had desperately written to Bohr invoking his aid.

The adviser was Otto Stern, Einstein's old colleague from the Prague days, who had crossed the Atlantic in 1934. Exactly how much he knew about the detailed progress of the bomb is not certain; there is every indication that it was considerable.

Stern paid a number of visits to Einstein, who after one of them said how terribly worried he was about the development of new weapons after the end of the war. No record of their discussions is likely to have been made, but their nature can be inferred from the climax that they produced.

This came in mid-December, 1944. Stern visited Einstein on Monday, December 11. Once again they discussed weapons. This time Einstein appears to have become gravely alarmed. The following day he sat down and wrote to Bohr. He wrote to him at the Danish Legation in Washington, and he appears to have dropped the "John Baker" pseudonym and addressed him plainly as Professor Niels Bohr.

Writing of the news that so greatly disturbed him, he urged that influential scientists such as Compton in America, Lindemann in England, and Kapitza and Joffé in Russia should bring pressure on the politicians to internationalize military power.

This letter could hardly have been more ill-timed; the names it mentioned could hardly have been more ill-chosen. In April, Bohr had received in London a letter from Peter Kapitza, which had invited him and his family to settle in Russia. He had shown it to the British intelligence authorities, who had vetted his warm but innocuous reply. In May he had secured a meeting with Churchill in London, largely through Lindemann's intervention, and had tried to impress on the British prime minister the need for bringing the Russians into a scheme for postwar control of nuclear energy. The interview was a tragic failure; Bohr was unable to explain, and Churchill was unwilling to listen. In August, Bohr was better received by Roosevelt who listened sympathetically for an hour, agreed that an approach should be made to Russia, and promised to raise the matter direct with Churchill, whom he was due to meet at Hyde Park the following month. But in September, Roosevelt and Churchill did more than rule out any idea of an approach to the Russians. They also initialed an aide-memoire, the last clause of which said: "Inquiries should be made regarding the activities of Professor Bohr and steps taken to ensure that he is responsible for no leakage of information to the Russians."

Bohr's friends loyally rallied to his support, but he was "distressed that the whole business had now become enmeshed in the interstices of American politics."

Bohr was in an awkward situation. He knew his Einstein. He knew that to a man of such trusting idealism the niceties of diplomatic protocol meant little. Whether he feared that Einstein might himself try to write to Kapitza or Joffé is not certain, but if he did, the fear—with all his knowledge of how "the secret" of the bomb was being kept from the Russians—must have haunted him. What is beyond doubt is that when Bohr received Einstein's letter from the embassy he hastened to Princeton; that in a long interview he persuaded Einstein to keep quiet; and that he reported in an official capacity on the incident to Washington in a private note that must have done much to vindicate the attitude of the "people...in Washington," who three years earlier decided to restrict Einstein's knowledge of the Manhattan Project.

He arrived at Mercer Street on Friday, December 22, and his report of what happened, dated merely "December 1944," was typed on quarto paper, apparently by Bohr himself and certainly in his own brand of English, with himself referred to as "B" and Einstein referred to as "X." It began by stating that he had visited Einstein to whom he had explained that it "would be quite illegitimate [sic] and might have the most deplorable consequences if anyone who was brought into confidence about the matter concerned, on his own hands should take steps of the kind suggested."

The note then continued, as follows:

> Confidentially B could, however, inform X that the responsible statesmen in America and England were fully aware of the scope of the technical development, and that their attention had been called to the dangers to world security as well as to the unique opportunity for furthering a harmonious relationship between nations, which the great scientific advance involves. In response X assured B that he quite realised the situation and would not only abstain from any action himself, but would also—without any reference to his confidential conversation with B—impress on the friends with whom he had talked about the matter, the undesirability of all discussions which might complicate the delicate task of the statesmen.

There is no reason to doubt the accuracy of Bohr's note. There is no reason to doubt that Einstein was here, as elsewhere, a man of his word. And the inevitable conclusion is that from December, 1944, until the dropping of the bombs on Japan eight months later, Einstein not only knew far more of the developing nuclear situation than any of his scientist friends realized but that he used his confidential and undisclosable information from Bohr to impress on them "the undesirability of all discussions which might complicate the delicate task of the statesmen."

315

First, he had to deal with Otto Stern. He waited until Christmas was half over. Then, on December 26, he sat down and wrote what must have been, even for Einstein, an extraordinarily difficult letter—one that prevented Stern from making any ill-advised move yet did not reveal the visit from Bohr; a letter, moreover, that would have been innocuous had it fallen into the wrong hands.

Here, as on previous occasions, Einstein had stepped into a dark arena and been tripped by his own ignorance of what was going on. Furthermore, his freedom of action, already limited by lack of official knowledge about the Manhattan Project, was now further hampered by what he had been told only in confidence. This was to be important in more ways than one. These arguments, and the earlier exchanges between Otto Stern and Einstein, were concerned with what was to happen after the war. Yet for practical purposes they also made it more difficult for Einstein to make his voice heard in any discussion that might be raised about use of the bomb in the Pacific or even in Europe, where a week before Bohr's visit the Germans had launched the Ardennes offensive, a salutary reminder that they were not yet beaten.

First questions about the actual use of the bomb were raised in March, 1945, by Leo Szilard, who since February, 1942, had been chief physicist at the Metallurgical Laboratory in Chicago. Germany was now seen to be within a few weeks of defeat, while it was already known to a few men, almost certainly including Szilard, that the Third Reich was nowhere near producing a nuclear weapon.

The story there had been strange. In the United States, Einstein had been kept virtually outside the nuclear effort once he had started it; in Germany there had been, by contrast, a movement that tended to rehabilitate the much-condemned "Jewish physics," which he represented. Certainly, a number of German physicists, fearful that the current denigration of theoretical physics would seriously hamper their country, held a meeting in Munich in November, 1940, and officially agreed that:

> 1. Theoretical physics is an indispensable part of all physics. 2. The Special Theory of Relativity belongs to the experimentally verified facts of physics. Its application to cosmic problems, however, is still uncertain. 3. The theory of relativity has nothing to do with a general relativistic philosophy. No new concepts of time and space have been introduced and 4. Modern quantum theory is the only method known to describe quantitatively the properties of the atom. As yet, no one has been able to go beyond this mathematical formalism to obtain a deeper understanding of the atomic structure.

The need to cloak relativity in particular and "Jewish physics" in general with a respectability enabling them to be used without reproach by German physicists was part and parcel of the nuclear research that in Germany paralleled the work being carried out

An aged Werner Heisenberg, who led Germany's wartime nuclear fission research. [Bildarchiv Preussischer Kulturbesitz]

in the United States and Britain. In all three countries the crucial decision whether to follow up laboratory work with industrial exploitation had to be taken in 1942. In Britain it was decided that industrial resources were inadequate, and the British effort was moved across the Atlantic. In the United States, America embarked on the multimillion-dollar Manhattan Project. In Germany, where the theoretical results were discussed at a high-level Berlin conference on June 4, 1942, the decision was the reverse. For a variety of reasons Heisenberg and his colleagues had not been as successful in their theoretical work as the Allies. But they had achieved quite a lot: they had demonstrated the theoretical possibility of a weapon. Yet no serious attempt to move on to the higher ground of industrial production was now made. This was sensible enough. During the first two years of the war the Germans had been so militarily successful that no need for nuclear weapons was foreseen. But now the balance had swung too much the other way:

> At the time [says Heisenberg of the 1942 meeting] the war situation was already too tense for long-term technical projects. An order is supposed to have been issued prohibiting technical developments which would require more than half a year for completion. The situation spared the German physicists the decision whether to plead for an attempt to produce atom bombs; they knew, on the basis of their technical experience, that such an attempt could not lead to success in less than three or four years. An attempt of this sort would have undoubtedly hastened German defeat, because the extensive manpower and materials necessary for it would have to be borrowed from other sources, thereby lessening the production of tanks and aeroplanes.

Heisenberg and his colleagues carried on. During the last months of the war he and the Kaiser Wilhelm Institute for Physics, of which he had been made Director in 1941, were evacuated to Hechingen, bringing the end of Germany's wartime nuclear fission story back to the little village where Elsa Einstein had been born. But they were still only at the stage of academic research—a fact that had become plain to an American mission in December, 1944. Code-named "Alsos"— curious choice since "groves," its translation from the Greek, was a clear lead to General Groves of the Manhattan Project—it had followed up the Allied advance across Europe. With the capture of Von Weizsäcker's papers in Strasbourg, it discovered that the Allies need fear no nuclear weapons from Germany. As Heisenberg himself said later, "Whatever one may think about the motives, it remains a fact that a serious attempt to produce atom bombs in Germany was not undertaken although in principle—but perhaps not in practice—the path to it had been open since 1942."

It seems that this was the case. But clinching evidence has been withheld. After the collapse of Germany in May, 1945, the leading German physicists who had been involved on nuclear research—Heisenberg, Hahn, and about a dozen others—were taken to France, and then unexpectedly brought to a house on the outskirts of Cambridge by Professor R. V. Jones, then director of scientific intelligence in the British Air Ministry. "I had them brought to Farm Hall," he has written, "to save them from a threat they never knew—for I had been told that an American general proposed to solve the problem of nuclear energy in post-war Germany by having them shot while they were still in 'Dustbin,' the Special Transit Camp in France." In England their rooms were fitted with secret microphones. Their conversations were recorded, and their reactions to the news of Hiroshima, provided by the radio, were taken down in detail. Small sections of the transcripts have been printed in English in General Groves' reminiscences; but the Germans have maintained that these are mistranslations. The original texts have not been made available—due largely, it appears, to British reluctance to admit that the incident ever took place.

During the closing months of 1944 information on the position of German nuclear research was made available in Washington to a few members of the Manhattan Project. It is most unlikely, says Goudsmidt, the Alsos leader, that Einstein was aware of it until well after the war. But Szilard was no doubt informed. And in the spring of 1945, Szilard began to ask himself, he records: "What is the purpose of continuing the development of the bomb, and how would the bomb be used if the war with Japan has not ended by the time we have the first bomb?" As in 1939, he wished to bring the matter to the notice of the president. As in 1939, he approached Einstein, visiting him in Princeton— and presumably being trailed by the Manhattan Project's intelligence agents, who followed him as they followed other leading members of the nuclear project.

In Princeton, Einstein gladly wrote another letter of introduction to the president.

Just how much additional information he had by this time gained either from Stern or from others is not clear. But there is a significant statement given in the June, 1945, edition of the *Contemporary Jewish Record*. This contains an interview with Einstein, which took place "shortly before" he retired from the Institute in April, 1945, four months before the bombs on Japan. The interviewer asked "whether the disintegration of atoms would not be able to release the tremendous atomic energies for warfare." "Unhappily," Einstein replied, "such a possibility is not entirely in the Utopian domain. When military art is able to utilise nuclear atomic energies it will not be houses or blocks of houses that will be destroyed in a few seconds—it will be entire cities." Taken with the correspondence of the previous December, this suggests that Einstein's assumed ignorance of what Szilard's memorandum concerned was no more than a euphemism to protect the author.

However, this does not mean that Einstein knew the details of Szilard's proposals. It is unlikely that he did. And this was probably just as well. For while the memorandum did question the use of the bomb in the war against Japan, it did so for reasons with which Einstein would not necessarily have sympathized. The consequence of its use, Szilard warned, might be that in the ensuing arms race the United States would lose its initial advantage. And he asked whether the chances of eventual international control of nuclear weapons might not be obtained "by developing in the next two years modern methods of production which would give us an overwhelming superiority in this field at the time when Russia might be approached."

Four months later Szilard was to be one of those who went clearly and unmistakably on record in opposition on moral grounds to the use of these bombs "in the present phase of the war." But the memorandum that Einstein supported was something different. "Scrambling his technology to cloak references to the hydrogen bomb," say the official U.S. historians, "Szilard divided atomic development into two stages. The first was reaching fruition. If the United States were well along on the second when it approached Russia, the better the chances of success. If international control proved a vain hope, the worst possible course would be to delay developing the second stage." This, one feels, was not exactly what Einstein had in mind as Szilard left Mercer Street in March with his letter to the president.

However, the effort was to be abortive as far as Roosevelt was concerned. Einstein's letter was dated March 25. "I decided to transmit the memorandum and the letter to the President through Mrs. Roosevelt, who once before had channelled communications from the Project to the President," Szilard has written. "I have forgotten now precisely what I wrote to Mrs. Roosevelt. I suppose that I sent her a copy of Einstein's letter—but not the memorandum. This I could not do. The memorandum I couldn't send her, because the memorandum would have been considered secret."

Mrs. Roosevelt gave Szilard an appointment for May 8. Shortly afterward, Szilard showed his memorandum to A. H. Compton, director of the Metallurgical Laboratory. "I hope you will get the President to read this," he said. "Elated by finding no resistance where I expected resistance, I went back to my office," he goes on. "I hadn't been in my office for five minutes when there was a knock on the door and Compton's assistant came in, telling me that he had just heard over the radio that President Roosevelt had died."

Some weeks later, Szilard took his memorandum to President Truman. Einstein's letter went, too, but there is no evidence that it had any influence on Truman, who read Szilard's document and said: "I see now this is a serious matter." He then referred it to Byrnes, the new secretary of state:

> President Truman asked me to see Szilard, who came down to Spartanburg (South Carolina, Byrnes' home), bringing with him Dr. H. C. Urey and another scientist [Byrnes has written]. As the Einstein letter had indicated he would, Szilard complained that he and some of his associates did not know enough about the policy of the government with regard to the use of the bomb. He felt that scientists, including himself, should discuss the matter with the Cabinet, which I did not feel desirable. His general demeanor and his desire to participate in policy-making made an unfavourable impression on me, but his associates were neither as aggressive nor apparently as dissatisfied.

Szilard, like many other scientists who attempted to influence U.S. policy during the next few months, failed in his purpose. In the words of the Frank memorandum, signed by many of the Manhattan Project scientists, and as summarized in the official U.S. history, "statesmen who did not realise that the atom had changed the world were laying futile plans for peace while scientists who knew the facts stood helplessly by." And after July 16, when the weapon was successfully tested in the New Mexico desert, the statesmen went ahead with plans for its use over Japan.

Einstein left Princeton for his usual summer holiday. At Saranac on August 6 he heard on the radio the news that his earlier views had, indeed, been a mistake: a chain reaction had given a proof of his $E = mc^2$ far more spectacular than any given in the laboratory. To a *New York Times* reporter who visited Einstein's house to tell him the news he said: "The world is not yet ready for it." It is also claimed by the editors of *Einstein on Peace* that he exclaimed: "Oh, weh!" At first he refused to make any public comment. Instead, Helen Dukas made a statement on his behalf. "Although it can be said that the professor thoroughly understands the fundamental science of the atomic bomb," this went, "military expediency demands that he remain uncommunicative on the subject until the authorities release details."

On August 11 he made his first public comment on the bomb, during a half-hour interview with Richard Lewis, an *Albany Times-Union* staff writer. He began by trying to damp down the hysteria that had swept the world. "In developing atomic or nuclear energy, science did not draw upon supernatural strength, but merely imitated the actions of the sun's rays," he said. "Atomic power is no more unnatural than when I sail a boat on

Saranac Lake." He was asked about reports of secondary radiation, which might cause sterilization or leukemia and answered: "I will not discuss that." He continued: "I have done no work on the subject, no work at all. I am interested in the bomb the same as any other person; perhaps a little more interested. However, I do not feel justified to say anything about it." He added that he thought it would be many years before atomic energy could be used for commercial purposes, but that substances other than uranium-235 might be found "and probably would be found" to accelerate its commercial use, an indication that he knew of the great U.S. achievement in manufacturing, on a commercial scale, the plutonium that had been used in the test bomb and in the second of those dropped on Japan. "You will do everyone a favour by not writing any story. I don't believe anyone will be interested," he concluded.

Einstein's wartime attitude toward the bomb has sometimes been described as muddled and ambivalent. It was, on the contrary, quite logical; once he had reluctantly agreed that force could only be met by force, as he had agreed in 1933, all the rest followed. When there seemed a chance that the Germans might be able to utilize a new weapon of frightening proportions, it followed that he should encourage the United States to counter it—even though he personally rated the danger very slight. When, in the summer of 1940, the nuclear project seemed likely to be stillborn, it was natural that he should further urge the authorities into the action that produced the Manhattan Project. When he learned in the winter of 1944 that the new weapon was, in fact, a practical proposition, this must have seemed to justify his earlier action: what was possible in the United States might well be possible in the Third Reich. When the war had been won, postwar control would be essential.

Later, as the background to the bombing of Hiroshima and Nagasaki began to be known, Einstein supported those scientists who claimed that the bombs should not have been used. This also followed. He agreed that force had to be met by force, and he supported the Allied bombing of German civilians as morally justified, yet he believed that justification could be stretched only to cover the minimum force necessary to achieve desired moral ends. On the facts available this did not include the Japanese bombings.

However, Einstein himself would have been the last to wriggle. The available facts do not make it absolutely certain that he would have agreed, even reluctantly, with the use of nuclear weapons against Germany if only this could have prevented its conquest of the world. But it is a strong assumption.

321

THE CONSCIENCE OF THE WORLD

An aging Einstein. [U.S. Department of Energy]

When the war with Japan ended in August, 1945, with the destruction of Hiroshima and Nagasaki by atomic bombs—and the threat of more to come although no more were yet ready—Einstein was sixty-six. He had officially retired from the Institute for Advanced Study in April, but the change in status was more formal than real. He still retained his study there. As he had for more than twenty years, he still worked on his search for the elusive field theory always a step ahead of him like a scientific will-o'-the-wisp. In some ways he appeared to have shrunk back into the Einstein of pre-1914 days, an almost quaint survival of the day before yesterday, smiling to the Princeton children from his own private world, occupied only with his science and the ways in which the laws of nature were ordered.

He was still the symbol of relativity, but that was an old song, as distant from the world of the United Nations and postwar problems as Queen Victoria or the Louisiana Purchase. In 1933 he had been a symbol of the world's distaste for what was happening in Germany; a rallying point for Jewish efforts to deal with the practical problems of the refugees. But all that, too, was now part of the past. The world had eventually taken up arms, fought the good fight, and was now faced with the problem of clearing up the mess. A defeated Germany and a defeated Japan had to be dealt with; an Italy whose status was what you liked to make it had to be encouraged to work its passage back into the council of nations. In Palestine it was becoming more and more clear that the British would be unable to hold Arabs and Jews apart much longer, and a question mark hung over what was to follow the mandate. Dominating all, there loomed the riddle of Russia's intentions and the grim thought that the worst of American and British suspicions might be justified. None of this seemed to belong to the world of Albert Einstein, a combination of the century's greatest brain and dear old gentleman.

The situation was transformed by the publication on August 11 of the Smyth Report—*Atomic Energy for Military Purposes*. The quiet recluse of Mercer Street suddenly became the man who had revolutionized modern warfare and upset both the apple cart of military power and the accepted morality of war. What is more, the $E = mc^2$ of 1905, and the 1939 letter to President Roosevelt came from the man whose reputation in science had been equaled only by his position as a vociferous pacifist. This was some consolation to scientists who did not really like responsibility for the death of 120,000 civilians, even in the best of causes, and to the nonscientific population, most of whom were glad that the decision to drop the bombs was no business of theirs. The outcome was inevitable. Almost overnight Einstein became the conscience of the world.

As such he wrote, spoke, and broadcast throughout the ten years that remained to him. Toward the end of August, 1945, he had written a laudatory letter to Raymond

Gram Swing of the American Broadcasting Company. This brought about a meeting between the two men. The result was Einstein's first major public statement on nuclear affairs, "'Atomic War or Peace,' by Albert Einstein as told to Raymond Swing." Although the "as told to" formula is often open to suspicion there is no reason to doubt the accuracy of this example; Einstein's views as outlined to Swing were those that he held for the rest of his life. They are extremely revealing, not least in the parallel they show between his attitude to the United Nations and to the League twenty years earlier.

Everything was in clear black and white. "I do not believe that the secret of the bomb should be given to the Soviet Union.... The secret of the bomb should be committed to a world government, and the United States should immediately announce its readiness to do so. Such a world government should be established by the United States, the Soviet Union and Great Britain, the only three powers which possess great military strength." All the rest sprang from this: the invitation to the Russians to present the first draft of a world government, "since the United States and Great Britain have the secret of the atomic bomb and the Soviet Union does not"; and the power of the world government "to interfere in countries where a minority is oppressing the majority and, therefore, is creating the kind of instability that leads to war."

Einstein himself admitted in the same article that the current advantage of the United States and Britain was a wasting asset since "we shall not have the secret of the bomb for very long." And he admitted that conditions in Spain and the Argentine "should be dealt with since the abandonment of non-intervention in certain circumstances is part of keeping the peace." Each of these two qualifications drove a coach and horses through his main argument. If Russia would soon have "the secret," there would be no incentive for her to surrender her hard-earned sovereignty to a world government whose two other members she had every reason to distrust. And "dealing with" Spain—or with the Argentine—would mean an aggressive war that would have been given little support by any world government.

Here, as on other occasions, Einstein handed a weapon to his enemies. Shortly before publication of the article, Congressman John Rankin, a Mississippi politician of ultraconservative views, strongly attacked Einstein in the House of Representatives for allegedly supporting an anti-Franco organization. "This foreign-born agitator would have us plunge into another European war in order to further the spread of Communism throughout the world," he claimed. "It is about time the American people got wise to Einstein." The slightly hysterical attack was off target since Einstein had made every effort to prevent the organization concerned from using his name. A few weeks later Rankin could more reasonably have asked how Spain could be "dealt with" without war.

Left: The ruins of Berlin after the Second World War. *[Culver Pictures]*

Right: Almost overnight in 1945 Einstein became the conscience of the world. As such, he wrote, spoke, and broadcast throughout the last ten years of his life. *[AIP Niels Bohr Library]*

Not all physicists were so remote from real life. Szilard had revealed in his March, 1945, letter to Roosevelt that he had a keen awareness of practicalities; even Bohr, in many ways the epitome of the idealist with his head in the clouds, had been brushed by circumstances into hard contact with the reality of what could and could not be accomplished in the immediate postwar world. And Einstein's friend Bertrand Russell also shared the vision he lacked. "I have no hope of reasonableness in the Soviet Government," Russell wrote to him on November 24, 1947, after Einstein had suggested alterations in a statement on nuclear weapons that Russell was preparing:

> I think the only hope of peace (and that a slender one) lies in frightening Russia. I favoured appeasement before 1939, wrongly, as I now think; I do not want to repeat the same mistake.... Generally, I think it useless to make any attempt whatever to conciliate Russia. The hope of achieving anything by this method seems to me "wishful thinking." I came to my present view of Soviet government when I went to Russia in 1920; all that has happened since has made me feel more certain that I was right.

Any doubts about the Russian attitude were dispelled in November, 1947, after Einstein had written an "Open Letter to the General Assembly of the United Nations" for *United Nations World.* This called for a strengthening of the United Nations, criticized the veto with which the Russians were obstructing operations, and made a further plea for world government. Russian reaction came the following month in an open letter on "Dr. Einstein's Mistaken Notions," signed by four leading Russian scientists including Sergei Vavilov and A. F. Joffé, Einstein's old friend of Berlin days. There was fulsome praise for Einstein followed by a recapitulation of Russia's struggle against Allied intervention after the First World War, and of its fight against Germany in the Second. "And now," the letter continued, "the proponents of a 'world super-state' are asking us voluntarily to surrender this independence for the sake of a 'world government' which is nothing but a flamboyant signboard for the world supremacy of the capitalist monopolies."

The reply—regarded even by Einstein as a "semi-official statement"—would have been enough to knock most men from the argument. Einstein hung on. But it is significant that when in April, 1948, the Emergency Committee of Atomic Scientists endorsed the idea of world government in a major policy statement, it noted that "this cannot be achieved overnight." Einstein had argued that something almost as instant was essential.

With headquarters in Princeton and offices in Chicago and on Madison Avenue, the Committee had already been active. On May 23, 1946, an appeal by Einstein had asked for two hundred thousand dollars to be spent on "a nationwide campaign to inform

324

Einstein and several famous American physicists gathered in Princeton, New Jersey, November 17, 1946, to launch an appeal for one million dollars to educate America on the implications of nuclear fission. In front (left to right): Harold C. Urey, Einstein, Selig Hecht; at rear (left to right): Victor J. Weiss-kopf, Leo S. Szilard, Hans A. Bethe, Thorfin R. Hogness, and Philip M. Morse. [United Press International]

the American people that a new type of thinking is essential if mankind is to survive and move toward higher levels," and less than a fortnight later he recorded a similar appeal for the newsreels. Yet it is clear from the papers of the Committee, as from the detailed analysis of the scientists' movement in America given by Alice Kimball Smith, that the effect of what Einstein said and did during this period was extremely limited. After the great wash of words subsided, the breakwaters still remained. Victor Weisskopf, a member of the Committee, puts it this way: "I do not remember that Einstein ever had any influence on our discussions. He very rarely took part in them. His only help was the influence of his name. He was not much informed about the details of the problems and tried to stay away from any decision-making discussions."

Apart from this—and from his obsession for getting back to the scientific work forever playing around in his brain, as dominant now as it had been when in a letter to Weizmann he had qualified the help he could give Zionism—Einstein's personal role was circumscribed by his ignorance of the scientific-military machinery that had been built as the Manhattan Project grew from 1942 onward. As Robert Oppenheimer once put it, "he did not have that convenient and natural converse with statesmen and men of power that was quite appropriate to Rutherford and Bohr, perhaps the two physicists of this century who most nearly rivalled him in eminence."

Einstein's strength lay less in diplomatic haggling and compromising than in the bold imaginative gesture outside the normal round. Thus it is doubly galling that he should have missed by a hair's breadth one great chance of making a decisive impact on the postwar nuclear debate. The chance was all but presented by Weizmann, who in December, 1945, conceived an ambitious idea for bringing Einstein to what was still Palestine. He planned to utilize Alexander Sachs, who had been brought in by Szilard six years previously, and if it was probably bad tactics to remind Einstein of the part he had played in prodding forward nuclear weapons, this is the only flaw in the scheme outlined in Weizmann's "Suggested Draft Letter to Professor Einstein." "Reflecting upon the impetus that you gave in 1939 to an enterprise that telescoped in a few years what otherwise might have taken a generation to accomplish," this went, "I have been moved to ask our good friend Alex to play once more an intermediary role and to submit to you some thoughts of mine regarding a unique service that I fervently hope you will find yourself in a position to render to the *Yishur* [general settlement] in Palestine and to the furtherance of science."

The cornerstone of a new Institute of Science was to be laid that spring:

In connection with the inauguration of this Institute [he went on] it has occurred to me that a select number of those who had contributed importantly to the telescoped

Left: Einstein and J. Robert Oppen-heimer (1904–1967) at the Institute for Advanced Study, Princeton, 1947. [AIP Niels Bohr Library]

Right: Oppenheimer with Dr. John von Neumann in front of an early computer. [Alan W. Richards]

fruition of atomic research and its application could be invited for the occasion, jointly by the Hebrew University and the Institute, and to contribute to a symposium on the import of that research for human progress and peace. Such a group—to be selected, with your aid, as representative of the ecumenical order of science instead of only the nations involved in the atomic bomb production—might thus issue from Palestine not only a synthesis of the current scientific views but a message for the healing of the nations and humanity.

This was the grand scheme that Weizmann conceived. He finally wrote on December 28, and shortly afterward the letter was in Sachs' hands. Sachs drove to Princeton, handed it over, and then took a short stroll with Einstein. During the walk they discussed the proposal, and on their return to Mercer Street, Einstein said he would consider making the journey if Sachs would come too. "But then," says Sachs, "some twinge experienced by him and reflected in his face led him to say: 'But my poor health doesn't permit.' The letter was handed back to me."

But the rejected invitation contained only the first half of Weizmann's initial idea, the visit to Palestine. There was no mention of atomic research, of a symposium on the importance of nuclear research for human progress and peace, or of a message "for the healing of the nations and humanity." What Einstein rejected was the idea of a simple visit. Whether he would have rejected the more significant appeal is another matter.

Einstein's influence on the development of postwar nuclear attitudes was thus at first glance a good deal less than mythology suggests. His ideas for world government in which he wrapped up so tightly the solution of the nuclear dilemma were considered wildly impractical by those with experience of day-to-day international relations; those who favored them rarely appreciated that they rested on force as surely as the policies of the Pentagon or the Kremlin. The hamstringing of the May-Johnson Bill, which would have put nuclear energy in the hands of the military and which Einstein disliked, was largely the work of men from the Manhattan Project, spurred on by Szilard. And it is difficult to point to any one act of Government, any decisive swing of public opinion, and unhesitatingly declare: "Without Einstein, things would have been different."

Yet Einstein was, to most, the one figure inextricably linked with the bomb, the man who sincerely regretted the way in which it had been used. His name still caught the eye. Even without the resplendent halo of hair that made him a photographer's delight, he retained more than a touch of the guru. Ordinary people listened to him. So, to varying extents, did the men who were in the front line of the postwar battle to control nuclear energy. It was not a popular battle to fight, and it was one in which their opponents could summon up—with different degrees of justification—patriotism, common sense, and

Einstein, former Vice-President Henry A. Wallace (left), and actor Paul Robeson (far right) in Princeton in 1947. Second from right is the newspaper columnist Dr. Frank Kingdon. [United Press International]

the will of the people. It was fortifying, therefore, that they could count on the moral support of a man like Einstein; however woolly his proposals for action might be, he was a man whom most people felt, and usually with good reason, sensed right from wrong with almost uncanny intuition. Therefore, it would not be right to underrate the unrecorded influence that Einstein may well have had on others: although he can be credited with no great victory, his mere presence added to the moral muscle of those who claimed that the great issues of nuclear weapons should be argued out with reason rather than emotion. He did more than his adversaries claimed even if he did less than his well-wishers sometimes imagine.

Einstein's concern with the nuclear debate logically drew him out into two other discussions. One dealt with the social responsibilities of science and scientists; the other with civil liberties and academic freedom, a subject that grew in importance as the rights and wrongs of nuclear armament became inextricably entangled with both national and international politics.

Yet he himself provides no guide to the place that scientists should or should not occupy outside their own fields. Einstein was, even more obviously than most human beings, a one-off model. His genius was linked with attributes not only of the saint but also of the rogue elephant, and scientists in government, at whatever level they operate or advise, must be counterbalanced by the more humdrum qualities. As Rutherford showed, they need not lack the sparks of the great imaginative mind; as Szilard showed, they can retain a quirkiness fringing on eccentricity. But if they are to serve without disaster, they must have something less than Einstein's white-hot fanaticism and must devote more time than he did to ordinary men and women.

On academic freedom, on the right of minorities to disagree, on what he considered the almost sacred duty of dissent, his emotion was tied in with his intellect, for his life had been marked by a long series of rearguard actions in support of temporarily retreating causes. But the editors of *Einstein on Peace* have stressed that "Einstein, who passionately defended the intellectual and moral freedom of the individual, frequently emphasised with equal conviction the obligations which a truly free individual must assume toward the community of which he is an integral part." Thus the long list of cases and letters that they quote exhibits a splendid reserve. Einstein is as careful to be fair, to hold the balance between individual and public interest, as he had been almost forty years earlier when helping to draw up the "Manifesto to Europeans."

But there was what it is difficult not to see as one blind spot in his civilized and civilizing attitude. Einstein was the German who had turned from his country twice, the German Jew who was appalled at the way the Germans had treated the Jews. Yet if the

327

Opposite: Einstein at a luncheon in Princeton, 1953. [© Ruth Orkin]

catalogue of war and recrimination was not to continue forever, generation by generation, someone had to stretch a hand across the gap that appeared to separate two different kinds of human and discover what was reality and what mirage. Two decades back Einstein had not looked on "reconciliation" as a dirty word.

But now, with the peace, his black detestation of all things German reasserted itself. It was not only the rearming of Germany as a providentially supplied weapon against Russia that he detested. That was enough to stick in the gullets of many decent men. Einstein's detestation went deeper, was more irrational, ignored the forgiveness of both Jews and Germans who had suffered far more than he. At heart, perhaps he could never forgive the fact that he himself had been born a German. The result looks today like a deep chink in his humanity.

He thought it was essential to prevent Germans from obtaining great political power. And the Einstein who had resigned from the League Committee when the French marched into the Ruhr, now believed that if the Ruhr were left to the Germans, the war would have been in vain.

His attitude toward Germany at the personal level was even more revealing than his views on the position that the country should occupy in the postwar world. Its tone was set in his uncompromising reply to Arnold Sommerfeld, who in October, 1946, invited him to rejoin the Bavarian Academy. Einstein had no wish to have any dealings with the Germans or even with the Academy. The only exceptions were men like Sommerfeld, and a few others.

These others presumably included Von Laue and Planck, as well as Hahn and Heisenberg, by now president and director respectively of the Max Planck Gesellschaft with which the Allied occupation authorities had replaced the Kaiser Wilhelm Gesellschaft.

Otto Hahn himself asked whether Einstein would become a foreign member of the new organization. He was met with a firm "No." Einstein refused to become an honorary member of a society much after his own heart, the German Association of World Government. He refused to become an honorary citizen of Ulm, or of West Berlin. And when President Heuss told him of plans to reform the peace section of the former Prussian order, *Pour le Merite*, he was told by Einstein that because of the Germans' mass murder of the Jews he had no interest in rejoining.

The same spirit was shown in letters to his old friend Born, now back in Germany. When Born retired from his post at Edinburgh in 1952 and moved to Bad Pyrmont in Northern Germany, he was taken to task for returning to a land of mass murderers. Born, noting that the German Quakers had their headquarters in Bad Pyrmont, replied in a letter that contained two barbs. "They are no mass-murderers," he

329

said, and "many of our friends there suffered far worse things under the Nazis than you or I." And then, no doubt remembering his own refusal to work on nuclear weapons and Einstein's letter to Roosevelt, he went on: "The Americans have demonstrated in Dresden, Hiroshima and Nagasaki, that in sheer speed of extermination they surpass even the Nazis."

This was perhaps a failure to compare like with like; and Einstein's feelings, like Born's, were those of the now-distant 1950s. Memories of the gas chambers, and of Dresden and Hiroshima, were stronger then than they are today. Some of Einstein's friends, putting in a plea of mitigation for his attitude, believe that a few more years would have made a difference.

This is possible; but it looks unlikely. By the end of the Second World War, Einstein was refusing to see Hitler as the scapegoat of the popular papers; what was wrong was not a madman but that such a figure could express the will of the thousands burning deep. Even had he experienced a twinge of doubt, even had he started to be influenced by Born's arguments, by the dictates of common sense, or by the growing evidence of a postwar German spirit that was different from the old, he might have thought it wrong to change his stance. By now he was too much a symbol of all that Jewry had suffered at Germany's hands; by now, for Einstein, reason would have been treason.

It was in this frame of mind that in the autumn of 1947 he heard of the death of Max Planck, that servant of the state whose first son had been killed at Verdun and whose second had been executed by his own countrymen after the attempt to kill Hitler in 1944. Einstein's attitude was curiously in contrast to that of Born. The physicist who had returned to live in "the land of mass murderers" wrote somewhat critically of Planck as the man in whom "the Prussian tradition of service to the state and allegiance to the government was deeply rooted...I think he trusted that violence and oppression would subside in time and everything return to normal. He did not see that an irreversible process was going on." Einstein remembered another side to Planck. He had, significantly enough, not written to him since the end of the war. Now the man who hated the Prussian spirit wrote to the widow of the man who typified at least some elements of that spirit.

Yet he wrote consolingly and without bitterness, recalling the fruitful period of physics through which both he and Planck had lived, stressing that Planck had been one of those rare men who had concentrated on the great truths of life but had yet remained human. When it came to Planck, and to the scientific spirit that he stood for, it was as if the years between 1913 and 1947 had not existed. It was a generous letter.

Einstein, who ruled out any reconciliation between Germany and the rest of the world in general, let alone between Germany and the Jews, still hoped for something similar between Jews and Arabs. For this reason he had campaigned against the creation of yet another nation-state. But in the postwar world other ethnic and religious groups were trying to give themselves the covering of political independence. It was certain that a Jewish state would arise from the ruins of the mandate.

Nor was this all. With the British desperately trying to restrict immigration during the last months of their control, extremists increasingly took the law into their own hands. It was not only the rise of Hitler that justified the use of force; in Palestine the situation quickly degenerated into guerrilla warfare. And now Einstein decided to swallow his pacifism once again.

In the spring of 1948 Lina Kocherthaler, Einstein's cousin in Montevideo, was approached by those wishing to raise funds for the Haganah, the Jewish resistance movement in Palestine. Would Einstein send them a letter that could be sold by auction? Einstein not only replied by return, on May 4, 1948, ten days before the end of the Palestine mandate, but enclosed a declaration headed: "To my Jewish brothers in Montevideo." On the letter's arrival in Montevideo it was decided to form a committee of Jewish academics and to hold a banquet at which it could be auctioned. The banquet was on July 17, and most of the money raised—roughly five thousand dollars—came from the sale of the Einstein letter.

Thus the instinctive pacifist was once more driven into admitting that force was necessary. Further, the arms that he detested were now to create a nation-state that he believed to be contrary to genuine Jewish needs. Einstein's regret at this, mixed with perplexity at the juxtaposition of good ends and evil means, remained with him for the rest of his life. With his failure to move opinion along the road to nuclear control through world government, and his refusal to budge from an almost Vansittartite approach to Germany, it completes a trilogy. Only science mitigated these tragedies, a field in which he was both humble enough to see his life as a link in a long chain, and confident enough to know that he had been essential.

Einstein walking on the campus of the Institute for Advanced Study, Princeton. [Alan W. Richards]

TWO STARS AT THE END OF THE ROCKET

Einstein's nonscientific interests after the Second World War were parallel to those that followed the war of 1914-18. Then he had wanted to abolish all weapons, to bring Germany back into the comity of Europe and help create a Jewish homeland that would not be a nation-state; now his aims were control of nuclear weapons, a Germany safe within an economic straitjacket, and the survival of Israel. There were other comparisons that suggest that outside science as well as inside it, Einstein would always be cast as the same lonely and tragic figure. Not least was the feeling that America of the later 1940s was tying him with the bonds he had first felt in the Germany of the 1920s. The country of his adoption seemed to be going the same way as the country of his birth.

Pessimism about America, an intuitive fear for its future, developed in Einstein long before it was felt by most of his American colleagues. There was reason enough for this. He worked on at the Institute as he had worked on at the Kaiser Wilhelm. He listened to the distortions of his own stand on nuclear weapons much as he had listened to descriptions of the General Theory as part of an international Jewish conspiracy. And as Senator Joseph McCarthy swam into power, kept afloat on a sea of ignorance, he no doubt remembered that "the great masses of the people...will more easily fall victim to a great lie than to a small one." The whole scene began to look uncomfortably familiar.

Attempts were made to coax him to Israel. "He said he was too old," reports Brodetsky, who visited him in 1948. "I told him that according to Jewish tradition, as he was only sixty-nine, he had another fifty-one years to live to reach the age of Moses. He repeated that he was too old. But I could see that he had many other claims at Princeton."

Quite apart from claims—notably those of people with whom he still worked at the Institute—there were ties, the most important being his own poor health. Since his breakdown of 1928, when he was approaching his fiftieth birthday, he had been forced to take life more easily. His smoking, which had always been strictly rationed by Elsa, was now more drastically cut. He compromised by keeping a tiny pipe and tobacco hidden in his desk, and would occasionally be tempted to half-fill it. Then he would go outside and borrow a match—not a box, for that would be too tempting and sinful, but a single match with which he might or might not get the pipe going. He had also been put on first a fat-free and later a salt-free diet by Dr. Ehrmann, his regular Berlin doctor, who had emigrated to New York before the war. Einstein hated it all, but he was never one to kick against the pricks.

The slow but steady deterioration in his condition would alone have tied him to Princeton. But there was also his work. Here, his principal worry was still the removal of determinacy from physics, which had been the main epistemological result of quantum mechanics, a result which to the end of his life he continued to regard as merely transitory. He suffered from no illusions. He knew that he was fighting a rearguard action against his colleagues, and he had no doubts about how they regarded him as a physicist whom physics had passed by.

With Max Born he continued to discuss, in the greatest detail, and with an almost pathetic attempt to reconcile the irreconcilable, the chasm that had opened up between him and so many of his contemporaries. He did not attempt to put forward a logical defense of his attitude. What he did was assert his belief, his "hunch," almost his faith, that physicists would eventually, and in all probability long after his death, provide a theory that would restore the balance to which he had been accustomed in the past: a theory in which law connected in a causal way not merely probabilities but facts. This stubborn belief continued to keep him the outsider, the old man mirroring the young rebel who had dared claim that light could be both wave and corpuscle and that time and space were not what they seemed to be.

Yet it was accepted that few men knew as much as Einstein about the nature of the physical world. Few were to have one of the new artificially created elements named after them: the einsteinium, which as the ninety-ninth was added to lawrencium, mendelevium, fermium, and curium—and was later joined by rutherfordium and hahnium. Even fewer knew as much about the spurs to creative scientific activity, and it followed as a matter of course that when Aydelotte retired from the directorship of the Institute in 1947, Lewis Strauss, one of the trustees, should seek his advice on a successor. Einstein would neither comment on the names put forward nor himself suggest any candidates. "I besought him to tell me, at the very least, what ideal qualities the trustees should seek in a director of the Institute," Strauss has written. "'Ah, that I can do easily,' he replied with a smile. 'You should look for a very quiet man who will not disturb people who are trying to think.'"

He might succeed in recommending a quiet man—it turned out to be Robert Oppenheimer—but his powers failed when it came to persuading the Institute to invite Max Born to Princeton. And Born, however hard he tried, could never coax Einstein back across the Atlantic. Thus their basic disagreements had to be shuttled back and forth through the mail. It was different with Einstein and Bohr, since Bohr, a nonresident member of the Institute, could visit Princeton whenever he wished. He came once in 1946, for the bicentennial celebrations of Princeton University, and again in 1948 for the spring semester at the Institute. On both occasions he had long exchanges with Einstein, carrying on the argument that had started at the Solvay Congresses two decades previously.

Einstein and the Polish physicist Leopold Infeld (1898–1968), with whom he collaborated in 1937 on *The Evolution of Physics*. Photographed in Princeton, 1938. *[Lotte Jacobi Collection]*

Those lucky enough to be present at the meetings watched an interplay between master and master that had a heroic quality quite distinct from its relevance to physics.

One such engagement occurred when Einstein attended a major address by Bohr in the Institute's main mathematics building. He was collected from Mercer Street by Dr. Mitrany who, accustomed to his friend's sweatered informality, was surprised to see him in dark suit, collar, and tie. They took their places in the lecture hall amongst an august company. Everyone settled down for a highly technical two-hour lecture that only Einstein and a handful of others could follow with more than polite interest. Bohr progressed toward the heart of the epistemological and scientific argument. Einstein listened, attentive from the start, then more than attentive, then with obviously mounting impatience. Finally, the strain was too much. He rose from his seat and walked to the platform in front of the long roller-blackboard that covered the entire wall. Then, chalk in hand, he interrupted the lecturer. What had been a monologue became a dialogue. Bohr understood. He, like Einstein, knew this was not arrogance but submission to fate. Only Einstein could adequately contradict what he believed was wrong even if he could not prove it was wrong. Not to do so would be dereliction of duty.

Bohr and Einstein continued their argument. They agreed to go on differing; Bohr confident that he had reached bedrock, Einstein as confident that they were still dealing with the lower subsoil of physics. Below, he continued to believe, lay the ideas that would bring back the world he had known half a century ago. If it were based on anything more than elderly optimism, the hope of restoring the images he had helped destroy during an iconoclastic youth was based on that old panacea for a fragmented physics, a satisfactory unified field theory. He still intuitively believed that this would allow the laws of quantum mechanics to be derived from nonstatistical laws governing not probabilities but facts, and he had pressed on relentlessly during his early years at the Institute, throughout the war and into the peace, still in hot pursuit of the set of equations that would show that God did not really play dice with the world.

He never completely despaired. He worked on, past his seventieth birthday, and at last began to see what he thought was light at the end of the tunnel. By the autumn he was ready with "A Generalised Theory of Gravitation." A typewritten copy of the manuscript was exhibited at the Christmas meeting of the American Association for the Advancement of Science, and the theory, with its twenty-eight mathematical formulas, appeared two months later as a fourteen-page appendix to the fourth edition of *The Meaning of Relativity*.

A new theory from Einstein, offering at the age of seventy a key to the riddle of the universe to replace the one he had provided at the age of fifty, caused a major stir in the scientific world, and its ground swell reached out to the man in the street. Low drew a cartoon that quickly became famous, showing Einstein bringing a giant key on New Year's Day to a Father Time exclaiming: "About time, too!" There were large and

334

Einstein with his son Albert and grandson Bernhard, 1932. [California Institute of Technology]

numerous headlines; phrases such as "master theory" were freely bandied about. Some of the more weighty journals began to outline what Einstein's thirty years of thought had yielded, a new and more convenient tool with which it was hoped that the laws of nature could be described.

What no one attempted to explain was how the tool could be used. The reason was simple. Infeld considered that he would need a year to understand it and added: "Like Chinese, you have to study it first." Harold Urey had not read it. "If I had," he said, "I would probably not have understood it."

However, it was not only the remoteness of the theory from even most scientific minds that was a stumbling block to acceptance. Unlike the General Theory of 1915, it could not apparently be tested. Einstein knew the limitations of what had been half a lifetime's work; typically, he made light of them, replying to any inquiry about the chances of experimental evidence: "Come back in twenty years' time."

Almost three decades later, Einstein's theory of a unified field remains unsubstantiated, and current thought veers away from the idea of the universe being built in this way. Tough realist that he was, Einstein would be only moderately put out by this view. He knew that at the least he was clearing a good deal of scientific weeds. He might be regarded as a scientific curiosity; nevertheless, he was spending his last years doing a job that could be attempted by only a handful of men in the world. Therefore, Einstein, a familiar figure on the tree-lined streets of Princeton in his shabby coat, old muffler, and black knitted cap, was still fired by an inner certitude no less invincible than in the days of Berne and Zurich. Then, he had been the silent dark horse, content to work on alone, confident of Albert Einstein. Now, the older version of the man was quite as sure of the work needing to be done, happy to ignore how the rest of the world regarded him. For half a century he had stuck to his last, a Mr. Standfast of physics. He had no cause to regret the decision now.

His routine was simple. He would breakfast between nine and ten, at the same time taking his "adrenalin cure"—reading the current political situation in the daily papers. In the winter he would be picked up from Mercer Street at about ten-thirty by the green station wagon from the Institute. He would usually walk home. In the summer he would walk to work and ride back in the early afternoon heat. On the way to the Institute, says Ernst Strauss, his assistant from 1944 until 1947, who accompanied him on occasions, a stranger would sometimes waylay him, and say how much he had wanted to meet him. "Einstein would pose with the waylayer's wife, children or grandchildren as desired and exchange a few goodhumored words. Then he would go on, shaking his head, saying: 'Well, the old elephant has gone through his tricks again.'"

At the Institute, he would work until one o'clock, sometimes alone, sometimes with his assistant, soaring up into the mathematical stratosphere where the battle had to be fought, always with his forces well-disposed, always optimistic of eventual success, even optimistic about failures which he would face with: "Well, we've learned some-

Einstein at the Institute for Advanced Study, Princeton. [Alan W. Richards]

thing." Soon after one o'clock he would put his notes into a thin worn briefcase and make for Mercer Street, sometimes stopping to chat with the two Oppenheimer children, occasionally accompanied by one of the younger faculty members or by one of the visiting professors. More frequently he walked alone. He did not like keeping good men from their duty and Helen Dukas, asking him on one occasion whether she should bring home a brilliant young mathematician just appointed to the Institute, was told: "No: let him get on with his work."

At one-thirty he would eat, then rest until the late afternoon when after a cup of tea he would work, see visitors, or more frequently deal with the correspondence that had been sorted by Miss Dukas earlier in the day. Supper came soon after six-thirty, and then there would be another bout of work or more letters. Sometimes he would listen to the radio, and occasionally there were private visitors. He had by this time given up his violin, saying that he was not good enough, but continued to play Bach or Mozart each day on his Bechstein grand.

On Sundays, friends would take him for a drive into the country or to the coast, which was only an hour away. He still hated to be seen in public, and he often repeated his old claim that like Midas he changed everything he touched—but in his case it turned not into gold but into a circus.

Such was the life that went on behind the barrier raised against inquisitive callers, visitors who wanted only a glimpse of the great man or of the place where he worked and lived, and correspondents who produced an echo of the crankeries with which he had had to deal during his first days of fame in Berlin.

But there were sometimes unexpected repercussions. Thus when the IBM Corporation invited him to the unveiling of a new computer, they failed to receive an answer. Dean Eisenhart of the Graduate School, Princeton University, was asked to investigate when a follow-up invitation, immaculately typed like the first one on an IBM executive machine, also failed to produce a reply:

> He explained [says his son, Churchill Eisenhart] that something must be amiss, because Dr. Einstein was scrupulous about replying to all such invitations. He walked over to Dr. Einstein's house and explained the situation. Dr. Einstein dumped the contents of a very large wastebasket on the floor and examined an item here and there. Finally his face lighted up. He handed one of the invitational letters to my father, saying: "It looks as if it were printed. I never read printed circulars."

Life at Mercer Street was quiet and unpretentious, homely and unaffected, not blatantly the life of a genius—in fact, a life in surroundings that were sometimes unexpected. In this house, more home of artist or polymath than theoretical physicist, Einstein was the centerpiece of a trio of women. Dominating it was Miss Dukas, since Elsa's death the person on whom the main burden of the household had fallen—the housekeeper and shopper, the cook and secretary, the organizer of peace and quite, the filer of correspondence who for lack of space was forced to store boxes of letters in the

336

Einstein and David Ben-Gurion (1886–1973), Princeton, 1951. [AIP Niels Bohr Library]

cellar and who often wished that Gutenberg had never lived. Only after Einstein's death was the priceless collection taken to the Institute to be housed in the room safe, guarded with entry door and combination lock, that had once held the miscellaneous nuclear secrets of the former director, Robert Oppenheimer.

Also at Mercer Street there was Margot, the stepdaughter who had grown so like Einstein in attitude and outlook that it was difficult to think of them as linked only by collateral lines on the family tree. Thirdly, there was Maja, two years younger than her brother, for whom he possibly felt more affection than for anyone.

Brother and sister read much together. From 1946, when she began to be crippled by arteriosclerosis, he would read to her every evening, and he continued to do so as, from the end of 1950, her condition became more critical. Margot nursed her. But, with intelligence scarcely impaired by advancing illness, Maja died in 1951.

Since the start of the century, Einstein's life had presented a series of unexpected contradictions. Now there was to come a final twist. In 1952 the image of the old eccentric, pottering along in his seventies, was to be brusquely shattered. Albert Einstein, the man who had always decried force, was invited to become president of Israel, that realization of Zionist hopes, the state that had successfully staked out its frontiers by force of arms and was defending them against all comers.

The proposal, practical, outrageous, or pathetic according to viewpoint, splendid in its audacity if grotesque in its implications, followed the death of Chaim Weizmann, who had become first president soon after declaration of the State of Israel in May, 1948. Weizmann died on Sunday, November 9, 1952, and a few days later Einstein was considered as a successor in the Tel Aviv newspaper *Maariv*. It seems likely that this was a test to discover public reaction. If so, it was flown by the prime minister, David Ben-Gurion.

Einstein, like most of his friends, refused to take the idea seriously, and when the *New York Times* asked for his reaction on the evening of Sunday the 16th, he refused to comment. Shortly afterward, the telephone in Mercer Street rang again, and the operator said that Washington was on the line. "Herr Gott," exclaimed Miss Dukas, who had answered: "Washington. What is wrong now?" This time it was Abba Eban, the Israeli ambassador to the United States who was making an informal inquiry. Would Einstein accept the presidency if it were offered by a vote of the Knesset?

His reply was in keeping with his reputation. "His main and urgent thought," says Professor Mitrany who was with him when the call came through, "was how to spare the ambassador the embarrassment of his inevitable refusal."

To Eban the situation was equally clear: "Einstein was visibly moved by the splendour and audacity of the thought," he has said, "but his rejection was firm and vehement: 'I know a little about nature,' he said, 'and hardly anything about men.' He implored me to accept his negative decision as final and do everything possible to divert and banish the press whose representatives were laying siege to his house in Mercer Street."

But Eban's instructions had come direct from the prime minister. He finally convinced Einstein that it would be improper for him to reject the proposal on the telephone, and the following day made a formal telegraphed request that he should receive his deputy to seek his "reaction on a matter of the utmost urgency and importance."

Einstein telephoned Eban, again declining the invitation. However, on Tuesday the 18th, a formal letter was brought to Princeton by the Israeli minister, David Goiten. "Acceptance would entail moving to Israel and taking its citizenship," said the letter. "The Prime Minister assures me that in such circumstances complete facility and freedom to pursue your great scientific work would be afforded by the government and people who are fully conscious of the supreme significance of your labours."

It was a persuasive appeal to a man for whom the creation of Israel was a political act of an essentially moral quality. Nevertheless, Einstein felt bound to refuse.

As his seventy-fifth birthday approached, there were still many ways in which it seemed that while age had matured him, it had hardly changed him basically. It was more than sixty years since he had decided to devote his life to a single quest, to order his days to an almost inhuman sense of priorities; nearly forty since he had reluctantly been drawn out into contact with the world of politics and power by the demands of Zionism and European peace. Yet what Einstein now stood for echoes his earlier beliefs in remarkable fashion, so that the *obiter dicta* of his last years ring like crystallized and polished examples of the casual ideas he had tossed off to fellow students at the E.T.H. or to colleagues who broke in on his thoughts while he was remaking man's picture of the universe.

As far as his own life was concerned, one thing seemed quite clear. "I made one great mistake in my life," he said to Linus Pauling, who spent an hour with him on the morning of November 11, 1954, "…when I signed the letter to President Roosevelt recommending that atom bombs be made; but there was some justification—the danger that the Germans would make them." In a message to the American Friends of the Hebrew University, he stressed the Jewish ideal of the person who enriched the spiritual life of his people and who repudiated materialism. It was a temptation to which he had never succumbed; enjoyment of "the pleasures that nature provides," was the nearest he came to it. So, too, with the more insidious temptations of great success. "The only way to escape the personal corruption of praise is to go on working," he said. "One is tempted to stop and listen to it. The only thing is to turn away and go on working. Work. There is nothing else."

Some of his last scientific judgments have been put on record by the Canadian astronomer, Dr. A. Vibert Douglas, Eddington's biographer, who traveled to Princeton in January, 1954:

He spoke [says Dr. Douglas] of the literary value, the beauty and brilliance of Eddington's writing in those books aimed at giving to the intelligent lay reader at least some understanding, some insight into the significance of the new scientific ideas—but with a smile he added that a scientist is mistaken if he thinks he is making the layman understand: a scientist should not attempt to popularise his theories, if he does "he is a fakir—it is the duty of a scientist to remain obscure."

This point, which Einstein also made in other places during his later years, was in strong contrast to his earlier attempts to explain relativity in simple language. It is difficult not to see here a reflection of the disillusion with the masses that surfaced during the latter part of his life:

In regard to the developments in the early years made by Weyl and Eddington, the later theories of the expanding universe of Friedmann, Lemaître and Eddington, the still later kinematic relativity of E. A. Milne, and the yet more recent theories of continuous creation of matter of Jordan, Bondi and Hoyle, the comments of Dr. Einstein were brief and critical [says Dr. Douglas]. He definitely disliked the hypothesis of continuous creation, he felt the necessity for a "beginning"; he regarded Milne's brilliant mathematical mind as lacking in critical judgment; he was not attracted by the idea of Lemaître's primeval atom; and he concluded by saying of his own and all the others: "Every man has his own cosmology and who can say that his own theory is right."

Thus, after two decades, what Thomson had said as a joke was repeated by Einstein in earnest.

Dr. Douglas knew that in Einstein's Berlin study there had once hung portraits of Newton and of Maxwell. Now all she saw was a portrait of Gandhi and another of a German musician. "The greatest man of our age," was how Einstein now described Gandhi; and, of Dr. Schweitzer, whose name was mentioned: "Yes, he too is a very great man."

"There remained one special thing I wanted to ask him—Who were the greatest men, the most powerful thinkers, whom he had known?" writes Dr. Douglas. "The answer came without hesitation, 'Lorentz.'"

Just as he dotted the i's and crossed the t's of his scientific beliefs during the last year or so of his life, so did he recapitulate his religious convictions. To Dr. Douglas he stated: "If I were not a Jew I would be a Quaker." And in an interview with Professor William Hermanns he said: "I cannot accept any concept of God based on the fear of life or the fear of death or blind faith. I cannot prove to you that there is no personal God, but if I were to speak of him I would be a liar."

As to what one could believe in, the answer was simple enough. "I believe in the brotherhood of man and the uniqueness of the individual. But if you ask me to prove what

I believe, I can't. You know them to be true but you could spend a whole lifetime without being able to prove them. The mind can proceed only so far upon what it knows and can prove. There comes a point where the mind takes a higher plane of knowledge, but can never prove how it got there. All great discoveries have involved such a leap."

As to the spur that pricked all men onward, that, too, was simple enough to explain. "The important thing is not to stop questioning," he said. "Curiosity has its own reason for existence. One cannot help but be in awe when [one] contemplates the mysteries of eternity, of life, of the marvellous structure of reality. It is enough if one tries merely to comprehend a little of this mystery each day. Never lose a holy curiosity."

Einstein had carried little of the emotional baggage that burdens most men. In some ways, of course, it made his task easier. He travels fastest who travels not only alone, but light; yet even in science this had brought items on the debit side. His inability to feel the human tragedy emotionally as well as intellectually had helped to disrupt his first marriage, a troublesome vexatious mistake that seems at times to have driven him to the point of desperation just when he wished to concentrate on the job in hand. These personal troubles had been overcome with his marriage to Elsa, who from 1919 helped to clear the path of greatness without complaint. To this extent the disabilities produced by his emotional isolation—by being, as he had described it to Besso as a young man, "rather cool and a bit of a hard nut"—had been overcome. He could get on with his work without worrying too much about anyone else. Outside that work, however, the aloofness that he did little to discourage brought its own reward: a man genuinely anxious to do good, he found the best of his intentions frustrated with maddening regularity.

Early in 1955 he was invited to conferences in Berne and Berlin to celebrate the fiftieth anniversary of his most famous paper. He declined.

He would have enjoyed the Berne meeting, even though its appraisal of the General Theory lacked the initial scientific rapture of 1919. The unqualified acceptance and the experimental verification that had long ago put the Special Theory beyond all dispute were still lacking here. While there was no doubt that gravity did affect light, the extent of its effect had become increasingly questioned as experimental methods improved. "A lot of work will have to be done before the astronomers really can say what is the value of the observed light deflection and whether the red shift is in existence at all," noted Freundlich at the Conference. Some of this work has now been done. But Born, to whom the General Theory continued to remain "the greatest feat of human thinking about nature," voiced qualifications that still hold. "Of the three observable consequences of the theory only the purely macroscopic one, the anomaly of the perihelion of the orbit of Mercury, is explained by Einstein's theory without doubt; the other two effects, the deflection of light-rays by the sun and the red shift of spectral lines (which are micro-phenomena), are still controversial, at least in regard to magnitude. I think that general relativity as we know it may be invalid in this domain."

The jubilee meetings could carry on well enough without him. Others could glitter in the scientific limelight while he, the man who had started it all, wound quietly toward the end of his life without fuss, an onlooker more than ever removed from the affairs of the world. Yet now, at almost the last minute of the last hour, Einstein was again to be drawn into the whirlpool of public affairs.

The offer of the presidency of Israel had come unexpectedly, a star blazing out through the twilight at the end of a long life. Now another arrived, and one that lit up a possible road to peace in a way that even now is not fully appreciated.

In mid-February he received a letter from Bertrand Russell. Both men had, in Russell's words, "opposed the First World War but considered the Second unavoidable." Both distrusted orthodoxy, and both had been appalled by the destructive possibilities of the hydrogen bomb. Yet if both had, in general, sought the same objectives, their methods had been as diametrically opposed as their characters. While Einstein had been content to continue with his work under the aegis of the Kaiser Wilhelm, Russell had gone to prison. While Einstein had aloofly despaired of the intelligence of mankind, Russell had protested by sitting on pavements. Einstein, for all his genuine feelings, had rarely stepped from behind the protection of his own interior world; Russell had insisted that he, too, should be heard, tormented, anguished, and combative.

But now Russell turned to Einstein for help. He was, he wrote on February 11, profoundly disquieted by the nuclear arms race. "I think that eminent men of science ought to do something dramatic to bring home to the public and governments the disasters that may occur. Do you think it would be possible to get say, six men of the very highest scientific repute, headed by yourself, to make a very solemn statement about the imperative necessity of avoiding war?" The statement would best be signed by men of opposing political creeds, and should deal not merely with the dangers of the hydrogen bomb but with those of bacteriological warfare, thus emphasizing "the general proposition that war and science can no longer co-exist." The letter added that the statement might appeal to neutral countries to set up commissions of their own nationals to investigate the effect, on them, of a third world war.

Einstein replied on February 16, 1955, with a letter that took Russell's proposal one step further. What he suggested was a public declaration, signed by a small number of scientists of international stature. Such men might even include Joliot-Curie, a leading communist, provided they were counterbalanced by others of different views. Bohr was an obvious candidate from the uncommitted countries, which Einstein hoped would supply half the signatures.

There followed another letter from Russell and a further reply from Einstein, who had by this time written to Bohr. Thus Russell's initial idea was considerably influenced by Einstein, and the outcome was quite rightly known as the Russell-Einstein Declaration. This was sent to Einstein by Russell on April 5; it recapitulated the dangers of contemporary war, with special emphasis on hydrogen bombs. And it ended with the following resolution, to be put to a world convention of scientists:

In view of the fact that in any future world war nuclear weapons will certainly be employed, and that such weapons threaten the continued existence of mankind, we urge the governments of the world to realise, and to acknowledge publicly, that their purposes cannot be furthered by a world war, and we urge them, consequently, to find peaceful means for the settlement of all matters of dispute between them.

While Russell's declaration was still in the mail with its accompanying letter, Einstein struck out on his own, writing to Nehru and in effect asking for his intervention in the area where an East-West war seemed most likely. This was in China, where the nationalist government's toehold on the offshore islands of Quemoy and Matsu threatened to lead the United States into an Asiatic quagmire. He enclosed with his letters a plan, prepared by Szilard, for the evacuation of the two islands for a definite period. Superficially this appeared the most obvious of nonstarters, but Einstein presumably felt that nothing but good would come of Nehru's intervention, whatever form it might take.

Three officers of the Society for Social Responsibility in Science now fortuitously called on him with a proposal for an open letter, which they hoped he might sign. He explained that something similar was already afoot, that Russell was behind the move, and that he had written to Russell saying: "You understand such things. You are the general. I am just a foot soldier; give the command and I will follow." But he seems to have known that he had little time left. "He was on the porch of his house as he spoke," writes one of his visitors. "Though it was not cold he was wrapped in a blanket. And somehow the air of parting was around."

Russell's letter had stirred Einstein in a way that few things had stirred him during recent years, and he now decided that the time had come to make a major statement on the position of Israel, whose Independence Day in May was to be held in circumstances even more ominous than usual. The threats from her ring of Arab neighbors were growing, while the announcement that Czechoslovakia and Russia were both to supply Egypt with arms added a new and more dangerous menace. Countermeasures were, in fact, already under way, and Mr. Dulles had agreed to release to the Israelis a dozen Mystère fighters from the U.S contingent to NATO as well as twenty-four Sabre jets from another source. But these measures were still unknown to the general public; this included Einstein—who only a few weeks earlier had claimed that the current Eisenhower administration was seeking "to win the sympathy of the Arab nations by sacrificing Israel."

He was, therefore, particularly receptive when, early in April, the Israeli authorities in Washington asked if he would make an Independence Day statement dealing with the country's scientific and cultural activities and stressing the peaceful uses of atomic energy. He would like to help, he replied on April 4. But, in the present circumstances, cultural and scientific developments were hardly relevant. What Einstein thought might be most effective was an analysis of western policies with regard to Israel and the Arab states.

Here was a unique opportunity. The Israeli ambassador, Abba Eban, seized it with both hands and on April 11 arrived at Mercer Street with the Israeli consul, Reuven Dafni:

> Professor Einstein told me [he later wrote] that he saw the rebirth of Israel as one of the few political acts in his lifetime which had an essential moral quality. He believed that the conscience of the world should, therefore, be involved in Israel's preservation. He had always refused the requests of television and radio networks to project his views to public opinion. This issue, however, seemed to him to be of such importance that he was actually taking the initiative, through me, of seeking the opportunity to address the American people and the world. He showed me the draft which he had begun to prepare. He had reached the end of a long preamble on the Cold War and wished to hear my views at greater length before discussing the political aspects of the Middle Eastern situation.

Eban and his colleague talked with Einstein for some time, and it was agreed that Dafni should return in a few days when Einstein had put the draft of his proposed address into more finished form.

On the same day, the 11th, he received the expected statement from Russell, and an accompanying list of scientists who would be asked to sign it. He agreed with the choice of names. And he signed the document. Thus he helped launch the manifesto, calling for a conference to appraise the perils of war and leading directly to the long series of influential Pugwash conferences attended by prominent scientists from the United States, Britain, and Russia, among more than a dozen countries.

The following day Einstein was in pain. But he refused to allow the doctor to be called, and it was without his knowledge that Miss Dukas telephoned Margot, then ill in the local hospital, and said that Einstein's personal doctor should be told.

Despite pain, Einstein worked on his Independence Day broadcast, to be further discussed with the Israeli consul the next day.

On the 13th, he was still in pain. But in the morning he received both the Israeli consul and Janos Plesch, who had come from New York. He went over his draft with Dafni. He also made additional notes. Some mystery surrounds their fate. The editors of *Einstein on Peace*, one of whom was Einstein's literary executor, describe them as "not available"; but they could find nothing to support a later rumor that the notes had been

stolen from the Princeton hospital. And they criticize a "reconstruction" of Einstein's planned address, based on information provided by Dafni, subsequently published in the *New York Times*. The most likely conclusion is that the notes, whatever happened to them, were too critical of "East," of "West," or of both sides in the power game, to be openly admitted as coming from Einstein.

Dafni left Mercer Street by midday. Soon afterward, Einstein complained of extreme tiredness and lack of appetite. After a light meal he lay down to rest: in mid-afternoon he collapsed. Miss Dukas, managing the situation singlehanded, called the doctor, who soon arrived with two colleagues, helped as an electrocardiagram was taken, fixed up a bed in the study, and prepared for a long vigil. The patient, given morphine injections, passed a quiet night.

Dr. Dean, who found Einstein "very stoical" and "his usual kind shy self," had diagnosed a small leakage of blood from a hardened aorta, and on the morning of Thursday the 14th, Dr. Frank Glenn, the cardiac and aortic surgeon, arrived from New York. So did Dr. Ehrmann and Dr. Bucky. One question had to be settled quickly; whether or not to operate. By 1955 this was possible, although the chances of survival during such an operation were still low—some experts put it at fifty per cent; without it they were minimal.

Years earlier, when Einstein had first learned of his condition and been told that his aorta might burst unless he took care, he had brusquely replied: "Let it burst." Now he was similarly uncompromising. He asked Dean how long death would take and was told that it might come in a moment, might take hours, or might take days. He was, his doctor said, "violently opposed" to surgery. To Miss Dukas, he later protested: "The end comes some time: does it matter when?" Just as in physics he had developed into the conservative revolutionary, so in medicine he tended to distrust what he thought of as radical innovations; it had once been impossible to operate on a man in his condition, and he would have none of it now.

Friday night passed quietly, and on Saturday morning he seemed to be better. Then, once again, there was intense pain, and he was unable to move. On the arrival of the doctor, hastily called by Miss Dukas, he at first refused to budge. Most patients would have been quickly overruled; but even now it was not easy to overrule Einstein. Finally, he was persuaded that hospital was best; characteristically, the argument that counted was that the nursing was too much for Miss Dukas.

On the way to the hospital he talked animatedly to one of the volunteer ambulance men. After arrival he began to feel better, and he soon telephoned Mercer Street. First, he wanted his spectacles; then, he wanted writing material. If there was still time left, it should not be wasted.

On Sunday, Margot was wheeled in to see him but almost failed to recognize him. He would go in his own time, and he insisted on one thing: "Do not let the house become a museum." He had already asked that his office at the Institute should not be

Opposite: Einstein in a photograph taken by Herman Landshoff. [© H. Landshoff]

preserved as he had used it, but passed on for the use of others. He did not want Mercer Street turned into a place of pilgrimage, and he would have had little sympathy for those who in later years called at Number 112 asking to see his study; for those who were to write to the Institute for mementos; or for the correspondents who from as far away as India wrote to his son Hans Albert pleading for a piece of anything that Albert Einstein had touched. He would have been surprised that an opera based on his life should be written for presentation in East Berlin, astonished at the million words that were cabled out of Princeton as the press moved in after his death. He would have exploded in one of his hearty gusts of laughter at the value of his signature and the hundreds of dollars that was soon to be the market price of his letters. He had wanted all this to die with him.

He had insisted that his brain should be used for research and that he be cremated; but his ashes were to be scattered at an undisclosed place. Again, no point of pilgrimage. He would have agreed with his literary executor, Otto Nathan, who was to write that the less published about Einstein's illness and the developments that led to his death, the better; Nathan did not see why the public should have an interest in the details, or why he and others should satisfy it if they had.

Hans Albert and Nathan arrived in Princeton on Sunday. With the first, Einstein discussed science; with the latter, politics and the danger of German rearmament. He was equable now, and late in the afternoon Dr. Dean even felt that the aneurysm might be repairing itself. With a recurrence of pain in the evening, Einstein was given another injection; but he was sleeping peacefully when Dean took a final look at 11 P.M.

In the small hours, soon after midnight, nurse Alberta Roszel, noticed a difference in his breathing. Becoming alarmed, she called for assistance, and with the aid of another nurse cranked up the head of the bed.

He was muttering in German, the language of his despised compatriots, still the only tongue with which he felt comfortable. It was with Germans that he had first won his spurs and in Berlin that he had first become world famous. It was only in German that he could contemplate the course of his life: his dedication to science and the subjugation of everything else; the self-imposed emotional asceticism; his belief that the human race was naturally aggressive and Germans more aggressive than the rest. It was in German that the last thoughts of one of the greatest brains since Newton's came to the surface through the unconscious mind.

Perhaps he should not have been so bearish about people? Perhaps he should never have gone to Berlin, made the way that much easier for the aggressors with his pacifism, or hated the Germans so much that he encouraged Roosevelt into the nuclear age? Perhaps he should not always have put science first? But on this there was, of course, no room for doubt, no cause for regret. As he took two deep breaths and died, it is unlikely that Einstein regretted very much, if he regretted anything at all. But Mrs. Roszel did not understand his German. And anyway, as Elsa had felt nearly twenty years before, dear God, it was too late now.

346

SOURCES AND BIBLIOGRAPHY

The original material for a life of Albert Einstein is scattered throughout the libraries and archives of Europe, the United States, and the Middle East. The largest single collections are the Einstein Archives, held by Princeton until the early 1980s and now in the Hebrew University, Jerusalem, and the Einstein-Sammlung der E.T.H. Bibliothek in Zurich. The first is particularly rich in records of Einstein's later years, but as his executor, Dr. Otto Nathan, has written: "Einstein himself was not greatly concerned with a systematic collection of his papers and correspondence; only in the last few decades of his life was sufficient attention paid to the preservation of the many important documents and letters that crossed his desk." The collection in the Eidgenossische Technische Hochschule (E.T.H.), Zurich, where Einstein both studied and taught, is naturally strong in the records of his years in Switzerland. These, however, are only two of the sources of original material.

Much of Einstein's long correspondence with Lorentz is divided between the Algemeen Rijksarchiv in The Hague and the Rijksmuseum voor de Geschiedenis der Natuurwetenschappen in Leiden. His meeting and early relationship with Erwin Freundlich is dealt with in the correspondence held until recently by the late Frau Freundlich. His friendship with Professor Lindemann—later Lord Cherwell—which began at the Solvay Congress in 1911 and continued to within a few years of his death, is covered by the Cherwell Papers in Nuffield College, Oxford. Light is thrown on his connections with the Solvay Institute by the papers used by Professor Jagdish Mehra for a history of the Congress, and on his move to Prague by the Adler Archives in Vienna. The Hale Papers and the Millikan Papers are among important material in the California Institute of Technology, dealing with Einstein's early visits to the United States.

The archives of the League of Nations Library in Geneva contain much new information on Einstein's membership of the International Committee for Intellectual Co-operation, while the Royal Library in Brussels contains his correspondence with H. M. Queen Elizabeth of the Belgians and details of his early visits to the Royal Palace at Laeken. The 190 pages of correspondence in the Weizmann Archives, Rehovot, and the Samuel Papers in the House of Lords Record Office, London, deal with Einstein's connections with Zionism from 1918 until the year of his death. And the Stadtarchiv, Ulm; the Israelitische Kultusvereinigung Württemberg und Hohenzollern; the Geheimes Staatsarchiv, Berlin; and many other German sources provide the documentary evidence for his birth, background, and citizenship.

The Rutherford Papers in the University of Cambridge; the Haldane Papers in the National Library of Scotland; the Bibliothèque Nationale, Paris; the Curie Laboratory Archives, Paris; the Russell Archives, McMaster University, Hamilton, Ontario; the Roosevelt Library, Hyde Park, New York; and the archives of the University of Utrecht all provide material dealing with his life and work. Two important unpublished manuscripts are Ehrenhaft's "My Experiences with Einstein," held by the Burndy Library, Norwalk, Connecticut; and "Comments on the letters of Professor and Mrs. Albert Einstein to Dr. Leon L. Watters," copies of which are held by the American Jewish Archives and by the California Institute of Technology.

Useful collections of private letters include the correspondence of Professor and Mrs. Einstein with Leon L. Watters, held by the American Jewish Archives; the Bucky letters, held by the University of Texas; the Koch letters, written by Einstein to his relatives in Belgium, held by the Université Libre, Brussels; the Kocherthaler letters, written to relatives in South America, in private hands in Montevideo; the correspondence with Dr. Janos Plesch, held by the Plesch family. In some ways the most important of all is Einstein's long correspondence with Michelangelo Besso, continuing for almost half a century, the various biographical aspects of which have been pointed out to me by Professor Jagdish Mehra of the University of Texas.

The Szilard Archives in San Diego contain much valuable background to the famous letter to Roosevelt, while the U.S. Atomic Energy Commission, the Office of the Chief of Naval Operations, and the National Archives and Records Service are among the official sources that hold material dealing with Einstein's work during the Second World War.

All these sources have been drawn upon, as well as the following:

Allgemeines Staatsarchiv, Munich; American Institute of Physics; Auswärtiges Amt, Bonn; Bureau Fédéral de la Propriété Intellectuelle, Berne; University of Chicago; Christ Church Library, Oxford; Library of Congress, Washington, D.C.; Deutsche Staatsbibliothek, Berlin; Deutsches Zentralarchiv, Potsdam; Perkins Library, Duke University, Durham, North Carolina; University of Edinburgh; Geheimes Staatsarchiv, Berlin; University of Göttingen; Landesarchiv, Berlin; MacArthur Memorial Archives, Norfolk, Virginia; University of Manchester; Max Planck Gesellschaft, Berlin and Munich; John Murray Archives, London; National Personnel Records Center, St. Louis, Missouri; Rhodes Trust, Oxford; Royal Netherlands Academy of Sciences and Letters, Amsterdam; Schweizer Schuler, Milan; Senatsverwaltung der Stadt, Berlin; University of Sheffield; Staatsbibliothek der Stiftung Preussischer Kulturbesitz, Berlin; Stanford University, Palo Alto, California; records of Swiss Federal Council, Berne; Swiss National Library, Berne; University of Syracuse; UNESCO Archives, Paris.

PRINTED MATERIAL

The bulk of Einstein's scientific work is contained in the papers listed in *Albert Einstein. A Bibliography of his Scientific Papers, 1901–1930* by E. Weil (London, 1937). Later bibliographies include that given in *Albert Einstein: Philosopher-Scientist* edited by Paul A. Schilpp (Evanston, Ill., 1949) and *A Bibliographical Checklist and Index to the Collected Writings of Albert Einstein*, Readex Microprint edition, compiled by Nell Boni, Monique Russ, and Dan H. Laurence (New York, 1960); both include Einstein's nonscientific writings, and bibliographical details of many interviews.

Einstein's key papers on relativity are printed, together with other relevant papers by H. A. Lorentz, H. Minkowski, and H. Weyl, in *The Principle of Relativity* (Methuen, London, 1923 and Dover, New York, 1952), while his own *Relativity: The*

Special and the General Theory is available in a succession of editions and translations from 1920 onward. His major papers on the Brownian movement are contained in *Investigations on the Theory of the Brownian Movement,* edited by R. Furth (London, 1926). Important material dealing with the birth of quantum mechanics is contained in *Letters on Wave Mechanics—Schrödinger, Planck, Einstein, and Lorentz,* edited by K. Przibram (Philosophical Library, New York and Vision Press, London, 1967), while Einstein letters dealing with science in general and with nonscientific subjects are contained in *Briefwechsel—Albert Einstein/Arnold Sommerfeld,* edited and with commentary by Armin Hermann (Schwabe, Basel and Stuttgart, 1968) and in *Briefwechsel 1916–1955—Albert Einstein/ Max Born* (Nymphenburger, 2 March, 1969; *Born-Einstein Letters,* London, 1971).

Books explaining relativity and putting Einstein's work in the larger context of science are as numerous as their quality is varied. Among the best are *Relativity Theory: Its Origins and Impact on Modern Thought,* edited by L. Pearce Williams (New York, 1968); Max Born's *Einstein's Theory of Relativity* (London, 1924); Pauli's *Theory of Relativity* (New York, 1958); Clement V. Durell's *Readable Relativity* (London, 1966); Lincoln Barnett's *The Universe and Dr. Einstein* (London, 1949); Freundlich's *The Foundations of Einstein's Theory of Gravitation* (Cambridge, 1920); Russell's *The A.B.C. of Relativity* (London, 1925); Bondi's *Relativity and Commonsense* (London, 1964); Charles Nordmann's *Einstein and the Universe* (London, 1922); and Cornelius Lanczos' *Albert Einstein and the Cosmic World Order* (London, 1965).

A number of Einstein's miscellaneous writings are contained in *The World As I See It* (London, 1935) and *Out of My Later Years* (London, 1950), and a selection of speeches and letters in *About Zionism* (London, 1930). Many of his early pacifist writings are included in *The Fight Against War,* edited by Alfred Lief (New York, 1933) and the bulk of them in *Einstein on Peace,* edited by Otto Nathan and Heinz Norden (London, 1963).

Einstein's autobiographical writings are limited to the —exclusively scientific—account of his development in Schilpp's *Albert Einstein: Philosopher-Scientist* (Evanston, Ill., 1949), and the brief notes in *Helle Zeit: Dunkle Zeit* (Zurich, 1956), a volume of reminiscences edited by Carl Seelig. The first attempt to give him a biographical background was made by Alexander Moszkowski in *Einstein the Searcher: His Work Explained from Dialogues with Einstein* (Berlin, 1921), a book that Einstein's friends ineffectively urged him to suppress. It was the first of the many. The husband of one stepdaughter produced a pseudonymous biography—*Albert Einstein* by A. Reiser (London, 1931)—to which Einstein gave his *cachet;* the husband of another produced, together with a journalist colleague, a book—*Einstein* (New York, 1944)—which Einstein repudiated. His doctor friend, Janos Plesch, devoted two chapters of his autobiographical *Janos* (London, 1947) to Albert Einstein; a writer-friend of his second wife, Antonina Vallentin, wrote a personal account of his life; while a Berlin acquaintance, David Reichinstein, wrote an *Albert Einstein,* which its subject unsuccessfully tried to suppress. Three lives written with varying degrees of blessing from their subject are

Philipp Frank's *Einstein: His Life and Times* (London, 1948), Carl Seelig's *Albert Einstein* (London, 1956), and Leopold Infeld's *Albert Einstein* (London, 1950).

The files of *Annalen der Physik, Nature, Science, The Times* and the *New York Times* have been used extensively, as have many other journals, magazines, and papers to which individual reference is made in the details of sources on pp. 353–360. The following is a select bibliography of the books and journal articles that have been found useful or to which specific reference is made below. For convenience, the bibliographical details of Einstein's main papers are given here; but the full list of his scientific publications runs to nearly forty pages and should be consulted, if required, in one of the bibliographies referred to above.

Adams, Walter S., "George Ellery Hale, 1868–1938," *Astrophysical Journal,* Vol. 87 (May, 1938), pp. 369–88.

Badash, L. (ed.), *Rutherford and Boltwood: Letters on Radioactivity,* New Haven, 1969.

Barker, Sir Ernest, *Age and Youth,* Oxford, 1953.

Barnett, Lincoln, *The Universe and Dr. Einstein,* London, 1949.

Baxter, James Phinney, *Scientists Against Time,* Boston, 1946.

Bell, E.T., *Men of Mathematics,* London, 1965.

Bell, G. K. A., *Randall Davidson, Archbishop of Canterbury,* London, 1935.

Ben-Gurion, David, *Ben-Gurion Looks Back in Talks with Moshe Pearlman,* London, 1965.

Bentwich, Norman, *The Hebrew University of Jerusalem 1918–60,* London, 1961.

Bentwich, Norman, *Judah L. Magnes,* Philadelphia, 1954.

Bentwich, Norman, *My Seventy-Seven Years: An Account of My Life and Times 1881–1960,* London, 1962.

Bentwich, Norman, *The Rescue and Achievement of Refugee Scholars,* The Hague, 1953.

Bentwich, Norman, *Wanderer Between Two Worlds,* London, 1941.

Bentwich, Norman and Helen, *Mandate Memories 1918–1948,* London, 1965.

Birkenhead, The Earl of, *The Prof in Two Worlds,* London, 1961.

Blumenfeld, Kurt, *Erlebte Judenfrage,* Stuttgart, 1962.

Bohr, Niels, *Essays 1958–1962 on Atomic Physics and Human Knowledge,* New York, 1963.

Bondi, Hermann, *Assumption and Myth in Physical Theory,* Cambridge, 1965.

Bondi, Hermann, *Relativity and Commonsense,* London, 1964.

Boorstin, Daniel (ed.), *An American Primer,* Chicago, 1966.

Bork, Alfred H., "The Fitzgerald Contraction," *Isis,* Vol. 57 (1966), pp. 199–207.

Born, Max, *Born-Einstein Letters, 1916–1955,* London, 1971.

Born, Max, *Einstein's Theory of Relativity,* New York, 1962.

Born, Max, *Natural Philosophy of Cause and Chance* (The Waynflete Lectures, 1948), Oxford, 1949.

Born, Max, *Physics in My Generation,* London, 1956, and New York, 1969.

Braunthal, Julius, *In Search of the Millennium,* London, 1945.

Brodetsky, Professor Selig, *Memoirs: From Ghetto to Israel,* London, 1960.

Buber, Martin, *The Knowledge of Man,* London, 1965.

Bucky, Thomas Lee, "Einstein: An Intimate Memoir," *Harper's Magazine* (September, 1964).

Byrnes, James F., *All in One Lifetime,* New York, 1958.

Campbell, Lewis, and W. Garnet, *James Clerk Maxwell,* London, 1884.

Clark, Ronald W., *The Birth of the Bomb,* London, 1961.

Clark, Ronald W., *Tizard,* London, 1965.

Cline, Barbara Lovett, *The Questioners: Physicists and the Quantum Theory,* New York, 1965.

Cohen, Harry A., "An Afternoon with Einstein," *Jewish Spectator* (January, 1969), p. 13.

Cohen, I. Bernard, "An Interview with Einstein," *Scientific American,* Vol. 193 (July, 1955), pp. 68–73.

Cohen, Morris Raphael, *A Dreamer's Journey,* Boston, 1949.

Cohen, Morris Raphael, "Einstein and His World," *The Menorah*

Journal, Vol. 24 (Spring, 1936), p. 107.

Cohen, Morris Raphael, *The Faith of a Liberal*, New York, 1946.

Compton, Arthur H., "The Scattering of X-Rays," *Journal of the Franklin Institute*, Vol. 198 (1924).

Dampier, Sir William, *A Shorter History of Science*, London, 1945.

De Broglie, Louis, *New Perspectives in Physics*, Edinburgh, 1962.

De Broglie, Louis, *The Revolution in Physics: A Non-Mathematical Survey of Quanta*, London, 1954.

De Sitter, Professor W., "On Einstein's Theory of Gravitation, and its Astronomical Consequences," *Monthly Notices of the Royal Astronomical Society*, Vol. LXXVI (October, 1916), pp. 699–728.

De Sitter, W., "From Newton to Einstein," *Kosmos: A Course of Six Lectures on the Development of Our Insight into the Structure of the Universe*, Cambridge and Harvard, 1932.

Deuel, Wallace, *People Under Hitler*, London, 1942.

Douglas, A. Vibert, "Forty Minutes with Einstein," *Journal of the Royal Astronomical Society of Canada*, Vol. 50, No. 3 (May–June, 1956), pp. 99–102.

Douglas, A. Vibert, *The Life of Arthur Stanley Eddington*, London, 1956.

Durrell, Clement V., *Readable Relativity*, London, 1966.

Eddington, Sir Arthur, *Relativity* (Eighth Annual Haldane Lecture, May 26, 1937), London, 1937.

Eddington, Sir Arthur, *Report on the Relativity Theory of Gravitation*, London, 1918.

Eddington, Sir Arthur, *Space, Time and Gravitation*, London, 1920.

Eddington, Sir Arthur, *The Theory of Relativity and its Influence on Scientific Thought* (Romanes Lecture, May 24, 1922), Oxford, 1922.

Ehrenhaft, Felix, "My Experiences with Einstein" (unpublished).

Einstein, Albert, *About Zionism: Speeches and Letters by Professor Albert Einstein* (edited and translated by Leon Simon), London, 1930.

Einstein, Albert, *The Fight Against War* (Alfred Lief, ed.), New York, 1933.

Einstein, Albert, *Ideas and Opinions*, London, 1964.

Einstein, Albert, *Investigations on the Theory of the Brownian Movement*, London, 1926

Einstein, Albert, *Lettres à Maurice Solovine*, Paris, 1956.

Einstein, Albert, *Out of My Later Years*, London, 1950.

Einstein, Albert, *The Theory of Relativity*, London, 1924.

Einstein, Albert, *Why War?* London, 1934.

Einstein, Albert, *The World As I See It*, London, 1935.

Einstein, Albert, and Max Born, *Briefwechsel 1916–1955*, Munich, 1969. (*Born-Einstein Letters, 1916–1955*, London, 1971)

Einstein, Albert, and Leopold Infeld, *The Evolution of Physics*, Cambridge, 1938.

Einstein, Albert, Erwin Schrödinger, Max Planck, and H. A. Lorentz, *Letters on Wave Mechanics* (K. Przibram, ed.), London and New York, 1967.

Einstein, Albert, and Arnold Sommerfeld, *Briefwechsel* (Armin Hermann, ed.), Basel and Stuttgart, 1968.

The following are Einstein's more famous scientific papers and lectures:

1905: "Über einen die Erzeugung und Verwandlung des Lichtes betreffenden heuristischen Gesichtspunkt," *Annalen der Physik*, Ser. 4, Vol. 17 (1905), pp. 132–148.

1905: "Über die von der molekularkinetischen Theorie der Wärme geforderte Bewegung von in ruhenden Flüssigkeiten suspendierten Teilchen," *Annalen der Physik*, Ser. 4, Vol. 17 (1905), pp. 549–60.

1905: "Zur Elektrodynamik bewegter Körper," *Annalen der Physik*, Ser. 4, Vol. 17 (1905), pp. 891–921.

1905: "Ist die Trägheit eines Körpers von seinem Energieinhalt abhängig?" *Annalen der Physik*, Ser. 4, Vol. 18 (1905), pp. 639–41.

1907: "Die Plank'sche Theorie der Strahlung und die Theorie der spezifischen Wärme," *Annalen der Physik*, Ser. 4, Vol. 22 (1907), pp. 180–90 and p. 800 (Berichtigung).

1907: "Über das Relativitätsprinzip und die aus demselben gezogenen Folgerungen," *Jahrbuch der Radioaktivität und Elektronik*, Vol. 4 (1907), pp. 411–62, and Vol. 5 (1908), pp. 98–99 (Berichtigungen).

1909: "Über die Entwicklung unserer Anschauungen über das Wessen und die Konstitution der Strahlung," *Physikalische Zeitschrift*, Vol. 10 (1909), pp. 817–25.

1911: "Über den Einfluss der Schwerkraft auf die Ausbreitung des Lichtes," *Annalen der Physik*, Ser. V, Vol. 35 (1911), pp. 898–908.

1913: "Entwurf einer verallgemeinerten Relativitätstheorie und eine Theorie der Gravitation," I. Physikalischer Teil von A. Einstein. II. Mathematischer Teil von M. Grossmann. Leipzig, 1913, Teubner, 38 pp. Sonderdruck aus *Zeitschrift für Mathematik und Physik*, Vol. 62 (1913), pp. 225–62 (Physikalischer Teil, pp. 225–44).

1915: "Erklärung der Perihelbewegung des Merkur aus der allgemeinen Relativitätstheorie," *Preussische Akademie der Wissenschaften, Sitzungsberichte*, 1915, Pt. 2, pp. 831–39.

1916: "Die Grundlage der allgemeinen Relativitätstheorie," *Annalen der Physik*, Ser. 4, Vol. 49 (1916), pp. 769–822.

1917: "Zur Quantentheorie der Strahlung," *Physikalische Zeitschrift*, Vol. 18 (1917), pp. 121–28.

1917: "Kosmologische Betrachtungen zur allgemeinen Relativitätstheorie," *Preussische Akademie der Wissenschaften, Sitzungsberichte*, 1917, Pt. 1, pp. 142–52.

1923: "Zur affinen Feldtheorie," *Preussische Akademie der Wissenschaften, Phys.-math. Klasse, Sitzungsberichte*, 1923, pp. 137–40.

1924: "Quantentheorie des einatomigen idealen Gases," *Preussische Akademie der Wissenschaften, Phys.-math. Klasse, Sitzungsberichte*, 1924, pp. 261–67.

and

1925: "Quantentheorie des einatomigen idealen Gases. 2. Abhandlung," *Preussische Akademie der Wissenschaften, Phys.-math. Klasse, Sitzungsberichte*, 1925, pp. 3–14.

1928: "Fundamental Concepts of Physics and Their Most Recent Changes," *St. Louis Post-Dispatch*, December 29, 1928.

1929: "Zur Einheitlichen Feldtheorie," *Preussische Akademie der Wissenschaften, Phys.-math. Klasse, Sitzungsberichte*, 1929, pp. 2–7.

1933: *On the Method of Theoretical Physics.* The Herbert Spencer Lecture delivered at Oxford, June 10, 1933. Oxford, 1933.

1933: *Origins of the General Theory of Relativity.* The George A. Gibson Foundation Lecture in the University of Glasgow, June 20, 1933. Glasgow (Glasgow University Publications, No. 30), 1933.

1935: "Can Quantum-Mechanical Description of Physical Reality Be Considered Complete?" with B. Podolsky and N. Rosen, *Physical Review*, Ser. 2, Vol. 47 (1935), pp. 777–80.

Eisenhart, Churchill, "Albert Einstein As I Remember Him," *Journal of the Washington Academy of Sciences*, Vol. 54 (1964), pp. 325–28.

Epstein, Jacob, *Let There Be Sculpture*, London, 1940.

Eve, A. S., *Rutherford*, Cambridge, 1939.

Fermi, Laura, *Illustrious Immigrants: The Intellectual Migration from Europe 1930–1941*, Chicago, 1968.

Fierz, M., and V. F. Weisskopf, *Theoretical Physics in the Twentieth Century: A Memorial Volume to Wolfgang Pauli*, New York and London, 1960.

Fisher, H. A. L., *The History of Europe*, London, 1936.

Fitzroy, Sir Almeric, *Memoirs, Vol. II*, London, n.d.

Flammarion, Camille, *Lumen*, Paris, 1873.

Flexner, Abraham, *I Remember*, New York, 1940.

Flückiger, Max, *A. E. in Bern*, Berne, 1961.

Frank, Philipp, *Einstein: His Life and Times*, London, 1948.

Frank, Philipp, *Interpretations and Misinterpretations of Modern Physics*, Paris, 1938.

Frank, Philipp, *Modern Science and Its Philosophy*, Cambridge, Mass., 1949.

Frank, Philipp, *Relativity—A Richer Truth*, London, 1951.

Freud, Sigmund, *Letters of Sigmund Freud, 1873–1939*, London, 1961.

Freundlich, Erwin, *The Foundations of Einstein's Theory of Gravitation*, Cambridge, 1920.

Furer, Admiral, *Administration of the Navy Department in World War Two*, Washington, D.C., 1959.

Gamow, George, *My World Line*, New York, 1970.

George, Hereford, *The Oberland and Its Glaciers, Explored and Illustrated with Ice-Axe and Camera*, London, 1866.

Gilpin, Robert, *American Scientists and Nuclear Weapons Policy*, Princeton, N.J., 1962.

Goldman, Nahum, *Memories*, London, 1970.

Goran, Morris, *The Story of Fritz Haber*, Norman, Okla., 1967.

Goudsmit, Samuel A., *Alsos,* New York, 1947.

Gowing, Margaret, *Britain and Atomic Energy 1939–1945,* London, 1964.

Grossmann, Kurt R., "Peace Movements in Germany," *South Atlantic Quarterly* (July, 1950), Durham, N.C.

Haas-Lorentz, G. J. de (ed.), *H. A. Lorentz: Impressions of His Life and Work,* Amsterdam, 1957.

Hadamard, Jacques, *An Essay on the Psychology of Invention in the Mathematical Field,* Princeton, N.J., 1945.

Hahn, Otto, *My Life,* London, 1970.

Haldane, R. B., *The Reign of Relativity,* London, 1921.

Hannak, Dr. J., *Emanuel Lasker: The Life of a Chess Master,* London, 1959.

Harrod, R. F., *The Prof,* London, 1959.

Hartshorne, Edward Yarnall, Jr., *The German Universities and National Socialism,* London, 1937.

Heisenberg, Werner, *Physics and Philosophy: The Revolution in Modern Science,* New York, 1962.

Helvetica Physica Acta, Supplementum IV, Basel, 1956.

Herneck, Friedrich, "Uber die deutsche Reichsangehörigkeit Albert Einstein," *Die Naturwissenschaften,* Heft 2, S 33, 1961.

Hewlett, R. G., and E. D. Anderson, Jr., *The New World, 1939–1946,* University Park, Penn., 1962.

Hoffman, Banesh, *The Strange Story of the Quantum,* New York, 1959.

Holton, Gerald, "Einstein, Michelson and the 'Crucial' Experiment," *Isis,* Vol. 60, Pt. 2, No. 202 (1969), pp. 133–97.

Holton, Gerald, "Influences on Einstein's Early Work in Relativity Theory," *American Scholar,* Vol. 37, No. 1 (Winter, 1967–68).

Holton, Gerald, "Mach, Einstein and the Search for Reality," *Daedalus* (Spring, 1968), pp. 636–73.

Holton, Gerald, "On the Origins of the Special Theory of Relativity," *American Journal of Physics,* Vol. 28 (October, 1960), pp. 627–36.

Hubble, Edwin, *The Observational Approach to Cosmology* (The Rhodes Memorial Lectures, 1936), Oxford, 1937.

Infeld, Leopold, *Albert Einstein: His Work and Its Influence on Our World,* New York and London, 1950.

Infeld, Leopold, "As I See It," *Bulletin of the Atomic Scientists,* Vol. 21 (February, 1965), pp. 7–14.

Infeld, Leopold, *Quest: The Evolution of a Scientist,* New York, 1941.

Inge, The Very Rev. W. R., *Diary of a Dean: St. Pauls 1911–1934,* London, 1949.

Inge, William Ralph, *God and the Astronomers,* London, 1933.

Jaffe, Bernard, *Michelson and the Speed of Light,* London, 1961.

Jeans, Sir James, *The New Background of Science,* Ann Arbor, Mich., 1959.

Jeans, Sir James, *The Universe Around Us,* Cambridge, 1930.

Jones, R. V., "Thicker than Heavy Water," *Chemistry and Industry,* August 26, 1967.

Karman, Theodore von, *The Wind and Beyond,* Toronto, 1967.

Kisch, F. H., *Palestine Diary,* London, 1938.

Klein, Martin J., "Einstein's First Paper on Quanta," *The Natural Philosopher,* Vol. 2, New York (1963), pp. 57–86.

Klein, Martin J., "Einstein and the Wave-Particle Duality," *The Natural Philosopher,* Vol. 3, New York (1964), pp. 1–49.

Klein, Martin J., *Paul Ehrenfest,* Vol. I, *The Making of a Theoretical Physicist,* Amsterdam, 1970.

Kuznetsov, B., *Einstein,* Moscow, 1965.

Lemaître, Georges, "The Beginning of the World from the Point of View of the Quantum Theory," *Nature,* Vol. 127 (1931), p. 706.

Lemaître, Georges, *The Primeval Atom: An Essay on Cosmogony,* New York, 1950.

Lief, Alfred (ed.), *The Fight Against War,* New York, 1933.

Lindemann, A. F. and F. A., "Daylight Photography of Stars as a Means of Testing the Equivalence Postulate in the Theory of Relativity," *Monthly Notices of the Royal Astronomical Society,* Vol. LXXVII, No. 2 (December 8, 1916), pp. 140–51.

Lindemann, F. A., "Einstein's Theory: A Revolution in Thought," *Times Educational Supplement,* January 29, 1920.

Lodge, Sir Oliver, "Einstein's Real Achievement," *Fortnightly Review,* DCLVII, new series (September, 1921).

Lorentz, H. A., *H. A. Lorentz: Impressions of His Life and Work* (G. J. de Haas-Lorentz, ed.), Amsterdam, 1957.

Lorentz, H. A., Albert Einstein, H. Weyl, and A. Minkowski, *The Principle of Relativity, A Collection of Original Memoirs on the Special and General Theory of Relativity,* New York, 1952.

Lovell, Sir Bernard, *Our Present Knowledge of the Universe,* Manchester, 1967.

Lowenstein, Prince Hubertus of, *Towards the Farther Shore,* London, 1968.

Mach, Ernst, *The Science of Mechanics,* Chicago and London, 1907.

Marianoff, Dimitri, and Palm Wayne, *Einstein: An Intimate Study of a Great Man,* New York, 1944.

Martin, Kingsley, *Editor; a Second Volume of Autobiography, 1931–45,* London, 1968.

Meitner, Lise, "Looking Back," *Bulletin of the Atomic Scientists,* Vol. 20 (November, 1964), pp. 2–7.

Michelmore, Peter, *Einstein: Profile of the Man,* London, 1963.

Millikan, Robert A., *The Autobiography of Robert A. Millikan,* London, 1951.

Millikan, Robert A., *The Electron,* Chicago, 1917.

Millikan, Robert A., *Time, Matter and Values,* Chapel Hill, N.C., 1932.

Milne, E. A., *The Aims of Mathematical Physics,* Oxford, 1930.

Milne, E. A., *Modern Cosmology and the Christian Idea of God,* Oxford, 1952.

Milne, E. A., *Sir James Jeans: A Biography,* Cambridge, 1952.

Moore, Ruth, *Niels Bohr: the Man and the Scientist,* London, 1967.

Mosse, George L., *Nazi Culture: Intellectual, Cultural and Social Life in the Third Reich,* London, 1966.

Moszkowski, Alexander, *Einstein the Searcher: His Work Explained from Dialogues with Einstein,* Berlin, 1921.

Mowrer, Edgar Ansel, *Germany Puts the Clock Back,* London, 1933.

Nathan, Otto, and Heinz Norden (eds.), *Einstein on Peace,* London, 1963.

Newton, Sir Isaac, *Mathematical Principles of Natural Philosophy,* Berkeley, 1960.

Newton, Sir Isaac, *Opticks,* New York, 1952 (based on the 4th ed., London, 1730).

Nobel Foundation (ed.), *Nobel: The Man and His Prizes,* Stockholm, 1950.

Nordmann, Charles, "Einstein à Paris," in *Revue des Deux Mondes,* Vol. 8, 7th series, Paris, 1922.

Nordmann, Charles, "Einstein à Paris," *L'Illustration,* April 15, 1922.

Nordmann, Charles, *The Tyranny of Time: Einstein or Bergson,* London, 1925.

North, J. D., *The Measure of the Universe,* Oxford, 1965.

Oppenheimer, J. Robert, "On Albert Einstein" (Lecture delivered at UNESCO House, December 13, 1965), reprinted in *The New York Review,* March 17, 1966.

Oppenheimer, J. Robert, *The Flying Trapeze: Three Crises for Physicists* (The Whidden Lectures for 1962), Oxford, 1964.

Pauli, W., *Theory of Relativity,* London, 1958.

Planck, Max, *The Origin and Development of the Quantum Theory* (Nobel Prize Address, June 2, 1920), Oxford, 1922.

Planck, Max, *Scientific Biography and Other Papers,* London, 1950.

Planck, Max, *Where is Science Going?,* London, 1933.

Plesch, John, *Janos: The Story of a Doctor,* London, 1947.

Polanyi, Michael, *The Logic of Liberty: Reflections and Rejoiners,* London, 1951.

Polanyi, Michael, *Personal Knowledge,* London, 1958.

Przibram, K. (ed.), *Letters on Wave Mechanics: Schrödinger, Planck, Einstein, Lorentz* (translated and with an introduction by Martin J. Klein), New York, 1967.

Rayleigh, Lord, *The Life of Sir J. J. Thomson, O. M.,* Cambridge, 1942.

Reichinstein, David, *Albert Einstein: A Picture of His Life and His Conception of the World,* Prague, 1934.

Reiser, Anton, *Albert Einstein: A Biographical Portrait,* London, 1931.

Ringer, Fritz K., *The Decline of the German Mandarins,* Cambridge, Mass., 1969.

Robb, Alfred A., *The Absolute Relations of Time and Space,* Cambridge, 1921.

Robb, Alfred A., *A Theory of Time and Space,* Cambridge, 1914.

Rolland, Romain, *Le Bund Neues Vaterland (1914–1916),* Lyons and Paris, 1952.

Rolland, Romain, *Journal des Années de Guerre 1914–1919,* Paris, 1953.

Rosenfeld, L., *Niels Bohr: An Essay,* Amsterdam, 1961.

Rosenfeld, Leonora Cohen, *Portrait of a Philosopher: Morris R. Cohen in Life and Letters,* New York, 1948.

Rotblat, J., *Pugwash,* Prague, 1967.

Rozental, S. (ed.), *Niels Bohr,* Amsterdam, 1967.

Russell, Bertrand, *The ABC of Relativity,* London, 1925.

Rutherford of Nelson, Lord, "The Transformation of Energy" (Watt Anniversary Lecture for 1936, delivered before the Greenock Philosophical Society, January 17, 1936).

Sachs, Alexander, *Background and Early History, Atomic Bomb Project in Relation to President Roosevelt,* Washington, D.C., 1945.

Samuel, Viscount, *Belief and Action: An Everyday Philosophy,* London, 1937.

Samuel, Viscount, *Essay in Physics,* Oxford, 1951.

Samuel, Viscount, *Memoirs,* London, 1945.

Samuel, Viscount, and Herbert Dingle, "A Threefold Cord: Philosophy, Science and Religion." *A Discussion Between Viscount Samuel and Professor Herbert Dingle,* London, 1961.

Schilpp, Paul Arthur (ed.), *Albert Einstein: Philosopher-Scientist,* Evanston, Ill., 1949.

Schonland, Sir Basil, *The Atomists,* Oxford, 1968.

Schrödinger, Erwin, *Mind and Matter* (The Tarner Lectures, 1956), Cambridge, 1958.

Scott, C. P., *The Political Diaries of C. P. Scott, 1911–1928,* London, 1970.

Seelig, Carl, *Albert Einstein: A Documentary Biography,* London, 1956.

Seelig, Carl (ed.), *Helle Zeit: Dunkle Zeit,* Zurich, 1956.

Shankland, R. S., "Conversations with Albert Einstein," *American Journal of Physics,* Vol. 31 (1963), pp. 47–57.

Shapley, H., *Through Rugged Ways to the Stars,* New York, 1969.

Shirer, William, *The Rise and Fall of the Third Reich,* New York, 1960.

Smith, Alice Kimball, *A Peril and a Hope: the Scientists' Movement in America, 1945–47,* Chicago, 1965.

Smith, Jean, and Arthur Toynbee (eds.), *Gilbert Murray: An Unfinished Autobiography,* London, 1960.

Smyth, H. D., *Atomic Energy for Military Power,* Washington, D.C., 1945.

Sommer, Dudley, *Haldane of Cloan: His Life and Times 1856–1928,* London, 1960.

Speight-Humbertson, Clara E., *Spiritism: The Hidden Secret in Einstein's Theory of Relativity,* Kitchener, Ontario, n.d.

Stein, Leonard, *Zionism,* London, 1925.

Stern, Alfred, "An Interview with Einstein," *Contemporary Jewish Record,* VIII (June, 1945), pp. 245–49.

Strauss, Lewis, *Men and Decisions,* London, 1963.

Stuart, James, *Within the Fringe,* London, 1967.

Szilard, Leo, "Reminiscences," *Perspectives in American History,* Vol. II, Cambridge, Mass., 1968.

Talmey, Max, *The Relativity Theory Simplified and the Formative Period of Its Inventor,* New York, 1932.

Templewood, Viscount, *Nine Troubled Years,* London, 1954.

Thirring, J. H., *The Ideas of Einstein's Theory,* London, 1921.

Thomson, Sir J. J., *Recollections and Reflections,* London, 1936.

Toynbee, Arnold J., *Acquaintances,* Oxford, 1967.

Tschernowitz, Dr. Chaim, "A Day with Albert Einstein," *Jewish Sentinel,* Vol. I (September, 1931).

Ulitzur, A., *Two Decades of Keren Hayesod,* Jerusalem, 1940.

Vallentin, Antonina, *Einstein: A Biography,* London, 1954.

Voss, Carl Hermann (ed.), *Servant of the People* (the letters of Stephen Wise), Philadelphia, 1969.

Watters, Dr. Leon L., "Comments on the Letters of Professor and Mrs. Albert Einstein to Dr. Leon L. Watters" (unpublished).

Weil, E., *Albert Einstein: A Bibliography of His Scientific Papers, 1901–1930,* London, 1937.

Weisgal, Meyer W., and Joel Carmichael (eds.), *Chaim Weizmann: A Biography by Several Hands,* New York, 1963.

Weizmann, Chaim, *Trial and Error,* London, 1950.

Weizmann, Vera, *The Impossible Takes Longer,* London, 1967.

Weyl, Dr. Harmann, *The Open World* (Three Lectures on the Metaphysical Implications of Science), New Haven, Conn., 1932.

Whitehead, A. N., *Science and the Modern World,* London, 1926.

Whitrow, G. J. (ed.), *Einstein: The Man and His Achievement,* London, 1967.

Whittaker, Sir Edmund, "Albert Einstein, 1879–1955," *Biographical Memoirs of Fellows of the Royal Society,* Vol. 1 (1955), pp. 37–67.

Whittaker, Sir Edmund, *History of the Theories of the Aether and Electricity,* 2 vols., London, 1951 and 1953.

Whyte, L. L., *Focus and Diversions,* London, 1963.

Wilson, Margaret, *Ninth Astronomer Royal: The Life of Frank Watson Dyson,* Cambridge, 1951.

Wolf, Edwin, II (with John F. Fleming), *Rosenbach: A Biography,* London, 1960.

Einstein on U.S. postage stamp issued March 14, 1966.

NOTES

Full details of the sources quoted, manuscript and printed, are given with bibliographical information in the "Sources and Bibliography."

Page

Chapter 1 German Boy

8 one of the follies of his life: Einstein-Janos Plesch, February 3, 1944. Material in hands of the Plesch family (afterward referred to as 'Plesch correspondence').

8 "pas très Juif": private note by Lord Samuel of conversation, October 31, 1930, Samuel Papers, House of Lords Records Office (afterward referred to as 'Samuel Papers').

9 Genealogical details: Rabbiner Dr. A. Tanzer, "Der Stammbaum Prof. Albert Einsteins," *Jüdische Familien-Forschung,* Jahrgang VII, December, 1931, and Israelitische Kultusvereinigung Württemberg und Hohenzollern. Genealogical trees of both the Einstein and the Koch families also exist in the Einstein Archives.

9 "His mode of life": Philipp Frank, *Einstein: His Life and Times,* p. 15 (afterward referred to as 'Frank').

10 "Exceedingly friendly": Einstein-Bela Kornitzer, *Gazette & Daily,* York, Pennsylvania, September 20, 1948 (afterward referred to as 'Kornitzer').

10 Ulm birthplace details: Stadtarchiv, Ulm.

13 "A true story": Kornitzer.

14 "Algebra is a merry science": Frank, p. 24.

14 Cäsar Koch details from documents in the possession of M. Jean Ferrard of Brussels, located by Professor Jagdish Mehra of the University of Texas and brought to my notice by Professor Jean Pelseneer of the University of Brussels.

15 "he could not even say": Antonina Vallentin, *Einstein,* p. 8 (afterward referred to as 'Vallentin').

16 "Is there any German person": Kornitzer.

17 "He was a pretty, dark-haired boy": Max Talmey, *The Relativity Theory Simplified and the Formative Period of Its Inventor,* p. 161.

17 living matter and clarity were opposites: Einstein-Hedwig, Born, January 15, 1927, Max Born, *Born-Einstein Letters,* p. 95 (afterward referred to as 'Born Letters').

17 "biological procedures": Carl Seelig (ed.), *Helle Zeit: Dunkle Zeit,* p. 64 (afterward referred to as 'Helle Zeit').

19 "to penetrate into the *arcana* of nature": Hereford George, *The Oberland and Its Glaciers, Explored and Illustrated with Ice-axe and Camera.*

19 " 'What we...strive for' ": Martin Buber, *The Knowledge of Man,* p. 156.

19 "I'm not much": Esther Salaman, "A Talk With Einstein," *The Listener,* September 8, 1955 (afterward referred to as 'Salaman').

19 "God is subtle but he is not malicious": for origin of phrase see p. 232.

19 "God does not play dice": for origin of phrase see p. 216.

20 "even he": David Ben-Gurion, *Ben-Gurion Looks Back,* p. 217.

20 "I was so surprised": Harry A. Cohen, "An Afternoon with Einstein," *Jewish Spectator,* January, 1969, p. 16.

21 "At the age of sixteen": Hans Einstein, quoted Kornitzer, *Ladies Home Journal,* April 1951, p. 136.

21 A paper to Uncle Cäsar in Stuttgart. Undated letter and MS, Einstein-Cäsar Koch, authenticated c. 1950 by Einstein, in possession of the Suzanne Gottschalk-Jean Ferrard family, Brussels. Preprint No. of "Albert Einstein's 'First' Paper" by Jagdish Mehra, CPT-82: AEC-31, January 8, 1971.

Chapter 2 Stateless Person

22 "was entirely his own fault": John Plesch, *Janos: The Story of a Doctor,* p. 219 (afterward referred to as 'Plesch').

22 "I was supposed to choose": Kornitzer.

22 a pleasant place: Einstein, *Aargauer Tageblatt,* February 19, 1952.

23 "Now, Einstein": quoted Carl Seelig, *Albert Einstein,* p. 19 (afterward referred to as 'Seelig').

23 "Sure of himself, his gray felt hat": Seelig, p. 14.

24 "he was by nationality a German": André Mercier, quoted G. J. Whitrow (ed.), *Einstein: The Man and His Achievement,* B. B. C. Third Programme Talks, p. 17 (afterward referred to as 'Whitrow').

24 "give up his passport": Walter Jens, "Albert Einstein," *Universitas,* Vol. 11, No. 3 (1969), p. 243.

24 formally ended Einstein's German nationality: Stadtarchiv, Ulm.

25 "When I was a very young man": Dr. Leon L. Watters, "Comments on the Letters of Professor and Mrs. Albert Einstein to Dr. Leon L. Watters," unpublished MS, American Jewish Archives, p. 26 (afterward referred to as 'Watters').

25 Fräulein Markwalder: quoted Seelig, p. 36.

25 "Heavens, no": Seelig, p. 15.

27 "intellectual women did not attract him": Vera Weizmann, *The Impossible Takes Longer,* pp. 102–3 (afterward referred to as 'Vera Weizmann').

27 "Personal matters": *The Observer,* London, April 24, 1955.

27 "He was devoid": Dr. Thomas Lee Bucky, "Einstein: An Intimate Memoir," *Harper's Magazine,* September 1964 (afterward referred to as 'Thomas Lee Bucky').

28 "the experience of the exterior world": "Jubilee of Relativity Theory," *Helvetica Physica Acta,* Supplementum iv, Basle, 1956, p. 19 (afterward referred to as 'Physica Acta').

28 "like so many": Morris Cohen, "Einstein and His World," *The Menorah Journal,* Vol. 24 (Spring 1936), p. 107 (afterward referred to as 'Menorah').

28 excellent teachers: Paul A. Schilpp (ed.), *Albert Einstein: Philosopher-Scientist,* p. 15, (afterward referred to as 'Schilpp').

28 Maxwell's work was not touched upon: Gerald Holton, "Influences on Einstein's Early Work in Relativity Theory," *The American Scholar,* Vol. 37, No. 1 (Winter 1967–68), p. 63.

30 "Maxwell's theory of the electromagnetic field": Max Born, "Physics in the Last 50 Years," *Nature,* Vol. 168 (1951), p. 625.

31 At home he studied the works: Schilpp, p. 15.

31 "the last man": E. T. Bell, *Men of Mathematics,* Vol. 2, p. 581, (afterward referred to as 'E. T. Bell').

31 "Colors, space, tones": quoted Gerald Holton, "Mach, Einstein and the Search for Reality," *Daedalus,* Spring 1968, p. 659 (afterward referred to as 'Daedalus').

31 "was not speculative in origin": typically, lecture, King's College, London, 1921, quoted *The Nation,* London, June 18, 1921.

31 a long philosophical pilgrimage: *Daedalus,* p. 636.

32 "You can do": quoted Margareta Niewenhuis von Uexkuell, "Erinnerungen an Einstein," *Frankfurter Allgemeine Zeitung,* March 10, 1956; also Uexkuell, "Albert Einstein nach meiner Erinnerung," E.T.H.

32 put off scientific work: Schilpp, p. 17.

33 A further letter followed: Einstein-Adolf Hurwitz, September 26, 1900, quoted Seelig, p. 49.

33 The work, though temporary: Einstein-Hurwitz, September 23, 1900, Seelig, p. 48.

33 "happy in Switzerland": Leopold Infeld, *Albert Einstein,* p. 119.

33 "perfectly in agreement": Stadtarchiv, Zurich.

33 "The process had not": Anton Reiser, *Albert Einstein,* p. 65, (afterward referred to as 'Reiser').

34 The people were humane: Einstein-Wisseler, August 24, 1948, Swiss National Library, Berne.

34 "Like other opponents of military imperialism": *Menorah,* p. 53.

35 heard through a student friend: Einstein-Heike Kamerlingh Onnes, April 12, 1901, Rijksmuseum voor de Geschiedenis der Natuurwetenschappen, Leiden (afterward referred to as 'Leiden').

35 teaching mathematics in a technical school: Einstein-Professor Alfred Stern, May 3, 1901, E.T.H.

36 "Albert was examined": Reiser, p. 65.

37 "Thorough academic education": Bureau Fédéral de la Propriété Intellectuelle, Berne, (afterward referred to as 'Bureau Fédéral').

Chapter 3 Swiss Civil Servant

38 "proved himself very useful": quotation from Friedrich Haller and details of salary and gradings, Bureau Fédéral.

39 "as the principal achievement of Einstein's work" and "crudeness in style": reports, E.T.H.

40 "More severe than my father": "Erinnerungen an Albert Einstein 1902–1909" (afterward referred to as 'Erinnerungen,' Bureau Fédéral).

40–41 first two papers: "Folgerungen aus den Capillaritätserscheinungen," *Annalen der Physik,* Ser. 4, Vol. 4 (1901), pp. 513–23, and "Über die thermodynamische Theorie der Potentialdifferenz zwischen Metallen und vollständig dissociierten Lösungen ihrer Salze, und eine elektrische Methode zur Erforschung der Molekularkräfte," *Annalen der Physik,* Ser. 4, Vol. 8 (1902), pp. 798–814.

41 three more papers: "Kinetische Theorie des Wärmegleichgewichtes und des zweiten Hauptsatzes der Thermodynamik," *Annalen der Physik,* Ser. 4, Vol. 9 (1902), pp. 417–33; "Eine Theorie der Grundlagen der Thermodynamik," *Annalen der Physik,* Ser. 4, Vol. 11 (1903), pp. 170–87, and "Zur allgemeinen molukularen Theorie der Wärme," *Annalen der Physik,* Ser. 4, Vol. 14 (1904), pp. 354–62.

41 "Walking in the streets of Berne": Einstein, *Lettres à Maurice Solovine,* p. vi (afterward referred to as 'Solovine').

42 "Einstein is 1.76 meters tall": Seelig, p. 40.

43 eating the caviar without comment: Solovine, p. x.

43 "A modest unassuming creature": Seelig, p. 38.

43 "her dreamy, ponderous nature": Seelig, p. 46.

44 "she has such a lovely voice": Seelig, p. 38.

44 "How it came about": Watters, p. 14.

45 "He was sitting in his study in front of a heap of papers": Dr. Hans Tanner-Seelig, E.T.H., and Seelig, p. 104.

45 "The door of the flat": David Reichinstein, *Albert Einstein: A Picture of His Life and His Conception of the World,* p. 25.

46 "blazing rockets": Louis de Broglie in Schilpp, p. 110.

46 a resume of things to come:

Einstein-Conrad Habicht, early 1905, Seelig, p. 74.

47 "These motions were such as to satisfy me": *Philosophical Magazine*, Pt. 4, 1828.

47 M. Gouy: *Journal de Physique*, (2), Vol. 7 (1888), p. 561.

47 Franz Exner: *Annalen der Physik*, Vol. 2 (1900), p. 843.

47 "On the Motion of Small Particles": "Über die von der molekularkinetischen Theorie der Wärme geforderte Bewegung von in ruhenden Flüssigkeiten suspendierten Teilchen," *Annalen der Physik*, Ser. 4, Vol. 17 (1905), pp. 549–60.

47 "To appreciate the importance of this step": Max Born, *Natural Philosophy of Cause and Chance*, p. 63 (afterward referred to as 'Born, *Cause and Chance*').

47 "the old fighter against atomistics": Arnold Sommerfeld in Schilpp, p. 105.

47 "The accuracy of measurement": Born, *Cause and Chance*, p. 63.

48 "fell like a bolt from the blue": Louis de Broglie, *New Perspectives in Physics*, p. 134 (afterward referred to as 'De Broglie, *New Perspectives*').

48 "to end his scientific life in sad isolation": De Broglie, *New Perspectives*, p. x.

48 "On a Heuristic Viewpoint": "Über einen die Erzeugung und Verwandlung des Lichtes betreffenden heuristischen Gesichtspunkt," *Annalen der Physik*, Ser. 4, Vol. 17 (1905), pp. 132–48.

51 "The discrepancy suggested": Sir Basil Schonland, *The Atomists*, p. 70 (afterward referred to as 'Schonland').

51 "After some weeks": Max Planck, *The Origin and Development of the Quantum Theory*, Nobel Prize Address, June 2, 1920, p. 3 (afterward referred to as 'Planck, Nobel Prize Address').

51 "Today, I have made": Max Born, "Obituary Notices of Fellows of the Royal Society," Vol. 6, No. 17 (November 1948), p. 161.

53 "not only prohibits the killing": quoted E. A. Milne, *Sir James Jeans*, p. 54.

53 "confronted with a novel kind": Niels Bohr, "The Solvay Meetings and the Development of Quantum Physics," in *Essays 1958-1962 on Atomic Physics and Human Knowledge*, p. 80 (afterward referred to as 'Bohr').

Chapter 4 Einstein's Relativity

54 "On the Electrodynamics of Moving Bodies": "Zur Elektrodynamik bewegter Körper," *Annalen der Physik*, Ser. 4, Vol. 17 (1905), pp. 891–921.

55 "From the time of Newton": J. Robert Oppenheimer, *The Flying Trapeze: Three Crises for Physicists*, p. 10 (afterward referred to as 'Oppenheimer, *Flying Trapeze*').

55 "Absolute, true and mathematical time": Sir Isaac Newton, *Mathematical Principles of Natural Philosophy*," p. 6.

55 "Absolute motion is the translation of a body": Newton, *Mathematical Principles*, p. 7.

58 "If Michelson-Morley is wrong": quoted Viscount Samuel and Herbert Dingle, *A Threefold Cord*, pp. 52-3.

58 Trouton and Nobel had tried: *Philosophical Transactions, A.*, Vol. 202 (1903), p. 165.

58 Both Lord Rayleigh and Brace had looked: *Philosophical Magazine*, December 1902, p. 678, and *Philosophical Magazine*, April 1904, p. 317.

59 "I am happy in the knowledge": quoted Lewis Campbell and W. Garnet, *James Clerk Maxwell*.

59 "the enormous stream of discoveries": Herman Bondi, *Assumption and Myth in Physical Theory*, p. 5.

60 "for me personally": quoted G. J. de Haas-Lorentz (ed.), *H. A. Lorentz*, p. 8.

61 "a logical consequence of several simultaneous hypotheses": Philipp Frank, *Interpretations and Misinterpretations of Modern Physics*, p. 39.

62 a spatially oscillatory electromagnetic field at rest: Schilpp, p. 53.

63 "I must confess": Alexander Moszkowski, *Einstein the Searcher*, p. 4 (afterward referred to as 'Moszkowski').

63 "worked for ten years": R. S. Shankland, "Conversation with Albert Einstein," *American Journal of Physics*, Vol. 31 (1963), pp. 47–57 (afterward referred to as 'Shankland'.)

63 "I pestered him for a whole month": Josef Sauter-Seelig, Seelig, p. 73.

63 "'You are the second'": "Erinnerungen," Bureau Fédéral.

63 "Einstein the eagle": Michelangelo Besso, quoted Seelig, p. 71.

64 "everybody had known": Born, *Physica Acta*, p. 251.

64, "Everybody knows that if you
66 are": Bertrand Russell, *The ABC of Relativity*, p. 28.

66 "the eternal struggle of the inventive human mind": Einstein and Leopold Infeld, *The Evolution of Physics*, p. vi.

66 "fey": Schonland, p. 56.

66 something in this idea: Plesch, p. 207.

68 "the notorious controversy": Max Born, *Einstein's Theory of Relativity*, p. 254.

68 "Asked if I consider": H. A. Lorentz at Mount Wilson Observatory, quoted *Contributions from the Mount Wilson Observatory*, Vol. XVII, Carnegie Institute of Washington (April 1928–November 1929), p. 27.

68 "When a rod is started": Sir Arthur Eddington, quoted by H. L. Brose in Erwin Freundlich, *The Foundations of Einstein's Theory of Gravitation*, p. viii.

69 Voigt: "Über das Dopplersche Prinzip," *Nachr. Ges. Wiss.* Göttingen (1887), p. 41.

70 two twins...age differently: Although novelists have often played tricks with time, one of the most extravagant examples was provided, some years before Einstein, by Camille Flammarion, the French astronomer. This was *Lumen*, published in 1873, the story of an adventurer who traveled back through time at 250,000 miles a second to witness, among other things, the end of the battle of Waterloo before the beginning. "You only comprehend things which you perceive," Lumen told the reader. "And as you persist in regarding your ideas of time and space as *absolute*, although they are only *relative*, and thence form a judgment on truths which are quite beyond your sphere, and which are imperceptible to your terrestrial organism and faculties, I should not do you a true service, my friend, in giving you fuller details of my ultra-terrestrial observations."

The weakness was, of course, shown years later by Einstein's revelation that c was the limiting speed in the universe since at the speed of light a body's mass would become infinitely great. Flammarion—in whose honor the 141st of the minor planets was named Lumen—believed in vegetation on the moon and in advanced and intelligent life on Mars, wrote many books of popular astronomy including *The Plurality of Inhabited Worlds*, which went through thirty editions, and late in life turned to psychic research.

71 "precisely because the old conceptions are so nearly right": F. A. Lindemann, "Einstein's Theory: A Revolution in Thought," *The Times Educational Supplement*, January 29, 1920 (afterward referred to as 'Lindemann').

71 "since everyday life": Russell, *The Observer*, April 24, 1955.

72 "Distance and duration are the most fundamental terms": Eddington, *The Theory of Relativity and Its Influence on Scientific Thought*, Romanes Lecture, May 24, 1922.

73 "The theory of relativity": Einstein, "Fundamental Concepts of Physics and Their Most Recent Changes," Lecture given Davoser Hochschule, printed *St. Louis Post-Dispatch*, December 29, 1928.

73 "replied that he had discovered": Hans Reichenbach, quoted Vallentin, p. 106.

73 "in science...the work of the individual": Speaking to National Academy of Sciences, Washington, D.C., April 26, 1921, quoted the *New York Times*, April 27, 1921.

73 "that this theory is not speculative": typically, lecture,

King's College, London, quoted *The Nation*, London, June 18, 1921.

73 "When I asked him": Shankland.

74 "the Michelson-Morley experiment had no role": Michael Polanyi, *The Art of Knowing,* p. 11.

74 "I naturally had before me": *Jewish Observer*, February 22, 1955.

74 ripe for discovery: Einstein-Seelig, *Technische Rundschau* No. 20, 47. Jahrgang, Berne, May 6, 1955.

75 "adopted Poincaré's Principle of Relativity": Sir Edmund Whittaker, "Albert Einstein 1879–1955," *Biographical Memoirs of Fellows of the Royal Society*, Vol. 1 (1955), p. 42.

75 "To discuss Einstein's Principle of Relativity": H. A. Lorentz, *Physikalische Zeitschrift*, Vol. 11 (1910), p. 1234, quoted Born, *Physica Acta*, p. 225.

75 "The genius of Einstein": *The Times*, May 25, 1931.

75 a brief paper: "Ist die Trägheit eines Körpers von seinem Energieinhalt abhängig?" *Annalen der Physik*, Ser. 4, Vol. 18 (1905), pp. 639–41.

76 "Are not gross Bodies and Light convertible": Newton, *Opticks*, p. 374.

77 "...it takes one's breath away": Hans Thirring, *The Ideas of Einstein's Theory*, p. 92.

78 "You haven't lost anything": Frank, p. 211.

78 "We use it": Oppenheimer, *Flying Trapeze*, p. 20.

79 "Relativism means the introduction": Frank, *Relativity—A Richer Truth*, pp. 29–30.

79 "Physical science does not": Sir James Jeans, *The New Background of Science*, p. 98.

79 "space and time": *The Tablet*, London, April 23, 1955.

Chapter 5 Fruits of Success

80 He did not care: Seelig, p. 113.

81 "was one of the keys to his character": James Stuart, *Within the Fringe*, p. 96.

81 "Whenever he felt": quoted Whitrow, p. 21.

82 "A new Copernicus": quoted Infeld, *Albert Einstein*, p. 44.

82 "Later, when Professor Loria": Infeld, *Albert Einstein*, p. 44.

83 "Although I was quite familiar": Born, *Physica Acta*, p. 247.

83 "I anticipate right away": W. Kaufmann, *Annalen der Physik*, Vol. 19 (1906), p. 495.

83 Kaufmann's results could not apparently be faulted: Einstein, "Über das Relativitätsprinzip und die aus demselben gezogenen Folgerungen," *Jahrbuch der Radioaktivität, und Elektronik*, Vol. 4 (1907), pp. 411–62 and Vol. 5 (1908), pp. 98–99 (Berichtigungen).

85 the law of causality: Frank, "Kausalgesetz und Erfahrung" ("Causality and Knowledge"), published in Ostwald's *Annalen der Naturphilosophie*, Leipzig, Vol. 6 (1907), p. 443.

85 "He approved the logic of my argument": Frank, *Modern Sci-*

ence and its Philosophy, p. 10.

85 an example of academic red tape: Einstein-Plesch, February 3, 1944, Plesch correspondence.

86 Shortly afterward, the decision was revised: Einstein-Plesch, February 3, 1944, Plesch correspondence.

87 "Because of this we feel compelled": Einstein, The Theory of Relativity, p. 62.

87 "This was displeasing to Einstein": Dr. Sciama in Whitrow, p. 34.

88 "to tell us whether he was": Lindemann, p. 59.

91 a reasonable theory of gravitation: Einstein, Origins of the General Theory of Relativity, George A. Gibson Foundation Lecture delivered Glasgow, June 20, 1933, p. 8 (afterward referred to as 'Gibson').

91 "great and brilliant period": Hermann Weyl, "David Hilbert," Obituary Notices of Fellows of the Royal Society, Vol. 4, No. 18 (November 1944), p. 547.

91 "whether he would ever have done it": E. Cunningham, Nature, February 17, 1921.

92 "the natural laws satisfying the demands": Einstein, The Theory of Relativity, p. 57.

92 "The non-mathematician is seized": Einstein, The Theory of Relativity, p. 55.

92 "from a 'happening' in three-dimensional space": Einstein, The Theory of Relativity, p. 122.

93 "the study of the inner workings": James Jeans, quoted Leon Watters, The Universal Jewish Encyclopaedia, New York, 1941, Vol. 4, p. 30.

93 "I do not know": Theodore von Karman, The Wind and Beyond, p. 51.

94 "felt herself at every moment": Statement for Curie Memorial Celebration, Roerich Museum, New York, November 23, 1935, printed Einstein, Ideas and Opinions, p. 76.

94 never met a real physicist: Infeld, Albert Einstein, p. 119.

94 "he said that it would be": Max Planck, Where Is Science Going?, p. 16.

94 "This seems to be rather amusing": Born, Physics in my Generation, p. 197.

95 "one of the landmarks": Wolfgang Pauli in Schilpp, p. 154.

95 a profound change in contemporary views: Einstein, "Uber die Entwicklung unserer Anschauungen über das Wesen und die Konstitution der Strahlung," Physikalische Zeitschrift, Vol. 10 (1909), pp. 817–25.

95 "At that time": Lise Meitner, "Looking Back," Bulletin of the Atomic Scientists, Vol. 20 (November 1964), p. 4.

Chapter 6   Moves Up the Ladder

96 "In my relativity theory": Frank, p. 96.

96 "We are on extremely good terms": Fritz Adler-Viktor Adler,

October 28, 1910, Adler Archives, Verein für Geschichte der Arbeiterbewegung, Vienna.

98 The details of Einstein's move to Prague are provided mainly by the Adler letters and are supplemented by Frank, pp. 98–101, who as Einstein's successor gives the most reliable general account of the move.

98 He was having a good time; Einstein-Lucien Chavan, July 5, 1911, Seelig, p. 129.

99 Einstein-George Pick correspondence: Einstein Archives.

101 "The problems of nationality": Frank, p. 107.

102 "Once in his strolls": Dmitri Marianoff and Palm Wayne, Einstein: An Intimate Study of a Great Man, p. 49 (afterward referred to as 'Marianoff').

102 another paper for the Annalen der Physik: Über den Einfluss der Schwerkraft auf die Ausbreitung des Lichtes" ("On the Influence of Gravitation on the Propagation of Light"), Annalen der Physik, Ser. 4, Vol. 35 (1911), pp. 898–908.

103 "Do not bodies act upon Light": Newton, Opticks, p. 339.

103 Soldner: Astronomisches Jahrbuch, Berlin 1804, p. 161.

104 the first Solvay Congress: The Conseil de Physique Solvay is usually translated into English as the Solvay Congress. However, Jean Pelseneer, Professeur Extraordinaire, Brussels University and the author of an unpublished "Historique des Instituts Internationaux de Physique de Chimie Solvay depuis leur fondation," points out that while a "Congress" involves a large number of scientists or others, Solvay's scheme was almost the reverse—the invitation of a small number of men representing the cream of European physicists. "Council" or "Conference" is suggested—but "Congress" is by this time probably too well used to be changed.

105 "Observing this shy genius": The Earl of Birkenhead, The Prof in Two Worlds, p. 37.

106 "I can still see Einstein": Max von Laue-Seelig, March 13, 1952, E.T.H.

107 about a trip to the Alps: Einstein-Madame Curie, April 3, 1913, Bibliothèque Nationale, Paris.

107 "I remember watching": Hyman Levy, in Whitrow, p. 43.

108 Einstein and Grossman published jointly a paper: Zeitschrift für Mathematik und Physik, Vol. 62 (1913), pp. 225–61.

108 "that they were not compatible with experience": Gibson, p. 11.

108 "speak of basic metaphysical concepts": Nahum Goldman, Memories, p. x.

109 "It was clear": Nature, Vol. 175 (May 28, 1955), pp. 926–27.

109 "Look. The blackboard moves": Felix Ehrenhaft, "My Experiences with Einstein," unpublished MS (afterward

referred to as 'Ehrenhaft').

111 "leaning directly on Einstein's treatment": Bohr, p. 84.

111 "Speaking with Einstein": George de Hevesy-Rutherford, October 14, 1913, Rutherford Papers, University of Cambridge.

111 "a stream of knowledge": Planck, Nobel Prize Address, p. 16.

111 to discover whether light was, in fact, bent: Forschungen und Fortschritte, Vol. 37, 1963, quoted in Daedalus, p. 645.

111 Details of Einstein's early friendship with Erwin Finlay-Freundlich are contained in a long series of letters between the two, including the following until recently held by the late Frau Freundlich (afterward referred to as 'Freundlich correspondence').

111 welcomed the help: Einstein-Freundlich, September 1, 1911

112 if the speed of light was affected: Einstein-Freundlich, August 1913.

112 "This morning I had a nice letter": Freundlich-Frau Freundlich, August 26, 1913.

113 "He writes to me that he has undertaken": George Ellery Hale-Einstein, November 8, 1913, Hale Papers, California Institute of Technology, Pasadena.

113 willing to contribute: Einstein-Freundlich, December 7, 1913, Freundlich correspondence.

Chapter 7   A Jew in Berlin

114 "at a profound disadvantage": R. B. Haldane, An Autobiography, London, 1929, p. 232.

115 had gone to Berlin: Einstein-Besso, March 26 (no year, but apparently 1911), Einstein Archives.

117 "This new interpretation of the time concept": Statement dated Berlin, June 12, 1913, E.T.H.

119 "At Easter, Einstein will move to Berlin": Walter Nernst-Lindemann, August 18, 1913, Cherwell Archives, Nuffield College, Oxford.

119 "In addition there were also personal factors": Frank, p. 136.

120 "the true artist will let his wife starve": George Bernard Shaw, Major Barbara.

120 "Prussian nationality which he acquired in 1913": Dr. Ernst Heymann, April 1, 1933, quoted Einstein, The World as I See It, p. 86.

120 no change in his nationality: Einstein-Academy, March 23, 1923 (18 Akad. Arch. II: IIIa, Bd. 23, B197) quoted Friedrich Herneck, "Uber die deutsche Reichsangehörigkeit Albert Einstein," Die Naturwissenschaften, Heft 2 (1961), S.33 (afterward referred to as 'Herneck').

121 a farewell supper for him: Louis Kollros, Physica Acta, p. 280.

122 "determined to keep himself as clear as possible": Einstein-Plesch, February 3, 1944,

Plesch correspondence.

122 "I have seen him": Viscount Samuel, Memoirs, p. 254.

122 He was also confident: Einstein-Besso, March 1914, Daedalus, p. 652.

126 "His resulting depression": Morris Goran, The Story of Fritz Haber, p. 66 (afterward referred to as 'Goran').

126 One of [his] great disappointments": Goran, p. 75.

126 "I am a sergeant": Goran, pp. 75–6.

127 "This is supposed to say": Sommerfeld, quoted Schilpp, p. 103.

127 Koppel as the man providing his Academy salary: Einstein-Freundlich, December 7, 1913, Freundlich correspondence.

128 his academic pay: Einstein-Hedwig Born, September 1, 1919, Born Letters, p. 12.

128 "Manifesto to the Civilized World": quoted Otto Nathan and Heinz Norden (eds.), Einstein on Peace, p. 4–6 (afterward referred to as 'Nathan and Norden').

128 Nicolai himself gives him credit: George Nicolai-Einstein, May 18, 1918, quoted Nathan and Norden, p. 7.

129 "very active": Kurt R. Grossmann, "Peace Movements in Germany," South Atlantic Quarterly (July 1950), p. 294 (afterward referred to as 'Grossmann').

129 "to work in any open way": Grossmann, p. 294.

129 he wrote with a mixture of resignation, pity, and disgust: Einstein-Paul Ehrenfest, August 19, 1914, and Einstein-Ehrenfest, December 1914, Einstein Archives; Einstein-Lorentz, August 2, 1915, Allgemeen Rijksarchiv, The Hague (afterward referred to as 'The Hague'); and Einstein-Ehrenfest, August 23, 1915, Einstein Archives.

130 "In looking at Einstein": Romain Rolland, Journal des Années de Guerre, 1914–1919, pp. 510–15 (afterward referred to as 'Rolland').

130 the cause of war on the aggressive nature: Das Land Goethes 1914–1916, Berliner Goethebund, 1916, Dokumentensammlung der Preuss. Staadtsbibliothek, Berlin-Dahlem.

131 irrevocable decision: Einstein-Besso, July 14, 1916, Besso correspondence.

132 "As his mind knows no limits": Plesch, p. 206.

132 "His utter independence": Hedwig Born, Helle Zeit, p. 36.

132 "He believed that nothing": Bucky, Helle Zeit, p. 65.

133 "I'm glad my wife doesn't know": Salaman.

134 "based on many years of experience": Frank, p. 156.

134 His letter was long and pessimistic: Einstein-Rolland, August 22, 1917, Rolland, p. 1205. (Given as Wednesday 21st, but Wednesday was the 22nd).

134 "I note once again the extreme injustice": Rolland, p. 1303.

Infeld, *Die Wahrheit*, March 15–16, 1969.

179 "My Answer to the Anti-Relativity Theory Company Ltd.": *Berliner Tageblatt*, August 25, 1920.

180 "Dear Einstein, You must not leave": Sommerfeld-Einstein, September 3, 1920, Sommerfeld, p. 65.

180 "referred to his lecturing at Oxford": Everett Skillings, "Some Recent Impressions in Germany," *The Oxford Magazine*, Vol. XXXVIII, No. 23, June 11, 1920.

180 suggesting Einstein for a post in Cambridge: Jeans-Rutherford, September 1, 1920, Rutherford Papers.

181 He was...tormented: Planck-Einstein, September 5, 1920, Einstein Archives.

181 "Most respected professor": Haenisch-Einstein, quoted the *New York Times*, September 26, 1920.

181 Bad Nauheim meeting: as with the famous confrontation between T. H. Huxley and Bishop Wilberforce at the Oxford meeting of the British Association in 1860, no complete verbatim record of the Lenard-Einstein exchange appears to have survived. Eyewitness accounts, recalled after half a century, are conflicting. The overall impression is that Planck just managed to keep the occasion in hand.

181 Lenard and (p. 182) Einstein and other speakers: *Physikalische Zeitschrift*, Vol. XXI (1920), pp. 666–68.

182 "was provoked into making a caustic reply": Born Letters, p. 36.

182 he would not allow himself to get excited again: Einstein-Born undated, Born Letters, p. 41.

182 "Berlin is the place": Frank, p. 206.

Chapter 11   Ambassador-at-Large

184 thorns in the side: Einstein-Plesch, February 3, 1914, Plesch correspondence.

185 "Calm yourself": Frank, p. 211.

185 "Einstein stayed in my house": Ehrenhaft, p. 5.

186 his English was practically nonexistent; and, following Manchester correspondence: Manchester University Archives.

186 "the excellence of his diction": *The Manchester Guardian*, June 10, 1921.

187 "I recall...I had invitations": Eddington-Lindemann, April 24, 1932, Cherwell Archives.

187 "Einstein arrives here": Haldane-John Murray, May 12, 1921, John Murray Archives, London.

187 "Will you do me the honor": Haldane-Einstein, Einstein Archives.

188 Haldane's comments to his mother on the Einstein visit are taken from the Haldane correspondence in the National

Library of Scotland. Sources for the dinner party on the 10th, include G. K. A. Bell and Sommer. Randall Davidson appears to have made a detailed record of the meeting.

188 "The Archbishop...can make neither": Lord Sanderson-J. J. Thomson, April 7, 1921, quoted Rayleigh, p. 203.

189 "I have never seen": Randall Davidson, quoted G. K. A. Bell, *Randall Davidson, Archbishop of Canterbury*, p. 1052 (afterward referred to as 'G. K. A. Bell').

189 "Lord Haldane tells us": G. K. A. Bell, p. 1052.

189 "The meaning of relativity has been": *Saturday Evening Post*, October 26, 1929, p. 17 et seq.

189 "Because clergymen are interested": Philipp Frank, "Einstein's Philosophy of Science," *Reviews of Modern Physics*, Vol. 21, No. 3 (July 1949), p. 349.

189 "especially in its mystical aspect": G. K. A. Bell, p. 1052.

189 "Mysticism is in fact": Seelig, p. 79.

190 "Einstein had no notes, no hesitations": *The Nation*, June 18, 1921.

190 "I am anxious to draw attention": *The Nation*, June 18, 1921.

191 "so firmly convinced": Hans Reichenbach, quoted Vallentin, p. 106.

191 "I think the German Ambassador was right": Haldane-Lindemann, June 15, 1921, Cherwell Archives.

192 The two fullest accounts of Einstein's Paris visit are given by Charles Nordmann in *Revue des Deux Mondes*, Vol. 8 (7th Series) 1922, and *L'Illustration*, April 15, 1922.

193 "The first impression": Nordmann, *L'Illustration*.

193 "On the subject of relativity": quoted Bernard Jaffe, *Michelson and the Speed of Light*, p. 101.

194 "All the students of Germany": Nordmann, *L'Illustration*.

195 Madame Curie now wrote: Madame Curie-Einstein, July 7, 1922, Curie Laboratory Archives, Paris.

196 Einstein's nationality: a major source is Herneck in *Die Naturwissenschaften*, which quotes extensively from Government and Academy documents.

197 "The Swiss Ambassador was surprised": Rudolf Nadolny, quoted Herneck.

197 award was received by the German ambassador: Nobel Foundation.

197 handed over at Einstein's request by Swiss Ambassador: Einstein Archives.

197 Ministerial report of January 13, 1923: quoted Herneck.

197 He gave them on March 24: Einstein-Ministry, March 24, 1923, quoted Herneck.

198 "On the whole the local visit of Einstein": report of German consul general, Barcelona, May 2, 1923, Deutsches

Zentralarchiv, Potsdam.

198 Einstein statement: February 7, 1924, quoted Herneck.

198 "a material side to the Nobel Prize": Lorentz-Einstein, May 1, 1923, Leiden.

198 a Japanese publisher: Einstein-Plesch, February 3, 1944, Plesch correspondence.

199 "It is an interesting commentary": Douglas, p. 44.

200 leaving the country...and canceling a dinner date: Einstein Archives.

Chapter 12   Unter den Linden

203 "Poor old Joffé": Plesch, p. 235.

204 "The stream continues": E. Cunningham, *Nature*, Vol. 109 (June 17, 1922), pp. 770–72.

204 "When you are twenty": Letter to author, October 22, 1968.

205 "But Albert": Ehrenhaft, p. 11.

205 "On occasions like this": quoted Marianoff, p. 85.

206 "I am happy because I want nothing": George Sylvester Viereck, "What Life Means to Einstein," *Saturday Evening Post*, October 26, 1929, pp. 17, et seq.

206 "I shall have to think about it": Frau Freundlich's statement to author.

206 "Einstein Tower": for details see Erwin Finlay-Freundlich, "How I Came to Build the Einstein Tower," *Physikalische Blätter*, Vol. 12, 1969.

208 "conviction that if a nuclear chain reaction": Leo Szilard, "Reminiscences," *Perspectives in Modern History*, Vol. II. p. 102 (afterward referred to as 'Szilard').

208 who create intellectual and spiritual life: Einstein-Professor Donnan, August 16, 1933, Szilard Archives, San Diego.

210 the whole theory would collapse: Einstein-Robert Millikan, July 13, 1925, Millikan Papers, California Institute of Technology, Pasadena.

210 "Not one of them thought": Michael Polanyi, *The Logic of Liberty*, p. 11.

212 very loath...to abandon complete causality: Einstein-Born, January 27, 1920, Born Letters.

212 "When, after a long absence": De Broglie, *New Perspectives*, p. 80.

212 "the suggestion made...purely on grounds": Polanyi, *Personal Knowledge*, p. 148.

212 "In the months that followed": De Broglie, *New Perspectives*, p. 139.

213 two-part paper for the Prussian Academy: "Quantentheorie des einatomigen idealen Gases," *Preussische Akademie der Wissenschaften, Phys.-math. Klasse, Sitzungsberichte*, 1924, pp. 261–67, and 1925, pp. 3–14 and pp. 18–25.

213 "the stepped-up realization": Schrödinger, "Our Image of Matter," *On Modern Physics*, London, 1961, p. 43.

214 "At sunset the top of Fujiyama":

L. Rosenfeld, *Niels Bohr*, p. 15.

215 "governed by statistical laws": De Broglie.

216 "It appeared experimentally proven": Schonland, p. 188.

216 "Einstein said partly as a joke": Frank, p. 260.

216 "A good joke": Frank, p. 261.

216 he was convinced that God did not throw dice: Einstein-Born, December 12, 1926, Born Letters, p. 91.

217 "At the Solvay meetings": Schilpp, p. 211.

217 "the impossibility of any sharp separation": Schilpp, p. 210.

218 "During a fairly long walk": De Broglie, *New Perspectives*, p. 182.

218 "Bohr's reasoning applied to any method": Barbara Cline, *The Questioners: Physicists and the Quantum Theory*, p. 240 (afterward referred to as 'Cline').

219 "On Mondays, Wednesdays and Fridays": Sir William Bragg, *Electrons and Ether Waves*, 23rd Robert Boyle Lecture, Oxford, 1921, p. 11.

219 "The advancing sieve of time": Lawrence Bragg-author, May 30, 1970.

219 "May the spirit of Newton's method": *Nature*, Vol. 119 (1927), p. 467.

220 "Today faith in unbroken causality is threatened": "Fundamental Concepts of Physics and Their Most Recent Changes," Translation of the Davos Hochschule Lecture published in the *St. Louis Post-Dispatch*, December 29, 1928.

Chapter 13   The Call of Peace

222 International Committee on Intellectual Co-operation: The English title was International Committee on Intellectual Co-operation, the French was Commission Internationale de Co-operation Intellectuelle. Both sides often swapped "Committee" and "Commission" as the spirit moved them —and in even official letters dropped the "Intellectual."

222 "not as representatives": League of Nations Archives, Geneva.

223 he had no desire to represent people: Einstein-Pierre Comert, July 4, 1922, League Archives.

223 "Einstein resigns": Inazo Nitobe-Gilbert Murray, League Archives.

223 "It is my belief": Henri Bergson-Nitobe, League Archives.

223 "I explained to you": Comert-Einstein, April 10, 1923, League Archives.

224 "I have recently become convinced": Einstein-League, March 21, 1923, League Archives.

225 useless to discuss rules of war: Einstein-Women's International League for Peace and Freedom, January 4, 1928, quoted Nathan and Norden, p. 90.

225 "On August 30th, 1930": *War Resistance*, Vol. 2, No. 23,

4th Quarter, p. 11.

226 "Even if only two per cent": Speech at Ritz-Carlton Hotel, New York, December 14, 1930, quoted Alfred Lief (ed.), *The Fight Against War*, p. 35.

226 suggesting that he should be replaced: Einstein-J. D. de Montenach, April 20, 1932, League Archives.

227 "One does not make wars less likely": quoted Nathan and Norden, pp. 168–70.

227 "This is not a comedy": Einstein, quoted Konrad Bercovici, *Pictorial Review*, February 1933.

Chapter 14   The Call of Zion

230 "I was to stir up Einstein": Kurt Blumenfeld has described his recruitment of Einstein into the Zionist ranks in his autobiography, *Erlebte Judenfrage*; in a lengthy article in the Belgian Zionist paper *La Tribune Sioniste*; and in various documents now in the E.T.H. They differ in wording, but not in significant detail.

230 "To my boundless astonishment": Blumenfeld.

230 "Einstein was young, gay and flirtatious": Vera Weizmann, pp. 102–3.

230 "explained his theory to me": Chaim Weizmann-Ossip Dymow, quoted Seelig, p. 81.

230 New York arrival: the main record of Einstein's day-to-day activities is taken from the *New York Times*.

232 "I have just got a new theory of Eternity": H. Shapley, *Through Rugged Ways to the Stars*, p. 78.

232 "God is subtle but he is not malicious": the famous remark, later to be carved into the mantelpiece of a Princeton University common room was, says Miss Dukas, overheard and remembered by Professor Veblen.

233 "Found him rather tired": F. H. Kisch, *Palestine Diary*, p. 29 (afterward referred to as 'Kisch').

234 "no holding back": *Palestine Weekly*, February 9, 1923.

234 "I consider this the greatest day": quoted *Palestine Weekly*, February 9, 1923.

234 "Interview with Deedes": Kisch, p. 30.

234 "an opening sentence *pro forma*": Samuel, *Memoirs*, p. 253.

234 He was impressed: Einstein-Weizmann, February, 11, 1923, Weizmann Archives, Rehovot.

235 "The Jews have produced no genius of rank": Norman Bentwich, *Wanderer Between Two Worlds*, p. 133.

235 "looked as happy": Norman and Helen Bentwich, *Mandate Memories*, p. 88.

235 "Ramassez plus d'argent": Kisch, p. 30.

236 asked for the withdrawal: Einstein-Magnes, December 29, 1925, Weizmann Archives.

236 Magnes declined: Einstein-Magnes, March 6, 1926,

Weizmann Archives.

236 to complain in stronger terms: Einstein-Weizmann, January 8, 1928, Weizmann Archives.

236 "Our income is entirely from voluntary subscribers": Weizmann-Einstein, June 8, 1933, Weizmann Archives.

237 Einstein's resignation: Einstein-Weizmann, January 8, 1928; Einstein-Weizmann, June 14, 1928; and Einstein-Weizmann, June 20, 1928, All Weizmann Archives.

237 "of an unusually momentous character": Weizmann-Einstein, May 29, 1929, Weizmann Archives.

237 "I am the Jewish saint"; statement to Sir John Simon; and visit to Frau Markwalder: personal information.

237 "the brave and dedicated minority": Einstein, quoted official report, 1. Council-Sitzung: Eroffnungsreden, p. 578.

Chapter 15   Preparing for the Storm

238 a preliminary paper: "Zur affinen Feldtheorie," *Preussische Akademie der Wissenschaften, Phys.-math. Klasse, Sitzungsberichte*, 1923, pp. 137–40.

238 "He agreed that the chance of success": A. A. Taub, quoted Whitrow, p. xii.

238 the outline of a unified field: "Neue Möglichkeit für eine einheitliche Feldtheorie von Gravitation und Elektrizität" *Preussische Akademie der Wissenschaften, Phys.-math. Klasse, Sitzungsberichte*, 1928, pp. 224–27.

238 "He has solved the problem": Elsa Einstein-Hermann Struck, December 27, 1928, quoted Stargardt Auction Catalogue, November, 1964.

239 the unified field theory paper: "Einheitliche Feldtheorie," *Preussische Akademie der Wissenschaften, Phys.-math. Klasse, Sitzungsberichte*, 1929, pp. 2–7.

239 "for the present, at any rate": *Nature*, Vol. 123, February 23, 1929.

239 "For my part, I cannot readily give up": *Nature*, Vol. 123, February 23, 1929, p. 281.

240 "in an agony of mathematical torment": *Helle Zeit*, p. 51.

240 "I had to explain to Boess": Plesch, p. 224.

242 "The conversation drifted back and forth": Dr. Chaim Tschernowitz.

242 "The kind of work I do": Frank, p. 147.

242 "Then Einstein spoke": Plesch, p. 210.

244 "I was disturbed by grim signs": Bentwich, *My Seventy-Seven Years*, p. 95.

245 the Queen's own notes in her agenda book: Royal Archives, Brussels.

246 "parce que je suis Rouge et Juif": note by Samuel, Samuel Papers.

246 "The result was better": Arthur

Fleming-Allan Balch, December 5, 1934, Millikan Papers.

248 "If you really want to send a message": the *New York Times*, December 3, 1930.

248 "within the brief quarter of an hour": the *New York Times*, December 12, 1930.

248 five crowded days: details, the *New York Times*.

252 "New observations by Hubble and Humason": the *New York Times*, January 3, 1931.

252 "the mathematician for
–53** whom symmetry": J. D. North, *The Measure of the Universe*, p. 118.

254 "Well, well, my husband does that on the back of an old envelope": as with many stories of the Einsteins in Pasadena, this is firmly believed even though evidence is lacking.

255 "Financial position movement and work Palestine": Weizmann-Einstein, cable, February 4, 1931, Weizmann Archives.

255 His first lecture was on relativity: Einstein's Rhodes lectures have never been printed. They are summarized in *Nature*, Vol. 127, pp. 765, 790, 826.

256 a graphic and pessimistic account: Einstein-Lindemann, June 9, 1931, Cherwell Archives.

256 proposed that Einstein should be made a "Research Student": details from Christ Church, Sir Roy Harrod, C. H. Collie, Cherwell Archives.

256 Einstein accepted without delay: Einstein-Lindemann, July 15, 1931, Cherwell Archives.

256 "Fleming read *not* his own letters": A. A. Noyes-Hale, October 8, 1931, Hale Papers.

257 "Board is of opinion": E. C. Barrett-Millikan, telegram, Millikan Papers.

257 "Now the seven thousand dollar figure which we talked about": Millikan-Einstein, October 11, 1931, Millikan Papers.

257 decided to remain in Germany for the winter: Einstein-Millikan, October 19, 1931, Millikan Papers.

257 Elsa wrote to Millikan: Mrs. Einstein-Millikan, November 14, 1931, Millikan Papers.

258 "I drove over to the Athenaeum": Abraham Flexner, *I Remember*, p. 381 (afterward referred to as 'Flexner').

258 "I had no idea that he would be interested": Flexner, p. 382.

259 "He was a charming person": R. F. Harrod, *The Prof*, p. 47.

259 "As it dawned on me": Flexner, p. 383.

259 "We sat on the veranda": Flexner, p. 384.

260 "Let Mrs. Einstein and me arrange it": Flexner, quoted in the *New York Times*, April 19, 1955.

260 "I cannot believe that annual residence for brief periods": Flexner-Millikan, July 29, 1932, Millikan Papers.

260 "maybe a solution will be found": Mrs. Einstein-Millikan, August 13, 1932, Millikan Papers.

260 "I have received leave of absence": the *New York Times*, October 16, 1932.

261 "a request which I know": Weizmann-Einstein, November 8, 1932, Weizmann Archives.

261 Einstein…was delighted to hear the news: Einstein-Weizmann, November 20, 1932, Weizmann Archives.

261 "Before you leave our villa": Frank, p. 273.

Chapter 16   Goodbye to Berlin

262 "to appropriate the sum": Wilber K. Thomas, Oberlaender Trust-Millikan, January 14, 1932, Millikan Papers.

262 "handled himself with a skill": Millikan-Thomas, January 16, 1933, Millikan Papers.

264 "As long as I have any choice in the matter": Interview with Evelyn Seeley, *New York World Telegram*, March 10 , 1933.

264 helping to save European civilization: Einstein-Alfred Nahon, July 20, 1933, *La Patrie Humaine*, August 18, 1933.

265 a visit to Princeton: details from the *New York Times* and Jewish Telegraphic Agency.

Chapter 17   Shopping for Einstein

267 "a scene which had not been witnessed in the Western world": William Shirer, *The Rise and Fall of the Third Reich*, p. 241 (afterward referred to as 'Shirer').

268 "The chief characteristic of this renascence": Professor Ernst Krieck, quoted *Science*, May 23, 1933.

268 "The Kaiser Wilhelm Society …begs leave": *Science*, Vol. 77, No. 2005 (June 2, 1933), p. 529.

268 "not yet hanged": Private information.

269 "But on my arrival in Cairo": Weizmann-Einstein, May 3, 1933, Weizmann Archives.

270 his reply to Weizmann: Einstein-Weizmann, May 7, 1933, Weizmann Archives.

270 "I can almost see Einstein now": C. H. Arnold-author, October 8, 1968.

271 suggesting that Einstein and he should meet: Weizmann-Einstein, June 4, 1933, Weizmann Archives.

271 a three-page letter: Weizmann-Einstein, June 8, 1933, Weizmann Archives.

271 firmly standing his ground: Einstein-Weizmann, June 9, 1933, Weizmann Archives.

271 "proposed radical changes in the administration": Bentwich, *Judah L. Magnes*, p. 168.

271 "It retired Magnes": C. H. Voss (ed.), *''Servant of the People,''* pp. 206–7.

Chapter 18   Of No Address

273 the times were out of joint: Einstein-J. B. Th. Hugenholtz, July 1, 1933, Nathan and Norden, p. 226.

273 "The husband of the second

fiddler": quoted Nathan and Norden, p. 227.

273 he had decided not to
–74 intervene: Einstein-H. M. King Albert, July 14, 1933, Royal Archives, Brussels.

274 "My dear Professor, I have received with great pleasure": H. M. King Albert-Einstein, July 24, 1933, Royal Archives, Brussels.

274 "would rather be hacked in pieces": Einstein, *Ideas and Opinions*, p. 10.

274 cheerfully accept military service: Einstein-Nahon, July 20, 1933, *La Patrie Humaine*, August 18, 1933.

274 "The apostasy of Einstein": Press Service of the International Antimilitaristic Commission.

275 "My ideal remains the settlement": Einstein public statement at Le Coq, Nathan and Norden, p. 234.

275 "My dear Prof, Someone has seen Einstein": Commander Oliver Locker-Lampson-Lindemann, July 20, 1933, Cherwell Archives.

276 "My name appeared in the French and English editions": quoted Press reports, Britain and America.

277 a small boarding house: information on Einstein's third, and final, journey to England in 1933, provided by Locker-Lampson's widow; Sir Walter Adams, former secretary of the Academic Assistance Council; the Rutherford Papers; contemporary newspapers; and other sources cited.

277 "I shall become a naturalized Englishman": *Daily Express*, September 11, 1933.

279 Lord Rutherford was in the chair: details from official and Press accounts of the meeting; also Sir Walter Adams to author.

280 looked forward to their next meeting: Einstein-Lindemann, October 5, 1933, Cherwell Archives.

281 "Einstein's boat was not yet at the pier in New York": Reverend John Lampe, July 7, 1956.

Chapter 19 Living with the Legend

282 "leaving 'the Physical World'": Cline, p. 15.

282 "Do you want to commit suicide?": Plesch-Einstein, September 22, 1947, Plesch correspondence.

282 "I have never known a place that to me was a homeland": Watters, p. 26.

283 "May I speak with Dean Eisenhart, please?": Churchill Eisenhart, "Albert Einstein As I Remember Him," *Journal of the Washington Academy of Sciences*, Vol. 54 (1964), pp. 325–28 (afterward referred to as 'Eisenhart').

283 his choice was Moses; and
–84 "Well, *my* husband always says": private source.

284 "Colonel MacIntyre...tele-

phoned the Institute": Report to White House Social Bureau, December 7, 1933, Roosevelt Library.

284 "With genuine and profound reluctance": Flexner-Roosevelt, November 3, 1933, Roosevelt Library.

284 he had not received it: Einstein-Mrs. Roosevelt, November 21, 1933, Roosevelt Library.

285 the original of the doggerel: The copy in the Roosevelt Library in Elsa's handwriting, was translated by the Department of State Translating Bureau, which provided a close and a rhymed version and were "careful not to fold or otherwise tamper with the original sheets." The original card, written by Einstein and addressed to Queen Elizabeth, is in the Royal Library, Brussels.

285 "One flower is beautiful": Watters, p. 20.

285 "Just as we were all seated at the table": Watters, p. 10.

286 "I am not tired": quoted Watters, p. 20.

286 Bucky-Einstein correspondence: The collection of letters is owned by the University of Texas at Austin.

286 "set up an excellent short-wave radio set": Watters, p. 19.

286 "perhaps the one thing": Plesch, p. 224.

286 "too snobbish": Bucky, *Helle Zeit*, pp. 60–5.

286 a childlike delight, Bucky, *Helle Zeit*, pp. 60–5.

287 "Burgess had made a number of drawings": Watters, p. 21.

287 "Once when out sailing with him": Watters, p. 21.

287 "While I never completely lost my awe of Einstein": Thomas Lee Bucky, p. 43.

288 "You know I can't make speeches": quoted in the *New York Times*, March 12, 1944, VI, p. 16.

288 "The theory was directed": Shirer, p. 250.

289 private evening of chamber music at his house: Shapley, p. 111.

289 "But doctor, what would you say": Charles A. Lindbergh-author, December 12, 1969.

290 "I would never ask the Professor to do that": Walther Mayer-author, December 4, 1968.

290 "I give her my understanding": Eisenhart.

290 "Einstein, absorbed in his intellectual pursuits": Watters, p. 150.

291 "Einstein, during my stay in Princeton": Infeld, "As I See It," *Bulletin of the Atomic Scientists*, Vol 21 (February 1965), p. 9.

291 "Probably I was regarded": Born, *Physics in My Generation*, p. 164.

292 "He replied 'No'": Leo Mattersdorf-author, May 7, 1969.

292 "Can Quantum-Mechanical Description of Physical Reality Be Considered Complete?": *Physical Review*, Ser. 2, Vol. 47 (1935), pp. 777–80.

293 "I have used this opportunity":

Bohr-Rutherford, June 3, 1935, Rutherford Papers.

293 Bohr published a paper: "Can Quantum-Mechanical Description of Physical Reality Be Considered Complete?": *Physical Review*, Vol. 48 (October 15, 1935), p. 696.

293 "Elementary Derivation of the Equivalence of Mass and Energy": American Mathematical Society, *Bulletin*, Vol. 41, pp. 223–30.

294 "This is not at all a stupid idea": Infeld, *Quest*, p. 311.

294 "I find my physical powers decreasing": Watters, p. 39.

Chapter 20 Einstein, the Bomb, and the Board of Ordnance

296 "playful suggestion": Sir William Dampier-Whetham-Rutherford, July 26, 1903, quoted Eve, p. 102.

296 "though the actual production": Planck, quoted in Born's obituary, p. 5.

297 Rutherford's warning to Lord Hankey: Ronald W. Clark, *The Birth of the Bomb*, p. 153 (afterward referred to as 'Clark, *Bomb*').

298 "The destiny of man has slipped": Desmond McCarthy, *New Statesman*, Vol. III (May 7, 1932), p. 585.

298 "It suddenly occurred to me": Szilard, p. 100.

298 "I assigned this patent to the British Admiralty": Szilard, p. 102.

299 the threat of the concentration camp: the story of Lise Meitner's escape from Germany is told in Otto Hahn's *My Life*.

299 "The picture was that of two fairly large nuclei": Clark, *Bomb*, p. 15.

300 "Clever, these physicists": Oppenheimer, *Flying Trapeze*, p. 52.

300 Tizard met the company's president, Clark, *Bomb*, p. 23.

300 building of a "uranium device": *Naturwissenschaften* Nos. 23/24, June 9, 1933.

300 "The show was going on": Dr. Vannevar Bush, *Boston Globe*, December 2, 1962.

300 Einstein's intervention: Leo Szilard's Archives are the most important single source of fresh information on the Roosevelt letter. Another is Alexander Sachs.

300 "Both Wigner and I began to worry": Szilard, pp. 111–12.

301 "had not been aware": Szilard-Seelig, August 19, 1955, E.T.H.

301 "That never occurred to me": Szilard-authors of *Einstein on Peace*, quoted p. 291.

301 "was deeply involved in his own work": Professor Aage Bohr-author, September 23, 1970.

302 "I have, to the best of my judgment": Bohr-Chadwick, message, quoted Sir John Cockcroft, *Obituary Notices of Fellows of the Royal Society*, Vol. 9, p. 45.

302 "I did not, in fact, foresee that it would be released": Einstein, "Atomic War or Peace," *Atlantic Monthly*, November 1945.

302 "he could scarcely believe that the universe was constructed": quoted Ronald W. Clark, *Tizard*, p. 301.

302 "Do you really think that the universe was made in this way?": Sir Henry Tizard, quoted Clark, *Tizard*, p. 301.

302 "my colleagues knew that I was opposed": Born-author, 1960, quoted Clark, *Bomb*, p. 83.

302 "Before contacting the Belgian Government": Szilard-Seelig, August 19, 1955, E.T.H.

303 "the danger to the Belgian State": Szilard Archives.

303 "at the time [of the visit]": Edward Teller-author, May 19, 1969.

304 Bernard Baruch or Karl Compton: Szilard-Einstein, August 2, 1939, Szilard Archives.

304 "be too clever": Einstein-Szilard, undated but apparently August 9, 1939, Szilard Archives.

304 "If such a note was written": Lindbergh-author, December 12, 1969.

304 "Lindbergh is not our man": Szilard-Einstein, September 27, 1939, Szilard Archives.

304 "Sachs confessed": Szilard-Einstein, October 3, 1939, Szilard Archives.

304 "Our system is such that national public figures": Alexander Sachs before Special Committee on Atomic Energy, U.S. Senate, November 27, 1945, *Background to Early History, Atomic Bomb Project in Relation to President Roosevelt*, Washington, D.C., 1945, pp. 553–73 (afterward referred to as 'Senate').

305 "read aloud his covering letter": R. G. Hewlett and E. D. Anderson, Jr., *The New World, 1939–1946*, p. 17 (afterward referred to as 'Hewlett and Anderson').

305 "pressure—by Einstein and the speaker": Senate.

305 "While we felt": Senate.

306 The letter, written to Sachs: Einstein-Sachs, March 7, 1940, Senate.

306 "the matter should rest in abeyance": Senate.

306 "a time convenient to you and Dr. Einstein": Roosevelt-Sachs, April 5, 1940, Senate.

306 "perhaps Dr. Einstein would have some suggestions to offer": Senate.

306 "It became clear": Senate.

306 "In case you wish to decline": Szilard-Einstein, April 19, 1940, Szilard Archives.

306 In the letter, the third that Einstein had signed: Einstein-Dr. Lyman J. Briggs, April 25, 1940, Senate.

307 "had a long conversation with the President," James Phinney Baxter, *Scientists Against Time*, p. 427.

307 "Though the Americans were aware": Arthur Holly Compton,

359

Atomic Quest: A Personal Narrative, London, 1956, p. 60.

307 "[It] gave Bush and Dr. James Conant what they had been looking for": Hewlett and Anderson, p. 43.

307 "Their optimistic report of July, 1941": Daniel Boorstin (ed.), *An American Primer,* p. 862.

308 Bush turned to Einstein for help: Dr. Frank Aydelotte-Bush, December 19, 1941; Bush-Aydelotte, December 22, 1941; Bush-Dr. Harold Urey, December 22, 1941; Urey-Bush, December 29, 1941; Bush-Aydelotte, December 30, 1941; U.S. Atomic Energy Commission, Documents Nos. 327–31.

309 "in my many discussions with President Roosevelt": Bush-author, December 27, 1968.

310 "It was in broken English": Shapley, p. 132.

310 links with the navy: Einstein-Bucky, July 26, 1943, and August 13, 1943, Bucky correspondence.

310 "Some friends of Einstein": Bush-author, December 27, 1968.

310 Einstein's engagement: dates and details from National Personnel Records Center, General Services Administration, St. Louis, Missouri.

311 "Since I happened to have known Einstein earlier": Gamow, p. 151.

311 "On the next day my project was moved": Gamow, p. 151.

312 "that the ultimate ethical values": Born Letters, p. 147.

312 "during the early part of World War II, Thomas Lee Bucky, p. 43.

313 "The uranium industry in 1943": *U.S. Minerals Yearbook,* 1943, p. 828.

313 "instigated some of the most important experiments": Margaret Gowing, *Britain and Atomic Energy, 1939–1945,* p. 264 (afterward referred to as 'Gowing').

314 influential scientists: Einstein-Bohr, December 12, 1944, diplomatic source.

314 a letter from Peter Kapitza: the fullest account of the Kapitza incident, the meetings with Churchill and Roosevelt, and the Hyde Park aide memoire, is given in Gowing, pp. 350–60.

315 Bohr memorandum, December 1944: diplomatic source.

316 a meeting in Munich: details and quotations, Samuel A. Goudsmit, *Alsos,* p. 152.

317 "At the time the war situation was already too tense": Werner Heisenberg, "The Third Reich and the Atomic Bomb," *Frankfurter Allgemeine Zeitung,* December 1967, reprinted, *Bulletin of the Atomic Scientists,* June 1968 (afterward referred to as 'Heisenberg').

317 "Whatever one may think": Heisenberg.

318 "I had them brought to Farm Hall": R. V. Jones, "Thicker Than Heavy Water," *Chemistry and Industry,* August 26, 1967, p. 1419.

318 "What is the purpose": Szilard, p. 123.

318 trailed by the Manhattan Project's intelligence agents: James F. Byrnes, *All in One Lifetime,* p. 285 (afterward referred to as 'Byrnes').

318 "Unhappily such a possibility is not entirely in the Utopian domain": *Contemporary Jewish Record,* VIII, June 1945.

319 "by developing in the next two years": Szilard memorandum, Szilard, p. 147.

319 "Scrambling his technology": Hewlett and Anderson, p. 342.

319 "I decided to transmit the memorandum": Szilard, p. 124.

319 "I hope you will get the President to read this": Szilard, p. 124.

320 "President Truman asked me to see Szilard": Byrnes, p. 284.

320 "statesmen who did not realise": Hewlett and Anderson, p. 342.

320 "The world is not yet ready": the *New York Times,* August 7, 1945.

320 "Oh, weh": Nathan and Norden, p. 308.

320 "Although it can be said": Helen Dukas, quoted in the *New York Times,* August 8, 1945.

320 "In developing atomic or nuclear energy": Einstein interviewed by Richard Lewis, the *New York Times,* August 12, 1945.

Chapter 21 The Conscience of the World

323 "'Atomic War or Peace,' by Albert Einstein as told to Raymond Swing": *Atlantic Monthly,* November 1945.

323 "This foreign-born agitator": Congressman John Rankin, October 5, 1945.

324 "I have no hope of reasonableness in the Soviet government": Bertrand Russell-Einstein, November 24, 1947, Russell Archives, McMaster University.

324 "Open Letter to the General Assembly": Einstein, *United Nations World,* October 1947.

324 "Dr. Einstein's Mistaken Notions": *New Times,* November 26, 1947.

324 "a nationwide campaign to inform the American people": this, and other appeal quotations, are taken from the Emergency Committee of Atomic Scientists papers, University of Chicago.

325 "I do not remember that Einstein ever had any influence": Victor Weisskopf-author, May 14, 1970.

325 "he did not have that convenient and natural converse with statesmen": Oppenheimer, "On Albert Einstein," Lecture delivered at UNESCO House, December 13, 1965, reprinted in *The New York Review,* March 17, 1966.

325 "Suggested draft letter to Professor Einstein": undated (penciled December 1945), Weizmann Archives.

326 "finally wrote on December 28": Weizmann-Einstein, December 28, 1945, Alexander Sachs.

326 During the walk they discussed the proposal: Sachs-author, May 7, 1970.

327 "Einstein, who passionately defended the intellectual and moral freedom": Nathan and Norden, p. 541.

329 if the Ruhr were left to the Germans: Einstein-Council for German Democracy, October 1, 1945.

329 no wish to have any dealings with the Germans: Einstein-Sommerfeld, December 14, 1946, Sommerfeld, p. 121.

329 Germans' mass murder of the Jews: Einstein-Heuss, January 16, 1951, Nathan and Norden, p. 578.

329 a land of mass murderers: Einstein-Born, October 12, 1953, Born Letters, p. 199.

329 "They are no mass murderers": Born-Einstein, November 8, 1953, Born Letters, p. 204.

330 Yet he wrote consolingly and without bitterness: Einstein-Frau Planck, November 10, 1947, Einstein Archives.

331 raise funds for the Haganah: Einstein-Lina Kocherthaler, May 4, 1948, Kocherthaler correspondence.

Chapter 22 Two Stars at the End of the Rocket

332 "the great masses of the people": Adolf Hitler, *Mein Kampf.*

332 "He said he was too old": Professor Selig Brodetsky, *Memoirs: From Ghetto to Israel,* p. 289.

333 no doubts about how they regarded him: Einstein-Habicht, summer 1948, Seelig, p. 209.

333 did not attempt to put forward a logical defense: Einstein-Born, March 3, 1947, Born Letters, p. 158.

333 "I besought him to tell me": Lewis Strauss, *Men and Decisions,* p. 271.

334 What had been a monologue became a dialogue: Dr. David Mitrany, statement to author.

335 "Like Chinese, you have to study it": Infeld, quoted *New York Herald Tribune,* January 1, 1950.

335 His routine was simple: Details of Einstein's postwar life are taken from conversations with Miss Helen Dukas; letters from Miss Dukas to Seelig, E.T.H.; and the more reliable of the correspondents who visited him.

336 "He explained that something must be amiss": Eisenhart.

337 "Herr Gott. Washington. What is wrong now": Mitrany statement.

337 There is some conflict of evidence about the details of how the offer of the presidency was made, as remembered by those directly concerned. The main facts are clear.

337 "Einstein was visibly moved by the splendor and audacity of the thought": Abba Eban, *The Jewish Chronicle,* October 2, 1959.

338 "Acceptance would entail moving to Israel": Eban-Einstein, November 17, 1952, Nathan and Norden, p. 572.

338 Einstein felt bound to refuse: Einstein-Eban, November 18, 1952, Nathan and Norden, p. 572.

338 "I made one great mistake": Einstein-Linus Pauling, quoted in Pauling's diary.

338 repudiated materialism: message to American Friends of The Hebrew University, 1954, quoted Bentwich, *The Hebrew University of Jerusalem, 1918–60,* p. 148.

338 "The only way to escape the personal corruption of praise": Einstein-Hermanns, interview by William Miller, *Life,* May 2, 1955.

339 "He spoke of the literary value": Douglas, "Forty Minutes with Einstein," *Journal of the Royal Astronomical Society of Canada,* Vol. 50, No. 3 (May–June 1956), pp. 99–102.

339 "I cannot accept any concept of God"; "the brotherhood of man"; "never lose a holy curiosity": Einstein-Hermanns, interview by William Miller, *Life,* May 2, 1955.

340 "A lot of work will have to be done": Freundlich, *Physica Acta,* p. 112.

340 "Of the three observable consequences": Born, *Physica Acta,* p. 225.

341 "opposed the First World War": Russell, quoted Nathan and Norden, p. xv.

341 "I think that eminent men of science": Russell-Einstein, February 11, 1955, Russell Archives.

341 a public declaration, signed by a small number of scientists: Einstein-Russell, February 16, 1955, Russell Archives.

342 "In view of the fact": Russell-Einstein, April 5, 1955, Russell Archives.

342 he had written to Russell; and "He was on the porch of his house": Paschkis-author, January 5, 1969.

343 He would like to help: Einstein-Israeli consul, April 4, 1955, Nathan and Norden, p. 639.

343 "Professor Einstein told me": Abba Eban, *The Jewish Chronicle,* October 2, 1959.

343 He agreed…And he signed the document: Einstein-Russell, April 11, 1955, Russell Archives.

345 almost failed to recognize him: Margot Einstein-Hedwig Born, Born Letters, p. 234.

CHRONOLOGY

1879	Albert Einstein born March 14 in Ulm
1880	Einstein family moves to Munich
1881	Maja Einstein, sister, born
1884–89	Einstein attends Catholic elementary school in Munich
1889–94	Einstein attends Luitpold Gymnasium, Munich
1894	Einstein's parents move to Milan. Einstein follows six months later
1895–96	Attends cantonal school, Aarau, Switzerland
1896	Einstein renounces German citizenship, enters Eidgenossische Technische Hochschule (E.T.H.), Zurich
1900	Receives diploma from E.T.H.
1901	Becomes Swiss citizen. Completes first scientific paper "Folgerungen aus den Capillaritäaserscheinungen" ("Consequences of Capillary Phenomena")
1901–2	Private tutor in Schaffhausen school
1902	Arrives in Berne. Obtains probationary appointment in Swiss Patent Office, Berne
1903	Marries Mileva Maric
1904	Birth of son, Hans Albert
1904	Patent Office appointment confirmed
1905	Papers on light quanta, Brownian motion, special relativity; and on a body's inertia— the last containing the $E = mc^2$ equation
1908	Receives degree from Berne University
1909	Joins University of Zurich
1909	Birth of son, Eduard
1911	Attends Solvay Congress in Brussels
1911–12	Professor of Physics at Prague University
1913	Publishes, with Marcel Grossmann, preliminary paper on general relativity
1914	Moves to Prussian Academy of Sciences, Berlin, and becomes director of Kaiser Wilhelm Institute of Physics there
1916	Publishes paper on general theory of relativity
1917	Publishes paper on cosmological implications of general relativity
1919	Divorce from Mileva Maric
1919	Results of eclipse expedition support general relativity
1919	Marries Elsa Lowenthal
1920	Death of Einstein's mother
1921	Visits United States and England
1922	Awarded Nobel Prize for Physics for research on the photoelectric effect
1922	Visits France and Japan
1923	Visits Palestine and Spain
1925	Visits South America
1929	First visit to Belgian royal family
1930–32	Three visits to California Institute of Technology and to England
1933	Temporary residence in Belgium, then emigration to the United States, where joins Institute for Advanced Study, Princeton
1936	Death of wife, Elsa Einstein, in Princeton
1939	Letter to President Roosevelt proposing research on nuclear weapons
1943–46	Consultant to U.S. Navy's Bureau of Ordnance
1946	Chairman, Emergency Committee of Atomic Scientists
1952	Offered presidency of Israel
1955	Signs Russell-Einstein Declaration, with which the Pugwash conferences were to be launched
1955	Dies, April 18, in Princeton

ACKNOWLEDGMENTS

I am grateful for permission to consult the Einstein Archives when it was held in Princeton. In addition, I wish to thank: Professor Jagdish Mehra, University of Texas at Austin, Texas, for reading the manuscript; and Professor Norman Bentwich, Josef Fraenkel, Professor N. Kemmer, Professor Sir Bernard Lovell, Dr. R. E. W. Maddison, Professor C. W. McCombie, the late Professor C. W. McCombie, Dr. David Mitrany, the late Heinz Norden, Dr. Peter Plesch, the late Sir George Thomson, and the late Lancelot Law Whyte for reading portions of the manuscript. A very large number of people in the United States, Europe, and the Middle East have been generous in providing documents and reminiscences. It is unfortunately impossible to name them all, but I would particularly like to thank the following, many of whom have died in the 1970s. Throughout the book, any opinions expressed, and the responsibility for the facts given, are entirely my own:

Sir Walter Adams, director, London School of Economics and Political Science; Professor Aage Bohr; Dr. Vannevar Bush; Dr. C. H. Collie; Professor A. Vibert Douglas; Eidgenössisches Amt für Geistiges Eigentum, Berne; Dr. H. A. Einstein; Churchill Eisenhart; Dr. Elizabeth Eppler, Institute of Jewish Affairs; Professor I. Estermann; Mme. M. Fawtier, UNESCO; Frau Kate Freundlich; Professor Dennis Gabor; Mrs. Barbara Gamow; Dr. Judith R. Goodstein, California Institute of Technology; Dr. Max Gottschalk; Kurt R. Grossmann; Sir Roy Harrod; Dr. J. van Herwaarden, Rijksuniversiteit te Utrecht, Universiteitsmuseum, Utrecht; Dr. Max J. Herzberger; Richard G. Hewlett, chief historian, U.S. Atomic Energy Commission; Professor Banesh Hoffmann; Alvin E. Jaeggli, Eidgenössische Technische Hochschule Bibliothek, Zurich; Bernard Jaffe; Miss Suzanne Christine Kennedy, Nuffield College, Oxford; Oscar Kocherthaler; Professor C. Lanczos, Dublin Institute for Advanced Studies; Dr. W. Lanzer, Verein für Geschichte der Arbeiterbewegung, Vienna; Colonel Charles A. Lindbergh; Dr. Jacob R. Marcus, American Jewish Archives; Julian L. Meltzer, Weizmann Archives; Professor Ashley Montagu; Mrs. B. Mulholland; Dr. John N. Nagy; Professor Linus Pauling; Professor J. Pelseneer, Université Libre de Bruxelles; Y. Perotin, League of Nations Archives, Geneva; Dr. Peter Plesch; Professor William Ready, McMaster University, Hamilton, Ontario; Professor Nathan Rosen; Professor Leonora Cohen Rosenfeld; Professor J. Rotblat; Dr. Alexander Sachs; Mrs. Esther Salaman; Mrs. Alice Kimball Smith; Dr. P. van der Star, Rijksmuseum voor de Geschiedenis der Natuurwetenschappen, Leiden; Dr. Gertrud Weiss Szilard; U.S. Department of the Navy; U.S. National Archives and Records Service; E. Vandewoude, Cabinet du Roi, Bruxelles; Dr. Charles Weiner and Mrs. Joan Warnow of the American Institute of Physics, for their help and guidance in the use of materials in the Niels Bohr Library for History and Philosophy of Physics; Jeremy Weston, The Royal Institution; Dr. G. J. Whitrow; Professor Eugene P. Wigner; E. T. Williams, The Rhodes Trust.

Finally, I wish to thank the large number of Jewish organizations in the United States, Britain, Israel, and elsewhere, who have helped to resolve specific problems; the numerous German bodies who have supplied information on the question of Einstein's nationality; the librarians and archivists of the universities and other sources listed in the section on references, who have helped to make my work less arduous; and the following for permission to quote copyrighted material:

Algemeen Rijksarchief, The Hague (H. A. Lorentz correspondence); *American Journal of Physics* (R. S. Shankland's "Conversations with Albert Einstein"); His Majesty King Baudouin of the Belgians (letter to Einstein from His Majesty King Albert of the Belgians); Professor Aage Bohr (letters of Professor Niels Bohr); Burndy Library (Ehrenhaft manuscript); California Institute of Technology Archives, Pasadena (quotations from the Hale and Millikan Papers); Cambridge University Press (Lord Rayleigh's *The Life of Sir J. J. Thomson*; Einstein and Infeld's *The Evolution of Physics*; Hermann Bondi's *Assumption and Myth in Physical Theory*; Sir James Jeans' *The New Background of Science*); Jonathan Cape Ltd. and Alfred Knopf (Philipp Frank's *Einstein*); Columbia University (1912 correspondence with Einstein); Thomas Y. Crowell Co. (*The Questioners*, by Barbara Lovett Cline); Deutsche Verlags-anstalt, Stuttgart, and Dr. H. Tramer (Blumenfeld's *Erlebte Judenfrage*); Eyre & Spottiswoode (Publishers) Ltd. (Anton Reiser's *Albert Einstein: A Biographical Portrait*); the late Frau Kate Freundlich (Freundlich correspondence); Victor Gollancz Ltd. (Leopold Infeld's *Quest: The Evolution of a Scientist*); Institute for Advanced Study, Princeton (letters of Dr. Frank Aydelotte and Dr. Abraham Flexner); Lady Jeans (Sir James Jeans' letter); Martin J. Klein (*Paul Ehrenfest*); Mrs. Henry R. Labouisse (correspondence of Madame Curie); Dr. Wanda Lanzer (Adler correspondence); executors of the late Lord Cherwell (Lord Cherwell's correspondence); McGraw-Hill Book Company (Max Talmey's *The Relativity Theory Simplified*); Mrs. B. Mulholland (Commander Locker-Lampson's letters); North Holland Publishing Company and Dr. Abraham Pais (*Niels Bohr*, ed. L. Rosenfeld); North Holland Publishing Company (*Niels Bohr: An Essay*, by L. Rosenfeld); Oxford University Press (Robert Oppenheimer's *The Flying Trapeze: Three Crises for Physicists*, the Whidden Lectures, 1962); Dr. Peter Plesch (*Janos*, by Janos Plesch); *Punch* (for poem, "Einstein and Epstein Are Wonderful Men"); Dr. Nesca Robb (Dr. A. A. Robb's poem); Mme Romain Rolland and Editions Albin Michel (Romain Rolland's *Journal des Années de Guerre 1914–1918*); The Hon. Godfrey Samuel and The House of Lords (Samuel material); Charles Scribner's Sons (Harlow Shapley's *Through Rugged Ways to the Stars*); *The Scientific American* ("An Interview with Albert Einstein," by I. Bernard Cohen); Raglan Squire (Sir John Squire's answer to Pope's epitaph on Sir Isaac Newton); Staples Press and Miss Joyce Weiner (Carl Seelig's *Albert Einstein*); the late Dr. Gertrud Weiss Szilard (Dr. Leo Szilard's letters and "Reminiscences"); The Master and Fellows of Trinity College, Cambridge (the writings of Sir Arthur Eddington); United Nations (League of Nations archival material); Mrs. G. W. Watters (writings of Dr. Leon L. Watters); George Weidenfeld & Nicolson Ltd. (Antonina Vallentin's *Einstein*); trustees of the Weizmann Archives (letters written by Chaim Weizmann).

R.W.C.

INDEX

The large number of photographs showing only Einstein are not indexed.

The pages with photographs of other people and places are italicized.

Herblock's cartoon which appeared
in the *Washington Post* after Einstein's
death in 1955.